THE CELEBRATED ELIZABETH SMITH

Jeffersonian America

CHARLENE M. BOYER LEWIS, ANNETTE GORDON-REED, PETER S. ONUF,
ANDREW J. O'SHAUGHNESSY, AND ROBERT G. PARKINSON, EDITORS

The Celebrated Elizabeth Smith

CRAFTING GENIUS AND
TRANSATLANTIC FAME
IN THE ROMANTIC ERA

Lucia McMahon

To Linda,
Happy Reading!!
Regards,
Lucia McMan
2023

UNIVERSITY OF VIRGINIA PRESS

Charlottesville and London

University of Virginia Press
© 2022 by the Rector and Visitors of the University of Virginia
All rights reserved
Printed in the United States of America on acid-free paper

First published 2022

1 3 5 7 9 8 6 4 2

Library of Congress Cataloging-in-Publication Data
Names: McMahon, Lucia, author.
Title: The celebrated Elizabeth Smith : crafting genius and
transatlantic fame in the Romantic era / Lucia McMahon.
Description: Charlottesville : University of Virginia Press, 2022. |
Series: Jeffersonian America | Includes bibliographical references and index.
Identifiers: LCCN 2022021133 (print) | LCCN 2022021134 (ebook) | ISBN 9780813947853
(hardcover) | ISBN 9780813947860 (paperback) | ISBN 9780813947877 (ebook)
Subjects: LCSH: Smith, Elizabeth, 1776–1806. | Women translators—Great Britain—
Biography. | Women scholars—Great Britain—Biography. | Women—Great Britain—
Intellectual life. | Romanticism—Great Britain. | Great Britain—Intellectual life—
18th century. | Great Britain—Intellectual life—19th century.
Classification: LCC P306.92.S6 M35 2022 (print) | LCC P306.92.S6 (ebook) |
DDC 418/.02092 [B]—dc23/eng/20220627
LC record available at https://lccn.loc.gov/2022021133
LC ebook record available at https://lccn.loc.gov/2022021134

Cover art: Portrait of Elizabeth Smith (circa 1807), included as a frontispiece in
Fragments, in Prose and Verse (Library Company of Philadelphia); *Easby Hall and
Easby Abbey with Richmond, Yorkshire in the Background,* George Cuitt,
ca. 1800 (Yale Center for British Art, Paul Mellon Collection)

For Liz and Jax, with love

CONTENTS

ILLUSTRATIONS

ACKNOWLEDGMENTS

I BEGIN BY ACKNOWLEDGING THE loss of my mentor Jan Ellen Lewis. So much of my academic journey remains shaped by imaginative "What Would Jan Do/Say?" moments. I also miss Dallett Hemphill's collegiality and generosity. Jan and Dallett provided essential feedback on early elements of this project, and I often wonder how this book would have been further influenced and enhanced by their insights and encouragement.

This book has been long in the making. My research on Elizabeth Smith's memoir was meant to be an article that would help me sort out my general interests in nineteenth-century female biography. Instead, the project took on a life (and afterlife) of its own. Along the way, life took some unexpected turns. Like Elizabeth Smith, I faced the disrupting and disorienting experience of losing my family home. I remember it all too well. The past few years have shown how choices and circumstances outside of our direct control can impact our lives in profound ways.

My family and friends have provided love, support, and comfort. My children, Liz and Jax, inspire me in countless ways. I am thankful for my siblings, Marie and Joey, and my nieces Skylar, Amanda, and Amber (#amberstrong) for cherished moments of love, laughter, and family time. My profound gratitude to Kelly Solloway, Ellen Pfeffer, and Raji Thron for creating spaces and communities for the practice of yoga. I am grateful to Bobbi and Steve Schlesinger for their kindness and support. Dear friends Debby Schriver and Jen Porat and their families offered valuable writing perspectives, kind encouragement, and generous hospitality. To Donna

Wallis, Jill Wilson, Mike Roulier, and the "trail trekkers," thank you for many moments of joy and inspiration (just another half-mile to go!).

I am grateful to William Paterson University (WPU) for Career Development funding in support of my research for this project. It should be acknowledged that those of us who do not teach at more prestigious universities often lack equitable institutional support and funding for our research efforts. This book was completed at a time when drastic cuts to travel and research funding models at WPU, along with my increased duties as chair of my department, made finding time and resources to research and write particularly challenging. I am grateful for my friends and colleagues at WPU for their smart, thoughtful, and engaged perspectives. Special appreciation to Jason Ambroise and Malissa Williams for their steadfast support and friendship.

I am indebted to archivists and librarians who facilitated my research requests and inquiries. The staff at the Library of the Society of Friends in London, the British Library, the American Antiquarian Society, and the Library Company of Philadelphia were especially helpful. I am also very grateful to the librarians who fulfilled my many interlibrary loan requests. Having access to materials through ILL was essential, especially during the final phases of revisions, when pandemic-related closures and constraints restricted my ability to travel to research archives and libraries.

The Society for Historians of the Early American Republic (SHEAR) continues to provide a scholarly home where I have been fortunate to meet so many generous, gracious scholars and friends. I am grateful to Will Mackintosh for our many SHEAR-or-bust travel adventures. Special thanks to Charlene Boyer Lewis (who lovingly and knowingly laughed when I long ago said that I wanted to write a "quick" biography), Nick Syrett (who nudged me to write that last chapter to get the book manuscript ready for review), and Rodney Hessinger (my longtime SHEAR comrade and dear friend). My heartfelt appreciation to Robyn Davis, Carolyn Eastman, Kara French, Cassie Good, Cathy Kelly, Mary Kelley, Beth Salerno, Christine Sears, and so many other lovely folk that I have gotten to know at SHEAR and other academic conferences. Thanks to Serena Zabin, Robert Churchill, Sara Gronim, Cami Townsend, Paul Clemens, and other Rutgers friends for camaraderie that has extended far beyond those long-ago graduate school days. Recently, I've enjoyed reconnecting with Chris Fisher and Pete Mickulas as we collaborate together on Ceres, a new book series for Rutgers University Press.

Many thanks to Nadine Zimmerli for her support and encouragement of this project, and to the staff at and affiliated with the University of Virginia Press who ably transformed the manuscript into a published book.

And to you, Dear Reader, thank you for finding this book and for taking the time to read about the celebrated Elizabeth Smith.

THE CELEBRATED ELIZABETH SMITH

"Under the Same Roof"

I N 1805, TWENTY-EIGHT-YEAR-OLD ELIZABETH Smith set off from her family home in Coniston, in the English Lake District, to visit Thomas Wilkinson, a family friend who lived about thirty miles northeast in Penrith. She was accompanied by her younger sister Kitty, her local friend Mary Dixon, and another friend visiting from Scotland. About halfway through their journey, the four women stopped in Patterdale for the night. The inn where the women lodged was very crowded, but Elizabeth Smith and her companions did not realize that the room designated as their "sitting room" had also been rented out to two male travelers for their overnight accommodations. The four women sat up talking for hours, unaware that two weary travelers were waiting for them to turn in for the night so that they could access their lodgings. For whatever reason, the two gentlemen did not simply ask the women for access to their quarters. Instead, "like the Watchman in London," they stood outside the window and called out the time. "11 o'clock. Half past 11 o'clock." It was well past midnight before the "Relentless Dames" finally retired for the night. Unaware of the inconvenience they had caused, Elizabeth Smith and her traveling companions also had no idea that the two men calling outside their window were none other than the celebrated authors Walter Scott and William Wordsworth. "Yet they slept under the same roof house, and never saw one another," recalled Wilkinson, who was friends with Wordsworth as well. The whole story only "came out after."[1]

During his 1819 travels through the Lake District, John Griscom, an American educator and chemist, followed the same route taken by Smith and her companions. After a "delightful" visit at Wordsworth's home, Griscom journeyed to Penrith to meet with Wilkinson. "We stopped a few moments in Patterdale, at Dobson's inn." There, as Griscom "afterwards learned," Walter Scott and his travel party "once lodged, during an excursion among the lakes. It happened on the same day, that Elizabeth Smith, (so justly celebrated for her piety and literary acquirements,) had stopped with her sister at this inn, also to repose during the night." Griscom included this story in his published travel narrative *A Year in Europe*, recounting the "subsequent regret of the parties" upon realizing they had been in such close proximity "without seeing each other."[2] By the time of Griscom's visit, Elizabeth Smith had died, but her legacy lived on both in Great Britain and in the United States.

For decades after her death, the story of Smith's night at the inn, along with other tales describing her intellectual accomplishments and adventurous explorations, circulated in local lore as well as within transatlantic cultures of print. When Walter Scott returned to the Lake District in 1825, William Wordsworth took him to the home of Lord and Lady Lonsdale, where he met with a "splendid circle of distinguished persons, who, like them, lavished all possible attentions and demonstrations of respect."[3] Thomas Wilkinson was among the distinguished guests that afternoon. He conversed with Scott "of historians and history, of poets and poetry; of Wordsworth, Southey, Coleridge, and Lord Byron." Wilkinson "also alluded to the adventure of Patterdale, of him and W. Wordsworth and Mary Dixon, Elizabeth Smith and her sister, twenty years ago."[4] Gone but not forgotten, Elizabeth Smith was "name-dropped" to Walter Scott in a conservation that referenced renowned literary figures associated with the Lake District.

Whoever tells the story—then as well as now—determines whose story it is and why it matters. For Thomas Wilkinson—the original teller of the tale—it was a lighthearted story that highlighted his extended network of friends, visitors, and travelers to his beloved Lake District home. For those more broadly interested in transatlantic literary studies, particularly the fame achieved by authors such as William Wordsworth and Walter Scott, this story offers an amusing anecdote about the temporary displacement of these celebrated writers and their inept, eccentric attempts to gain entrance to their lodgings. But what about the "Relentless Dames" who were so wrapped up in their own conversations that they did not heed the calls outside their window? As this story suggests, women often traveled the same roads, occupied the same spaces, and shared the same intellectual interests as prominent literary men. Both groups of travelers in this story actively participated in larger historical and literary developments, including picturesque travel, Romanticism, and expanding transatlantic cultures of print.

While these two sets of travelers inhabited shared physical and printed spaces, they operated under different norms. In the language of the era, men such as Wordsworth and Scott were often referred to as "literary lions," while Elizabeth Smith and her companions would have been described as "learned ladies." Literary lions attracted the admiration of the world, earning transatlantic fame for their works in their own lifetimes and beyond. Learned ladies, however, frequently faced cultural criticisms and gender prescriptions that sought to curtail their ambitions. Male authors were generally free to issue forth their literary productions (and their night calls) without fear of censure. They might face criticism of their work, but they rarely had their right to *pursue* that work challenged, or had their personal identities called into question for their choices of careers. Nor did male authors typically have to defend their physical inhabiting of public spaces—indeed, more likely, they were fêted by admirers everywhere they traveled, rather than expected to wait outside. By contrast, any woman who took up her pen risked censure of her identity, character, and femininity, rather than just critical assessments about the quality of her poetry or prose.

Various commentators on "female authors" could not imagine what "prompts a woman to obtrude herself on the public."[5] And while women such as Elizabeth Smith often traveled without male companions, prescriptive writers tended to brand such physical autonomy as unladylike or dangerous. Rather than view women's explorations with respect or admiration, pundits often presumed that women were inexperienced "tourists" in need of male escorts and protection. Women thus had to learn to navigate the literary public sphere—as well as inns and other public spaces—with gendered caution.

There is another key difference between these two sets of travelers. Whereas Wordsworth and Scott continue to occupy center stage in the literary and historical record, Smith and her companions have been all but forgotten.[6] *The Celebrated Elizabeth Smith* deliberately puts the forgotten subject at the center of the story, offering new insights into the making of Romantic-era genius, literary celebrity, transatlantic culture, and gendered norms. Scholars have spent decades recovering women's historical experiences and literary contributions, yet many of our interpretative frameworks continue to center a select group of men most closely associated with Romanticism.[7] Despite important scholarly interventions, many still presume that there was something distinct and incomparable about how such renowned men of talent approached the world. Yet all along the way, learned women traveled the same scenic routes and literary paths that were so instrumental in shaping the sensibilities of key Romantic figures such as Wordsworth and Scott.

The Celebrated Elizabeth Smith views the experiences and contributions of Elizabeth Smith and other learned women as central, not incidental, to our understandings of the cultural, literary, and tourist landscapes that defined the age of Romanticism. Refocusing our gaze, we can see that ambitious, talented women such as Elizabeth Smith and her companions were, in essence, often "hiding in plain sight." We can recover their experiences by exploring the inns, parlors, libraries, landscapes, and letters in which women spent countless hours enacting learned and fulfilling lives. It is worth considering why Romantic-era contemporaries (and subsequent generations of scholars) did not fully recognize learned women's aspirations or always notice their presence in spaces typically thought to be the province of men. Part of the story, then, is to examine how cultures of print and picturesque travel scenes were often deliberately less receptive to learned and adventurous women, and to explore why. That is the story I wish to tell in *The Celebrated Elizabeth Smith*.

Who was Elizabeth Smith? Born in 1776 in northeast England, she was a young woman with seemingly boundless intellectual curiosity. The Smith family home in Durham provided land, comfort, and respectability, but her parents sought to elevate their socioeconomic status. During Elizabeth's childhood, her family moved to an impressive estate located along the Wye River Valley, a renowned spot on any travel map of picturesque spots. Surrounded by scenic vistas, young Elizabeth spent countless hours studying astronomy, botany, geometry, mathematics, history, and poetry. With little formal training, she mastered several languages, including Latin, Greek, Hebrew, French, Spanish, German, and Arabic. She accomplished all of this even as her family faced a financial crisis and experienced a "genteel poverty" marked by years of geographic dislocation. After her family settled in the Lake District, Elizabeth Smith translated the Book of Job from Hebrew, as well as the German letters of Frederick and Margaret Klopstock, work she found "very delightful," as it provided "something to engage my thoughts [and] to fix my attention."[8]

In part because she lacked a permanent family home for several years, Elizabeth Smith was an adventurous traveler who rambled through scenic landscapes, explored historic ruins, and literally climbed mountains. She lived in regions celebrated as picturesque tourist destinations—first at Piercefield, near the popular ruins of Tintern Abbey, and later in the English Lake District. She made regular visits to Bath, noted for its circles of accomplished women. She loved to take long solitary walks, often sketching the beautiful and sublime scenes that she encountered. She was a fearless explorer who scaled Snowdon in Wales and the many mountains near her Lake District home. Although deeply inspired by Romanticism's veneration of the sublime and picturesque, Smith also retained a proper sense of Christian piety, along with a quiet resignation to God's will. That her talents were cut short by her tragic death at the age of twenty-nine in 1806—well, that was a plot line that could have come straight out of a sentimental novel.

A family friend described "Bess, lower in stature," as "pretty, her eyes blue, her complexion fair, and her fine hair of a light brown" (fig. 1). While alive, she was known for her "reserve" and unassuming nature: "We knew not then of the treasures of intellect and goodness which lay beneath that modest and retiring exterior."[9] Smith's quiet disposition reflected her fear of disapproving critics. As her mother recalled, "She was a living library, but locked up except to a chosen few . . . for her dread of being

FIGURE 1. Portrait of Elizabeth Smith (circa 1807), included as a frontispiece in editions of *Fragments, in Prose and Verse,* published in 1809 and later. (Library Company of Philadelphia)

called a learned lady, caused such an excess of modest reserve."[10] Although Smith shared her intellectual interests and travel adventures with trusted friends and family, she often made deliberate decisions to keep her talents selectively "locked up."

Elizabeth Smith came of age in a world that offered learned women both fresh possibilities and gendered constraints. Her extensive intellectual pursuits, along with her daring physical explorations, illustrate that women were active contributors to the era's cultural, literary, and tourist developments. Women frequently occupied the same literary and literal spaces as their male counterparts, yet their actions and behaviors were subjected to gendered assessments that assumed a male subject as the "norm." As she explored her place in this world, Smith self-consciously sought to achieve a delicate balance between social acceptance and individual accomplishment. "A woman must have uncommon sweetness of disposition and manners," she reflected, "to be *forgiven* for possessing superior talents and acquirements."[11] Smith sought *forgiveness*—that is, to avoid criticism—for her various interests by cultivating an amiable disposition. Her concerns demonstrate the powerful ways that cultural criticism could inform learned women's experiences and expectations.

What makes Elizabeth Smith so fascinating as a historical subject is that much of her story took place after her death in 1806, when her literary "afterlife" began. Unlike male authors such as Scott and Wordsworth, who achieved widespread fame within their own lifetimes, Smith's celebrity status developed largely posthumously. Although Smith was known within local literary circles before 1806, her rise to fame truly began in 1808, two years after her death, when her friend Henrietta Maria Bowdler published Smith's memoir, helping to assure a place of honor for Smith (and for Bowdler as editor) in the literary public sphere.[12] Between 1808 and 1818, over two dozen editions of Smith's memoir, *Fragments, in Prose and Verse: By a Young Lady, Lately Deceased,* along with various works of translation that she prepared before her death, were published in both Great Britain and the United States.

Through acts of personal and public remembrance, Elizabeth Smith achieved posthumous fame across transatlantic cultures of print. Her literary afterlife endured for decades, extending far beyond the initial publication of her works. Throughout the nineteenth century, numerous individuals on both sides of the Atlantic celebrated Smith's life and writings in scores of manuscript and printed sources, including collective biographies, conduct literature, travel narratives, and tribute poetry. In various accounts, "the celebrated Elizabeth Smith" was described in effusive terms: "a female of uncommon talents and acquirements"; a woman "whose character was as interesting as her genius was extraordinary"; "whatever she did was well done."[13]

Uncommon. Interesting. Extraordinary. Such descriptions, however celebratory, implied that Elizabeth Smith represented a unique exception to gendered norms. Smith certainly possessed impressive intellectual talents and an adventurous spirit, but do those traits make her unusual or uncommon? Her scholarly achievements and travel explorations, as well as her dread of criticism and posthumous fame, were *all* emblematic of the age in which she lived. Smith was as much a product of her time as celebrated men such as William Wordsworth and Walter Scott, or more well-known women writers such as Hannah More and Mary Wollstonecraft. What these individuals shared, along with many of their contemporaries, was a desire to explore the world around them, to put pen to paper, and to gain access to an expanding literary marketplace in which to disseminate their ideas. In these respects, Smith was not that unusual or uncommon, yet such labels reveal the ways in which cultural gatekeepers in British and American society sought to relegate accomplished women to the margins, both during their lifetimes and in cultural memory.

Rather than focus on Elizabeth Smith as an exceptional figure, *The Celebrated Elizabeth Smith* explores the expansive constellation of relationships, practices, spaces, and attitudes that shaped women's lives and legacies in the late eighteenth and early nineteenth centuries. Smith and other learned women were keenly invested in Romanticism's key tenets, including travel explorations of sublime, picturesque landscapes; artistic venerations of mythical past glories; and the privileging of imaginative and creative impulses. Both men and women approached places, poetry, and prose with these concepts in mind.

The rise of domestic tourism and picturesque travel that developed in eighteenth-century England was a key component of Romanticism, venerating the nation's mythic ruins and inspiring landscapes. A number of women travelers enthusiastically participated in visits to acclaimed spots on the picturesque travel map. In contemporary accounts and subsequent scholarship, however, the ideal traveler was presumed to be white, male, adventurous, and unafraid to wander off "the beaten track" in search of authentic experiences and sublime locations. Most travel narratives published in the late eighteenth and early nineteenth centuries centered the experiences of elite white men, emphasizing the physical efforts, skills, and courage required to explore sublime and picturesque regions.[14] Women who traveled tended to record their experiences in private journals or letters and produced fewer published travel narratives. In the cultural imagination, then, a "female adventurer" represented an anomaly in need of explanation. Critics portrayed women adventure-seekers as atypical and exceptional, typically expressing disdain, rather than admiration, for their aspirations and explorations. Men earned commendations for their daring travels and writings, but women were often overlooked, dismissed, or criticized when they expressed similar interests.

Gendered concepts also defined the era's evolving understandings of authorship, celebrity, and print. Extensive local, national, and transnational networks enabled an increasingly wide circulation of books, pamphlets, and other printed materials.[15] In eighteenth-century England and France, expanding cultures of print, along with visual media and public exhibitions, helped usher in new forms of celebrity for authors, actors, and other public figures. Literary celebrity culture initially spotlighted the achievements of British male authors such as Walter Scott, Lord Byron, and William Wordsworth. As celebrity culture took further root within transatlantic cultures of print, a number of authors from both sides of the Atlantic gained publicity, and in some cases notoriety, through ardent public interest in their lives and writings.[16]

At the same time that men such as Walter Scott and Lord Byron achieved notable transatlantic fame, a number of British women, including Hannah More, Elizabeth Carter, and other "literary ornaments," also "greatly distinguished themselves in the higher branches of composition."[17] The achievements of these celebrated women helped promote advancements in women's educational opportunities and literary productions in both England and America.[18] In 1807, an American essayist explicitly called on his countrywomen to emulate the "intellectual excellence" of accomplished British women: "Such a noble example is worthy of imitation."[19]

By the early nineteenth century, the success achieved by a growing number of women authors on both sides of the Atlantic evoked celebration *and* condemnation, highlighting the complex, sometimes contradictory ways in which cultures of print have served to promote *and* censure women's ambitions.[20] One London essayist enthusiastically proclaimed that "a distinguished female writer is the *effect* of civilization carried to a very high point," yet also cautioned that "an increase of knowledge, much as we value it," should not come "at the expense of their social or domestic virtues."[21] Commentators acknowledged women's intellectual capacities yet also warned that such pursuits were ill-suited to their prescribed gender roles. Summarizing these ambiguous attitudes, one male essayist conceded "that many female pens are wielded with an ability that would by no means discredit the most enlightened understanding," but tempered his praise by suggesting, "we admire them more as authors, than esteem them as women."[22] Critics asserted an incompatibility between women's literary talents and their femininity without declaring any comparable incongruity for male authors.

In frequently setting the terms "woman" and "author" as oppositional, rather than synonymous, critics posited a seemingly fundamental contradiction between women's intellectual outputs and their feminine identities. Women authors thus often had to defend the very notion of their intellectual ambitions and literary careers—not just the quality of their writings—from gender-specific criticisms. Even the very possession of intellectual capacity was gendered, as some commentators doubted whether it was possible for *any* woman to embody the unique, elevated type of genius at the heart of Romanticism. Terms such as "female author" or "learned lady" reveal gendered constraints embedded within categories—author or learned—that were seemingly gender neutral but implicitly coded male. Such classifications implied that a woman could succeed at being an author or scholar, or at maintaining a sense of respectable womanhood, but could seldom achieve both simultaneously. The terms "female author" and "learned lady" contributed to the notion that it was anomalous for *any* woman to engage in scholarly and literary productions, at the very moment that an increased number of women were doing so on both sides of the Atlantic.

These tensions dramatically shaped Elizabeth Smith's life and legacy. She came of age at a time when even those who supported the growth of educational and literary opportunities for women often insisted that certain intellectual gains came at the expense of true womanhood. As one essayist noted, "A lady may be intelligent and well informed, but in the present state of society she can rarely be a scholar." Significantly, this same author held up Elizabeth Smith as a "rare" specimen: "She was not only a scholar, but a woman—omni laude cumulate." Smith was regarded as an exception to the widespread belief "that every advance in abstruse science or profound learning by a lady is gained at the expense of domestick honour—of *household good*."[23] Smith was celebrated for successfully inhabiting an identity as a scholar *and* a woman, in an era that was often deeply suspicious of the compatibility of those two categorizations.

Elizabeth Smith—or any other learned lady who somehow achieved the seemingly elusive equilibrium as a "woman" and a "scholar"—was labeled "exceptional" or "extraordinary," rather than recognized as conventional or representative. Yet if there was anything atypical about Smith, it was not that she was an accomplished scholar or curious wanderer but rather the posthumous praise she received for having a proper sense of femininity, *despite* her achievements. In other words, Smith was regarded as not only intellectually *exceptional* but also socially *acceptable*. Typically presented as a dutiful daughter with an unblemished character, she was venerated not merely for her impressive acquirements but because of her seemingly ideal balancing of learning, modesty, and piety. Although Smith produced poetry and several works of translation, she did not establish a public career as an author (at least while living) or openly promulgate radical ideas about women's equality. Deeply accomplished but seemingly unambitious, she was regarded as a counter to more troubling examples of women authors who willingly entered the literary marketplace or directly sought to challenge prescribed gendered norms.

The era's conflicting attitudes toward women authors are often attributed to the "Wollstonecraft moment." First published in 1792, Mary Wollstonecraft's *A Vindication of the Rights of Woman* brought renewed debates about women's intellectual, political, and social equality to the forefront of transatlantic cultures of print. If Wollstonecraft's intellectual ideas had radical undertones, her personal life was of even more concern to some critics. When Wollstonecraft's husband, William Godwin, published a posthumous memoir about her in 1798, his candid account of her love affairs and illegitimate pregnancies tarnished Wollstonecraft's transatlantic reputation and cast a long shadow on intellectual women in general.[24] Wollstonecraft came to epitomize all that critics of women's literary ambition feared—a woman who developed radical notions of equality and pursued an unconventional lifestyle. Yet despite the controversy, there was no abrupt shift in reception; women were not welcomed as authors at first and then denounced after 1798 (or vice versa). Before and after Wollstonecraft, critics offered both praise and condemnation of women authors, sometimes even in the same work. Richard Polwhele, who fiercely attacked Wollstonecraft in his *Unsex'd Females,* expressed admiration for British bluestockings such as Elizabeth Carter, Elizabeth Montagu, and especially Hannah More, "whose productions have been appreciated by the public as works of learning or genius."[25]

Unlike Mary Wollstonecraft, whose posthumous reputation was largely tarnished and vilified, Elizabeth Smith was *forgiven* for her many talents. She was seen as modest, reserved, and pious—not brash, pedantic, or ambitious. Both the positive acclaim Smith inspired and the critical reception Wollstonecraft generated represented two sides of the same coin. Both women served as cautionary tales—as warnings to other women that there were plenty of "wrong" ways to be a learned lady and seemingly very few "right" ways. By insisting that it was uncommon for a woman to be so intellectually accomplished, especially a woman who was also perfectly feminine, writers evoked Elizabeth Smith as the rare "exception" that proved the rule, implying that it was more common for learned women to exhibit problematic, unfeminine, and unattractive characteristics. In both life and death, accomplished women often provoked a contested set of cultural reactions.

Ambivalence about learned ladies reflected the egalitarian potential and persistent contestation that developed within local, national, and transnational cultures of print. By 1800, authors and readers from a variety of racial, ethnic, and socioeconomic groups enjoyed expanded access to print. Scholars have addressed how such tensions shaped the literary receptions of writings by and about Black and Indigenous individuals. As eighteenth-century authors such as Phillis Wheatley, Samson Occom, and Olaudah Equiano gained transatlantic fame, their stories were often framed in terms of their "exceptional" characteristics or unique talents, or used to make broad assessments about the intellectual potential of Black and Indigenous people.[26] By contrast, even the most favorable—or critical—reviews of an individual white male author's works did not typically include declarative assessments about white men's collective intellectual capacities or deficiencies. Genius was defined as unique and rare but also as inherently white and male. These standards influenced how critics assessed various writings, particularly works by individuals whose identities did not match the expected norms.

Recognizing that Elizabeth Smith benefited from privileges associated with her whiteness and socioeconomic status, I seek to avoid reproducing frameworks that define intellect, authorship, and genius as implicitly white and male. The recovery of Smith as a biographical subject *and* a posthumous literary celebrity encourages us to rethink the problematic concept of the *exceptional* figure. Viewing her achievements as singular or unique retains a limited lens. The key to unlocking her historical significance is not to try to prove that yes, she actually possessed impressive scholarly talents and linguistic abilities indicative of genius. That seems clear, but the mere existence of a woman's achievements should not be so noteworthy or surprising. Rather, Smith's life and legacy help us to recognize and interrogate the cultural and structural conditions that sought to regulate women's literary productions and physical adventures. Smith's efforts to enact a learned life, as well as the various responses her efforts inspired in others, aptly illustrate larger cultural trends that opened up— and simultaneously sought to limit—intellectual possibilities and creative opportunities for elite women at the dawn of the nineteenth century.

At the heart of Elizabeth Smith's story is an enigma: how did a woman who dreaded public censure *in life* become celebrated for her achievements *in death*? Paradoxically, the idea that Smith deliberately avoided recognition for her many talents during her lifetime contributed to her enduring posthumous fame. As the Boston-based *Christian Observer* remarked in its 1808 review of Smith's memoir *Fragments, in Prose and Verse:* "The excellent and amiable being, towards whom the public eye is now attracted, never sought it for herself. She was contended to live and die in privacy. . . . Her life, therefore, consists of only a few dates, which mark little more than the commencement and close of her career."[27] The characterization of Smith as an unknown woman whose life included "no incidents" and little more than "a few dates" seems like a rather dismissive notion of her life's worth—a far cry from the type of memorialization literary lions such as Wordsworth or Scott inspired. Still, the

Christian Observer devoted fourteen pages of its August 1808 issue to Smith's life and writings, suggesting that there was indeed much more to her story. The publication and promotion of posthumous memoirs such as *Fragments* helped create expanded notions of whose stories were worth telling.[28]

In exploring both the lived experiences and posthumous representations of Elizabeth Smith as a learned lady, I interrogate intriguing intersections between the fields of biography, literary studies, and print culture. Scholars have examined how cultural constructions of womanhood were inscribed into a variety of literary forms, deepening our understandings of the relationship between gender and print.[29] Models of exemplary womanhood that were produced, sustained, and reshaped by print highlight fascinating interplays between literary representations and lived experiences. Several influential works of biography further indicate how women's lives were shaped by prescriptive ideologies, as well as by family life, sociability, and other cultural factors.[30] Through such studies, we have a better understanding of how individual women influenced, and at times challenged, the dominant models of womanhood that attempted to govern their conduct and behavior. This was especially true in Elizabeth Smith's lifetime, when women such as Mary Wollstonecraft, Jane Austen, Hannah More, Maria Edgeworth, Judith Sargent Murray, and Susanna Rowson actively helped to shape cultural and literary representations of womanhood. These well-known authors, however, represent only a fraction of women's manuscript and printed writings produced at the turn of the nineteenth century. As we recover more literary productions by understudied or unknown women, we are, as Anne K. Mellor notes, beginning "to see the entire spectrum of women's writing in the Romantic era."[31]

Of course, our ability to recover women's writings and experiences depends on the availability and accessibility of source materials. Sometimes women's stories come to us through fragments—and this is particularly true for Elizabeth Smith. The correspondence and writings of Walter Scott, William Wordsworth, and other literary lions have been carefully preserved and are widely available in a variety of published and digitized formats. By contrast, the source base relating to Elizabeth Smith is fragmented but full of potential. To date, I have uncovered just one fragment

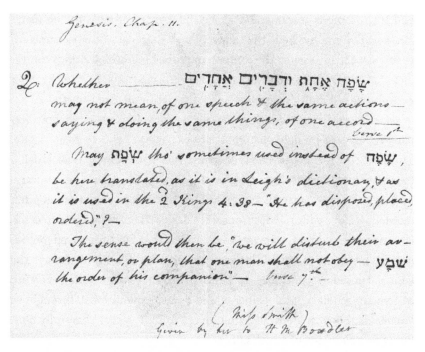

FIGURE 2. Fragment of Elizabeth Smith's handwriting (circa 1800–1805), from a nineteenth-century autograph collection. (© British Library Board, Evelyn Papers)

of a source written directly in her own handwriting, in an autograph collection held at the British Library (fig. 2).[32]

The main source for this project is Elizabeth Smith's posthumously published memoir, *Fragments, in Prose and Verse*. Edited by Henrietta Maria (known as Harriet) Bowdler, *Fragments* contains a carefully curated cache of Smith's "literary remains," including selections of her poetry, correspondence, and journals. Perhaps best known for her efforts at "bowdlerizing" Shakespeare, Bowdler's heavy editorial hand is evident throughout Smith's memoir.[33] *Fragments* offers a bowdlerized account, by an actual Bowdler, of Smith's life story and writings. With this in mind, Bowdler's mediated representations must be used with caution. Various excerpts from Smith's writings included in *Fragments* reveal how she eagerly spent hours puzzling over mathematical equations, fiercely defended her favorite authors, and fearlessly wandered through ancient ruins and mountainous terrains. Yet at key moments throughout the memoir, Bowdler emphasized "the modesty and simplicity of her character," even—especially—when the content and tone of Smith's writings contradict that notion.[34] Through her editorial interventions, Harriet Bowdler actively shaped Smith's legacy as a modest, accomplished woman.

Often regarded as a diluting, moralizing form of censorship, bowdlerizing removes seemingly unsuitable or offensive context to create a safe, sanitized text for respectable readership. In *Fragments*, the bowdlerizing takes on more subtle forms, reflecting Harriet Bowdler's keen awareness of the ambivalence and outright hostility that learned women often faced. Bowdler's editorial decisions were designed to create a positive, celebratory reception for *Fragments*—to assure that Smith received *forgiveness* for her many talents. It is worth considering that Bowdler made the editorial decision to include—rather than expunge—compelling evidence of Smith's scholarly achievements and travel explorations. Throughout *Fragments*, Bowdler's bowdlerizing serves to blur, rather than fully blot, intriguing elements of Smith's life story.

Fragments, in Prose and Verse is a particularly fitting title for Smith's memoir. Only fragments of her life story and writings are accessible to us. There are significant chronological and narrative gaps throughout her memoir, and accordingly much of Smith's everyday life remains hidden from view. To further research her life, I have searched for and uncovered various fragments of evidence in scattered manuscript and printed sources, including correspondence written by family and friends, genealogical and financial records, and contemporary accounts of the geographical places where she lived and visited. Together, these materials enable me to reconstruct more biographical details. The correspondence of her friends Harriet Bowdler, Mary Hunt, and Mary Ann Burges, coupled with the personal and printed writings of several literary figures who knew and admired Smith, such as Thomas Wilkinson, Hannah More, and Mary Leadbeater, yielded additional references to Smith's lived experiences, while also illuminating the personal and professional networks that supported her intellectual aspirations and travel adventures. Further research into everything from conduct literature to travel narratives gave me useful insights into the everyday lives and cultural representations of learned women.

After her death, references to Elizabeth Smith popped up in scores of printed and manuscript materials—from published tribute poetry to the travel diary of a young woman who wept at Smith's grave. Retracing Smith's afterlife has involved a careful search for and sifting through archival, print, and digital source materials. This research patchwork underscores the challenges and possibilities that scholars face when seeking to recover the histories of individuals who do not leave traditional archival "footprints." Piecing together fragmented sources materials requires methodological approaches that recognize gaps, uncertainty, and supposition.[35]

To reconstruct Elizabeth Smith's life and legacy, *The Celebrated Elizabeth Smith* is organized into two parts. Part 1 examines Smith's lived experiences from her birth in 1776 to her death in 1806. Given the fragmented archival record, this section employs a thematic, rather than a traditional "cradle-to-grave" biographical approach. I have developed a series of narrative arcs that offer important vistas into the era's cultural and literary landscapes. Inspired by her night at the inn, I pay close attention to the geographical and physical locations that sparked Elizabeth Smith's intellectual curiosity and adventurous spirit. The four chapters in part 1 are focused around places central to her life story: her childhood home in the Wye Valley, a popular tourist region; her frequent stays in Bath, noted for its community of literary women; her travel adventures throughout England, Wales, and Ireland; and her residence in the English Lake District, celebrated for both its poets and landscapes. The geographical locations at the heart of Smith's life story remind us that women occupied many spaces thought to be the province of men, while also serving as symbolic vistas for surveying her place in the world as a learned woman.

While part 1 sheds new light into what it meant to be a learned lady in an era noted for its literary lions, critical parts of Elizabeth Smith's story began only after her death in 1806. Part 2 explores how a relatively unknown British woman became a celebrated literary figure with transatlantic reach. This section retraces the production, dissemination, and reception of her literary afterlife within local circles, British culture writ large, and across the Atlantic in the United States. Here too place mattered, as her posthumous fame became closely linked to key locations where Smith lived and explored. In both America and England, readers crafted imaginative connections to Smith across time, place, and print.

The second half of the book explores what was at stake as individuals told and retold particular stories about Elizabeth Smith—stories that served as larger cultural assessments about gender, genius, and authorship. Writers often followed Harriet Bowdler's lead, memorializing Smith in ways that emphasized her seemingly modest nature, rather than her ambitions and adventures. Many nineteenth-century commentators were more drawn to an oft-repeated story of Smith baking a tart, for example, than to her bold account of ascending Mount Snowdon. Her legacy became that of an uncommonly exceptional woman frozen in time, rather than a problematic (living) scribbling woman or adventurous mountain climber. From beyond the grave, Elizabeth Smith's literary "ghost" garnered effusive admiration more effortlessly than most learned ladies could expect to receive during their lifetimes. But such praise came at a cost. Smith's literary afterlife often included the erasure of those aspects of her personality and behavior that did not fit larger cultural narratives about how women should conduct themselves. Employing Smith as a symbolic character, various commentators appropriated and even exploited her memory to serve their own prescriptive agendas. In time, the truth about whether or not the "real" Elizabeth Smith bore any resemblance to the idealized characterizations written about her became less and less relevant.

Together, Elizabeth Smith's life story and her enduring afterlife reveal a larger narrative about women's abilities to pursue fulfilling lives for themselves during the age of Romanticism, and the cultural reactions such aspirations inspired. In life and in death, Smith was embedded within social and literary worlds that nourished—and yet also sought to contain—the possibilities of women's intellect and ambition. Her story also urges us to confront the politics of forgetting, to consider how and why a woman who maintained a literary reputation on both sides of the Atlantic for decades received so little attention as the nineteenth century came to an end. Smith's story ends not with her actual death but rather with her eventual historical obscurity. Her rise and fall as a renowned figure raises fundamental questions about how literary and historical genres—as well as celebrity status—have been shaped (and reshaped) over time.

In popular culture, celebrity not only depends on individual talent but waxes and wanes in strength and popularity according to audience reception and media coverage.[36] Like celebrity status, literary prominence and historical significance are not fixed entities; these categories continually shift in response to evolving determinations about whose stories are worth telling and why. Elizabeth Smith's life, legacy, and subsequent obscurity offer revealing vistas into cultural and prescriptive norms about women, genius, and celebrity in the Romantic era and beyond.

Elizabeth Smith's story also illuminates the enthusiasm and fortitude of a well-traveled woman who stayed up past midnight, actively enacting a learned life while Walter Scott and William Wordsworth waited outside. Let's begin by retracing her journey, along with some of the people and places she encountered along the way.

PART I

❧

A Learned Life

1

❦

"Rocky Precipices"

I LOVE YOUR FLOWERY MEADOWS, and murmuring streams; but I cannot help preferring rude mountains, roaring torrents, and rocky precipices," Elizabeth Smith reflected to a friend in July 1792. In contrasting flowery meadows and rude mountains, fifteen-year-old Elizabeth was ardently defending the "grandeur" of Ossian, her then favorite poetry.[1] In the process, she evoked a set of competing cultural sensibilities that attempted to shape life for young women coming of age in the late 1700s. Conduct literature and gender ideology stressed feminine modesty, gentleness, benevolence, and piety. Elizabeth's longing for bold adventures, however, was emblematic of the restless spirit and search for unique, authentic experiences that defined the age of Romanticism.[2] Her descriptions—rude, roaring, rocky—indicated her decided preference for sublime summits over sequestered vales.

As a young woman coming of age in late eighteenth-century England, Elizabeth Smith grew up in the cultural, physical, and gendered spaces between domestic quietude and daring adventure. Even the two family homes Elizabeth inhabited in her youth reflected these competing standards. For the first decade of her life, Elizabeth lived at Burn Hall, the Smith family estate in northeast England. Burn Hall symbolized the staid values of genteel family life, rooted in patriarchal traditions of male privilege and landed inheritance. In 1785, the Smith family relocated to Piercefield, an estate in southeast Wales near the popular resort towns of Bath and Bristol. With the family's move to Piercefield, Elizabeth found herself literally living in the middle of a cultural project. Her new home—with its sweeping vistas of the Wye River Valley and located in close proximity to the ancient ruins of Tintern Abbey—regularly attracted discerning travelers in "search of the picturesque."[3] The Smith's new home in Wales epitomized Romanticism's veneration of sublime landscapes as sources of creativity and inspiration.

Rooted in old-world traditions, life at Burn Hall stressed duty and deference, whereas Piercefield exemplified the transcendent and imaginative elements of Romanticism. At Burn Hall, calm, gentle fields abounded; at Piercefield, rocky cliffs beckoned. As she came of age, Elizabeth Smith made a geographic and symbolic shift away from quiet meadows and toward expansive new heights.

"Great Improvements"

Born in December 1776, Elizabeth Smith was the second child and eldest daughter of George Smith (1751–1822) and his wife, Juliet Mott Smith (1754–1838). The Smith family of Durham valued piety, learning, and tradition. George Smith's grandfather, also named George Smith (1693–1756), was "a man of learning and high character" who had studied history at Queen's College, Oxford. This elder George Smith became a bishop and was known for his edition of Bede's historical works, a task first begun by his father. After receiving an inheritance, he purchased Burn Hall in Durham in 1717. Five years later, this George Smith married Christian Bedford (1704–1781), the daughter of Bishop Hilkiah Bedford. Their eldest son, John Smith (1723–1752), became a doctor and in 1750 married Anne Shuttleworth. The couple's son—Elizabeth's father, George—was born in 1751. John Smith died just one year after his son's birth, so it was young George Smith who inherited Burn Hall after his grandfather's death in 1756.[4]

When he came of age, George Smith "made great improvements to his seat and adjacent lands."[5] Given his family's roots in northeast England, George Smith seemed destined for a life devoted to maintaining the family estate. Many landed gentry were able to generate their yearly income from land rentals and various investments. The lands and farms attached to Burn Hall generated approximately £400 annually in rents, a respectable but not overly prosperous income.[6] In late eighteenth-century England, income among members of the landed gentry varied greatly, from £200 to £2,000. (At the upper echelon of British society, members of the nobility achieved earnings ranging from £4,000 to £20,000.)[7]

In 1774, as he settled into the role of family patriarch, George Smith married Juliet Mott, the "daughter and sole heiress of Richard Mott of Carlton, Suffolk."[8] Described by friends as "pious and accomplished," Juliet Mott was a woman of worth.[9] Little is known about her upbringing, although her girlhood was captured on canvas. As a young girl, Juliet had her portrait painted by the celebrated artist Thomas Gainsborough, who presented it to Juliet's father in gratitude for the care he received while a guest at the Mott house. The portrait was later praised as "one of the sweetest of pictures of girls."[10] As the only surviving child of her parents, the sweet girl grew up into a young woman with considerable financial assets.[11] On the eve of her marriage to George Smith, twenty-year-old Juliet Mott was set to receive "the sum of One thousand pounds if she shall live to attain the age of 21 years" from the Suffolk estate of her uncle Thomas Mulliner. This settlement also entitled Juliet to "recive and take thereout to their his and her own respective use and uses One clear yearly sum or rent charge of two hundred pounds of lawful money" from Mulliner's land holdings in Suffolk.[12] Juliet Mott Smith's inheritance, along with the two-hundred-pound annual income generated from her uncle's land holdings, illustrate the potential economic benefits of eighteenth-century marriage. These resources would augment the newly married couple's wealth, providing funds to spend on items associated with gentry status, including furniture, entertainment, education, and charitable donations.

As George and Juliet Smith's eldest daughter, Elizabeth was born into a genteel world that privileged comfort and affluence. At Burn Hall, she undoubtedly was taught the importance of family tradition, polite manners, and enlightened sociability. British family values were tethered to the gendered ideology of "separate spheres" in this period, with men supposed to be "active in the world as citizens and entrepreneurs" while women maintained a sense of order and stability in the home.[13] Although the realities of late eighteenth-century life inevitably complicated the sharp demarcations prescribed by separate spheres ideology,

these gendered notions nonetheless played instrumental roles in orga-
nizing families' understandings of home and work.

By the late eighteenth century, various works of conduct literature
published in transatlantic cultures of print stressed gendered understandings of family life. Advice writers repeatedly reminded young
women that "within the circle of her own family and dependents lies
her sphere of action."[14] That sphere of action related to both the physical
labor associated with running an eighteenth-century household as well
as the emotional work of sustaining family values. Undoubtedly Burn
Hall was staffed with servants to assist with the endless everyday tasks
of cooking, baking, sewing, cleaning, and childcare. Most middle-class
and genteel families employed at least one to three servants, with larger
estates requiring additional household labor.[15] Whether they directly
engaged in particular domestic chores or not, women of all classes were
expected to play key roles in maintaining household order and domestic
tranquility. "If *men* are expected to distinguish themselves by science,
valour, eloquence, or the arts," conduct writer John Bennett argued, "a
woman's greatest praise consists in the order and good *government* of her
family."[16]

In both England and America, idyllic family life embodied the perfect balance of material, emotional, and intellectual comfort. By the late
eighteenth century, a neat, tasteful home, conveying a "restrained elegance," was the domestic ideal in England and America. Transatlantic
markets gave British and American families access to a variety of consumer goods representative of these shared cultural and material standards. Everything in a home, including its furniture, tea service, wallpa-
per, carpets, paintings, and other decorative items, signified a family's
affluence and taste.[17] In describing her visit to one amiable family, Smith
family friend Harriet Bowdler noted how the home's inhabitants and
objects contributed to a scene of domestic harmony: "They were always
surrounded by such delightful society, they had such a noble Library, and
so much to interest and amuse; Globes, Telescopes, Drawing, Music, &c.
&c., that every day was too short."[18] As such praise suggests, the rituals
of "delightful society" required both material comforts and instructive
entertainments. Gathered together in a tastefully decorated parlor or

library, family members might examine a globe or read aloud from a book of poetry while listening to melodious music played on a nearby piano or harp.[19] Such scenes evoked idealized expressions of tranquil domesticity at the heart of elite British and American family values.

This worldview promoted particular notions about how to best educate women so that they could possess "taste and information enough" to participate in the family social circle.[20] Training in "ornamental" accomplishments such as needlework, painting, and music offered women the skills necessary to augment both the decorative sensibilities and polite sociability of the family home. "If you have any acquired talent of entertainment, such as music, painting, or the like," Hester Chapone advised young women, "your own family are those before whom you should most wish to excel."[21] While an emphasis on proper refinement molded the ornamental accomplishments of young women, by the late eighteenth century genteel families increasingly sought to provide their daughters with more substantial forms of learning.[22] As Hannah More, a conduct writer with wide popularity in both England and America, asserted, "Merely ornamental accomplishments will but indifferently qualify a woman to perform the *duties* of life."[23] To properly fulfill those duties, young women required a careful combination of sense and sensibility.

By the late eighteenth century, prescriptive writers on both sides of the Atlantic recommended that young women study a variety of subjects, including history, geography, natural history, botany, and astronomy, "to enrich the mind with useful and interesting knowledge suitable to their sex."[24] Scores of conduct books and educational treatises promoted the benefits of providing young women with a diverse, well-rounded body of knowledge. Both ornamental arts and scholarly subjects were valued as means of cultivating women's social and domestic graces. Whether women studied music or history, the main purpose of any educational pursuit, as Hannah More insisted, was to inspire "a relish for domestic life, the most desirable temper in the world for women."[25] Writer John Bennett agreed, urging young women to "let your knowledge be *feminine,* as well as your person."[26] The primary purpose of education remained focused on preparing women for their prescribed social and familial roles, rather than developing independent ambitions.[27]

As women were being educated for home life, rather than professional careers, overly rigorous academic training was deemed unnecessary. Relatively few formal institutional opportunities existed for young women in eighteenth-century England, but by the century's end, educators established a number of boarding schools to meet the demands of the expanding professional middle class, who viewed education of both sons and daughters as a means of social mobility. In post-revolutionary America, similar trends developed, as hundreds of female academies served the educational aspirations of families of various socioeconomic backgrounds.[28] Despite these developments, women's access to standardized schooling came at a slow, uneven, and unsystematic pace on both sides of the Atlantic. In England, concerns about both the quality of instruction and moral conduct at boarding schools led to a general climate of distrust. As a result, many families remained "averse to boarding schools, as inspiring a young person with improper notions and undermining the taste for pure simplicity and domestic worth."[29] Like many other families of this era, the Smiths chose home instruction for their daughters. Education at home, under the supervision of a governess or one's mother, remained standard practice for many elite British families.[30]

The first years of Elizabeth Smith's childhood at Burn Hall provided ample room for both genteel refinement and intellectual development. Even as a young child, as her mother Juliet recalled, Elizabeth's actions and behaviors were marked by an "utmost regularity," as she approached life with "an apparent reflection far beyond her years." At three years old, Elizabeth already displayed signs of a strong intellect, as she regularly left "an elder brother and younger sister to play and amuse themselves" while she "made herself mistress" of the books in the nursery. By age four, Elizabeth "read extremely well."[31] In 1782, when she was six years old, Elizabeth's intellectual precociousness gained additional support. At the time, the family temporarily left their family home in Durham and relocated to Suffolk, so that Juliet Smith could help care for her ailing uncle. Juliet hired a young woman to serve as a "companion" for her three young children. As Juliet discovered this woman's extensive intellectual abilities, she became more of a "governess," providing basic educational training for young Elizabeth, along with her older brother, George-Thomas (b. 1775), and her younger sister, Kitty (b. 1778).[32]

In 1784, Juliet Smith's uncle died and the family returned to Burn Hall, leaving their governess behind but taking with them increased family fortunes. The Smiths received an inheritance that enabled George Smith to purchase Piercefield in Monmouthshire, Wales, while retaining the Burn Hall estate.[33] The family's subsequent move to Wales marked not only their rising socioeconomic status but also a symbolic and geographic embrace of Romanticism's inspirational impulses.

"The Romantic Walks of Piercefield"

While Burn Hall denoted old world, traditional family values, Piercefield revealed new outlooks. Even before the Smiths acquired Piercefield, the estate and its surrounding grounds, along with the region in general, were well-known destinations for discerning travelers. In the mid-eighteenth century, Valentine Morris, the estate's previous owner, developed a series of scenic walks and viewpoints and regularly opened up the grounds to visitors.[34] Morris's improvements helped put Piercefield on the map as a "must see" location in the popular Wye River Valley (fig. 3).

Located in close proximity to and within easy access from the resort towns of Bath and Bristol, the Wye Valley was home to historical sites such as Tintern Abbey and Chepstow Castle. Often described as the "birthplace of British tourism," the region gained popularity as eighteenth-century travelers flocked to experience its sublime, magnificent scenery.[35] The Wye Valley held particular appeal for tourists, offering spaces of genteel "picturesque recreation" as well as a landscape "whose topography and historical vestiges" created a sense of "dislocation and radical otherness."[36] With its rocky cliffs and ancient ruins, the Wye River region evoked a mythical landscape in which the beauties of the natural terrain combined with the remnants of olden glory. Tintern Abbey and picturesque spots along the river's edge provided inspiring scenes ideal for sketchbooks and paintings. For the more adventurous, the region's ragged precipices and wooded areas highlighted nature's untarnished wonders.

FIGURE 3. Piercefield Walks (circa 1803), showing the rocky cliffs and picturesque landscapes near Elizabeth Smith's home. (© British Library Board)

By the end of the eighteenth century, travelers to Bath and Bristol considered a trip to the Wye Valley a requisite part of their itinerary. Many visitors to those popular resort towns "cannot withstand the allurement of a passage to the other side" of the Severn River, to experience "the solemn ruins of Tintern abbey, and the romantic walks of Piercefield."[37] A local travel industry developed featuring carefully curated tours and services for the steady stream of individuals seeking to explore the Wye Valley.[38] As interest in the region grew, guidebooks provided travelers with practical information on securing coaches to the boathouse and booking ferry passages across the Severn, as well as recommending notable establishments for dining and lodging.

In addition to offering practical travel tips, guidebooks included appealing descriptions of the region's attractions to persuade visitors that a visit across the river was worth their time and effort. One of the most influential books was William Gilpin's *Observations on the River Wye*, first published in 1782, based on his 1770 visit to the region. Gilpin noted that Morris's "improvements" to the house and property at Piercefield were "much worth a traveller's notice."[39] Gilpin's "bewitching description of the river Wye" inspired numerous individuals to travel and record their observations on Piercefield, often as they made their way to or from Tintern Abbey.[40] These descriptions were almost universal in their enthusiastic praise for Piercefield's landscape, which, according to one guidebook, "waves almost imperceptibly in a grand outline, on the brow of the majestic amphitheatre of cliffs impending over the Wy[e]." Piercefield's winding paths unexpectedly revealed several scenic views, "from meadows and lawns, to rocks and precipices, and from the mild beauties of English landscape to the wildness of Alpine scenery."[41] As the 1791 edition of the *New Bath Guide* noted, Piercefield's "most beautiful and magnificent scenery" was varied and inspired, including "stupendous rocks, immense woods, distant prospects, and all the softer beauties of elegant improvements, [which] render Piercefield a scene that fills the beholder with the most ravishing admiration."[42] The result, according to another guide, "contributed to form a picture, which can neither be conceived nor described, without detracting infinitely from its charms."[43] By the end of the eighteenth century, the "celebrated Walks of Piercefield" were renowned within British tourism circles.[44] "I could not think of leaving this country without visiting Piercefield," one traveler asserted.[45]

In choosing to live in a region noted for its domestic tourism, and at a well-known spot on the picturesque travel scene, George Smith made a status-seeking decision about his family's home life. The choice to purchase an entirely new home rather than remaining at Burn Hall indicated his desire to reinvent himself and redirect his family fortunes. He appeared eager to distinguish himself from the long line of John and George Smiths of Burn Hall that had come before him. With the move to Wales, he was now George Smith of Piercefield. In addition to his status as a member of the landed gentry, Smith embarked on a new career, establishing the Monmouthshire Bank with his partner John Curre. To further promote ties to his new place of residence, he served a term as sheriff of Monmouthshire in 1788.[46]

With the move to Piercefield, George Smith sought to transform his family's genteel country life into a prominent, public display of affluence.[47] The desired effect, according to an 1801 description of Piercefield, was to create a living environment "equally calculated for private comfort or public splendor."[48] Piercefield was a particularly inspiring location for those in search of public splendor, but this style of living was not for the faint of heart. As one traveler noted after his 1787 visit, Piercefield "is very fine thing to see, but not a desirable place to inhabit." The residence and extensive grounds at Piercefield took considerable costs to maintain. "I know not Mr. S's income; but it is not a station of retirement, or for a man of small fortune; being for ever on an exhibition, and in a glare; and so famed, that an owner, and his servants become shew men."[49] Such performative rituals helped showcase George Smith's rising status but required significant investments of time, money, and energy.

While George Smith viewed Piercefield as an opportune place to elevate his status, the family's new home inspired his bright, curious daughter as well. Elizabeth would have agreed with the many travel writers who praised her new home as "this enchanting spot" full of places to explore, "where nature wantons in such variety, and combined so great a portion of the beautiful, the picturesque, and the sublime."[50] While most travelers spent only a day or two taking in the sublime sights, Elizabeth experienced the wonders of Piercefield every day. Surrounded by scenic walkways, historic ruins, and wooded paths, she had ample space for physical and mental explorations.

Having already demonstrated signs of intelligence at an early age, Elizabeth's powers of mind blossomed at Piercefield. She made "most rapid" progress in her studies, demonstrating a seemingly unquenchable thirst for knowledge.[51] In 1786, the Smith family's former governess resumed her employment, primarily to teach the children French and Italian.[52] With the births of Elizabeth's younger siblings Charles Felix, Juliet, and John Henry Bedford between 1786 and 1788, a governess undoubtedly offered Juliet Smith welcome childcare assistance. When their governess left after three additional years with the Smith family, Elizabeth was accomplished enough that she "became a sort of governess to her younger sisters."[53] Elizabeth also continued her own intellectual pursuits, studying history and mathematics and learning several languages in addition to French and Italian.

Even in an era marked by growing support for women's education, Elizabeth's ardent intellectual pursuits, especially in languages, might have garnered controversy or disapproval. Advice writers warned that only a woman possessed with "particular genius" was capable of engaging in the study of "learned languages," and only if she intended to "make a modest and proper use of them." In particular, critics insisted that women's study of classical languages such as Latin and Greek was potentially pedantic and ostentatious. "The danger of pedantry and presumption in a woman," conduct writer Hester Chapone warned, should be enough to steer women away from extensive studies of languages and other scholarly pursuits.[54] As such remarks illustrate, even those who promoted improvements in women's access to education warned that *too* ardent an approach "would render you unwomanly indeed."[55]

In this respect, Elizabeth was fortunate to receive encouragement for her extensive scholarly interests, not only from her supportive mother and governess but also from her growing connections with other like-minded women. In 1789, Elizabeth met Henrietta Maria (known as Harriet) Bowdler (1750–1830), the woman who would significantly shape her intellectual character. The Bowdler family made their home in Bath and were active participants in that town's renowned social and literary scenes. Described by her friends as "very amiable and ingenious," Harriet Bowdler surrounded herself with accomplished, learned women.[56] The Bowdlers enjoyed warm friendships with a number of influential literary figures of the era, including Fanny Burney, Hester Piozzi, and Eleanor Butler and Sarah Ponsonby, the famed Ladies of Llangollen.

When she first met Elizabeth Smith in 1789, Harriet Bowdler had recently edited and published a volume of her deceased sister's poetry. The volume was initially published without attribution and presented as an act of benevolence to support a charity hospital in Bath. In the volume's preface, Harriet (anonymously) insisted that the poems and essays were not written out of any desire for literary fame but rather for the benefit of "the humble and pious Christian" seeking "support and consolation."[57] It is significant but not surprising that Harriet Bowdler positioned her foray into print within traditional notions of femininity, respectability, and benevolence. She understood that such pious, modest refrains could help mitigate prevailing critiques that viewed women's literary productions as "unwomanly" or outside of their prescribed sphere.

As Juliet Smith later reflected, meeting Harriet Bowdler, who visited Piercefield for a month with her mother, Elizabeth Bowdler, was a pivotal moment in her daughter Elizabeth's life: "I date the turn of study which Elizabeth ever after pursued, and which, I firmly believe, the amiable conduct of our guests first led her to delight in."[58] Upon first meeting the Bowdlers, Elizabeth expressed "extreme timidity" and was reluctant to join in conversations with her guests. Despite Elizabeth's reticence, Harriet and her mother immediately recognized her "very uncommon talents." Elizabeth's intellectual abilities continually "astonished" the Bowdlers. According to Harriet, Elizabeth "excelled in every thing that she attempted," including "Music, Dancing, Drawing, and Perspective." Just as she had done in the nursery as a young child, Elizabeth spent countless hours reading with "unwearied attention." Although Harriet worried that her young friend "might injure her health" by spending too much time with her books, she eagerly offered Elizabeth intellectual, emotional, and moral support.[59] Nearly forty at the time, Harriet took the thirteen-year-old Elizabeth under her wing. Their difference in age was not seen as an impediment to friendship. Conduct writers such as Hester Chapone urged young women to pursue close friendships with "some person of riper years and judgment, whose good-nature and worthy principles may assure you of her readiness to do you service."[60] Older and wiser companions, Chapone and other prescriptive writers believed, could impart invaluable advice to young women.

Harriet Bowdler developed a warm, mentoring friendship with Elizabeth Smith, while Elizabeth Bowdler served as a trusted elder, offering guidance to their accomplished young protégé. Upon Elizabeth Smith's confirmation in December 1791, Elizabeth Bowdler wrote a letter to commemorate this symbolic moment as the commencement of "the most important period of life." She advised Elizabeth Smith to develop a clear sense of herself: "We must be considered as thinking and acting for ourselves." Elizabeth Bowdler emphasized the importance of cultivating a purposeful life through piety, self-study, and thoughtful attention to one's duties. To guard against pride and "many other failings," she presented her young friend with a series of framing questions: "How can I best serve God?. . . . How can I employ my time and my talents to the best advantage? What are the errors into which I am most likely to fall?" Elizabeth Bowdler sought to guide fifteen-year-old Elizabeth Smith with her transition to adulthood. "I should wish every one who really aims at Christian perfection," she advised, "to make out in writing a plan of life suited to his particular situation and character, and resolutely determine to act up to it."[61]

Filial devotion and Christian piety were at the heart of the era's notion of femininity, but significantly, Elizabeth Bowdler also emphasized the importance of putting one's talents to good use. Driven since childhood by her keen intellect, Elizabeth Smith may have found such advice particularly appealing. As Elizabeth contemplated her plan of life, the romantic vistas of Piercefield offered expansive paths for exploration.

"A Pretty Little Fiction"

In summer 1792, just months after receiving Elizabeth Bowdler's thoughtful advice, fifteen-year-old Elizabeth Smith was out on one of her frequent walks among the grounds surrounding Piercefield, where she discovered the remains of an ancient building, including "several round towers, a moat, &c." Elizabeth wondered if the ruins once belonged to Llewelyn, the Prince of Wales. "I have a great mind to believe that our Castle in the wood is the Castle of Buillt," she eagerly reported to her friend Mary Hunt.[62] Elizabeth acknowledged that her theory was most likely "a pretty little fiction" but insisted that the notion was "so harmless, that I really must believe it."[63] This "pretty little fiction" provided a compelling outlet for her developing intellectual and imaginative powers. For the next several months, Elizabeth devoted herself to researching these ruins with what Harriet Bowdler described as "indefatigable application." "I remember walking over the spot where her lively imagination had built a Castle," Harriet recalled, "of which she drew a plan from the slight traces which remained."[64]

As she ruminated on her ancient ruins, Elizabeth turned to her friend Mary Hunt, who was then working as a governess for the Simcoe family in Devonshire. Mary learned that Margaret Graves, an aunt to the Simcoe daughters, had access to a Welsh manuscript that promised to provide "invaluable" leads. "Has Mrs. Graves shewn the manuscript to any person who understands Welsh?" Elizabeth asked impatiently, hoping that the translation of this document "will settle all our doubts." Elizabeth understood that uncovering the mystery of her ruins required dedication and persistence: "We are obliged to fight hard, with every body we meet, in maintaining our cause," she reported excitedly to her friend.[65] Elizabeth also gained valuable assistance from her mentor. Harriet Bowdler reached out to the Welsh barb Edward Williams, who was then at work "writing the history of Monmouthshire."[66] At the time, Edward Williams, who also went by the Welsh name Iolo Morganwg, was attracting attention from leading literary circles for his efforts to promote Welsh history, language, and culture.[67] Williams expressed interest in the project, and as Elizabeth reported, "told us that Buillt, where it has been said he [Llewelyn] died, is somewhere near this place; he does not know where it is, but we will find it out."[68]

Perhaps it seems somewhat audacious that a young woman would expect a leading Welsh literary figure to assist with her "pretty little fiction," but both Harriet Bowdler and Juliet Smith already had connections to Edward Williams. In February 1791, the two women met with Williams and "invited me to their Patronage," encouraging his efforts to secure key social and literary contacts.[69] In both Great Britain and the United States, elite women often served as patrons for aspiring literary figures. Women used their social connections to promote authors, to solicit subscriptions for their works, and to help build their literary reputations.[70] These types of activities illustrate how women frequently played indirect but influential roles within local and national literary circles.

As Elizabeth Smith explored her ruins, Edward Williams was navigating the "many mysteries of Authorship," meeting with literary figures, and traveling to London to solicit subscriptions for a volume of poetry he hoped to publish.[71] Throughout the 1790s, he continued to gain support and celebrity for his historical and literary endeavors, particularly his efforts to search for a supposed lost tribe of Welsh-speaking Native Americans. As Harriet Bowdler reported in one of her letters to Edward Williams, "Mrs. Montagu and some of the *first-rate Litterati*" of Bath were curious for updates on findings related to this "lately discovered Welsh Colony in America."[72] Harriet Bowdler's enthusiasm for Williams's efforts waned somewhat once she learned that he somehow managed to spend "all the money which was subscribed" for his volume of poetry without seeing it printed. As the project dragged on for months without any progress, Harriet began to express doubts. Williams's lengthy absence from his home in Wales, as she wrote, seemed "injudicious in itself" to some people, and "very unfortunate for your Family," who were, "as I hear much distressed without you." By drawing on concerns about his reputation and familial responsibilities, Harriet Bowdler tried to use feminine virtue to coax Edward Williams into right action. Although concerned about his misspent funds, Harriet reported that her mother agreed to send "eight guineas" so that he could buy the paper needed for printing but "says she hopes you will give her the satisfaction of knowing that it has answered the purpose intended, by sending her the Printers' receipt for the Paper."[73] Having invested their time and money into Williams's project, the Bowdlers were eager to see their patronage bear fruit.

When *Poems, Lyric and Pastoral* was finally published in 1794, after what even he admitted was "a pretty long delay," Edward Williams publicly praised Harriet and Elizabeth Bowdler in the book's preface as "most amiably benevolent Ladies." The Bowdlers were among the volume's list of subscribers whose names appeared in italics, to indicate that Williams counted them as "my most distinguished friends." Italicized entries for "*George Smith*, Esq. Piercefield, &c." and "*Mrs. Smith*, ditto, &c." also appeared on the subscription list. In one of the volume's poems, Williams enthusiastically celebrated "Nature's charms" and beauties found at Piercefield.[74]

Piercefield was an enchanting, inspiring location for poets and travelers, so it is not surprising that Elizabeth Smith was eager to commemorate the discoveries she had made during her explorations. At first, she tried without success to persuade Mary Hunt to write a poem about the location's historical significance. It is understandable why Elizabeth initially asked her friend for assistance. In 1786, Mary Hunt composed a poem, "Written on Visiting the Ruins of Dunkeswell-Abbey, in Devonshire, Sept. 1786," near the Simcoe family home in Devonshire. Published anonymously in the *Gentleman's Magazine*, her poem underscored the appeal of ruins as sites of creative contemplation: "Though now in ruin'd majesty they lie, / The fading reliques of departed days . . . / Whose solemn shades reflection's powers invite."[75] In 1792—right as Elizabeth Smith was exploring her ruins—Mary Hunt's poem was also included in Richard Polwhele's published collection *Poems, Chiefly by Gentlemen of Devonshire and Cornwall*.[76] As Elizabeth Simcoe noted, "Miss Hunt, has, at last, at the solicitations of her friends, consented to have her name affixed to the Verses on Dunkeswell Abbey."[77]

In attempting to persuade her friend Mary to compose a set of verses about the ruins at Piercefield, Elizabeth proposed, "You must say that it is translated from an old Welsh bard, and that will set the matter beyond a doubt."[78] Had she known the truth about his efforts, Elizabeth might have asked Edward Williams for help with this specific task, as he was dedicated to "recovering, and where necessary inventing an illustrious Welsh literature tradition."[79] After his death, it was discovered that Williams had forged many of the Welsh manuscripts he presented to the public as authentic historical texts. Perhaps he would have gladly lent his pen in the aid of Elizabeth's pretty little fiction.

Dissatisfied with the historical materials she consulted in her research, Elizabeth Smith may have understood Edward Williams's desire to invent a new literary tradition. "All those old authors copy after each other, and make nothing but confusion," she complained in a letter to Mary Hunt. "I prefer my own way of making the history just as I please, without consulting one of them."[80] To make her own history, Elizabeth turned to poetry. "A Supposed Translation from a Welsh Poem, Lately Dug up at Piercefield, in the Same Spot Where Llewellyn at Grynfyd Was Slain, Dec. 10th, 1281," represents her stylized attempt to give voice to her ruins. Her deliberate use of the phrase a "supposed translation" alerted the reader to the poem's true origins, while calling attention to the historical significance of its setting. The verses echoed the sensibilities of Welsh history by evoking resonant themes of loss, glory, and mourning:

> To Piercefield's Cliffs I'll now a pilgrim go,
> Shed o'er my Prince belov'd the tears of woe;
> There will I seek some deep and rocky cell,

Amidst the thick entangled wood to dwell;
There indulge my plaintive theme,
To the wan moon's icy beam,
While the rocks responsive ring,
To my harp's high-sounding string;
Vaga stops her rolling tide,
List'ning to her ancient pride;
Birds and beasts my song attend,
And mourn with me our country's fatal end![81]

Elizabeth Smith's first significant poem—forged from months of research, curiosity, and collaboration—represented a pivotal moment in her life. Elizabeth had shown signs of intellectual talent as a young girl at Burn Hall, but life at Piercefield provided her with both the physical and imaginative frameworks to take her efforts to the next level. Just fifteen when she composed these verses, Elizabeth was relatively new to poetic expression and perhaps a bit unsure of her developing literary voice. She insisted that she composed these verses because her friend Mary refused her earlier request to write a poem, and "because you desire me to continue rhyming." She expressed tentativeness about the quality of her productions, coupled with gratitude that Mary was eager to read the poem. "Without making use of any of the modesty for which you so kindly give me credit," Elizabeth demurred to Mary, "I must see that I do not deserve all that you say about the subject." Despite her reservations, Elizabeth did not refrain from sharing opinions, efforts, or poetry with Mary and other trusted friends. Rather, she drew courage from their encouragement. "However, if it be your true opinion, you must be delighted at being desired to read this volume of nonsense," she wrote to Mary, "and if it not be, I have taken the most effectual method to cure you of complimenting."[82] Elizabeth may have dismissed her own pretty little fiction as a "volume of nonsense," but she was grateful for her friends' support.

Harriet Bowdler would later insist that Elizabeth Smith's hesitancy about sharing her poem was evidence of her protégé's overly modest nature, but Elizabeth's enthusiastic approach to this project hardly seems indicative of a restrained personality. While her self-deprecating remarks could be read as reflections of excessive modesty, it is possible they were part of her efforts to construct an acceptable framework for her extensive, exhaustive pursuits. The disclaimers Elizabeth used—modesty, self-effacement, deference to her friend's wishes—served to justify her rigorous research process and her desire to put pen to paper. Such modest refrains were useful for any young woman seeking to avoid charges of selfish literary ambition that were often directed at learned ladies. Just as Harriet Bowdler strategically presented her sister's verses for publication under the guise of Christian piety and resignation, Elizabeth Smith was careful to situate her initial literary efforts within the "safe" world of female friendship. Writing poetry at the behest of a trusted friend was an acceptable pastime for a young woman, located within the boundaries of respectable feminine activity.

Moreover, to see her poem merely as some modest, amateur effort would be to place Elizabeth Smith at the margins, rather than at the center, of the geographical and cultural landscape that she literally called home. Living at Piercefield, Elizabeth regularly encountered the steady streams of travelers who eagerly visited the estate's celebrated walks, along with the nearby ruins of Tintern Abbey (fig. 4). Although Romantic-era men (and subsequent generations of scholars) have identified this search for the picturesque as "culturally coded male," Elizabeth's residence at Piercefield pointedly demonstrates that women were also active participants in these literary and cultural patterns.[83] Significantly, she experienced these trends not in the abstract but as notable, up-close parts of her everyday life.

Inspired by her picturesque surroundings, Elizabeth Smith was also informed by the era's heightened interest in Welsh history and culture. Living in the Wye River Valley and in such close proximity to Tintern Abbey, Elizabeth saw firsthand how remnants from the past were especially popular among Romantic-era tourists, poets, and artists. Haunting ruins, set amid inspiring natural landscapes, evoked mythical connections with the past, sparking lingering "questions about the relationship between man and nature."[84] Both lyrical poetry and domestic tourism were key components of the era's revitalized interest in the regional cultures of the British Isles. As a burgeoning domestic tourism industry developed in

FIGURE 4. Tintern Abbey (1815), showing tourists standing among the ruins and overgrown foliage. (© British Library Board)

late eighteenth-century England, men and women alike flocked to sites such as Tintern Abbey, where remnants of the past presented themselves in haunting, overgrown landscapes.

Elizabeth Smith understood that poetry highlighting connections between her ruins and the Prince of Wales could infuse the site with heightened appeal. By presenting her poem as a "supposed translation," Elizabeth deliberately conjured an image of a "lost" Welsh past, a vision that also inspired figures such as Edward Williams. Romantic poets were drawn to "authentic folk tradition" from Wales, Scotland, and Ireland as sources of creative inspiration. Poetry glorifying these regions' mythical pasts reflected literary and cultural movements that sought to maintain distinct traditions and legacies across the British Isles.[85]

It is also worth noting that Elizabeth's poetic efforts imitated the style and format of her then-favorite poet. Ossian's epic tales of adventure, battles, and lost love, set against a dramatic historical background, evoked imaginative and romantic themes easily adaptable to Piercefield's rocky cliffs. The poetry of Ossian was first published in the 1760s by Scottish poet James Macpherson, who claimed to have discovered and translated the poems from ancient Gaelic originals. Subsequently, Ossian's poems were translated into several languages and generated international acclaim. Almost immediately after publication, however, disputes about Ossian's authenticity created a literary scandal, with prominent authors weighing in on both sides. Samuel Johnson was convinced that the poems were forgeries, but supporters such as Hugh Blair defended Macpherson's claims. The debate lasted for decades without clear resolution. Despite the controversy, Ossian was widely admired by many key figures, including Thomas Jefferson, who in 1773 described Ossian's poetry as a "source of daily and exalted pleasure."[86] Walter Scott felt that Ossian's poems held particular "charms for youth," recalling how he had "devoured rather than perused" them, committing long passages to memory. Scott eventually accepted that Ossian was forged but softened his critical appraisal by explaining that he believed Macpherson "*thought* almost every word of Ossian in Gaelic, though he wrote it down in English."[87]

The spirit of Romanticism, along with expanding publication markets, encouraged innovative literary practices, and in the process enabled individuals to reinvent themselves. At the very moment that Elizabeth Smith contemplated her ruins, James Macpherson was a wealthy, if controversial, literary figure serving in Parliament, while Edward Williams, a stonemason by trade, was successfully soliciting subscriptions for his volume of poetry and making a name for himself as Iolo Morganwg. Walter Scott's historical poetry and novels would soon launch him toward new heights of literary celebrity, but in 1792 he was a young lawyer working in Edinburgh. Although he tempered his youthful love of Ossian, Scott retained a desire to present compelling narratives focused on epic, historical themes. By turning to historical fiction, he avoided the controversies that surrounded Macpherson and Williams.

Despite the differences in their career trajectories, these men's authorial ambitions were fueled by key literary, cultural, and physical landscapes that shaped the Romantic era. Like these more well-known male literary figures, fifteen-year-old Elizabeth Smith was also eager to fashion a new plan of life, one that would enable her to contribute to the era's evolving intellectual and cultural trends. But her ability to do so was impeded not just by her age and inexperience but by her gender. While an increasing number of women took up their pens during this era, prescriptive literature sought to dissuade young women from cultivating literary ambitions, encouraging them instead to find contentment in more modest, tame pursuits. Conduct literature repeatedly promoted the virtues of quiet domesticity, warning young women not to develop overly romantic or sensationalized notions of life. As Hannah More advised, "Teach her that human life is not a splendid romance, spangled over with brilliant adventures."[88]

Elizabeth Smith's explorations at Piercefield suggest that young women were often drawn to "brilliant adventures," even as cultural prescriptions sought to steer women away from such activities. Thriving travel scenes and literary networks inspired many young women to imagine new vistas for themselves. At picturesque Piercefield, Elizabeth's thirst for adventure had ample room to develop. As she devoted countless hours to her research and explorations, Elizabeth received support and encouragement, rather than criticism or condemnation. As a young woman, she was learning that her intellectual and imaginative pursuits were worthy endeavors. Her friend Mary Hunt's poem on the ruins near Devonshire was published to positive acclaim. Such publications reflected larger trends, as a number of women authors of the era incorporated local historical writings into their poetry, novels, and various works of nonfiction.[89] The Bowdler and Smith families had actively helped shepherd Edward Williams's poetry into print at the same moment that they encouraged Elizabeth Smith's pretty little fiction. And if a stonemason could become a poet, why not an intelligent young woman living on the picturesque banks of the River Wye?

The subject and tone of her verses provide further insights into Elizabeth Smith's aspirations. These were not gentle, feminine verses set in calm meadows and murmuring streams. Her rocky cliffs and wistful tales revealed Elizabeth's desire to forge something magnificent from the ruins. She was drawn not to tame, feminine vales but to Romanticism's celebration of the epic, heroic, and daring. However, at just fifteen years old, Elizabeth was not yet in charge of her own plan of life. It had been her father's decision to relocate the family home to Piercefield. The family's fortunes, and by extension Elizabeth's future, ultimately remained in his hands.

"A Change of Fortune"

While Elizabeth was ruminating on the past, her father was planning for the future. The opportunity to purchase Piercefield came as a result of its previous owner's economic misfortune, a lesson George Smith might have considered more closely as he took on such grand living quarters. After investing heavily in improvements to the property, Valentine Morris left Piercefield in 1772 to return to the West Indies, where his family had made their fortunes on sugar estates. Over the next decade, Morris fell deeply into debt. In 1778, an attempt to sell Piercefield for £24,000 fell through, and the estate was occupied for several years by tenants who did not adequately maintain Morris's extensive walkways. The house and grounds suffered from a decade of neglect and decline and were in need of improvement when George Smith purchased the estate in July 1784 for a price below its original value.[90]

Enthusiastic about the prospect of showcasing his new home, George Smith solicited John Soane's architectural expertise. At the time, Soane was an aspiring architect eager to make a name for himself. As he built his reputation, Soane relied largely on private commissions, often arranged through his supportive network of friends. It was George Smith's cousin Rowland Burdon (who had met Soane in Italy) who helped the architect secure work for the Smith family.[91] As the poet Edward Williams learned, one's professional success in the eighteenth century often depended not only on personal talents but also on the valuable contacts and patronage an individual secured along the way.

George Smith initially hired John Soane in 1783 to renovate the cowbarn at Burn Hall. As one biographer noted, Soane took on the project because he believed "that not even a manger was too lowly for a talented architect eager for work."[92] Ultimately, Soane hoped his aesthetic designs would lead to a distinguished public career. Eager to promote himself, Soane displayed his plans for the cowbarn at the 1784 exhibition of the Royal Academy of Arts. Soane may have hoped that such an unusual choice for a submission would garner attention. The barn (which was large enough to house thirty cows) featured a "high-arched entrance and pavilion ends." Visitors to the Royal Academy might have been impressed with Soane's aesthetic sensibility, but ultimately construction of the cowbarn required modifications for its practical use.[93]

George Smith also hoped to renovate the living quarters at Burn Hall, but he abandoned those plans after purchasing Piercefield. Instead, Soane prepared a set of designs that reflected Smith's desire to add a heightened sense of grandeur to his new home.[94] Piercefield was perhaps the perfect location for Soane to apply his neoclassical design sensibility, which had been influenced by his travels to Rome and Naples and reflected his interests in "romantic literature and picturesque theory."[95] Soane's initial plans, drafted in 1785, included an expansion of the existing three-story home to include "a library with a bow front, large vestibule, a dining room and withdrawing room at the south-east and north-east corners."[96] This would be an ambitious and expensive project. Costs to build or renovate country houses in late eighteenth-century England varied, but other projects that John Soane worked on during the 1780s ranged between £3,700 and £16,000 in expenditures.[97]

Due to Piercefield's status as a popular tourist destination, word spread that George Smith, "the present proprietor, is erecting a magnificent mansion near the spot."[98] Visitors hoped that the "native charms" of Piercefield would remain safe from George Smith's "alterations."[99] Writers expressed concerns that Smith's lavish plans to renovate the house would mar the natural, sublime beauty of Piercefield's landscape. "Unless directed by a very rare taste," one critic argued, any changes "will rather injure than embellish those charming scenes, which, hitherto, *improvement* has not deformed. Happily, whatever a *pretty* taste may do within, it cannot extend to the scenery without."[100] Others complained about his decision to limit visitors' access to Piercefield. As the 1791 *New Bath Guide* noted, Smith "will not suffer it [Piercefield] to be seen on any day but Thursdays."[101] Choosing to enact one's family life as a cultural project attracted its share of both supporters and critics.

For unknown reasons, George Smith's renovation plans for Piercefield seem to have stalled for several years. In 1790, John Soane again drew up "3 fair drawings of design" and "talked over plans" with George Smith. Two years later, Soane sent additional drawings for review. By summer 1792—the same year Elizabeth Smith was hard at work exploring her ruins—renovations to the house at Piercefield were finally underway. Soane's plans for the project reflected a "simpler and more economical" vision than the sketches originally prepared in 1785.[102] Yet even in their scaled-back form, the renovations created major upheaval. "Could you see the state our house is in," Elizabeth wrote to her friend Mary that August, "you would not think it possible to live in it; half the walls pull'd down, foundations dug, and heaps of rubbish every where."[103] By the fall of 1792, Juliet Smith left Piercefield, "not being able to stay here any longer." Elizabeth's mother seemed to have only limited patience for her husband's ambitions. With the support of her extended network of friends, Juliet was able to escape the disruptive renovations. Elizabeth and her siblings remained at home, with plans to reunite with their mother in Bath at Christmas. "I live in hopes," Elizabeth wrote to Mary as she planned her next steps.[104]

At the end of the year, Elizabeth made the journey to Bath to reunite with her mother and also spent "many happy hours" with dear friends Mary Hunt and Harriet Bowdler.[105] As the sixteen-year-old prepared to travel back to Piercefield at the end of February 1793, her prospects seemed bright. Elizabeth looked forward to reuniting with the rest of her family and to entertaining friends in her newly renovated home: "I hope to have more time at Piercefield, where we are now all to meet, after having been scattered over the face of the earth for the last half year."[106] Elizabeth's hopes for the future, however, were quickly put to test by the realities of the present. Within days of her arrival home in late February 1793, a dark cloud descended on the Smith family. On February 20, George Smith informed his architect that "his notes would be stopt payment tomorrow."[107] England's war with France in response to the French Revolution had created financial panic that had far-reaching personal and business consequences across the kingdom.[108] George Smith's Monmouthshire Bank was among the many that failed that year, plunging him into financial ruin.

With bankruptcy imminent, Piercefield was scheduled to be seized by creditors, creating turmoil for the Smith family. At ten o'clock in the evening on Saturday March 2, "the Under-Sheriff, &c. came to take possession of the house." The Smiths secured Piercefield "so that they could not enter." The family survived what Elizabeth referred to as the "night of storms," and George Smith's attorney arrived from London to stop the "execution."[109] The reprieve was only temporary. A bankruptcy was issued against George Smith and his partner John Curre, who were "required to surrender themselves to the Commission" to "make a full Discovery and Disclosure of their Estate and Effects." Creditors met in London that summer to assess the situation and "to receive Proof of the separate Debts of the said George Smith."[110]

During the bankruptcy inquiries, it was uncovered that George Smith had earlier drawn up a bond of £40,000 to John Curre, his business partner, to help lend credibility to his banking business: "John Curre having permitted his name to be made use of therein at the special instance and request of the said Geo. Smith in order to add reputation to the said bank." In exchange for Curre's support, George Smith had "agreed to indemnify the said Jn. Curre from all Risk Loss and Damage." Other case notes indicated creditors' concerns about Smith's character: "Smith committed several acts of bankruptcy, [and] absented himself from his dwelling house to avoid his Creditors." Due to the intermingling of George Smith's personal and business finances, it was considered "a most serious Case."[111]

Juliet Smith attempted to mitigate the impact of her husband's bankruptcy by calling on John Soane for financial assistance. Soane expressed his wish "to render any service in my power to any part of your family" but noted that he was unable to fulfill her request of "raising the Sum wanted."[112] The bankruptcy proceedings determined that the Smith family would lose their home at Piercefield, along with the family's land holdings in Durham and the Suffolk property that Juliet Smith had inherited. The properties were scheduled to be auctioned off by creditors in late 1793. Piercefield and its extensive land holdings were assessed as generating £2,000 in annual rents, with the Smith's various land holdings in Durham county providing an additional £700 annually.[113]

George Smith's financial failure devastated the family's fortunes. As one family friend later recalled, "Within a few years he had experienced a great reverse of fortune. He had enjoyed large possessions, and his wife had brought him £50,000. He unfortunately engaged in a bank, which failed, leaving him in comparative poverty."[114] The family enjoyed considerable prospects before the bank failure, in no small part due to the assets Juliet Smith had brought to the marriage. While supportive friends blamed the war for Smith's bankruptcy, it is likely that George Smith's own actions placed the family's financial future at risk even before international events muddied the waters. An architectural history of Piercefield suggests that Smith's bank and another local bank were "bitter rivals" before the widespread bank failures of 1793, contributing to his financial instability. By 1792, George Smith had mortgaged part of the Piercefield estate, presumably to help finance the renovations. When he defaulted on a £10,000 loan, he had to forfeit a portion of his property holdings.[115]

The long delay in beginning renovations at Piercefield supports the idea that George Smith may have overextended his financial prospects in choosing to relocate and set up a grand home and banking business in Wales. Although John Soane was first commissioned to draw up plans in 1785, renovations to Piercefield did not begin until 1792, and on a more modest scale than George Smith had initially envisioned. Evidence from the architect's business records also indicates that Soane lent money to Smith in 1790.[116] These fragments of information suggest that George Smith's various financial decisions, and not merely the chaos created by war, led to the decline of his family fortunes.

In any case, central to the Smith family story is a fundamental tension between the family model promoted by separate spheres ideology and the ways in which George Smith's ambitious plans and subsequent bankruptcy fundamentally disrupted the family's socioeconomic status. The prescriptive ideology of separate spheres rested on the notion of a male breadwinner, with the "home as haven from the market."[117] In leaving Burn Hall to raise his family fortunes at Piercefield, George Smith embarked on a grand plan to reinvent himself. Piercefield's romantic, sublime scenery provided an inspired site for such aspirations, but when his vision led to

financial ruin, the Smiths found themselves without the comfort and stability of a home to call their own. As part of the bankruptcy proceedings,
George Smith was forced to sell the home at Piercefield and also forfeit
the family estate at Burn Hall. The family retreated to Bath to stay with
friends and figure out their next steps.

As Harriet Bowdler reported, such "a change of fortune, so sudden, and
so unexpected was a great trial." Leaving Piercefield behind must have
been difficult for Elizabeth Smith. The picturesque family home, according to Harriet Bowdler, was "one of the finest places in England," where
Elizabeth "enjoyed all the elegant comforts of affluence."[118] At Piercefield,
Elizabeth was relatively free from domestic burdens and had ample time
to pursue a variety of intellectual activities and physical explorations,
aided by a supportive network of family and friends. She had dwelled
in the possibilities of a romantic landscape that offered vistas far more
expansive than the quiet domestic scenes prescribed by the era's conduct
literature. Elizabeth must have wondered whether she would be able to
maintain her lofty pursuits given her family's reduced financial circumstances. Yet she apparently handled the change with quiet resignation.
As her mother recalled, "I do not recollect a single instance of murmur
having escaped her, on account of the loss of fortune."[119]

"These Steep and Lofty Cliffs"

Had her family remained at Piercefield, Elizabeth Smith might have
met her future neighbor William Wordsworth, who first visited the Wye
Valley in the summer of 1793, just months after the Smith family's abrupt
departure to Bath. Two years later, the poets Robert Southey and Samuel
Coleridge, then traveling the region on a lecture tour, were invited by
publisher Joseph Cottle to "visit Piercefield and Tintern Abbey; objects
new to us all." With their "ladies elect," the group set out "in high spirits,
anticipating unmingled delight in surveying objects and scenery, scarcely
to be surpassed in the three kingdoms."[120] The visit inspired Coleridge to
write the following verses:

Dim coasts, and cloud-like hills, and shoreless ocean.
It seemed like Omnipotence! God, methought,
Had built him there a temple; the whole world
Seemed imaged in its vast circumference.[121]

Coleridge's verses aptly illustrate the Wye Valley's appeal to those in search of the sublime and picturesque. Expansive landscapes provided sources of daring and adventure that sparked individuals' creativity and imagination. Such longings were at the heart of Romanticism and clearly inspired the travels and writings of poets such as Coleridge and Wordsworth. When he revisited the Wye Valley in 1798, Wordsworth also famously set to verse "these steep and lofty cliffs / Which on a wild secluded scene impress."[122]

Like Wordsworth and Coleridge and countless other romantic sojourners, Elizabeth Smith found inspiration in those same lofty cliffs. Although the prescriptive literature of the era attempted to steer young women toward more gentle paths, Elizabeth Smith could not help her preference for rude mountains and rocky precipices. As she contemplated her future away from her beloved home at Piercefield, Elizabeth stood at a precipice. Undeterred by her family's financial collapse, she relied on her intellectual curiosity and adventurous nature to forge something new from the ruins.

2

🌿

"Well Furnished at Present"

A COMMUNITY OF LEARNED LADIES

FTER HER FAMILY WAS forced to leave Piercefield in March 1793, Elizabeth Smith spent the rest of the year in Bath with her friend Harriet Bowdler. As Harriet recalled, Elizabeth regretted leaving behind "the sublime scenes of Piercefield, which furnished an infinite variety of subjects for the pencil," and particularly the family library, "of which she so well knew the value."[1] Despite these losses, sixteen-year-old Elizabeth found ways to continue her extensive range of studies. "I have a nice collection of German books, which Miss Bowdler has borrowed for me. There is the Iliad, which seems to me a very good translation," she reported to her friend Mary Hunt that October. "There is the Messiah, which I am reading a second time with more pleasure than the first. A very pretty collection of poems by different persons; a Novel; and a book of Plays; so you see I am well furnished at present. I wish I had you to enjoy them with me."[2] Even without a home to call her own, Elizabeth remained "well furnished" with many books.

Elizabeth Smith's extended visit to Bath in 1793 marked the beginning of a new lifestyle. For the next several years, the Smith family "had no home of our own" and were forced to rely on the generosity of family and friends who offered recurring invitations for extended visits to their homes.[3] Despite the loss of her family home at Piercefield, Elizabeth Smith found fresh outlets for social relationships and intellectual opportunities. "We entered on a regular course of history, both ancient and modern," Harriet Bowdler recalled. "At other times we studied Shakespeare, Milton, and some other English poets, as well as some of the Italians. We took long walks, and often drew from nature."[4] Like other Romantic-era figures, Elizabeth Smith and her circle of friends were drawn to poetry, drawing, and history as ideal subjects for developing their creative impulses.

Bath was a particularly welcoming spot for Elizabeth Smith and her family to regroup from the loss of their Piercefield home. A 1793 guide-book proudly declared that "in beauty and elegance it far exceeds any view of London."[5] Bath was a soothing place for both body and mind. The town drew a steady stream of visitors, some who came in search of its healing waters and others who were drawn to the town's notable social and literary exchanges (fig. 5). The *New Bath Guide* promoted the resort town as "one of the *most agreeable* as well as *polite* places in the kingdom."[6] After George Smith's bankruptcy, Elizabeth's family may have especially appreciated Bath's relatively affordable standard of living. Although rents could be expensive, overall Bath was considered an appealing loca-tion for "folks of small pecuniary means."[7] Those seeking a "genteel life," one visitor observed, were able to "live in that rank of society cheaper

FIGURE 5. Bath, England (circa 1750), known for its community of women authors and philanthropists. (© British Library Board)

than elsewhere." Bath was a relatively safe and well-ordered town, where "ladies may walk in the streets after candle light alone in perfect security." For these and other reasons, the town was known as "the great retreat of widows & unmarried ladies."[8]

During the eighteenth century, Bath was home to a number of accomplished women who were successful authors, literary patrons, and benevolent reformers.[9] In Bath, Elizabeth Smith regularly encountered learned women engaging in a variety of social, literary, and charitable pursuits. As she cultivated friendships with like-minded women, Elizabeth found support and validation for her scholarly interests, along with respite from her family's financial uncertainty. Through her studies and sociability, Elizabeth made herself at home among Bath's community of learned women.

"She Is, I Believe, a Blue-Stocking"

Having left behind the inspiring ruins at Piercefield, Elizabeth Smith discovered a variety of inspiring scenes in her new temporary home. As Harriet Bowdler's houseguest, Elizabeth had access to Bath's extensive social, literary, and benevolent networks. The Bowdler family enjoyed friendships with a number of learned women who resided in or visited Bath, including Fanny Burney, Hannah More, Sarah Holroyd, and Margaret Holford. When she first visited Bath in 1780, Fanny Burney, author of the celebrated novel *Evelina*, was warmly welcomed by Harriet Bowdler and other members of Bath society. "Your time could not be better employd," a family friend wrote with approval of her visit. "You are now at school,—the great school of the world; where swarms of New Ideas, & new Characters will continually present themselves before You."[10]

Eighteenth-century Bath was a place to see and be seen. At a number of events, including dinner parties, salon gatherings, and public assemblies, Bath residents and visitors privileged the practices and rituals of well-mannered sociability. The town was home to "two sets of Assembly-Rooms," where "fancy balls" and concerts were held regularly, with admission by subscription. An official set of "rules and regulations" governing dress, dance, and admission sought to assure orderly, refined socializing. Bath's carefully curated gatherings represented a self-conscious creation of community—offering a "vortex of amusement" that privileged polite, well-regulated sociability. As the *New Bath Guide* surmised, "No place in England, in full season, affords so brilliant a circle of polite company as Bath."[11] Of course, well-mannered company could be found across England and America, but Bath's reputation distinctly reflected the influence of the women who resided there.

By the time of Elizabeth Smith's 1793 visit, women in Bath had created well-regarded venues for polite sociability. Several women regularly hosted large, informal gatherings in their homes. At weekly events held at the "handsome" home of one Bath hostess, as visitor Kathryn Plymley observed in 1794, guests freely mingled in two large "drawing rooms open into each other, one is appropriated to cards, the other to conversation & work." At such events, "form is excluded & the meeting is pleasant."[12] Women crafted warm, welcoming spaces that gave Bath its well-known reputation as an agreeable resort town. As Plymley reflected after her stay, "We are much impressed with the great civility & indeed kindness that we have received there."[13]

Bath's varied venues for socializing and entertainment meant that "every one may in a great measure chuse their own society."[14] The Bowdlers and their circle of friends often favored small "tranquil and rational" gatherings with like-minded company. In 1786, Harriet Bowdler and author Fanny Burney visited the Bath home of scientist Jean-André Deluc and his wife. "We had a very sociable and sensible evening," Burney mused. "There was no other company, and Miss Bowdler consented to show us several books of drawings, which she had taken from nature, chiefly in Wales, and which were extremely pretty and interesting."[15] Encouraged by the positive feedback she received from her trusted friends, Harriet Bowdler later exhibited her artwork to admiring public audiences in Bath. During her 1794 visit to Bath, Kathryn Plymley went "to see Miss Bowdler's drawings" on public display, including a sketch of Tintern Abbey, located near Elizabeth Smith's former home in the Wye River Valley.[16]

At a variety of large and small gatherings, women were particularly pleased to find men who openly expressed admiration for the notable women they encountered. After one assembly, Fanny Burney related a conversation she had with a gentleman present: "He told me he had very lately met with Hannah More,—& then mentioned Mrs. Montagu & Mrs. Carter, whence he took occasion to say most high & fine things of the Ladies of the present age,—their writings & talents. . . . I soon found he had no small reverence for us *Bluestockingers*."[17] Harriet Bowdler's brother shared similar sentiments; Fanny Burney described him as "a man of much cultivation, and a searcher of the *bas bleu* all his life."[18] Such examples of male admiration, along with Fanny Burney's proud self-identification as a bluestocking, provide important insights into Bath's community of learned women.

As Fanny Burney's comments suggest, the term "bluestocking" was originally positive and self-referential, used "by way of pleasantry" to describe a particular group of women *and* men in eighteenth-century England known for their intellect, wit, and sociability.[19] Elizabeth Carter, Elizabeth Montagu, Anna Seward, Hannah More, and other bluestockings were praised for their contributions to the worlds of polite sociability and literary criticism.[20] Through their salons, correspondence, and patronage, as well as their literary productions, the bluestockings "assumed a strong public identity" in eighteenth-century England.[21] Well-known in their own lifetimes, the bluestockings were the subject of poetry and paintings in their honor, and evoked in numerous articles and essays as highly recognizable symbols of women's accomplishments. Writers on both sides of the Atlantic acknowledged that "the present age has produced a most brilliant constellation of female worthies."[22] The celebration of accomplished women performed important cultural work, creating visions of national identity and cosmopolitan sociability rooted in enlightened notions of progress, refinement, and civilization.[23]

From its positive origins, however, the term quickly took on pejorative connotations, serving as a stereotype to denigrate and parody intellectual women.[24] The word invited controversy, reflecting the era's contested responses to women's intellectual and literary aspirations. By the early nineteenth century, even fictional characters risked reproach for behaving "more like a philosophick member of the *blue-stocking* club than a young woman commencing the impassioned career of life"—that is, marriage and motherhood.[25]

Shifting ideas about bluestockings influenced how women approached social and public spaces. Among supportive company, Bath women felt comfortable showcasing their many talents. But women understood that outsiders and critics could be less receptive. Upon meeting Harriet Bowdler in 1787, Sir Gilbert Elliot, the Earl of Minto, remarked on her character: "She is, I believe, a blue-stocking, but what the colour of that part of her is must be mere conjecture, as you will easily believe when I tell you that, talking of the operas, and amongst the rest of the dancers, she said she never looked at the dancing, but always kept her eyes shut the whole time, and when I asked why, she said it was so indelicate she could not bear to look."[26] Another commentator on Bath society referred to Harriet Bowdler and her sister as "blue-stockings both, of very deep complexion."[27] Such references indicate how the term *bluestocking* operated as a cultural shorthand to convey unspoken assumptions about women's aspirations and identities.

Quips about bluestockings served as a way to assess women's behavior and actions. What Gilbert Elliot perceived as excessive modesty likely reflected Harriet Bowdler's desire to mitigate the negative connotations that were increasingly associated with bluestockings. Implicitly or explicitly, learned women understood that one way to escape charges of brash or pedantic behavior was to exemplify proper feminine traits, especially piety and modesty. It is possible that Harriet Bowdler would have preferred to appear overly modest in public than be labeled a loud and overbearing bluestocking. Writing to a friend, she conveyed sentiments that challenged Elliot's characterization of her as overly prim and prudish: "I can see no harm in music (in moderation) & much good in a good play or poem. Music, Drawing, &c, add much to domestic happiness, and whatever increases our power of giving pleasure is *good*."[28] People who knew Harriet Bowdler more closely, such as Fanny Burney, described her personality in more gentle tones, as "the soft repose of good sense, good humour, urbanity, and kindness" (fig. 6).[29]

As shifting connotations of bluestockings illustrate, Elizabeth Smith came of age in an era that offered women expanded educational and literary opportunities but also expressed ambivalence and hostility toward women who sought to openly exercise their powers of mind.[30] By the 1790s,

FIGURE 6. Portrait
of Henrietta Maria
Bowdler, by Isaac
Wane Slater,
published in 1830
by Thomas Cadell.
(© Trustees of the
British Museum)

learned women faced both celebration and condemnation, and often from
the same critics. "No age has been more distinguished by the learning of
its women than the eighteenth century," one essayist declared, "nor has
the world been slow in bestowing the tribute of applause so justly due to
their writing." Such praise, however, was tempered by remarks disparaging women's intellectual ambitions, asserting, "I know no way of render-
ing classical knowledge so ridiculous, as by cloathing it in petticoats."[31]
Such characterizations posited an incompatibility between serious scholarship and feminine learning, suggesting that it was unusual and even
"ridiculous" for women to exhibit certain types of knowledge, especially
in public settings. Even as they eagerly pursued a variety of scholarly
activities, learned women were well aware of the negative connotations
and sharp criticisms their aspirations might inspire in others.

Such lessons were not lost on Elizabeth Smith. Within the safety of supportive social spaces and in personal letters shared with trusted friends,
Elizabeth was expressive and unapologetic about her scholarly pursuits.
However, she tended to be noticeably reserved in more formal social settings. As Harriet Bowdler's houseguest, Elizabeth was introduced to key

literary figures who visited or resided in Bath, including the acclaimed author Hannah More, one of Harriet Bowdler's "old friends."[32] More later recalled her interactions with Elizabeth Smith fondly: "I knew and admired her long ago, before I suspected what knowledge lay concealed under that modest countenance."[33] As such comments suggest, Elizabeth often made a self-conscious decision to keep her talents hidden in public settings to avoid scrutiny or criticism. As her mother recalled, Elizabeth was "a living library, but locked up except to a chosen few," explaining that her daughter's "dread of being called a learned lady, caused such an excess of modest reserve."[34]

Elizabeth Smith's modesty was a guarded response, designed to avoid criticism by those who might label her interests as pedantic and ostentatious. Sensitive to potential censure, learned women in Elizabeth's social circle made strategic decisions about how to represent themselves. In public settings where they were uncertain about the responses their learned lives might inspire, women might self-consciously downplay their ardent intellectual pursuits or adopt an air of modesty. In their supportive relationships, women freely and unapologetically pursued intellectual interests, confident they would receive support and validation. In Bath, Elizabeth looked for opportunities to choose her own society of likeminded friends.

"The Companion of Our Studies and Our Pleasures"

During her extended visit to Bath in 1793, Elizabeth Smith actively cultivated friendships that nourished her learned aspirations. With Harriet Bowdler as her trusted guide, Elizabeth developed connections with a number of accomplished women who resided in or visited Bath. Along with the support she received from the Bowdler family, Elizabeth's time in Bath was made more enjoyable when her friend Mary Hunt arrived for a visit in April 1793. Their friendship had blossomed the year before, when Mary accompanied Harriet Bowdler on a visit to Piercefield. Bonded by their "similarity of talents and pursuits," Elizabeth and Mary became close friends.[35] If Harriet served as a trusted older mentor, in Mary Elizabeth found a kindred spirit. Writing in 1786, one gentleman described Mary Hunt as having a "great force of intellect, an acute and well furnished understanding," noting with approval that "her heart is as amiable and pure as her genius is vigorous and splendid."[36] Mary was known both for her genius and for her good character. This combination, as Elizabeth and her circle of friends understood, was most likely to earn a learned woman praise instead of criticism.

Born in 1764, Mary Hunt was twenty-nine at the time, twelve years older than Elizabeth. Mary was the daughter of Rowland Hunt (1707–1785) and Ann Wells Hunt (d. 1801). Her father served as a well-respected rector of Stoke Doyle, a village in Northamptonshire. After Rowland Hunt's death in 1785, his widow and daughter sought additional sources of income. Employment as a governess or lady's companion were the most common options for genteel women in similar circumstances.[37] By 1793, Mary Hunt and her mother were working as governesses and caregivers for the Simcoe daughters at Wolford Lodge, their Devonshire home, while John and Elizabeth Simcoe traveled to Upper Canada to take up his post as lieutenant governor.

The main purpose of Mary Hunt's visit to Bath in 1793 was to accompany Eliza Simcoe, one of her charges, on a visit to her aunt Margaret Graves, who had lived with the family before taking up full-time residency in Bath in late 1792. Upon moving to Bath, Margaret Graves suggested that the Simcoe daughters live with her during their parents' time in Canada. Elizabeth Simcoe expressed her desire that the Hunts "remain at Wolford with the children," conveying her "utmost reliance and confidence in your care of them, and approbation of your method of educating them." Elizabeth Simcoe's faith in the Hunts signified her high regard for their skills and characters, especially since she had the option of sending her daughters to live with their aunt. Margaret Graves still expected her nieces to visit regularly, however, and Elizabeth Simcoe understood that such invitations "certainly could not be refused." As Eliza Simcoe prepared for her visit to Bath, her mother was careful to instruct the Hunts that "we do not wish her stay longer than six weeks because we would not stop her education or separate her from her sisters for a longer time."[38] Even though her daughter was accompanied by her governess, Elizabeth Simcoe recognized that Eliza's formal course of studies would be interrupted by the extended visit to her aunt's house, as well as by Bath's many diversions and entertainments.

Although the purpose of Mary Hunt's visit to Bath was to serve as a companion to Eliza Simcoe, she had plenty of free time to spend with her friends Elizabeth Smith and Harriet Bowdler.[39] During her four-month stay in Bath in 1793, Mary became "the companion of our studies and our pleasures," as Harriet recalled, assisting Elizabeth "in Botanical and other pursuits, as well as in different branches of the Mathematics."[40] During this visit, Mary encouraged Elizabeth to study German—a language Elizabeth confessed her brother had once tried to teach her, but he "either found me too dull, or was too lazy to go on."[41] With Mary's support, Elizabeth made substantial progress in German and other language studies. "How much am I obliged to you for teaching me German!" Elizabeth later reflected.[42]

Mary Hunt served as an intellectual guide and trusted friend, and was instrumental in expanding Elizabeth Smith's circle of like-minded companions. Mary introduced Elizabeth and Harriet to Eliza Simcoe and her sisters, young women who were also pursuing extensive studies under Mary's guidance. Elizabeth Simcoe may have worried less about her daughter's time in Bath had she known that Mary Hunt's social circle devoted so much time to their intellectual pursuits. Through their connections to Mary Hunt, Elizabeth Smith and the Simcoe daughters benefited from a growing network of learned women. On a subsequent visit to Bath with her sisters, Eliza Simcoe informed Mary that "Miss Bowdler and the Miss Smiths were so good as to take us to Weston to see your house, with which we were excessively pleased."[43] Over time, Harriet became especially close to Eliza, the eldest Simcoe daughter, mentoring her in ways that paralleled her relationship with Elizabeth Smith. "Mrs. Bowdler has been all kindness to me," Eliza Simcoe reflected during one of her frequent visits with Harriet in the years that followed.[44] Mary Hunt and Harriet Bowdler helped Elizabeth Smith forge connections with other learned women with similar intellectual interests.

Almost immediately after Mary Hunt's return to Devonshire in the summer of 1793, another member of the Simcoe circle made her way to

Bath. In September 1793, Mary Ann Burges, a close friend and neighbor of Elizabeth Simcoe, also traveled to visit Margaret Graves. Upon arriving in Bath, Mary Ann called on Harriet Bowdler, presumably at Mary Hunt's request.[45] "I liked Miss Bowdler very much," Mary Ann later reflected. "Her conversation is very sensible, and all of her sentiments are such as it is impossible not to admire."[46] That fall, Elizabeth Smith's interactions with Mary Ann in Bath were brief, limited to a "formal visit with the rest of our party." She wished to call on Mary Ann directly but was afraid "that she could not possibly have the same wish to know me that I had to know her."[47] Elizabeth's relationship with Mary Ann initially seemed more deferential than the warm friendships she shared with Harriet and Mary. In 1793, Mary Ann Burges was thirty years old—about the same age as Mary Hunt, while thirteen years older than Elizabeth Smith and thirteen years younger than Harriet Bowdler. Given Elizabeth's close relationships with Harriet and Mary, the age difference does not, on its own, explain Elizabeth's seeming obsequiousness toward Mary Ann. As their interactions in Bath were limited to larger group gatherings, rather than more intimate settings, Elizabeth lacked the opportunity to become as closely connected to Mary Ann as she wished.

Although her relationship with Mary Ann Burges was not as intimate as the friendships she shared with Mary Hunt and Harriet Bowdler, Elizabeth Smith expressed warm admiration, "both from what I have heard you say," she wrote to Mary, "and from the very little I have seen of her myself."[48] Mary Ann Burges devoted her days to intellectual pursuits, mastering several languages, including German, Spanish, and Swedish. Describing one "extremely busy and comfortable" day, Mary Ann noted that she "studied Swedish, composed two Songs, drew several hours, Botanized, and read an Octa. Volume on Solitude."[49] Elizabeth's interest in learning Spanish was likely inspired by Mary Ann, who in turn had encouraged Mary Hunt to study the language. "I think learning Spanish and reading Euripides and Cicero, have been of great use to her," Mary Ann wrote about Mary in October 1793.[50]

Through her friendships with Harriet Bowdler, Mary Hunt, Mary Ann Burges, and other members of their growing social circle, Elizabeth Smith benefited from supportive interactions with learned women. Despite differences in ages and circumstances, these women were linked together by mutual interests, trust, and admiration. Events showcasing their literary and artistic talents were a common feature of these women's patterns of socializing. Eliza Simcoe wrote to Mary Hunt after attending a "little Party" at a Mrs. Davis's house in Bath, where she was asked "to read your Poems aloud."[51] On a visit to another friend's Bath home, Mary Hunt spent the evening "listening to Miss Holford who is to read to her some of her beautiful poetry."[52] At such events, Elizabeth Smith would have discovered that women were celebrated, not shunned or criticized, for their talents.

In Bath, Elizabeth repeatedly encountered women who crafted well-furnished spaces and creative outlets for their learned pursuits. Surrounded by other intellectually accomplished women, Elizabeth would not have felt unusual or exceptional for her ardent scholarly interests.[53] Through such encounters and friendships, Elizabeth found inspiring examples to shape her own conduct and behavior.

"A Very Learned Dispute"

The friendships Elizabeth Smith cultivated during her stay in Bath provide evidence of how learned women navigated a variety of personal relationships and social spaces. In like-minded company, these women freely made their talents known. When Mary Hunt first arrived in Devonshire, Mary Ann Burges quickly noticed that the new Simcoe governess excelled in subjects that Mary Ann thought were her own areas of expertise. "Indeed she has adopted such pursuits of mine, as were not her own before," Mary Ann reflected to a friend in April 1793, confessing that "in Astronomy she has left me far behind." Mary Ann sometimes found it challenging, as she admitted, to apply "myself equally to her studies."[54] Mary Hunt and Mary Ann Burges took note of each other's array of studies, aware they had each met an intellectual match.

Mary Ann Burges was not the only one to take notice of Mary Hunt's impressive scholarly abilities. Within their Devonshire circle, Mary Ann Burges noted that a "dispute" developed between Margaret Graves and

Mary Hunt's mother over "whether Miss H[unt] or I, is the most learned." As Mary Ann reported to her friend Elizabeth Simcoe, she was "accosted with a variety of questions, commonly in History," as Margaret Graves sought to prove Mary Ann's intellectual superiority. Mary Ann resented such attempts, as "this sort of involuntary rivalry totally destroys the comfort that might otherwise arise from what similarity there is in our pursuits." Mary Hunt agreed, confessing to Mary Ann that she grew weary "at hearing perpetually from Mrs. G. that I knew all the things she did not."[55]

It is worth noting that Margaret Graves and Mrs. Hunt's "dispute" was driven by their fundamental respect for and recognition of Mary Ann Burges's and Mary Hunt's extensive talents. Whether or not it was appropriate for these women to engage in ardent intellectual pursuits was *not* up for debate—rather, the rivalry focused on who was the "most learned." Within their own supportive communities, learned women's scholarly interests were not subject to disparagement or considered inappropriate. There were no criticisms about the types of knowledge these women acquired or concerns they were spending too much time with their studies. Although Mary Hunt and Mary Ann Burges expressed frustration at the older women's constant quizzing and comparisons, on some level they may have realized that such assessments reflected deep admiration of their scholarly accomplishments. In this sense, the older women's debate represented a far different response than what learned women might encounter in more conventional social circles or within transatlantic cultures of print, where they might be pejoratively labeled as bluestockings or learned ladies.

A variety of social interactions and cultural commentaries repeatedly served to remind women that "there are many prejudices entertained against the character of a learned Lady."[56] Shortly after returning home from her 1793 visit to Bath, Mary Ann Burges learned from a friend that she would not be welcome at a certain gentleman's home, "as he desired no such company." When Mary Ann's friend asked why, "all he would say was that he heard I was a learned lady."[57] Those who knew Mary Ann Burges were more generous in their assessments of her character. Her brother praised her extensive "acquirement of every species of knowledge," particularly in languages and scientific studies, while also describing her

"admirable" character, particularly "that modest retiredness of disposition which led her to shrink from the celebrity to which the extent and
application of her talents so justly entitled her."[58] In the company of other
learned women, Mary Ann freely showcased her extensive talents rather
than "modest retiredness." Supportive friendships provided learned
women with a sense of belonging and validation that served as a bulwark
against societal criticisms and judgments.

Rather than view each other as rivals, Mary Ann Burges and Mary
Hunt forged strong bonds of friendship rooted in their common scholarly ambitions. As Mary Ann reflected, "Miss Hunt and I suit each other.
I really like her very much, and think she has very amiable quality; I am
a great deal with her."[59] The two women developed a close relationship
characterized by shared intellectual interests but not always shared sentiments. "When we read together, we seldom agree," Mary Ann noted.
But a lack of intellectual harmony on particular subjects or books did
not detract from their friendship. "Miss Hunt and I had a very learned
dispute about innate ideas," Mary Ann reported to Elizabeth Simcoe
in September 1793, shortly after Mary's return home from her visit to
Bath.[60] The two women regularly engaged in "great dispute" over materials they read without sacrificing their friendship.[61] Indeed, one of the
striking aspects of the friendships within Elizabeth Smith's social circle
was their freedom to disagree with each other. Typically, young women of
the era were socialized to be diffident and deferential, not argumentative
and outspoken. Harmony and affinity were privileged as key standards
governing social and personal relationships. Within their supportive relationships, learned women could be more candid and opinionated, rather
than demure and reserved.

Within her growing social circle, Elizabeth Smith learned that intellectual discord was acceptable, even welcomed, as such exchanges were predicated on mutual trust and candor. Even when she disagreed with them,
Elizabeth demonstrated no dread of criticism from her friends, confident that they shared and supported her enthusiastic approach to scholarly activities. Mutual respect meant that any particular disputes about
specific authors or books would not disrupt their fundamentally shared
affinities as learned women. In one letter to Mary, Elizabeth admitted

that she was "engaged in an argument with my dear Miss Bowdler" about poetry. Elizabeth expressed her preference for her then-favorite poet Ossian, confidently asserting, "I support him against all other poets . . . for I really *love* his poems beyond all others." Elizabeth did not defer to her mentor but strongly presented her own opinions. "Surely in 'the joy of grief,' and in night scenes," Elizabeth insisted, "there is nothing equal to him." "All of his heroes are so *good*," she asserted, and "every word is poetry."[62] Elizabeth did not feel the need to couch her love of Ossian within deferential tones, even in discussions with her older mentor. Her passionate defense of Ossian indicates a young woman enthusiastically articulating her ideas to trusted friends while developing her own voice and literary tastes.

With such support, Elizabeth Smith gained confidence in her intellectual powers, along with an eagerness to express herself on a number of subjects. Her growing friendships with other learned women provided her with opportunities to share her scholarly interests without restraint, modesty, or fear of censure. In her letters to trusted friends, Elizabeth excitedly described her intellectual interests—puzzling over mathematical equations or learning several languages—with an almost breathless enthusiasm. "My favourite study just now is Algebra," she reported to Mary, reminding her friend of the time they spent together "measuring squares and circles."[63]

Through both face-to-face encounters and a world of letters, Elizabeth and her friends crafted a fulfilling world of intellectual expression.[64] Shared practices of studying and reading together, even when separated by geographical distance, helped to strengthen the bonds among learned women. Friends eagerly kept track of each other's scholarly pursuits, recommending particular authors and books to one another and creating shared opportunities for intellectual exchange. In November 1793, Elizabeth reported reading Klopstock's *Messiah* again, noting, "There is more of it than there was in Miss Burges's, which was, I believe, only fifteen books." Upon reading the full twenty-two books, Elizabeth uncovered additional information about one of the characters, which she requested Mary pass onto Mary Ann: "Pray inform Miss Burges of this, for I remember hearing her regret his fate."[65]

Although scholars often focus on the emotional comfort and companionship that friendships provided for women, within Elizabeth Smith's social circle intellectual interests were an equally important component for sustaining friendships.[66] Being able to share scholarly pursuits created strong bonds of affinity among learned women. As Elizabeth Simcoe reflected to Mary Hunt about her growing friendship with Mary Ann Burges, "you will certainly rival me in her affection if you have learnt Spanish."[67] Shared intellectual pursuits provided the basis for ardent and long-lasting friendships. The emotional bonds women forged were rooted in and sustained by a sense of shared appreciation and validation for their learned aspirations. Such friendships provided women with sources of both emotional *and* intellectual nourishment. After Mary Hunt left Bath, Elizabeth lamented her friend's absence: "We never take a pleasant walk, or read anything interesting, but some one says, 'I wish Miss Hunt were here;' and you may be sure that nobody contradicts it." Elizabeth particularly missed being able to share her newfound love of German with Mary. "I want to shew you every pretty passage I meet with in German," she commented, confessing that "I do not like half so well now that I have no one to enjoy it with me."[68]

There was a candor and freedom to these friendships that serve to highlight the pride and pleasure women took in their scholarly accomplishments. Free from disapproving eyes, learned women felt at ease in each other's company. "If you should ever receive a letter from me written like copper-plate," Elizabeth Smith remarked in one letter to Mary Hunt after apologizing for her handwriting, "depend upon it I am going to quarrel with you."[69] Elizabeth understood that if she presented a polished and refined "copper-plate" version of herself to a trusted friend, it would be an act of artifice—not a representation of her true identity. She regarded a copperplate presentation of herself—either in person or in letters—as a strategy designed with prescribed social mores and potential critics in mind. Such a carefully curated persona could serve as a useful safeguard in less hospitable environments but was contrary to the close bonds of friendship and trust cultivated among learned women.

In Bath, as Elizabeth Smith and her friends discovered, women found welcoming spaces for their talents, along with persistent reminders about the importance of balancing their intellectual aspirations with social acceptance. For women who sought to expand their scholarly ambitions beyond the close-knit realms of personal friendships, a copperplate presentation could be particularly valuable.

"The Author Is Called Upon to Avow It"

The friendships that Elizabeth Smith cultivated were representative of Bath's communities of accomplished women. In Bath, a number of women actively enacted learned lives, inhabiting vibrant social and literary circles. Throughout the eighteenth century, a number of well-known British women authors, including Catharine Macaulay, Sarah Fielding, and Sarah Scott, made Bath their home. Their aspirations were fictionized in Sarah Scott's utopian novel *Millenium Hall,* first published in 1762. Scott used her novel to promote a vision of women living together in a close-knit community. Drawn together after experiencing individual misfortunes, these women value Christian piety, reform, and education. Even as their notions of ideal womanhood remain framed by conventional standards, the women of *Millenium Hall* forge a new, fulfilling home for themselves. At its heart, the novel demonstrates a desire for female autonomy and self-agency, mirroring the lived experiences of many learned women who made Bath their home.[70]

Like the fictional world described in *Millenium Hall,* Bath women created social spaces and learned rituals to pursue a variety of social, benevolent, and literary activities. By the time of Elizabeth Smith's 1793 visit, Bath women were well known for their distinctive social and literary exchanges. One of the most celebrated spaces in eighteenth-century Bath was led by Lady Anna Miller (1741–1781), who regularly hosted poetry competitions at her estate located in Bath Easton.[71] Although Lady Miller passed away before the time of Elizabeth Smith's visit, her influence endured within Bath's cultural memory. Members of the Bowdler family had attended Miller's gatherings; other notable guests included women authors such as Fanny Burney and Anna Seward. Lady Miller's events generated considerable public attention, with publications such as the

1778 *New Prose Bath Guide* providing detailed accounts of her poetry competitions. Her ritualized contests centered around "an antique Vase, into which the Ladies and Gentlemen put Copies of Verses." The submissions were read aloud in company, and "the Majority of them determine which Piece has the most Merit, and then the Author is called upon to avow it." Winning authors were presented with a "Wreath of Myrtle."[72]

Lady Miller's poetry competitions were well attended but also sparked a degree of ridicule and resentment from outsiders who disapproved of such seemingly unconventional expressions of local literary culture. Before her visit to Bath in 1780, author Fanny Burney confessed, "Bath Easton is so much Laughed at in London." Yet she acknowledged that Miller's gatherings were well known outside of Bath, indicating that many out-of-town visitors coveted an invitation: "Nothing *here* is more *tonish* than to visit Lady Miller, who is extremely *curious* in her Company, admitting few people who are not of *Rank* or of *Fame*."[73] The elite, insider nature of Miller's competitions fueled both curiosity and jealousy. Bluestocking Anna Seward, a contributor to Lady Miller's contests, recalled that her hostess was sometimes criticized by individuals "who were disappointed in their expectations of being summoned to her intellectual feast."[74] Others viewed the events with derision, perhaps in part because of Miller's eccentric nature. Male critics such as Horace Walpole dismissed Miller's competitions as "folly," while Samuel Johnson apparently "held them very cheap."[75]

Such critiques, however, did little to dissuade Lady Miller and her guests. The renown surrounding her gatherings inspired Miller to publish the poetry originally submitted for her competitions.[76] The published volumes of *Poetical Amusements at a Villa near Bath* demonstrate how local social gatherings could serve as springboards to the larger worlds of print and publishing. While the publications grew out of Miller's select soirees, the first volume of *Poetical Amusements* was so popular that its initial edition sold out "within ten days." A second edition of the first volume, along with a second volume of additional poems, was published in 1776.[77] A total of four volumes appeared in print before Miller's death in 1781.

Poetical Amusements provides evidence of a vibrant social and literary culture cultivated by women and men alike but was carefully presented to the reading public with a set of comforting refrains to avoid the scorn of critics who might have judged the work—or its many female contributors—harshly. The book's preface explains that the poems were not originally composed with publication in mind: "Their authors did not foresee their appearance under their present form." The preface also explicitly implores potential "Critics" to consider the "novelty" of the poems' compositions, informing readers that "any little profit arising from its sale" would be donated to "one of the most deserving and importunate Charitable Establishments."[78] In taking care to explain the friendly origins and charitable purposes of the published poems, *Poetical Amusements* sought to disarm potential critics who might have questioned the propriety of publishing what could be considered amateur poetry. This emphasis sought to cast Miller's literary productions as innocent "amusements" shared among a benevolent circle of local friends rather than as ambitious designs for literary fame. Yet in publishing *Poetical Amusements*, Lady Miller made a deliberate choice to take poems originally shared in person and present them to a larger reading public.

Poetical Amusements was marked by another publishing practice common among eighteenth-century women writers. Many poems appeared without author attribution or featured dashes to partially hide the names of authors. On the surface, the dashes were devised to protect the identities of individuals. However, they provided only the slightest veil of anonymity for members of Bath society. Local readers would have been able to decipher names such as "Miss El—k—r" or "G. P—tt, Esq," especially since these poems had been previously read aloud at Miller's gatherings.[79] The authorship of many pieces was already known within Bath's select social circles. As the preface acknowledged, "the greater part of these poems were acknowledged by their Authors in numerous assemblies" and shared widely in manuscript form before being collected for publication.[80]

One of the contributors to Lady Miller's *Poetical Amusements* was Harriet Bowdler's sister Jane, whose poem "On Love" was included as an anonymous entry in the first volume.[81] The same poem later appeared in a volume that Harriet prepared for publication after Jane's death in 1784. This posthumous volume of Jane Bowdler's writings, originally titled *Poems and Essays by a Lady Lately Deceased*, was initially published anonymously in 1786.[82] Jane Bowdler already had a local reputation for her poetry through her contributions to Lady Miller's literary gatherings, so the identity of the "lady lately deceased" was an open secret within Bath social circles. Subsequent editions published as early as 1787 identified Jane Bowdler as the author, and the work was retitled *Poems and Essays, by the Late Miss Bowdler*. Over the next several years, Jane Bowdler's *Poems and Essays* went through several editions. The seventh edition of Bowdler's work was published in 1793, the same year Elizabeth Smith visited the Bowdlers in Bath. In 1798, a tenth edition was published, including "an Essay which was never before printed" about Jane's lengthy illness, which included the permanent loss of her voice.[83] Anna Seward was "pleased" by the work, noting to a friend that the poems "contain no great resplendence of genius" but aptly revealed "the effusions of a pure, a gentle, and cultivated mind."[84] Jane Bowdler's posthumously published writings emphasized the qualities she embodied during her life. According to Fanny Burney, Jane Bowdler remained "perfectly resigned, & very mild & patient" despite her illness.[85]

Given her close connections to the Bowdler family, Elizabeth Smith was familiar with literary productions such as Lady Miller's *Poetical Amusements* and Jane Bowdler's *Poems and Essays*. In 1798, she wrote to a friend praising "the new edition of Miss Bowdler's Essays."[86] Elizabeth likely noted that these works were published to benefit local Bath charities, a strategy that served as a particular means of "legitimating women's writing" by promoting acceptable notions of femininity, piety, and benevolence.[87] The varied reactions to Lady Miller's social circle would have reminded Elizabeth Smith and other learned women that their activities could be the source of either praise or condemnation, depending on the company. Bath offered a variety of fulfilling social and literary exchanges, but within cultures of print, a woman could not always choose the reception that awaited her.

"The Work of a Female Pen"

As works such as Lady Miller's *Poetical Amusements* illustrate, Bath offered women access to a variety of social and literary gatherings that could also serve as avenues to public recognition and publication. Bath had a growing reputation as a local publishing center, especially for women. Although London remained the literary capital of England, smaller publishing centers such as Bath proved particularly receptive to women authors.[88]

Within her social circle, Elizabeth Smith saw up-close and personal examples of women entering the literary marketplace as published authors. The Bowdler family maintained ties with Richard Cruttwell, a Bath printer, as well as with Cadell and Davies, a major London publishing firm. By the early nineteenth century, Harriet Bowdler, her siblings, and their mother Elizabeth all had various works appear in print. By 1802, proceeds from Jane Bowdler's *Poems and Essays,* edited by Harriet, yielded six hundred pounds for a local Bath hospital.[89] Harriet Bowdler also anonymously published *Sermons on the Doctrines and Duties of Christianity,* a popular work that went through numerous editions.[90] "Her sermons as so popular here," Fanny Burney remarked, "that they are not only the general Sunday reading" for families unable to travel to church "but they are even preached from the pulpit by various divines."[91] Later, Harriet was an unattributed contributor to her brother Thomas's famous work *The Family Shakespeare* (1807), helping to create the carefully excised, or bowdlerized, editions of the works associated with the family name.[92]

Less is known about Mary Hunt's literary career. Her poem "Written on Visiting the Ruins of Dunkeswell-Abbey" was published in eighteenth-century periodicals and included in Richard Polwhele's 1792 collection of poetry.[93] Evidence also indicates that she anonymously published two works, a children's textbook on astronomy and a translation from the French of Charles Vilette's *Essay on Happiness of the Life to Come.*[94] Both of Mary Hunt's books appeared without author attribution and were published by Richard Cruttwell in Bath and Charles Dilly in London. As Mary Ann Burges explained to Elizabeth Simcoe, "Miss Hunt, if I recollect rightly, told you that she had written some easy lectures on Astronomy for the use of your Children. By the advice of the Bowdlers, they are now printed, & I believe sell very well; Miss Hunt's name, however, is concealed."[95] The decision to remain "concealed" in print did not preclude women from sharing their literary productions with supportive friends.

Mary Ann Burges engaged in similar strategies to navigate the literary marketplace. In 1794, Burges anonymously published *The Cavern of*

Death, an early gothic-style novel, and she later authored *The Progress of the Pilgrim Good-Intent,* written as a kind of sequel to the steady-selling *Pilgrim's Progress.* In addition to these publications, Mary Ann was a longtime friend and collaborator of Jean-André Deluc, a Swiss scientist who served as a reader to Queen Charlotte at Windsor Court. The prefaces to *The Progress of the Pilgrim Good-Intent* and other published works acknowledged Mary Ann Burges as having contributed significantly to Deluc's published work on geology.[96]

Even when they published anonymously, the women in Elizabeth Smith's circle expressed concern over the reception of their works. When her novel was first published in early 1794, Mary Ann Burges reported to a friend: "My Brother has sent me the Cavern of Death, which I am frightened and ashamed beyond measure to see in its present shape." Specifically, Mary Ann regretted seeing "mistakes in the printing," but she also insisted that "I do not care for the fame of my works," expressing her preference to "continue unknown."[97] After the first edition quickly sold out and a second edition was printed, Mary Ann still wished to remain anonymous: "I believe I am perfectly safe, and keep my countenance perfectly well when people talk about it to me, as is very frequently the case, for it is honoured with a place in the circulating library at Honiton, so that all the Misses of the country have read it."[98] Given her ardent intellectual interests, such disclaimers were most likely strategic, a way to deflect potential criticism. Although her work was a literary success, Mary Ann Burges remained reluctant to draw public attention to herself as a published author.

The London *British Critic* described *The Cavern of Death* as "not only a moral but an interesting tale" and praised its "elegant" language and entertaining narrative.[99] Mary Ann Burges was pleased that the "*British Critic* has been much more civil to me than I had any expectation of." The praise the book inspired may have derived from its anonymous publication. As she informed a friend, "But nothing pleases me so well as that they say nothing of 'presuming from the style of this performance that it is the work of a female pen'; which is the observation of all others that have never read of any book, without thinking it."[100] In possibly presuming that *The Cavern of Death* was the work of a male writer, the *British Critic* reviewed the book on its own terms, rather than as "the work of a female pen." Mary Ann

Burges clearly understood that such a fair assessment was more than many women authors received at the hands of male critics. "When we learn it is the work of Lady," one essayist admitted in 1789, "however highly we may prize her productions, we must pity that error of judgement which could engage her in pursuits so repugnant to female delicacy."[101] Such critiques undoubtedly influenced Mary Ann Burges and other women who decided to publish their works without public attribution.

The literary productions of the women in Elizabeth Smith's circle provide detailed evidence of what literary scholar Eve Tavor Bannet has termed the publishing practice of "semi-anonymity." Women authors who published anonymously often freely shared "the secret of authorship" within their own social and literary networks.[102] Their decision reveals one strategy some women adopted as they grappled with how to best negotiate the literary marketplace. Even well-known bluestockings such as Sarah Scott and Elizabeth Montagu initially chose to publish anonymously.[103] Women's reticence to publish openly undoubtedly was motivated, at least in part, by the ambivalent, often hostile climate for women authors that existed within transatlantic cultures of print. Both in England and America, women writers could face sharp rebukes from critics skeptical of any "work of a female pen."

Concerns about criticisms, particularly at the hands of male reviewers, did not stop women from publishing their works. They made deliberate, strategic decisions about how, when, and where to publish—but publish they did. By the early nineteenth century, the literary marketplace, particularly for novels, "was both in reality and in perception dominated by women writers."[104] Cultural commentators recognized that the era represented a watershed moment for women's intellectual productions. As one London essayist noted in 1813, "there are now alive, or at least there have lived, within the last twenty years, more women distinguished for their literary talents, and whose works are likely to immortalize their names, than in the twenty centuries that had elapsed."[105] Several of these women, including Hannah More and Elizabeth Carter, attained notable financial gains from their publications. Their literary careers challenged prescriptive models of marriage and domesticity that assumed women's dependence on male breadwinners. Women's commercial success prompted a cultural backlash, even though there was no abrupt shift in reception, no time when women were welcomed as authors and then when they were denounced (or vice versa). Women authors received both praise and criticism at the same time, as the circumstances that enabled women's intellectual expressions to flourish also sought to constrain their literary ambitions. The more inroads they made in the literary marketplace, the more women were warned that they risked both their femininity and respectability by taking up their pens.

The success enjoyed by an increasing number of women writers brought to the surface the uncomfortable idea that women might be eager to claim space in the literary spotlight. Increasingly, critics questioned the appropriateness of women writers in broad, sweeping judgments. "I never knew a female author," one critic bemoaned, "whose excellence was sufficient to atone for the violation offered to nature in stepping out of her original sphere.... It is a melancholy sight where the philosopher is built upon the destruction of the woman."[106] The idea of a woman purposely pursuing a literary career was often met with such hostility that many women writers explicitly referenced economic hardship—a husband's death or financial ruin—to justify their forays into the world of print. Other women strategically confined their literary efforts to domestic fiction and similar seemingly "safe" genres such as sentimental poetry.

Many women who earned approval in the literary public sphere typically supported, rather than directly challenged, such prescriptive models. Writers such as Hannah More advocated relatively conservative notions of womanhood, even if they, as individuals, pursued more public and ambitious lives. More asserted that the true aim of women's education was to "carefully cultivate intellect, implant religion, and cherish modesty." While pursuing a career as an author and advocating for improvements in women's education, More insisted that women's learning needed to remain cloaked in piety and humility: "Far be it from me to desire to make scholastic ladies or female dialectians."[107] The tenor and tone of such advice advocated private and domestic roles for women, even as a number of learned women occupied influential roles in social, literary, and print circles.

To navigate often hostile cultural attitudes toward women writers, the women in Elizabeth Smith's circle employed what we might think of as copperplate presentations of themselves in public and in print. Cautiously representing themselves and taking care to avoid offense, these women developed public personas as mild, meek, and pious, which provided "safe" entrances into the world of print. Publishing anonymously, pseudonymously, or as acts of benevolence in support of local charities represented tactics that learned women such as Harriet Bowdler and Mary Ann Burges employed to offset criticisms of their literary aspirations. Through such approaches, learned women hoped to avoid charges that their writing was motivated solely by a desire for literary fame, enabling them to claim identities as reclusive, even reluctant, participants in the literary marketplace.

Behind the scenes, learned women benefited from fulfilling relationships that intertwined their personal, social, and literary aspirations. As they made the transition to the world of print, the women in Elizabeth Smith's circle actively used their relationships to support each other's publications. Well aware of how critics regulated the literary marketplace, women adopted strategies to help assure a positive reception for their works. After the publication of *The Family Shakespeare*, Harriet Bowdler asked Eliza Simcoe to "*puff* my Shakespeare a little, for so many Booksellers and library people, Reviewers &c. &c. are interested in other editions, that they will not allow this to be *known*." Despite what she perceived as a lack of support from mainstream literary channels, Harriet was pleased to report that *The Family Shakespeare* "has been introduced at Court, and is liked very much; but do make some of your *great people* bring it into fashion. Mrs. Burges has been most kindly interested for it, and made Mr. DeLuc recommend it at Windsor, as did Mrs. Kennicott."[108] Harriet Bowdler and other women authors actively utilized personal networks to influence the sale, dissemination, and reception of their literary productions.

The experiences of women such as Harriet and Jane Bowdler, Mary Hunt, and Mary Ann Burges offer important insights into the status of women authors in late eighteenth- and early nineteenth-century cultures of print. Their strategic efforts to navigate literary markets add important nuance to conventional understandings of how the typically male-dominated world of printers, booksellers, and publishers functioned. Their literary careers suggest the existence of what we might think of as a counterculture of print, demonstrating how women utilized personal and social relationships to navigate the larger worlds of print and publishing. Fulfilling friendships cultivated in local communities served as supportive channels for women seeking to publish their literary productions. Women did not have to navigate publishing worlds alone but were buttressed by the support of their friends. These connections helped to sustain the more "visible" workings of print culture in ways that often went unnoticed or unsung in public. Much of this behind-the-scenes work was deliberate and calculated, as women developed self-conscious strategies to avoid public censure for their literary ambitions.

"I Am Very Impatient"

Elizabeth Smith's time in Bath was well spent. Surrounded by the work of several female pens, she took note of how to craft a well-furnished life. In September 1794, Elizabeth prepared "to leave Bath and its neighbourhood; not, I assure you, without great regret at leaving our good friends here. . . . We are so happy here," she wrote to Mary, "that I know not how we shall bear the change."[109] Bath's community of learned women provided inspiring examples of literary sociability, charitable benevolence, and successful authorship. In Bath, Elizabeth enacted a learned life, enthusiastically engaging in scholarly pursuits and polite sociability. Rather than feel exceptional or isolated for her scholarly ambitions, she found support and validation among an expanding circle of like-minded friends. Elizabeth saw firsthand how women in her social circle entered the literary marketplace as "unknown" or anonymous authors, balancing their concerns for female respectability with desires for literary success. Within such a supportive environment, the possibilities to enact a learned life must have seemed as inspiring as the rocky cliffs of Piercefield.

Encouraged and assisted by her friends, Elizabeth continued to pursue a variety of scholarly interests, and in particular focused on honing her language skills. She studied German, Persian, Arabic, and Spanish, and hoped "to begin Hebrew" and Latin.[110] The next year, after visiting friends with a well-stocked library, Smith was able to immerse herself in Latin studies. "I have read Caesar's Commentaries, Livy, and some volumes of Cicero," she proudly informed Mary. "I am very impatient to begin Virgil."[111] As she pursued a variety of language studies, Elizabeth continued to rely on her friends for support and inspiration. "I wish I had your patience to translate from one language to another," she wrote to Mary in April 1794, "for I believe it is the only way of being perfect in any."[112]

At the time, Elizabeth doubted her abilities in writing "of any kind, that I never like to attempt it."[113] Yet the more Elizabeth studied, the more she expressed a desire to express herself in that fashion. She began to keep "pocket-books" containing a series of reflections.[114] Elizabeth found it "improving, as well as amusing, to write down" her thoughts. Through her continued studies and writings, Elizabeth began to imagine new possibilities for herself that would enable her to put her scholarly talents to use. Fearing that "a great part of my life is wasted in foolish imaginations and idle dreams," she sought to transform her youthful romanticism into a more purposeful life.[115]

Over the next several years, however, Elizabeth Smith continued to lack a permanent family home and spent much of her time sojourning from one place to another on extended visits with family and friends. This nomadic lifestyle fueled her restless spirit and longing for adventure. As she traveled through England, Wales, and Ireland, Elizabeth relied on her friendships to keep her well furnished with sources of creative and intellectual inspiration.

3

"At the Foot of the Tower"

PICTURESQUE WANDERINGS AND THE SEARCH FOR HOME

D URING A TRIP TO Wales in May 1798, Elizabeth Smith visited
key tourist sites, including the celebrated ruins of Conway Castle. Delighted by her surroundings, Elizabeth wished that her
friend Mary Hunt was with her to explore "the dark winding passages
and broken staircases of this beautiful Castle." One of the castle's towers, Elizabeth mused, "would make the nicest dwelling in the world." The
tower "stands on a rock overhanging the river," offering "the finest view
imaginable." Unfortunately, "this fairy castle" remained out of reach,
Elizabeth noted, "for the timbers are entirely gone, and I pine in vain
to get into the little niche." While acknowledging the infeasibility of her
plan, Elizabeth imagined carving out a home for herself in the tower: "It
certainly would be very *snug,* filled exactly as one would wish; but any
place would do, so filled, therefore let us be content at the foot of the
tower."[1] Uncertain about the future, Elizabeth longed for contentment
and a place to call home.

After her father's bankruptcy and the loss of her family home at
Piercefield, Elizabeth Smith adapted to a lifestyle marked by visits to
locations such as Bath, London, Wales, and Ireland. Her travels provided moments of both inspiration and unease. "Our fate is still uncertain," Elizabeth wrote from Wales, while maintaining a hopeful out-
look toward the future. She was determined to "make the best of the
present, and let the future shift for itself." During this unsettled time,
Elizabeth relied on her supportive friendships, scholarly pursuits, and
travel adventures to sustain her. "I think I am content," she mused to

Mary after her visit to Conway Castle, "and yet to be sure I should like to have you here."[2]

Throughout the 1790s, Elizabeth Smith visited or resided at several sought-after travel spots across the British Isles. Locations such as Piercefield, the Smith family's former home in South Wales, or Conway Castle in North Wales, where Elizabeth longed to dwell, were among the most celebrated destinations for discerning travelers engaged in "the search for the picturesque."[3] Romantic-era figures regarded visits to such historic ruins, scenic landscapes, and mountainous terrains as spring wells of creative vision and authentic experience. William Wordsworth, Samuel Coleridge, and other poets composed verses venerating key sites, while artists such as John Smith and Joseph Turner captured inspiring visions of sublime scenery in their sketchbooks and paintings. Most well-known travel writings, sketches, and poetry from the era were produced by men, leading both contemporary observers and modern scholars to view picturesque travel as "culturally coded male." Eighteenth-century travel guides privileged the male gaze, celebrating the bravery and adventures of men who explored sublime locations off "the beaten track."[4] Women also traveled, but they were more likely to be dismissed as mere "tourists" in need of male escorts and protection. Moreover, many women tended to record their travel experiences in personal letters and journals, rather than published narratives, contributing to the notion that picturesque travel was primarily the province of men.[5]

Elizabeth Smith's adventures help to highlight women's active participation in the picturesque travel scene. Throughout the 1790s, she explored ancient castles, sketched scenic vistas, and literally climbed mountains at the very same locations that male travelers celebrated in their various poems, paintings, and guidebooks. Like other romantic wanderers, Elizabeth was particularly drawn to sublime landscapes and ragged ruins, reflecting her longstanding preference for rocky precipices rather than tame meadows. Her journeys encourage us to consider how such experiences shaped learned women's sense of their place in the world. Whether she stood at the foot of a castle tower or at the top of Mount Snowdon, Elizabeth Smith contemplated expansive vistas, surveying the landscape for a welcoming home.

"I Know Not Where This Will Find You"

With the future uncertain, Elizabeth Smith was not the only member of her family looking for a new place to reside. Having lost his home and business to bankruptcy, George Smith was seeking ways to rebuild his good name and support his family. In early 1794, he considered relocating to Canada. The idea of starting over somewhere new and far away, of being able to leave behind both his creditors and his fallen reputation, must have appealed to a man needing to reinvent himself. It is very likely that George Smith considered relocating to Canada as a result of the friendships that his daughter and wife cultivated. At the time, Mary Hunt was serving as a governess to the Simcoe daughters, who remained in England during their father's appointment as lieutenant governor in Upper Canada. Mary Ann Burges, a close friend of John Simcoe's wife, Elizabeth, developed a warm relationship with Mary Hunt, and through her was introduced to the Smith family. George Smith recognized that these relationships, which were so intellectually and emotionally important to his daughter, might also be utilized to help him secure a position in Canada.

In March 1794, as Mary Ann Burges traveled to Bath for a visit, she learned that George Smith "has a prodigious fancy to go with his family to Upper Canada" and agreed to meet with him to share her knowledge of John and Elizabeth Simcoe's life there. Juliet Smith, however, was strongly opposed her husband's "prodigious fancy." Still recovering from the disruptive and humiliating effects of losing their family fortunes, Elizabeth's mother was not seduced by the promise of a fresh start so far from home. Against the daunting prospect of a cross-Atlantic voyage and move away from her network of supportive family and friends, Juliet Smith set her own plan into action. Juliet and her friends urged Mary Ann Burges to "represent it [Canada] in the most uninviting light possible." Therefore, when Mary Ann Burges and George Smith met in March 1794, "I talked to him about Rattle Snakes & Indians . . . and if I did not succeed in dissuading him from the journey, I at least very considerably increased the disinclination of his Wife & daughters to accompany him. I think they will carry their point at last."[6] Less than two weeks after this meeting, Mary Ann reported that her efforts were successful: "Mr. Smith has been prevailed upon by my eloquence to give up present thoughts of going to Canada."[7]

The willingness of Juliet Smith and Mary Ann Burges to conspire together to thwart George Smith's Canada "scheme" suggests a weakening of his influence at home. George Smith had turned to his wife's and daughter's relationships as potential sources of professional patronage, but the very connections he hoped would grant him favor with John Simcoe were instead secretly conniving against his plans. With the help of her supportive friendships, Juliet Smith engaged in her own scheming to avoid relocating her family to Canada. These women's behind-the-scenes work represented a shadowy but powerful and effective form of female influence that enabled Juliet Smith to exert some control over her family's future.

Writing to Mary Hunt in April 1794, Elizabeth Smith thanked her friend for "all the trouble you took about Canada," confirming that the idea was "entirely given up." Elizabeth noted that the decision was made "against my will, for I was delighted with the idea and wished excessively to go."[8] Unlike her mother, Elizabeth viewed the prospect of a new life in Canada as an appealing adventure. She longed for an inspiring place to call home—whether it was in Canada or the ruins of a castle tower in Wales. For the next several years, however, the Smith family remained in a state of prolonged uncertainty about their future residence. With his Canada plans thwarted, Elizabeth's father secured a commission in the army and was assigned to a regiment in Ireland.[9] While George Smith was stationed in Ireland, Juliet Smith and her daughters spent weeks or months staying with relatives and friends in Bath, London, and other locations. While such extended visits were common, they were typically expressions of sociability, not necessity. The hospitality of family and friends provided Juliet Smith and her children with essential shelter and support during the years they spent without a home of their own.

Elizabeth's studies and friendships served as important anchors during this unsettled time. She continued to enjoy opportunities for scholarly exploration, as generous friends opened not only their homes but also their libraries. "I am very rich in German books just now," Elizabeth informed Mary, pleased that a family friend in Bath "has given me the entré of his library, to take whatever I like."[10] With such support, she pursued a wide array of intellectual interests, including astronomy, geometry, history, and poetry, as well as extensive language studies in German, Spanish, Latin, Greek, Hebrew, and Arabic. Extended visits to friends' homes likely created lengthy stretches of leisure time for Elizabeth, who, as a guest, presumably would not have been expected to devote hours to the domestic duties that women typically engaged in while maintaining a family household.

No matter where she journeyed, Elizabeth longed to share her scholarly pursuits and travel adventures with her trusted circle of friends. In the summer of 1795, during one of her many visits to family friends in south London, Elizabeth wistfully wrote to Mary after finding "a new Atlas" of the stars. "I would shew it to you," she mused, "if you would meet me on the wing of Pegasus, or any other convenient place you will appoint in the upper regions, for it does not seem probable that we should soon see each other in these below."[11] The Pegasus represented a symbol of flight and freedom and appealed to Elizabeth's imaginative nature. Her longing for a magical means of conveyance suggested a desire to stay connected with friends despite her frequent travels.

Lacking the power of flight, Elizabeth instead relied on letter writing to maintain her intellectual and emotional bonds with Mary and others. Letters enabled friends to "partake of our pleasure" of shared intellectual pursuits. Even when separated by distance, Elizabeth and her friends kept track of each other's reading habits and scholarly interests, offering recommendations and commentaries on various works for each other's enjoyment. Writing to Mary in October 1795, Elizabeth provided a summary of her recent reading habits: "I have not seen Gellert. Oberon I have read, and was much pleased with some parts of it." Elizabeth remained well furnished with a variety of reading materials. "I have just finished Froissard, which, though rather tedious, I found very entertaining," she continued in this same letter. "I read the Memoirs of Petrarch. . . . With this book I was excessively pleased. It is impossible not to love Petrarch."[12] Elizabeth's extensive reading habits—from German poetry to the works of Italian Renaissance writer Petrarch—reflected elite literary tastes popular during the Romantic era.[13] Through their letters, learned women helped each other to stay informed about what authors and books were likely to be discussed in select social and literary circles.

Letters provided opportunities for intellectual exchanges among absent friends, but never being fixed in one location for too long sometimes presented challenges in sustaining a correspondence. Elizabeth was not always sure where to have letters directed, and due to inevitable lapses or gaps in writing, she was not always up to date on her friends' various travels. "Now I know not where this will find you," Elizabeth wrote to Mary in October 1795. "I will however direct to Bath, hoping your comfortable party is not yet dissolved, though I have little chance of finding you together," she lamented, "as the time of our transplantation appears very uncertain." During this period, Elizabeth's letters sometimes took on wistful tones. "It was very good of you to wish for me by the sea-side," she wrote to Mary after hearing of her friend's travels. "I know nothing I should have enjoyed so much as seeing it for the first time with you." Elizabeth feared that time and distance might be eclipsing her place in Mary's heart. "I cannot help thinking the companions you had were more agreeable than I should have been," she noted with an air of self-deprecation. Such statements reflected a desire for reassurance, for emotional comfort to ease the pain of physical separation. In this period, romantic couples often engaged in episodes of "testing" each other's affection, particularly during periods of geographical distance. This emotional dynamic could also be experienced in homosocial friendships, as Elizabeth and Mary's correspondence reveals.[14]

In spring 1796, Elizabeth accompanied her mother to Ireland on a trip that had the potential to decide the family's fate. As Elizabeth informed Mary, "I strongly suspect that we shall either take up our abode in Ireland, or go abroad wherever the regiment may happen to be ordered." The Smiths were eager to settle down and reunite with George Smith, but Juliet Smith seemed to regard the prospect of relocating to Ireland as unappealing as her husband's earlier Canadian scheme. "We talk of returning in the autumn," Elizabeth confided to Mary, "and I am glad it is talked of, because it makes my mother quit England with less reluctance than she otherwise would."[15]

While she had considered a possible move to Canada with enthusiasm, Elizabeth contemplated the trip to Ireland with mixed emotions: "On the whole, I am extremely pleased with the idea of our expedition;

for besides my natural love of rambling, and of seeing and knowing every thing that is worth the trouble, I am weary of the world." Elizabeth was an avid adventurer who typically welcomed opportunities for travel and exploration. Yet with her family's future residence uncertain, she was uneasy at the thought of leaving England behind, even temporarily, "the only world with which I am acquainted, the scene of all our miseries." Elizabeth was experiencing "the positive pain of leaving some very dear friends" and expressed "great regret" at parting with her beloved younger sister Kitty, who was not accompanying Elizabeth and her mother to Ireland.[16] Elizabeth's comments reflected continued uncertainty about her family's future, as well as concerns about maintaining long-distance connections with loved ones.

For someone who usually embraced adventure, Elizabeth's thoughts on her upcoming trip had an unusually gloomy tone to them. "I may be drowned, I may never return, I may never see you again till 'the life to come,'" she mused to Mary. "Do not forget me; and be assured whatever changes may happen to me, of fortune, or habitation, my sincere affection for my MARY will never change. Adieu, perhaps for ever!"[17] Elizabeth's emotional angst in part reflected the potential dangers and inconveniences of the journey to Ireland. From Bath, Elizabeth and Juliet Smith would travel over 200 miles northwest across Wales, in order to cross the Irish Sea at either Liverpool or Holyhead. Once they reached Dublin, they faced an overland journey of over 130 miles to reach George Smith's barracks at Sligo, located in the northwest region of Ireland.[18]

There was one bright spot, however, that made Elizabeth and Juliet Smith's trip to Ireland particularly appealing. As they journeyed across Wales, Elizabeth and Juliet stopped at Llangollen to visit Eleanor Butler and Sarah Ponsonby, two of the era's most renowned learned ladies. "Lady Eleanor Butler and Miss Ponsonby have sent us a most obliging invitation to their house, and I hope we shall pass a day and a night there. Do you not envy us this visit?" she wrote to Mary. Excited about her visit to the famed "Ladies of Llangollen," Elizabeth wished that "we could carry you and our beloved friend [Harriet Bowdler] with us."[19] Whether she was learning new languages, reading inspiring books, exploring new lands, or meeting other learned women, Elizabeth was most fulfilled when she shared such meaningful experiences with her closest friends. It is no wonder, then, that she longed for Mary Hunt's and Harriet Bowdler's company when meeting the Ladies of Llangollen, two learned women who successfully created a life and home of their own, on their own terms.

"Fancied Myself in a Fairy Palace"

In receiving a personal invitation to the home of Eleanor Butler and Sarah Ponsonby, Elizabeth Smith would have indeed been the envy of many late eighteenth-century travelers. By the time of Elizabeth Smith's visit in 1796, the Ladies of Llangollen's "romantic friendship" had earned them a heightened degree of fame and notoriety. After their elopement to Wales in 1778, the two women set up a household together in Llangollen—a daring act of autonomy that rejected conventional, heteronormative constructions of eighteenth-century marriage. They lived off modest inheritances, enough to maintain their own home in North Wales. Butler and Ponsonby quickly attracted widespread attention and curiosity, achieving celebrity status for their independent lifestyle.[20]

As their fame grew, Butler and Ponsonby's cottage in Llangollen became renowned as a requisite stop for many tourists journeying through Wales, or those traveling between Dublin and London. The poet Anna Seward, who visited Llangollen a year before Elizabeth Smith, enthusiastically described Sarah Ponsonby and Eleanor Butler as "women of genius, taste, and knowledge,—sought, in their beauteous retirement, by the great, the literary, and the ingenious."[21] Having self-consciously devoted themselves to a life of retirement, the Ladies were protective of their home and their time. Resentful toward uninvited guests, Butler and Ponsonby admitted that they often "refused them with proper contempt."[22] Travelers wishing to visit Butler and Ponsonby had to write to them upon arrival in Llangollen and hope to be granted an invitation. Catherine Hutton, who toured Wales in 1796 (the same year as Elizabeth Smith), considered requesting an invitation but "was told that the frequent exhibition of their house to strangers had become troublesome to the ladies; and I did not think it right to intrude upon them for my own gratification."[23] Those without an invitation had to content themselves, as another traveler noted in 1797, with "a passing view of the simple, elegant, and picturesque residence of Lady Eleanor Butler and Miss Ponsonby."[24]

Along with curious tourists, a number of key literary figures, including Walter Scott and William Wordsworth, visited Eleanor Butler and Sarah Ponsonby. (It's worth noting, however, that Elizabeth Smith's 1796 meeting occurred decades before the arrival of Wordsworth and Scott, who did not visit the Ladies until 1824 and 1825, respectively.) The literary lions regarded the Ladies of Llangollen as exceptional and eccentric, reflecting the range of responses Butler and Ponsonby inspired during their lifetimes. By the 1820s, the Ladies often wore masculine-style top hats and black riding attire, fashion choices that sparked curious commentary. During Walter Scott's visit, his son-in-law dismissively described the Ladies of Llangollen as "odd and extravagant beyond report," representing "the spirit of blue-stockingism."[25] Quips about bluestockings, as learned women knew all too well, represented familiar forms of disparagement. William Wordsworth was more generous, writing a sonnet in praise of their "Vale of Friendship" and referring to Ponsonby and Butler as "Sisters in love, a love allowed to climb, / Even on this earth, above the reach of Time!"[26] Wordsworth's tone was favorable but his use of the word "allowed" called to mind the condescending tolerance, rather than true acceptance, learned women often faced.

While many regarded their relationship as unconventional, Eleanor Butler and Sarah Ponsonby shared much in common with other accomplished women from the era. Their home, which included an extensive library, was a self-conscious creation of space devoted to their ardent scholarly interests (fig. 7). As Anna Seward noted, "This saloon of the Minervas contains the finest editions, superbly bound, of the best authors, in prose and verse."[27] In her journal, Eleanor Butler recorded the delight she and Sarah Ponsonby experienced in spending "warm and comfortable" days at a "table strewed with Books, pens, Ink, paper, every implement for Drawing."[28] Discerning about which visitors to welcome, the Ladies of Llangollen were particularly pleased when they were able to spend time in the company of other learned women. In 1788, Eleanor Butler expressed favorable impressions toward one visiting family: "We felt quite sorry when

FIGURE 7. Portrait of the Ladies of Llangollen, Lady Eleanor Butler and Sarah Ponsonby (circa 1836), shown in the library of their Llangollen home. (© Trustees of the British Museum)

they took leave. Most charming and wonderfully accomplished family, perfect mistresses of Latin, Italian, French and painting."[29]

Eleanor Butler's and Sarah Ponsonby's interests in language studies, reading, and drawing were similar to those that provided the substance of Elizabeth Smith's warm friendships with Mary Hunt, Harriet Bowdler, and other learned women. In addition to their shared intellectual pursuits, members of Elizabeth's social circle and the Ladies of Llangollen considered Harriet Bowdler a trusted friend. Bowdler maintained a steady correspondence with the Ladies, visited them several times, and was among the very few who were "invited to stay the night" at their cottage.[30] Writing to Eleanor Butler in 1798, Anna Seward noted, "I rejoice that your beloved Miss Bowdler will soon visit it daily."[31]

Friends of Harriet Bowdler, including Elizabeth Smith, could thus expect to receive a warmer welcome than strangers who considered the Ladies of Llangollen's cottage a requisite tourist stop. As Harriet later recalled, "The visit in Llangollen Vale more than answered the expectation of my friends, and the very obliging manner in which they were received, was highly gratifying to me."[32] Unfortunately, Elizabeth Smith's account of her visit to Llangollen has not survived. However, we can glean some sense of how the encounter may have gone based on the experiences of Eliza Simcoe, a member of Elizabeth Smith's social circle, who traveled to Llangollen in 1809.[33]

After her visit, Eliza Simcoe wrote a lengthy letter to Mary Hunt, her former governess, describing her meeting with Eleanor Butler and Sarah Ponsonby. By then, the Ladies of Llangollen had grown increasingly weary of the constant stream of curious visitors, and Eliza doubted that she would get the opportunity to meet them. Harriet Bowdler had provided Eliza with a careful set of instructions: "The etiquette was to write a note to them—as they knew my name perhaps they would see me." Before Eliza could work up the courage to write, "to my surprise on Sunday morning I received a most polite invitation to drink tea with them that evening, and bring the friends who were with me."[34]

Eliza Simcoe's personal invitation to visit Eleanor Butler and Sarah Ponsonby's cottage, like the one Elizabeth Smith received in 1796, was made possible due to her close connection with Harriet Bowdler. "You cannot think how kindly they received me having long known me they said as a favorite child of Mrs. Bowdler's—indeed she is too good to me," Eliza reported to Mary. Eliza was charmed by the "amiable and fascinating" women and impressed by their extensive intellectual interests. "I believe Lady Eleanor shewed me every Italian book that ever was written," wrote an awestruck Eliza. She was especially pleased when Eleanor Butler asked after Mary Hunt and "wanted to know what Spanish books you were reading." Overwhelmed by Butler's and Ponsonby's intellectual stores as well as their generous hospitality, Eliza Simcoe "fancied myself in a Fairy Palace."[35]

As Eliza Simcoe's glowing description suggests, many learned women admired the Ladies of Llangollen. Most eighteenth-century women would not and did not make the unconventional decision of largely cutting themselves off from their families to create homes of their own. Nonetheless, the Ladies of Llangollen offered learned women an enchanting vision of a fulfilling and rewarding life dedicated to scholarship and sociability. Eleanor Butler and Sarah Ponsonby had, in fact, made a home for themselves "filled exactly as one would wish"—bringing to life Elizabeth Smith's musings from the foot of Conway Castle.[36] As she left Llangollen and continued the journey to Ireland, Elizabeth renewed her hopes of crafting such a well-furnished life.

"Our Millenium Hall Scheme"

After her visit with the Ladies of Llangollen, Elizabeth Smith's dread about the trip to Ireland faded. Along the way, however, she and her mother inevitably encountered some of the physical inconveniences of eighteenth-century travel. Juliet and Elizabeth made the last leg of their trek to George Smith's barracks at Sligo on horseback through a heavy rainstorm. When they arrived, "dripping wet," Juliet was frustrated to learn that their baggage had not arrived, "and owing to the negligence of the Quarter-master, there was not even a bed to rest on." As she considered their dismal surroundings, which lacked the comforts of home, Juliet was "forlorn." Elizabeth quickly offered reassurances to her mother, pointing out "a little cupboard" in a corner as "a blessing." "I dried my tears," Juliet recollected, "and endeavoured to learn fortitude from my daughter."[37] Elizabeth's strong sense of loyalty to her family inspired her to seek contentment even under stressful circumstances. Recovering from their bleak arrival at Sligo, she reported that "we are very well, and much amused with the little misfortunes that happen to us."[38] Her cheerful attitude toward the "misfortunes" of travel, including their inhospitable lodgings, was indicative of Elizabeth's love of rambling. While her mother felt miserable in their uncomfortable situation, Elizabeth focused on making the most of her time in Ireland.

Although her 1796 visit to Ireland was made with a specific purpose and destination in mind—to see her father—Elizabeth embraced the opportunities for adventure, exploration, and friendship that travel afforded.[39] As she explored Ireland's "green hills, rivers, lakes, and fine woods," Elizabeth's sense of adventure took flight.[40] Inspired by her surroundings, Elizabeth once again found herself drawn to rugged mountains instead of calm meadows. If Mary was with her, Elizabeth mused, she would insist that her friend join her as she explored, "to make you wander through a valley, between mountains tossed together in all the wild and rugged forms imaginable, with an hundred cascades dashing from the summits, and forming a beautiful lake at the bottom." In Ireland, Elizabeth encountered the types of sublime landscapes depicted in the poetry of her beloved Ossian: "I never before knew so well what Ossian meant by the thick mist of the valley, and the ragged skirts of a cloud as it sails slowly over the dark heath."[41] Immersing herself in such environs fueled Elizabeth's imaginative, wandering impulses.

During her visit to Ireland, Elizabeth also found fulfillment in the warm friendship she developed with Lady Isabella King, the daughter of the Earl of Kingston, whose home the Smiths had stayed at while on route to George Smith's barracks. Elizabeth looked forward to forging new bonds of friendship based on shared intellectual interests. Just as Mary Hunt had inspired Elizabeth's love of languages, Elizabeth encouraged her new friend to study German, "because your Ladyship is one of the very few people I think worthy to understand German."[42]

Returning to England after four months in Ireland, Elizabeth reflected on the hours that she and Lady Isabella had spent together walking, talking, and planning for the future. "Our Millenium Hall scheme appears so distant," she wrote to her new friend, "that I fear we shall be grown cross disagreeable old maids before we can put it in execution."[43] Elizabeth's reference to Sarah Scott's utopian novel *Millenium Hall* revealed her persistent desire to craft an ideal space that she could share with her close friends. Scott, one of several eighteenth-century women writers who made Bath their home, used her novel to present a vision of independent, single women living together in a close-knit community. During Elizabeth's lifetime, *Millenium Hall* served as a cultural shorthand to describe places considered particularly receptive to accomplished women. Traveling in 1791, one woman praised a lodging near Worcestershire, England, remarking, "I assure you, in some respects it reminds me of Mrs. Scott's Millenium Hall: it seems almost to be that charming imaginary society realized," and further commenting that "every one here has an air of cheerfulness and content."[44]

Elizabeth Smith's Millenium Hall scheming with Isabella King about a cheerful, content home to call their own may have seemed "distant," but it was not that far-fetched. Her friendship with Lady Isabella developed directly after her visit to Sarah Ponsonby and Eleanor Butler in Llangollen, two women who had succeeded in forging an unconventional, independent life for themselves. Elizabeth was also personally familiar with Bath's vibrant community of learned women, the real-life inspiration for Sarah Scott's novel. In both fact and fiction, she repeatedly encountered inspiring examples of women successfully enacting learned lives. Many of these women avoided conventional marriage and motherhood, forging alternate paths for themselves that were conducive to their intellectual interests. Elizabeth's various experiences during her travels through Wales and Ireland—her encounters with rugged landscapes, meeting the Ladies of Llangollen, and even casual garden walks with a new friend—all sparked her desire to find a place for herself in the world. Where that home was located was perhaps less important than the life she could pursue as a learned woman in the company of supportive friends. "Any place would do, so filled," she mused while imagining such a home from the foot of the castle tower in Wales.

Upon returning to Bath after her visit to Ireland, however, Elizabeth lacked even a room of her own. As a houseguest, she had little privacy, "for there are so many of us that we have no separate rooms, but all sit constantly together." In January 1797, Elizabeth apologized for her delay in answering her new friend's letter, noting that she had "been waiting in hopes of being left alone to write to my dearest Lady Isabella." Elizabeth viewed letter writing as a space to converse freely to close friends without apologies or restraint, to discuss topics with "as many variations as you please." Such letters were meant to convey personal, trusted sentiments that "the rest of world will hear with indifference, perhaps with ridicule, as not understanding or entering into the sentiments of the writer." Echoing sentiments she had declared to Mary Hunt, Elizabeth mused to her new friend: "It is a maxim of mine, that whoever writes me a copper-plate letter does not love me, and *vice versa*." Not surprisingly, Elizabeth found it difficult "writing to any one I love when any human creature is present; it is as bad as talking in mixed company." Even reading around others was sometimes challenging for Elizabeth, who resorted to creating "a kind of solitude by hiding my face with it [her book] when I come to a passage which particularly pleases me."[45]

Elizabeth longed for a place to call her own, where she could engage in intellectual and imaginative pursuits without interruption or obser-vation. Whenever possible, she relied on forms of solitary reflection— burying herself in a book, or long rambles through the countryside—to carve out some space for herself. Her self-conscious seeking of "a kind of solitude" enabled Elizabeth to create some kind of distance between herself and the stream of company she must have frequently encountered during recurring visits to friends and family. Her shy, reserved demeanor provided a copperplate presentation and plausible explanation for those moments when Elizabeth did not wish to contribute to the various con-versations going on around her.

Elizabeth spent much of 1797 and part of 1798 visiting with Harriet Bowdler in Bath. Although grateful for the support of her friends, she felt adrift, having endured nearly five years without a family home. At times, Elizabeth must have felt that her Millenium Hall vision grew ever more distant, but the seemingly unfeasible nature of her musings did little to quell her longings. In a journal from this time period, Elizabeth reflected, "The most difficult vice to conquer, is pride; I mean a high idea of our own merits, and a spirit of rebellion. This came in Eve's way; she fell, and perhaps there is not one of her posterity who would not have done the same."[46] Eve's desire for knowledge was considered the cause of her fall, but as Elizabeth mused, few learned women would be able to resist such temp-tation. Elizabeth's sympathetic response to the "original sin" of a woman longing for a learned life provides some insights into her own sense of self. Cultural prescriptions urged women to be mild, meek, and submissive, but learned women such as Elizabeth Smith possessed a degree of pride in their "own merits." Her persistent desire to enact a fulfilling life suggests how learned women often struggled to find space for themselves within the prescriptive constraints of eighteenth-century womanhood.

In spring 1798, Elizabeth was on the road again, traveling to North Wales for a sightseeing tour with her mother and Louise Smith, the wife of her brother George-Thomas. While Elizabeth embraced opportunities for exploration that travel afforded, the scenic vistas she encountered also sparked a growing sense of restlessness. "If we stay much longer amongst these delightful scenes," she confided to Mary during her 1798 stay in Wales, "I shall grow completely and irrecoverably idle." By midsummer, Elizabeth and her companions had become "such vagrants" that she rarely found the inclination to write, "even to you." Elizabeth imagined that Mary, by contrast, was "studying hard, and enjoying, peace, quietness, and leisure, in your comfortable little retreat." Elizabeth enjoyed traveling but also longed for the comforts and stability of a home to call her own. Still, in the face of continued uncertainty about the future, Elizabeth sought contentment wherever her family's travels led her. She "determine[d] never again to be *anxious* about any thing, persuaded that all events are much better disposed than if *I* had the management of them."[47]

Elizabeth Smith strove for contentment yet she found it challenging to conquer her restless nature. Her "spirit of rebellion" found expression in her ardent intellectual pursuits, her longings to explore rocky terrains, and her imaginative flights of fancy. In Wales, Elizabeth's restless nature found new inspiration during her explorations of enchanting castles and rugged mountains.

"Ramble with Me"

During her 1798 visit to Wales, Elizabeth and her family were active participants in the picturesque travel scene. They explored expansive landscapes and crumbling castles, took "delightful walks, and find great use for our sketch-books."[48] While in Wales, Elizabeth visited popular tourist locations, including Caernarvon Castle, the well-visited birthplace of Edward II that was described as having "the greatest appearance of any castle" in Wales.[49] As she recounted her visit to Caernarvon, Elizabeth again imagined that Mary was there to "ramble with me through dark passages without end or number." She wished that her friend could "ascend with me to the Eagle Tower, and count if you can the number of steps, for indeed I forgot to reckon, and having no book of travels from which to extract a journal, I cannot tell you." Describing the expedition for Mary's benefit, Elizabeth related various anecdotes shared by her tour guide, including his attempt to "refute the opinion of Mr. Pennant," a popular travel writer, about which room Edward II was born in. "Come on into another little room," Elizabeth continued, "and if you chuse to be remembered amongst fools, write your name upon the planks which still remain." After hearing more stories from the tour guide, Elizabeth was led to "hurry away from the Castle, wishing to spend days and weeks in examining it."[50]

Elizabeth's references to a "book of travels," to Thomas Pennant's famous guidebook on Wales, and to the ritual of visitors recording their names on castle planks reveal her familiarity with the literary and material culture that guided eighteenth-century picturesque travel. Guidebooks provided practical and useful information about lodgings, roads, and attractions, as well as cultural commentary on prevailing travel practices and rituals. Before setting off on a journey, sightseers were encouraged to procure various "travelling 'knick-knacks,'" including maps, pedometers, looking glasses, and sketchbooks.[51] These travel accoutrements served as recognizable material and symbolic markers informing how one was "supposed" to experience key spots.[52]

As they made their way to select locations, individuals used information gleaned from various sources to guide their journeys. Yet in the process of such careful preparation, travelers risked creating experiences that seemed pre-scripted and conventional. Elizabeth's quip that some visitors focused primarily on counting their steps while climbing a castle tower, or her complaint at being rushed through rooms instead of being able to explore freely, suggest some of the ways that eighteenth-century tourism could be a highly mediated experience. The "search for the picturesque"

was marked by tensions between the longing for authentic, unique experiences and the well-known, ritualistic expectations associated with particular locations on the travel map.

A variety of personal and published travel writings reflected apprehen-
sions regarding individuals' expectations and experiences of picturesque
tourism. To highlight the unique aspects of their own adventures, many
sought to record their personal observations through sketching or journal-
ing. Travelers focused on conveying their "first impression"—encouraged,
whenever possible, to write or sketch directly "on the spot" to capture the
most genuine account of their initial encounter with sublime or picturesque locations. Such spontaneous productions—even if fragmented and
incomplete—were thought to provide more authentic and individualized
representations than writings or drawings that were later edited or polished for public dissemination.[53] Yet having already "encountered" their
destinations through various guidebooks, sketches, and poems, some
individuals wondered what new insights they could add. Setting off for a
tour of North Wales in 1784, one male traveler confessed, "I shall be more
fearfull of describing the country I mean to visit . . . because the ground
has been lately so much trod; & every particular so well brought forward
by able pens and pencils."[54] Individuals worried that their own reflections
might seem formulaic and derivative in comparison to more well-known
writings. As travel narratives proliferated in both manuscript and published form, some feared that "there are so many travels written, the world
is tired of them."[55]

Despite concerns about the inauthentic or formulaic elements of tourism and travel writing, many men and women strongly believed that there
was something unmatched and transcendent about picturesque travel.
"What a multitude of adventures may be grasped within the narrow circle
of a day," a Bath resident reflected in 1797, "by those ramblers who have
spirit to investigate; curiosity to enquire; and attention to observe."[56] As
Elizabeth Smith well knew from her residence at Piercefield, eighteenth-
century travelers were drawn to past ruins and mountainous terrains as
embodiments of the sublime, picturesque, and romantic. The wonders of
nature and crumbling remnants of old buildings were particularly celebrated for their association with a venerated past vision of the British

Isles. An 1801 poem by William Sotheby captured the powerful appeal of must-see locations on the picturesque travel scene:

> Whether he gaze from Snowdon's summit hoar,
> Or scale the rugged heights of bold Lodore,
> Down Wye's green meads, white cliffs, and woodlands sail,
> Catch inspiration from Langollen's vale,
> In Dove's still dell the world's far din forsake,
> Or hermit visions feed on Lomond's lake.[57]

Sotheby's poem evokes a vision of a solitary male traveler seeking inspiration from rugged cliffs and scenic vales. A well-traveled woman, Elizabeth Smith spent time in nearly all of the key locations on the picturesque travel scene celebrated in Sotheby's poem and other influential travel writings. Significantly, Elizabeth not only visited but lived in two of the regions evoked by Sotheby—the Wye River Valley in South Wales and, after 1800, the English Lake District. She also spent time in Ireland, where, as we have seen, she was enchanted by the region's rugged landscapes. Along with other Romantic-era figures, Elizabeth Smith understood the appeal of such places as sources of creativity and inspiration. She had begun her own youthful poem about the ruins at Piercefield by evoking Snowdon's key symbolism within the Welsh landscape: "Round Snowdon's shaggy brows grim darkness hung."[58] Drawn to sublime, picturesque, and romantic scenes since her youth, Elizabeth expressed a persistent longing for rocky precipices and rugged terrains. And during the summer of 1798, Elizabeth Smith accomplished one of the ultimate travel adventures of the era—*she* would "gaze from Snowdon's summit hoar."

"Go with Me to the Top of Snowdon"

Climbing Snowdon was considered both the literal and symbolic pinnacle of the picturesque travel map in Wales.[59] Many Romantic-era travelers expressed their desire "to traverse Snowdon and its dependencies; to visit the summit of the highest mountain in the three kingdoms."[60] Described as "a compound of wonder, grandeur, and terror," the mountain's

FIGURE 8. Mount Snowdon, Wales, by Samuel Alken (after John W. Smith), illustration published in William Sotheby's *Tour through Parts of Wales* (1794). (© Trustees of the British Museum)

awe-inspiring summit was celebrated in a variety of poetry, prose, and paintings (fig. 8).[61] "Raised o'er the rocky scenery sublime," William Sotheby enthused, "Thee, Snowdon! King of Cambrian mountains hail!"[62]

Mountain climbing was an embodied experience that required a degree of courage, determination, risk, and effort. Such physical aspects associated mountain climbing with masculinity, as did the fact that most travel narratives about climbing published during this era focused on the experiences of men. Romantic-era poets, including Samuel Coleridge and William Wordsworth, were particularly drawn to Snowdon and other mountainous terrains due to the "perceived link between sublime experience and poetic production." The physical challenges involved in scaling a mountain evoked a sense of exhilaration and accomplishment believed to spark creative and imaginative impulses.[63] Wordsworth's trip to Snowdon inspired him to muse about how "circumstances awful and sublime" stirred "a mind sustained / By recognitions of transcendent power."[64] From the vantage point of a rocky precipice or mountain summit, all things seemed possible.

Snowdon presented particular challenges and complications for those wishing to make the climb, or once at the top to see clearly. "Multitudes of people go to see Snowdon," Catherine Hutton noted during her 1797 tour of North Wales, "but it is the lot only of a few to say that they have seen it."[65] The mist and fog often thwarted hopeful climbers, and so did trepidation. Some travelers who found themselves at the foot of Mount Snowdon, as travel writer William Gilpin confessed, "felt but little inclination to ascend higher."[66] The trek required physical prowess and stamina, particularly for those hoping to reach the elusive summit. In 1797, Bath resident Richard Warner and his traveling companions were initially unable to begin their climb, grounded by "impenetrable mist." Their local guide eventually led them to an alternate path but warned that it was even "more steep and disagreeable" than the typical route. It took over "two hours of very severe labour" to reach "the summit of Snowdon." Up top, Warner and his travel party were briefly rewarded with "a wide, unbounded prospect" for a few moments, until a cloud "once more infolded us in its chilly embrace."[67] Many who made the trek often had to be content with "the satisfaction of saying he was there, but not that he cou'd see anything at the top," since "so rare it is to have a clear view from such amazing heights."[68]

Such obstacles were not insurmountable for Elizabeth Smith. Throughout her years of rambling, Elizabeth's wish to explore rude mountains, rather than quiet meadows, had not dissipated. Thus, when Elizabeth literally found herself at the foot of the mountain, she eagerly began climbing. "And now you must mount your old friend Pegasus," Elizabeth wrote to Mary, "and go with me to the top of Snowdon to adore the rising sun." As she recorded an account of her climb for Mary, Elizabeth expressed concern that "my travels [are] so much more tedious in the recital than in the performance."[69] Despite such disclaimers, Elizabeth was eager to share her adventures with a trusted friend who was well acquainted with her longing for rocky precipices and inspiring vistas.

"Quitting the Castle," Elizabeth, accompanied by her mother and sister-in-law Louise, "took a most delightful walk beside the river on which it stands" before returning to their inn for supper. Conscious to avoid the clichéd writing common in many travel narratives, Elizabeth spared her friend "the description of every dish, and how much was paid for it, because I have forgotten both." Such comments indicate that Elizabeth was well familiar with the criticisms leveled against formulaic travel writing. In any case, as Elizabeth emphasized, the "enormous supper" served a practical purpose—to provide sustenance for the adventure to come.[70]

Elizabeth, Juliet, and Louise Smith began their journey to the mountain at eleven o'clock at night. If climbing Snowdon was regarded as the pinnacle of the picturesque travel scene in Wales, doing so overnight was the ultimate experience. As William Wordsworth reflected about his nighttime Snowdon climb: "With eager pace, and no less eager thoughts / Thus might we wear a midnight hour away."[71] An overnight ascent enabled individuals to experience the sublime thrill of being on the summit for sunrise, which occurred around four or five in the morning during the summer months.

After traveling eight miles by "moon-light," the Smith women arrived "at a little hut where the guide lives." They gathered supplies and "began our march at a quarter past one." Elizabeth, Juliet, and Louise planned to ascend Snowdon overnight, accompanied only by a local male guide, a remarkable feat indicative of their determined spirits. Walking in the darkness, under heavy clouds that threatened rain, Elizabeth and her companions reached "the first range of hills" around two in the morning. A "violent wind" began to blow, which "frightened" her sister-in-law. "Seeing a very steep ascent before her," Louise decided "she would sit down and wait for our return." Juliet Smith volunteered to wait with her daughter-in-law back at the guide's hut but "very kindly insisted" that Elizabeth continue the climb.[72] Juliet must have recognized how much her daughter wished for an adventure to call her own.

Left alone with her guide, "who could not speak a word of English," Elizabeth continued her ascent up Snowdon. As the pair "toiled up several mountains" to reach the uppermost summit, Elizabeth occasionally stopped to pick up some moss or plants but was generally "disappointed in the botanical way." Elizabeth "went on as fast I could, without stopping," occasionally taking "a moment to look down on the mountains under my feet, as clouds passed over them." She kept a brisk pace, anxious to reach "the top before sun-rise." As she "was ascending the last step in ambition's ladder," Elizabeth remembered that her mother and sister-in-law "would be very impatient for my return" and wondered if "they would find their way back to the hut" in the middle of the night. Elizabeth was contemplating turning back to rejoin her companions when she suddenly found herself at the foot of "an immense chasm, all in darkness" that stretched for at least a hundred feet.[73]

As she later explained to Mary, Elizabeth viscerally experienced Snowdon's disorientating effects—the feeling, as one eighteenth-century travel writer described, of being "kept in continual suspense."[74] As she described this state of uncertainty, Elizabeth's narrative briefly switched to the present tense, suggesting the intensity of the experience and its strong association in her memory: "You think you are now at the top, but you are mistaken. I am standing indeed at the top of the abyss, but with a high rocky peak rising on each side of me, and descending very near perpendicularly into the lake at the bottom." From this vantage point, Elizabeth was awestruck by "a beautiful rose-coloured light, while the opposite part still casts a dark shade." She experienced "delight" and "ecstasy" in her surroundings. "The guide seemed quite delighted to see me so pleased," she recounted to Mary, "and took care in descending to lead me to the edge of every precipice, which he had not done in going up."[75] The guide recognized the evident joy Elizabeth experienced in climbing new heights.

Continuing the climb, Elizabeth "set off along the brink of the cavity for the highest peak," where she "saw a view, of which it is impossible to form an idea from description." Surrounded by mountaintops and clouds, and with the whole scene "bounded by the sea," she "was enjoying the finest blue sky, and the purest air I ever breathed." As the sun rose, it appeared to be "still hanging over the sea." From her vantage point, she sketched the impressive view and "sat down, for the first time" since beginning the climb to snack on "bread and milk" with her guide. At half past four and "almost frozen," they "began to descend." Remembering her waiting companions, and perhaps feeling a tinge of guilt for having made the journey without them, Elizabeth and her guide made their way down the mountain in "all possible haste" to rejoin her mother and sister-in-law. Elizabeth "found them safe in the hut at ten minutes past six." From there, Elizabeth, Juliet, and Louise Smith took a carriage ride to breakfast, visited the famed Devil's Bridge, and returned to their lodgings at Caernarvon for dinner and an evening walk. She finally "went to bed after *thirty-nine hours* of almost constant exercise."[76]

Elizabeth Smith's successful climb of Snowdon challenges the dominant narrative that presumes only male adventurers participated in such exhilarating acts of exploration. Moreover, climbing Snowdon at night placed her among the upper echelon of travelers from the era. It is significant that Elizabeth would not turn back when her sister-in-law refused to climb, and that she was willing to make the trek without anyone but a local guide to accompany her. A young, unmarried woman, alone on a mountain in the middle of the night with only a male guide, certainly seems a noteworthy achievement. Yet for Elizabeth, scaling Snowdon represented one in a long series of adventures, rather than a singularly extraordinary experience.

How exceptional was Elizabeth Smith's accomplishment in climbing Snowdon? Although a number of eighteenth-century women traveled through and explored Wales, it is unclear how many attempted to reach Snowdon's summit, especially overnight. Catherine Hutton was an avid traveler who took several tours of Wales in the 1790s with her father, but she did not accompany him when he climbed Snowdon. From the foot of the mountain, she "saw Snowdon in perfection . . . and I looked at him as if I would get acquainted with every atom." Although Catherine Hutton rambled over miles of rugged landscapes, she did not attempt Snowdon's challenging climb. "Had I been on his summit," she mused, "he would have had no competitor," but her views of Snowdon were limited to those "from below."[77]

Catherine Hutton remained at the foot of the mountain, but her father's *Remarks upon North Wales*, published in 1803, included a story he heard about "two gentlemen and a lady, in September, 1797, [who] began to climb this famous mountain." When the party reached the top after enduring a wet, windy climb, "the lady, elated with success, though she could see nothing, pulled off her hat and cap, and huzzaed for joy." William Hutton's retelling of the story presented a largely unfavorable impression of this unknown woman, describing her actions as inappropriately assertive and outside the boundaries of proper feminine behavior:

"The Amazonian lady, no doubt, was the leader of the party, and designed, like some others of her sex, to govern ours." A woman's wish to climb Snowdon somehow translated, in Hutton's mind, into her desire to rule over men. Such misplaced ambitions, he asserted, were no match for the mountain: "The lofty Snowdon, however, reduced the more lofty spirit of the female adventurer. She fell into fits, her life was despaired of, and she was brought in a chaise the next morning to Caernarvon at four, in a state of distress which excited pity."[78]

William Hutton was frequently accompanied by his daughter in his travels, yet there were evident limits to his understandings about women's participation in certain adventures. His presumptions failed to accord women the same respect given to men who sought to experience the feat of mountain climbing. Rather, his account indicates how women adventurers were often regarded in contemptuous tones, rather than celebrated for their aspirations. Hutton's dismissive account masculinized this unknown female climber ("Amazonian") but also implied that she was too delicate ("fell into fits") to handle reaching the summit. He assumed that her adventurous spirit meant that she sought to "govern" men, rather than serving as a reflection of the same impulses that inspired male mountaineers. The implication was that mountain climbing and other physically demanding travel adventures were well outside the bounds of proper feminine behavior.[79] In the cultural imagination, a "female adventurer" represented an anomaly in need of explanation. As William Hutton's account suggests, such efforts were likely to inspire condemnation rather than praise.[80]

Any woman who climbed mountains—especially any woman who dared to climb Snowdon at night—would have been regarded as exceptional and even suspect. For Elizabeth Smith, the adventure was worth it. She scaled Snowdon with a courage, strength, and skill that matched the most determined male mountaineer. She did not succumb to "fits" or suffer any physical or emotional harm from her climb. "After this I think you will not take the trouble to enquire after my health," Elizabeth wrote to Mary, as "it must be tolerably good." Elizabeth was clearly energized by her climb. "I am delighted that I have been," she wrote to Mary, "and would not for any thing give up the recollection for the sublime scene." She wished only for more time to enjoy the scenery, and of course for "some one to enjoy the expedition with me."[81] Reaching Snowdon's summit at sunrise further reinforced Elizabeth's love of rambling and her longstanding preference for rocky precipices over tame, domesticated scenes.

"To Give a Fillip to My Ideas"

Climbing Snowdon was an impressive feat—the kind of achievement meant to be recorded and shared. Many who reached the summit scratched their names on rocks or on scraps of paper to be found by subsequent trekkers.[82] Elizabeth Smith did not mention if she participated in this specific travel ritual or if she was aware of other women who had successfully scaled Snowdon. The "particular account" that she penned about her Snowdon adventure offered a personal narrative written for a close friend, rather than a more public, ritualistic chronicling. Learned women often used their correspondence with friends as safe, trusted places to express themselves. Writing about her travel adventures represented an important act of self-fashioning that clearly conveyed her sense of accomplishment and pride. Elizabeth worried that her friend's "patience is exhausted" by her account, and as a result she "suppressed at least half of what I wish to say."[83] Climbing Snowdon clearly sparked Elizabeth's desire to say and write and do more.

At some point, Elizabeth also composed an essay consisting of various "Observations in North-Wales." While only a fragment remains, these "Observations" were much more stylized and formal than the account she composed for her friend's benefit. This composition seemed intended for a broad, general audience. Instead of a breathless account of the "ecstasy" she felt in ascending the summit, Elizabeth focused on the botanical and geological features of the mountain landscape she encountered. "Vegetation does not cease at the top of Snowdon: several sorts of moss, and lichen . . . grow even to the summit," she dryly recounted. The composition also contained some general observations on local customs, content common in many travel guides from the era.[84] While only a small portion of this document remains extant, its prose style suggests that Elizabeth was contemplating writing a copperplate account suitable for publication. For whatever reason, it does not appear that she ever moved forward with this plan.

When Elizabeth Smith climbed Snowdon in 1798, there were only a handful of published travel accounts written by women. British authors Mary Morgan and Ann Radcliffe published their travel narratives in the 1790s, but most women travelers during this era were more likely to record their observations in personal letters or journals. Women who published accounts often adopted familiar strategies, including apologetic disclaimers and anonymous publications, to justify their forays into the genre of travel writing. In the preface to her Wales travel narrative, Mary Morgan insisted that it was her friends who "wished me to collect, and publish" the writings that she originally shared with them during her 1791 travels. Morgan presented her printed narrative with a familiar disclaimer, asserting that she "does not flatter herself that the Public can be much gratified with the perusal of a Work, which was written only for the amusement of a few friends."[85] Morgan claimed that she had no deliberate ambitions to become an author but was eventually persuaded by friends to do so.

Although a number of women participated in the picturesque travel scene, cultural attitudes presented challenges for those seeking to record and publish their experiences. In 1802, the London *Monthly Magazine* published an account by "L.A." describing her recent travels through Wales. This woman and her traveling party completed the "arduous and fatiguing ascent" of Snowdon during the daytime, reassuring readers that they experienced "none of the perils and dangers described by tourists." Did this woman feel safe and protected traveling in a group, or did she deliberately seek to downplay dangerous aspects of the climb? Perhaps she lacked perspective about Snowdon's summit, where her party found "everything wrapped in an impenetrable veil of clouds—not a glimpse is to be had of the wild prospect below." In any case, this anonymous woman self-consciously presented her account as "the simple unvarnished narrative of one who described, on the spot, what she saw, and nothing else."[86] Having completed the climb safely during the day with companions, she seemed somewhat unsure how to frame her narrative.

These concerns may explain why some women travel writers sought to remain anonymous. In 1803, another woman wrote to the publishing firm

Vernor and Hood about the possibility of publishing a "Manuscript copy of a Tour through various parts of England and Scotland" but expressed reservations about revealing her identity in print: "As I am far from being desirous of the appellation of an *Authoress* I must decline having my name affixed to the publication."[87] This writer understood that any "authoress" risked censure and ridicule at the hands of male critics. Given the era's expressed ambivalence toward women writers in general, travel writing may have seemed a particularly risky genre.

Concerns about literary reception may explain, on a broad level, why there are relatively few publications before the 1800s that actively highlight women's experiences with the picturesque travel scene and also specifically account for why Elizabeth Smith did not seek publication of her Snowdon adventure. Indeed, when Elizabeth learned that Mary had shown her account of climbing Snowdon to mutual friends, who in turn shared it with others, she expressed discontent. Elizabeth gently chided Mary for being "a *blab*" and asserted her hope that the "insipidity" of her current letter would "not be put in the trumpet of fame, and blown to the four quarters of the world."[88] Elizabeth understood that once her writings were out in wider circulation, they could be subject to various critical assessments beyond her control. Conscious of the unconventional nature of her accomplishment, perhaps she was reluctant to be mocked either as an "Amazonian climber" or "Authoress." These framings, Elizabeth understood, tended to call attention to women's ambitions and aspirations in problematic ways.

Her trepidation was not unfounded. In 1811, Eliza Simcoe wrote to Mary Hunt as she was preparing "my Tour of Wales," an account based on her own recent travels. It is unclear whether Eliza hoped to publish her narrative, as she seemed somewhat unsure of its merits. "I have no idea of describing scenery, nor any pleasure in recording the most brilliant observations of a Country," she confided to Mary, her former governess. She turned to their mutual friend Elizabeth Smith's writings for inspiration. "On looking over Miss Smith's account of Snowdon, I feel disappointed," Eliza confessed. In particular, she was struck that Elizabeth Smith "could describe so awful so glorious a scene so lightly, or rather in so lively a manner." Elizabeth's "lively" account of Snowdon seemed surprising to

Eliza: "I should have supposed it would have made such different impressions upon her from those she appears to have felt—perhaps she was more used to mountainous scenery, or perhaps she was in better spirits than I was, but yet I do not quite understand it."[89] Elizabeth's bold, fearless descriptions did not align with Eliza's experiences nor did it match the handful of published accounts by women available at the time. If a sympathetic member of her social circle seemed unsure of how to interpret Elizabeth's confident tone, how might the reading public respond?

Although unwilling to have her travel writings shared with a wider audience, Elizabeth Smith could not deny a growing desire for something more. The tone and tenor of the narrative she produced for her close friend indicates the profound effect that climbing Snowdon had produced. After reaching the summit, Elizabeth realized how challenging it would be to remain content at the foot of the tower. In a letter written to Lady Isabella King shortly after her Snowdon trek, Elizabeth offered advice to her friend that was equally applicable to herself: "I am entirely of your opinion, that *you* must seek for happiness in more rational employments, for which you are well qualified." Elizabeth believed that Isabella had talents that "*should* not be thrown away, and I am persuaded will *not*." As she encouraged her friend to make proper use of her talents, Elizabeth recognized that she had to take her own advice to heart. "The lack of new objects, and new subjects, has very nearly occasioned a stagnation of ideas in my mind," she confessed. Eager for new avenues of creative expression, Elizabeth called upon her friend for inspiration: "I want something to interest me, and therefore I beg you to write to give a fillip to my ideas, which will otherwise be congealed into a mass of ice this winter."[90]

In the meantime, the Smith family's peripatetic lifestyle continued, making it challenging for Elizabeth to direct her energies toward any specific purpose. Elizabeth remained intellectually curious—pursuing language studies; reading widely in a variety of works; enjoying various "amusements, such as seeing the British Museum"; and engaging in astronomical observations with the aid of a "good telescope." She envied her friend Mary Hunt, who was able to gaze on the stars through the telescope of her neighbor Dr. William Herschel, one of the most famous astronomers of the day.[91]

After years of wandering, Elizabeth looked forward to the prospect of settling down. "We are going, to my great satisfaction," she reported with enthusiasm to a friend, "to settle somewhere in a cheap and romantic country." George Smith still preferred Ireland, but Juliet Smith remained unconvinced and instead "talks of Wales, Scotland, or the Lakes in Cumberland." Elizabeth's mother expressed a particular preference for the Lake District, another key tourist destination on the picturesque travel scene. "If my Father could come to us when he liked it, I should be perfectly content," Elizabeth noted, acknowledging that her mother was likely to win the family battle over where to reside, just as she had successfully sabotaged George Smith's Canada scheme.[92] After years of enduring a nomadic lifestyle, Juliet was determined to prevail in the matter of her family's choice of residence.

As they imagined life in their new home, Elizabeth and her sisters eagerly worked out a plan for how the household would be run: "Kitty is to work in the garden under my Mother's inspection; Juliet is to feed the poultry; and I am to manage to dairy."[93] The Smith women evoked romanticized notions of an idyllic rural retreat harmoniously sustained by their collaborative efforts. George Smith was conspicuously omitted from this imagined household management plan, suggesting that Juliet Smith and her daughters had grown quite accustomed to his prolonged absences from home. After experiencing economic downturn and the loss of their home at Piercefield, the Smith women sought to reinvent themselves in a household that privileged female domestic economy. In essence, Elizabeth and her sisters were developing something of a Millenium Hall scheme for themselves. Their musings may seem idealistic, but they indicate that the Smith women were eager to forge a new life and home for themselves.

Before moving to the Lake District, Elizabeth and her family "removed to Ireland" in the summer of 1799 to reunite with George Smith.[94] Juliet Smith enjoyed Ireland much more than she had on her 1796 visit, in part due to the friendly welcome she received during the family's extended stay in Ballitore. According to Mary Leadbeater, a poet and writer from the area, Juliet Smith self-consciously cultivated her family's reputation, as she adjusted to "moving in a lower sphere of life than that to which they were entitled." Leadbeater recalled that the Smiths "dressed richly, yet with modest elegance." Elizabeth and her sisters "took long walks into the surrounding country; they were very dexterous with the needle, and very charitable," especially on behalf of a "poor little orphan, whom they fed and clothed, and for whose schooling they paid."[95] Despite their financial losses, the Smith women carefully conveyed a sense of gentility and benevolence—markers of feminine virtue and respectability. Immersing themselves in local social, literary, and benevolent circles, Juliet and her daughters earned the "attention and sympathetic regards" of friends in Ireland, who assisted in their efforts to find "a peaceful retreat" in the Lake District.[96]

Perhaps after such positive experiences in Ballitore, George Smith may have hoped that his wife might be persuaded to make their home in Ireland, but Juliet Smith "greatly disliked the country as a place of residence."[97] In 1800, the Smiths left Ireland to settle in the Lake District. The family rented in Patterdale for several months before purchasing a farm in Coniston for their new residence. Awaiting the move to their new home, Elizabeth mused, "We look forward to the land of promise."[98] Eight years after losing their home at Piercefield, the Smith family was finally putting down roots in the Lake District. Once again, Elizabeth Smith found herself living in a key tourist destination, one made famous by William Wordsworth, Samuel Coleridge, and other celebrated literary figures. Like Piercefield, the Lake District offered both the comforts of a family home as well as expansive vistas to explore. Mature and self-assured from her travel adventures, scholarly pursuits, and supportive friendships, Elizabeth was ready and eager to give a fillip to her ideas.

4

"Rejoice in Their Own Energy"

ENACTING A LEARNED LIFE

WITH ITS MANY MOUNTAINS, lakes, and scenic vistas, Elizabeth Smith's new home in the Lake District inspired her to propose an amendment to Edmund Burke's famous remarks about the sublime, which he defined as "occasioned by terror." Instead of terror, she reflected, "I think he would have defined it better" to consider the sublime as "something incomprehensible to the mind of man, something which it struggles to take in, but cannot." Elizabeth conceptualized the sublime as "an extent of space of which the eye sees not the bounds." Such expansive space could provide a viewpoint more pleasing than terrifying: "The pleasure occasioned by the idea of sublimity seems to me to consist in the exertion of the mind," she mused, "which, when violent, overpowers weak minds, as violent exercise does weak bodies, but makes strong ones feel and rejoice in their own energy." Elizabeth considered herself in possession of both strong mind and body, and thus capable of encountering awe-inspiring scenes without being overpowered by them. To fully appreciate the sublime, one also needed a proper sense of perspective, as "the same perpendicular height gives a more sublime idea to a person on the summit than at the base, because the eye cannot so easily measure the height."[1] No wonder she frequently sought out new heights to explore.

In the years since her father's bankruptcy in 1793, Elizabeth Smith had conducted her share of both physical adventures and scholarly pursuits. She regularly drew inspiration from rugged landscapes as well as from the many accomplished women that she met in Bath, Wales, Ireland, and other travels. A variety of explorations and encounters fueled her optimistic hopes of crafting a fulfilling, well-furnished life. The Lake District offered what Elizabeth Smith had longed for during her many years of wandering: ample space for adventure, along with a fixed place to call home.

In her new home, Elizabeth found validation for her belief that both intellectual pursuits and physical adventures were necessary for one's health and well-being. "Study is to the mind what exercise is to the body," she reflected. "Neither can be active and vigorous without proper exertion."[2] Advocates in England and America increasingly emphasized the importance of physical exercise for both men and women but also tended to reify gendered understandings of masculine strength and feminine daintiness as normative. Conduct writer John Bennett promoted "exercise in the open air" as a way for women to "cheer the mind and invigorate the spirits," before observing that "attention to a *garden* is a truly *feminine* amusement."[3] A variety of prescriptive writings attempted to direct women toward tame meadows and gentle pastimes, but Elizabeth Smith had been drawn to bold ramblings, mountain climbing, and travel explorations since her girlhood. The Lake District offered Elizabeth—now in her twenties—an ideal setting to pursue an "active and vigorous" life.

Like the Smith family's former home in the Wye River Valley, the Lake District was a popular destination on the picturesque travel map. According to guidebook author Thomas West, the region offered myriad forms of nature—"the soft, the rude, the romantic, and the sublime." With such varied scenes, there were seemingly endless opportunities for exploration: "Something new will open itself at the turn of every mountain." The association of noted figures such as William Wordsworth, Samuel Coleridge, and Thomas Clarkson with the region further increased the Lake District's popularity among "persons of taste, genius, and observation."[4] Along with the growing number of discerning travelers drawn to the Lake District, Elizabeth Smith was eager to explore the picturesque and sublime vistas that surrounded her at every turn.

Inspired by her surroundings, Elizabeth enacted a learned life filled with various forms of creative expression. She enthusiastically roamed the region's numerous mountains, lakes, waterfalls, and scenic paths. These explorations inspired her to compose poetry and other writings on varied topics, and to continue her extensive language studies. Taken together, these endeavors reflected Elizabeth's desire to rejoice in her powers of body *and* mind.

"A More Prominent Situation"

Upon their move to the Lake District, Juliet Smith informed a family friend that Elizabeth "I believe likes it better than she expected."[5] Juliet did not elaborate, but this comment suggests that her daughter had some initial reservations about their new home. The region's remoteness may have contributed to Elizabeth's initial reticence about the move. The Lake District was geographically distant from her close friends Harriet Bowdler and Mary Hunt. These friendships had long provided fulfillment and support, but changing circumstances meant fewer opportunities for face-to-face visits. In 1801, Mary Hunt began working as "Sub Governess" for Princess Charlotte of Wales. This was a prestigious position but one that left her little free time for personal travel.[6] Whenever possible, Elizabeth continued to visit friends in Bath, London, and other parts of England. One summer, she enjoyed an extended stay with family friends near London who "are such admirers of Bess," as her mother noted, "that they can never find any reason for her return, and are always half offended at her leaving of them."[7]

Elizabeth's initial misgivings also may have stemmed from her father's continued uncertainty about his future. When Juliet and her daughters first arrived in the Lake District in the autumn of 1800, George Smith was still in Ireland with his regiment. "My Family are anxious that I should make a trial of the place, and mode of Life," he noted, "before I finally give up my situation in the army."[8] Several months later, he was able to "dispose of his Commission," just before his regiment was ordered to Egypt as part of the British expedition during the Napoleonic War.[9] Unfortunately, the income derived from the sale of his officer commission was lower than expected, and "Mr. S. with it [reduced] to half pay for life." This development, as Juliet Smith lamented, "vanishes all my Castles in the Air!"[10] Despite continued financial insecurity, George Smith was finally able to reunite with his family in their new home, nearly a decade after declaring bankruptcy.[11]

After renting in the Lake District for several months, the Smith family, with the assistance of a local friend, found "a more prominent situation and pitched on by Consitone [*sic*] Lake which was purchased and they are now there."[12] By spring 1801, as the family prepared to "be planted" in their new home in Coniston, Elizabeth expressed hope for the future "and flatter ourselves all will be better in the next house."[13] Her mother was pleased with their "home prospect" at Coniston, which she described as "the most desirable I ever saw."[14] Friends agreed that "the situation is indeed enchanting," but the house was small, damp, and in need of repairs. During a visit to the Smiths in 1802, author Elizabeth Hamilton reported on the family's living situation. "I wish I could say that the house was comfortable," she wrote to Harriet Bowdler, "but in truth it is not." Despite the dwelling's shortcomings, the family "seem determined against building at present," willing to put up with uncomfortable lodgings until they achieved more financial stability. The Smiths settled on a "judicious plan" that focused first on improving their farmland to "double its value."[15] In truth, Juliet Smith wished to renovate her new home, but her initial plan "unfortunately exceeds the bounds of my shallow purse." She pragmatically scaled back the renovations to fit her modest budget. "I cannot exceed 500£," she acknowledged, even if that meant living in a house that was "inconveniently small."[16]

There were also social considerations guiding Juliet Smith's plans for her new home. "My Friends in the South"—perhaps in Bath or south London—had encouraged her to "settle amongst them," but Juliet had "many objections" to the idea. "The Southern modes of Life are not calculated for my narrow Income," she confessed to a trusted friend. Nearly a decade after her husband's bankruptcy, Juliet still felt the humiliating effects of her family's financial misfortunes. "I cannot so entirely forget my former situation, as to think I could feel comfortable in a Neighbourhood where I was look'd down upon."[17] Significantly, Juliet repeatedly used singular, first person references to "my" friends, income, and situation, signifying an independent spirit forged from years of living apart from her husband. Having finally found a place to reside, Juliet Smith resolved to maintain control over her family fortunes.

A friend from Ireland sympathized with her concerns, remarking that the family had consciously chose the "peaceful retreat" of the Lake District, as "they prefer nature's haunts to more studied artificial allure."[18] Against the often stylized and formal rituals of British elite society, where rank and status determined one's place in the world, the Lake District offered the possibility of a fresh start. Juliet Smith's new friend Elizabeth Hamilton agreed, writing to Harriet Bowdler that "remoteness from what is called *good neighbourhood* is another great advantage, for there they can preserve the dignity of retirement."[19] Although the Lake District was a popular tourist destination, it was a relatively remote area and thus provided a less stressful environment for the Smiths to reestablish themselves after years of disruptions.

Having chosen her new home with care, Juliet Smith set to work forging valuable social connections. She was pleased by the "respect and attention" she received from various Lake District residents and visitors.[20] Juliet expressed warm admiration for the Scottish author Elizabeth Hamilton, who was introduced to the family by Harriet Bowdler. Hamilton, "a wonderfully clever Woman!" was a "bright constellation" in the Smith social circle.[21] During their extended visits to the Lake District, Hamilton and her sister enjoyed socializing "with the ever-charming" Smith family, who were adapting well to their new home, "improved in spirits, and enjoying an increase of fortune and of comforts."[22] Juliet and her daughters also became friends with Mary Dixon, the daughter of John Smeaton, an engineer who earned widespread admiration for the Eddystone Lighthouse and other civil projects. Beloved by her father as "the companion and sharer of his intellectual tastes," Mary Dixon lived with her husband near Lake Windermere.[23] Meeting women respected for their intellectual achievements must have helped the Smiths adjust to their new home. Through such friendships, Juliet Smith and her daughters continued to enjoy the inspiring companionship of like-minded women.

The Smiths also benefited greatly from their evolving friendship with Thomas Wilkinson (1751–1836), who was introduced to the family through their mutual friend Mary Leadbeater of Ireland.[24] A Quaker poet who loved long rambles and quiet contemplation, Wilkinson was an esteemed figure in the Lake District. William Wordsworth wrote his poem "To the Spade of a Friend" in Wilkinson's honor, extolling his "industry of body and of mind."[25] Wilkinson was delighted with the "worthy family of Smith." In a February 1801 letter to their mutual friend Mary Leadbeater, he praised Juliet Smith's "great animation and good sense" and expressed fondness for her daughters, remarking that "there seems an innocence and intelligence about them, clothed in the garb of modesty, which is very engaging."[26] To another friend, he commended Elizabeth and her sisters for their "Solidity, Innocence, and Intelegance." He reserved special admiration for Elizabeth, informing a friend that she "understands 10 or 12 different Languages, can translate from the Persian, Arabic, etc., and with her Pencil delineates our Mountain Scenery with uncommon skill."[27]

As their friendship developed, the Smiths occasionally made the trek to visit Thomas Wilkinson's Yanwath home, located near Penrith, about thirty miles from Coniston. It was during one of these visits that Elizabeth Smith and her traveling companions had their close encounter at the Patterdale inn with William Wordsworth and Walter Scott. At other times, Wilkinson visited the Smiths at their Coniston home. "I have never received a visitor with more Joy, than I always receive you," Juliet Smith affectionately wrote to him.[28]

Although Juliet Smith was disappointed by her family's continued financial precarity, she succeeded in creating social ties that were essential to the family's elevated status and reputation. She cultivated connections with well-known residents of and visitors to the Lake District, including the Wordsworths and Clarksons, families who also maintained friendly ties with Thomas Wilkinson. In June 1802, she informed Wilkinson that she "called on the Wordsworths, whom I wished to introduce to Miss Hamilton."[29] Through such efforts, Juliet Smith made sure that her family had a welcoming home in Lake District society.

With her mother hard at work securing social contacts, Elizabeth was free to wander the landscape. Supported by family and friends, Elizabeth eagerly took advantage of varied opportunities for physical exploration and creative expression, ready to exercise her body and mind.

"Gave Birth to Both Verse and Prose"

Elizabeth Smith and her sisters delighted in exploring the Lake District's scenic vistas. Their new friend Thomas Wilkinson shared their love of wandering. One such "long ramble" with "the lasses," as he reflected in an 1801 letter to a friend, "gave birth to both verse and prose."[30] His narrative provides evidence of Elizabeth's enthusiastic pursuit of adventure in her new home. The day began early in the morning with a row across Coniston Lake. As they rowed, Thomas Wilkinson and the Smith sisters quietly reflected on the scenery, "our minds exulting amidst the glories of nature, and glowing with benevolence." The explorers continued their journey, passing "scattered cottages," "immense caverns," and "lofty mountains," until they "arrived at the foot of the mountain."[31] The travel party eagerly began their ascent up Langdale Pikes, a formidable mountain range located about ten miles from Coniston (fig. 9). According to William Green, a local artist and Smith family friend, "a more dignified and

FIGURE 9. Langdale Pikes (circa 1800–1826), by William Green, local Lake District artist and Smith family friend. (© British Library Board)

impressive assemblage of mountain lines, scarcely exist in the north of England."[32] Lake District resident Dorothy Wordsworth expressed similar sentiments, referring to Langdale Pikes as "most grand and majestic."[33]

As they made their ascent up Langdale Pikes, "we sometimes turned round," Thomas Wilkinson recalled, "to survey the sinking vales, and diminished objects beneath us, and found, that objects which appeared great when we were among them, were, from the point we surveyed them, now dwindled into mere nothing." Continuing the climb, Wilkinson discovered that mountains that had seemed "scarce discernible" from a distance became "mighty and overwhelming." He was astounded by their sublime surroundings: "Indeed all these mountainous regions rise in masses of immense rocks, that are beheld with horror." Wilkinson admitted that he was "the first to express any thing like fear," while his "intrepid companions" were ready to forge ahead: "Kitty, who feels a kindness for the whole creation, offered me her hand; while Elizabeth, with a courage I had never met with before, proposed to explore what remained, and winding round the corner of a rock, presently ascended out of sight."[34]

Thomas Wilkinson beheld the sublime with a sense of terror and dread, echoing the sensibilities expressed by Edmund Burke and others. By contrast, Elizabeth Smith displayed courage and eagerness. Just as she had done at Snowdon, Elizabeth enthusiastically went in search of new heights, even when her companions were ready to turn back. She was eager to traverse new terrains, but for those left behind, "the absence of Elizabeth was a period of dreadful suspense." As she climbed out of her companions' line of vision, they could not determine where she was, "whether she might be clambering up the cliffs above us, or falling down the precipices below." Finally, the party heard "her calling to us from the cliffs over head. In her descent she missed her way, and got on the shelf of rocks higher than that on which we sat; however, we soon got all together again."[35] Although her companions expressed concern about her safety, Elizabeth understood that missteps were often a necessary part of exploration.

Throughout the day's adventures, Thomas Wilkinson remained impressed by the fortitude, tenacity, and cheerfulness of his "amiable conductors." As they made their return to Coniston, the party was "drenched" by rain storms and rising waters, yet the Smith sisters remained calm and composed, never complaining about the arduous journey. "After being eleven hours on our feet," Wilkinson reported, "and walking between 20 and 30 miles, we arrived home in safety."[36] Mary Leadbeater, who knew the Smith family from their stay in Ireland, enjoyed the account, commenting on Kitty's "benevolent" nature and "the venturous Bessy (I shared in your anxiety which she occasioned)." As Leadbeater noted, the Smith sisters were well suited to make the most of their new Lake District home: "The pouring rain served to exhibit the unvarying good humour of these lovely damsels, and is as beautiful a scene as any in the picture!"[37]

First shared with friends and then published in 1812 as "A Day's Tour in the North of England," Thomas Wilkinson's account provides vibrant evidence of the Smith sisters' active participation in the sublime adventures venerated by Romantic-era writers and artists. Many published accounts from the period tended to focus on men's experiences, but sources such as Wilkinson's essay, as well as a variety of personal letters and journals, remind us of women's presence in these inspiring spaces. The writings of Lake District resident Dorothy Wordsworth indicate that she regularly took long walks in the surrounding countryside, often accompanied by her brother and their guests. Her 1818 account of climbing Scafell Pikes was included without attribution in her brother's 1822 *Guide to the Lakes*, leading readers to presume it was William Wordsworth who made the trek.[38] Whether or not they were recognized in print, a number of women enjoyed rambling in the Lake District.[39]

Given her previous residence in the picturesque Wye River Valley, as well as her extensive travels in Wales and Ireland, Elizabeth Smith was an experienced adventurer by the time of her family's move to the Lake District. Retaining her youthful love of rocky precipices and mountainous terrains, Elizabeth explored her new surroundings with enthusiasm and confidence. Either alone or with her sisters, she delighted in "Pedestrian exercise" while soaking up the region's majestic scenery. One day, Elizabeth and her sisters walked "38 miles," their mother reported to Thomas Wilkinson, and yet "Bess and Kitty were not at all fatigued."[40]

Elizabeth Smith often set off by herself for long rambles, unaccompanied by any companion or guide. She felt free to do so, unencumbered by gendered notions of propriety or concerns about physical danger. Her mother sometimes worried about her daughter's boundless energy. Upon hearing about another one of Thomas Wilkinson's potentially dangerous adventures, Juliet Smith recognized his kindred spirit with her daughter: "I think no one (except my own Bess) would have been so *fool-hardy*."[41] In gently chiding her friend, Juliet wondered why he would "tempt Providence," and the same could be said for her daughter. "Her enthusiastic admiration of the sublime and beautiful," Juliet later reflected, sometimes led Elizabeth to stray "beyond the bounds of prudent precaution with regard to her health." But Juliet recognized that these explorations boosted her daughter's spirits. Elizabeth loved to roam for miles, returning home without fatigue and "more cheerful than usual."[42]

The Lake District was an ideal setting for Elizabeth Smith, Thomas Wilkinson, and other wanderers. Residents and visitors often described the region with a sense of wonder and awe. The Lake District offered, as resident William Wordsworth reflected, "an ascent of almost regular gradation from elegance and richness to the highest point of grandeur and sublimity."[43] During her 1794 visit to the Lake District, author Ann Radcliffe and her companions "perceived ourselves to be in the mid-way between beauty and desolation, so enchanting was the retrospect and so wild and dreary the prospect."[44] Another traveler celebrated the endless adventure he encountered, as "every turn of the road, and every valley, gave us a new scene;—the prospects were ever changing and diversified."[45]

Travelers often described the Lake District's mesmerizing landscapes as being infused with a supernatural, magical quality. "This is the very region," Ann Radcliffe contemplated, "which the wild fancy of a poet, like Shakespeare, would people with witches, and shew them at their incantations, calling spirits from the clouds and spectres from the earth."[46] Traveler William Hutchinson agreed, describing scenic vistas that "seemed like inchanted haunts, where driads met with naids, in the happy regions of the genius of the Lakes."[47] Travel guides noted that "stories of apparitions, witches, fairies, etc.," and other "strange occurrences" remained common "fire-side tales" among local residents.[48]

When she first moved to the Lake District, Elizabeth found it "astonishing" that "the belief in ghosts and witches is still in full force" among some residents. Initially, Elizabeth was skeptical about such superstitions, lamenting that "the poor people believe *at least* as firmly as they do in the Bible," she reported to her friend Mary Hunt. "When I come to witchcraft," she scoffed, "you will think it is time for me to leave off."[49] Despite her disparaging tone, the region's supernatural connotations soon found their way into Elizabeth's consciousness. In February 1801, she composed a poem to reflect on an incident that occurred one winter's day as she rambled "alone on the pathless steep" in search of a "foaming waterfall." Along the way, she slipped down a "steep slope" and found herself in a "dark abyss." Initially, Elizabeth could see no way out and feared she would "perish." As she attempted to resign herself to the "will of God," she came to a realization:

> Across my mind th' idea flash'd—
> 'Twas not by his command I hither came;
> 'Tis I, who wickedly have thrown away
> 'That life which He for nobler ends had giv'n.[50]

Seized with a sense that her life had purpose, Elizabeth prayed not for passive resignation to God's will but for deliverance from her predicament. In her poem, she described what happened next:

> Instant I rais'd my eyes, I know not why,
> And saw my sister stand a few yards off;
> She seem'd to watch me, but she could not help.

Elizabeth then imagined that she saw herself falling into a stream and being tossed "from rock to rock" as her sister ran to "meet below my mangled lifeless limbs." This vision of her own death as her sister helplessly watched spurred Elizabeth to action. "Life then had value," she decided, determined to save herself:

> It was worth a struggle, to spare her soul
> That agony.—I pass'd, I know not how,
> The danger; then look'd up—she was not there,
> Nor had been! 'Twas perhaps a vision sent
> To save me from destruction.[51]

Elizabeth referred to this "vision sent" as an extraordinary but authentic occurrence. She ended her poem by crediting God with having saved her life, but in her telling, it was the supernatural apparition of her beloved sister that prompted Elizabeth to find her way out of the abyss and back toward safety. The experience had a profound effect on Elizabeth, inspiring her to use the medium of poetry to give voice to what had transpired, as well as to contemplate the "nobler ends" of her life's purpose.

As this unusual experience suggests, the sublime and picturesque scenery of the Lake District provided Elizabeth Smith with numerous opportunities for physical adventure while also sparking her creative impulses. Like her friend Thomas Wilkinson, Elizabeth was eager to have her adventures give "birth to both verse and prose." Her encounters with the region's bold landscapes inspired her to put pen to paper. Another poem she composed in early 1801 focused on a moment of calm respite after "the storm is past; the raging wind no more." Her poem describes a gathering around a warm fire that sparks renewed energy and inspiration: "Amid the burning pile / A voice, as of a silver trumpet, speaks." The voice carries a call to action but also a note of caution:

> Children of Taste! Nature's enthusiasts!
> Ye, who, with daring pride, attempt to paint
> These awful scenes; is this offering fit
> To great Ulswater's Genius? Is it thus
> Ye adore the picturesque, the beautiful?
> Is this your homage to the dread sublime?[52]

In her poem, Elizabeth directly addressed "Nature's enthusiasts," that is, those interested in picturesque travel and sublime landscapes. Her poetic voice wondered if Lake District explorers possessed the literary and artistic skills necessary to do justice to the region's awe-inspiring scenery. Given her own wandering impulses and growing desire for creative expression, the poem can also be read as a reflection of Elizabeth's ambitions. As she pursued a variety of physical explorations and intellectual endeavors, Elizabeth wondered what proper "homage" she could contribute to do justice to her picturesque and sublime surroundings. Living in a region full of possibility and potential, she employed her strength of body *and* mind to explore her place in the world as a learned woman.

"It Is Not Learning That Is Disliked in Women"

Before her move to the Lake District, Elizabeth had resolved "to try and make amends for past negligence, by employing every moment I can command to some good purpose."[53] In her new home, she was ready and eager to find her purpose and place in life. Inspired by her physical explorations of the region's landscapes, Elizabeth increasingly took up her pen as a means to explore the "extent of space of which the eye sees not the bounds." In addition to poetry, Elizabeth composed several "reflections on various subjects," including her thoughts on intellect, ambition, vanity, humility, happiness, and religion.[54] Most of the reflections that Elizabeth composed (and that were subsequently included in her posthumously published memoir) are undated. According to Harriet Bowdler, some were written in the 1790s during Elizabeth Smith's sojourns in Bath, but many were composed around the time of her move to the Lake District. It is unclear what form these reflections originally took—whether they were kept as part of a journal or commonplace book, or written separately on individual sheets of paper. It is also unknown whether Elizabeth shared these writings with anyone during her lifetime. While she freely expressed her ardent scholarly interests in conversations with and letters to trusted friends, these writings may have provided a more solitary outlet for honing her powers of observation and analysis.

By putting pen to paper, Elizabeth was writing herself into being, crafting an identity for herself that sought to make good use of her many talents.[55] Her writing was an important form of self-expression that allowed Elizabeth to contemplate her persistent desire to enact a useful, purposeful life. In one written reflection, she used the example of learning to play an instrument to examine the general "progress of understanding." Musicians typically began by practicing and "playing the music of others" before attempting to compose original pieces. From emulation sprung originality. Developing one's powers of mental reasoning, she mused, followed the same pattern: an individual began "by reading and hearing the opinions of others, and then forms his own."[56] Through reading and writing, she learned to fine-tune the instrument of her own mind.

Given her varied interests, it is not surprising that several of Elizabeth's writings focused on the forms, uses, and effects of women's intellectual capacities. These reflections suggest that Elizabeth was well aware of, but also sought to challenge, the criticisms women often faced for their intellectual ambitions. In one significant entry, she offered her assessment on the era's evolving attitudes toward learned women:

> It is not learning that is disliked in women, but the ignorance and vanity which generally accompany it. A woman's learning is like the fine clothes of an upstart, who is anxious to exhibit to all the world the riches so unexpectedly acquired. The learning of a man, on the contrary, is like hereditary rank, which having grown up with him, and being in a manner interwoven with his nature, he is almost unconscious of possessing it. The reason of this difference is the scarcity of the commodity amongst females, which makes every one who possesses a little, fancy herself a prodigy. As the sum total increases, we may reasonably hope that each will become able to bear her share with a better grace.[57]

Elizabeth Smith expressed confidence in women's scholarly abilities, along with a sympathetic understanding of how challenging it could be to enact an identity as a learned woman. She acknowledged that *some* women who sought to "exhibit" their newly acquired intellectual acquirements might be guilty of vain or pedantic behavior. Unlike prescriptive writers who sharply criticized women for such conduct, Elizabeth regarded learned women with empathy and support. Until recently, she explained, most women lacked access to educational opportunities that men had long enjoyed. It was understandable, then, that some newly educated women were perhaps a bit too eager to celebrate their newfound intellectual "riches." The solution was not to criticize individual women for any propensity toward pedantic behavior but rather to encourage the "sum total" of *all* women's educational attainments, so "that each will become able to bear her share with a better grace." If educated women could become as commonplace as educated men, women too could treat their intellect as an unconscious possession, or "heredity rank." Elizabeth thus sought to transform concerns about female pedantry into justifications for even greater educational opportunities for women. As more women became educated, their collective confidence would erase any desire for ostentatious displays of learning.[58]

Elizabeth maintained a strong faith in women's intellectual attainments, along with a recognition of gendered constraints. "It is the fashion now to consider the abilities of women as being on an equality with those of men," she mused. "I do not deny that there may be many women, whose abilities, and still more their powers of conversation, are superior to those of the generality of men; but there never was among women a Milton, a Newton, &c."[59] With this comment, Elizabeth asserted that learned women's intellectual capabilities were comparable, or even "superior," to "the generality of men" but still seemed to privilege the notion of extraordinary male genius.

In calling attention to men's and women's seemingly differing levels of intellectual attainment, Elizabeth Smith tuned in to prevailing transatlantic debates about whether exceptional genius was inherent or acquired. Her comments help underscore how the origins and meanings of genius were subject to evolving and overlapping definitions on both sides of the Atlantic. Throughout most of the eighteenth century, genius was commonly understood as a trait that an individual *possessed*—much like wit or cleverness. For example, Mary Ann Burges wrote about struggling "against the full bent of my genius" in her efforts to keep up with Mary Hunt's extensive intellectual talents.[60] Eighteenth-century genius was more often identified with men of exceptional talents ("a Milton, a Newton") than with women, yet there was at least some acceptance that genius was not limited to men. Moreover, this understanding of genius as a trait was grounded in a belief in its potential development and refinement. While an individual was perhaps born with natural aptitude or intellect, genius could be *cultivated* through individual study and effort. This notion reflected a broad enlightened faith in the powers of reason, intellect, and education.

During the Romantic era, understandings of genius came to increasingly focus on innate identity. That is, one was considered "a Genius," rather than in *possession* of genius. This shift reflected Romanticism's strong emphasis on individualism and the imaginative. Increasingly, "true genius" referred to an individual who, by his very nature, was creative, original, unique—and capable of producing new ideas. Not surprisingly, this evolving understanding of innate genius was framed as almost exclusively male.[61] Yet the flourishing of even seemingly innate genius, as Elizabeth Smith came to realize, required proper conditions: "It is not surprising that so few, so very few geniuses appear in the world, if we consider how many circumstances are necessary to their production."[62] As scholars such as Megan Marshall have noted, male geniuses frequently relied on the willingness of unsung muses, usually women, who sustained the material and household conditions needed in order to devote themselves to scholarly or creative lives. Women such as Ralph Waldo Emerson's wife Lydia or William Wordsworth's sister Dorothy sublimated their own intellectual ambitions in the service of their husbands or brothers.[63] These talented men were considered to be innate geniuses, but their creative powers thrived in part because others—typically women—were taking care of them and their households.

Elizabeth Smith's insights respecting the circumstances needed to nurture genius were particularly true for women. Nature, she contemplated, may have "given to a woman a spirit of curiosity able to make useful discoveries in every branch of science, which, from a narrow prejudice, must be confined to the affairs of her neighbors." Women's prescribed roles did not typically provide the conditions necessary for their creative powers to develop fully. Confined to domestic duties and family life, most women had few avenues to explore the kind of creative life indicative of genius. "Thus I am persuaded genius often exists," Elizabeth concluded, "but lies concealed, sometimes even from the possessor of it, for want of occasions to call it forth."[64] In recognizing these cultural and gendered constraints, Elizabeth came to realize that there were larger forces explaining why "there never was among women a Milton." Her evolving ideas about genius reveal a keen understanding of how prescribed gender roles often thwarted women's intellectual ambitions. Determining whether or not *any* individual woman might have been considered a "true genius" was perhaps less important than recognizing how gendered constraints attempted to keep *all* women from reaching their full potential. Women's lack of access to educational, professional, and creative opportunities hindered their development as geniuses, not their innate capacities. How many women geniuses unknowingly or unwillingly kept their intellectual powers hidden and untapped?

Elizabeth Smith's evolving comments on the nature of genius were a reflection of and response to the ambivalence, and sometimes open hostility, often expressed toward the growing number of women seeking educational and literary opportunities in both England and America. Even those who generally supported women's intellectual capacities worried that too much attention to scholarly pursuits would lead to women's abandonment of their domestic and familial responsibilities and a breakdown of social norms. "Girls might be made excellent scholars as well as men," a Boston conduct writer surmised in 1808, "but then, other things must be neglected."[65] As they acquired knowledge, women were encouraged to keep their prescribed gender roles in mind. Any woman who sought to devote herself to a scholarly life was likely to be considered selfish, egotistical, and unwomanly, rather than celebrated for her intellectual ambitions. As one London essayist quipped, "We could wish them to have a taste for learning, not a voracious appetite."[66]

With such criticisms in mind, Elizabeth Smith thought carefully about how to best enact a learned life. In both her conduct and writings, she repeatedly expressed a desire to pursue her scholarly interests and wandering impulses while also seeking to make those endeavors palatable to others. "A woman must have uncommon sweetness of disposition and manners," she mused, "to be *forgiven* for possessing superior talents and acquirements."[67] Her comment about forgiveness suggests a self-conscious understanding that her own aspirations were likely to cause condemnation rather than celebration, unless they were tempered by an amiable and agreeable demeanor. Accordingly, Elizabeth took care to present herself in ways that others would find difficult to criticize. She did not issue a direct, radical call for women's equality, yet sought, in her own way, to challenge the constraints learned women faced.

Since her youthful days at Piercefield, Elizabeth Smith had carefully crafted a copperplate presentation designed to evade criticism. She perfected the art of concealing her ambitions and accomplishments by enacting perceived feminine traits such as sweetness, modesty, and humility. "The more talents and good qualities we have received," she noted, "the more humble we ought to be."[68] To avoid charges of pedantic and conceited behavior often directed at learned women, Elizabeth stressed the importance of modesty and humility. "I should think it wrong to stir my finger *on purpose* to gain the good opinion of the whole world," she noted. "Not that I despise it," she qualified, admitting that it was "difficult to guard against the desire of being admired." Elizabeth bristled against admiration without merit, or "to be better thought of than I deserve." She did not want to be viewed as a "fraud," that is, for having "made something pass for more than it was worth." She wanted the opportunity to pursue her varied interests in a purposeful fashion—but not out of vanity or a desire for fame. Any praise bestowed by others was "a valuable part of our reward," she concluded, but "ought never to be the *motive*."[69] Significantly, Elizabeth critiqued men who sought literary fame but who were willing to "overturn all the principles of the world, and publish the most extravagant doctrines, merely to be talked of." Some male writers, she suggested, were primarily motivated by "the vanity of advancing something new," rather than the quality or veracity of the ideas expressed.[70] Learned women, Elizabeth understood, could not afford to be as brash or bold. Literary lions could get away with confident, even conceited behavior that would have likely earned learned ladies harsh criticism.

Such reflections indicate that Elizabeth Smith was searching for a way to make her mark on the world but was careful to adopt strategies that made her ambitions acceptable to others. Her friend Thomas Wilkinson clearly admired Elizabeth's courage while scaling mountains but noted that she was cautious in social settings: "In company she kept back so much, that some would be in danger of forgetting she was there; but when called on to speak, she did it so much to the purpose, so pleasingly, and so unaffectedly, that one wished no one to speak but herself."[71] Elizabeth could be pleasing, charming, and erudite, but she did not like to draw too much attention to herself, or come across as vain and ostentatious. She was influenced by her circle of learned friends, including the author Elizabeth Hamilton, one of the family's Lake District associates. In praising their accomplished friend, Juliet Smith mused, "Miss H. has real Learning, but like all those whom I have observed of my own Sex, who *know most*—She is not desirous of displaying it, and it is only insensibly in the course of conversation that it appears."[72] Even a celebrated, well-known woman author understood that she risked censure for daring to display knowledge openly in certain situations.

Like other learned women in her social circle, Elizabeth Smith self-consciously cultivated a modest exterior but also repeatedly emphasized the importance of putting one's talents to good use. "A certain degree of respect to ourselves is necessary," she reflected in another entry. "Too low an opinion of ourselves will also prevent our undertaking what we are very able to accomplish," Elizabeth stressed. It was essential that individuals properly understood and cultivated their own abilities, so "that we may employ them to the best advantage."[73] As she settled into life in Coniston, Elizabeth sought to employ her talents to their best advantage. Inspired by her sublime surroundings, she found the courage to step onto a new precipice—this time in search of scholarly heights.

"Employed in Something Which Might Interest the Public"

The Lake District provided Elizabeth Smith with a renewed sense of purpose. As she explored the landscape, she also exercised her mind. In addition to writing poetry and various reflections, she focused on honing her translation skills. In 1803, Elizabeth completed what she referred to as "my Sunday work"—"translations of Job," as well as "different parts of the Old Testament," from Hebrew.[74] Several commentators would later offer praise "in the highest terms" for "her critical sagacity" in translating Hebrew.[75] Elizabeth's knowledge of Hebrew was entirely self-taught. "I never read Peters on Job, nor any thing about the Hebrew language, except the book of Dr. Kennicott's which you lent me," she explained to Harriet Bowdler. "Parkhurst [a Hebrew dictionary] has been my only guide, but I fancy he is a very good one."[76]

As she developed her translation skills, Elizabeth sought to address and counter stereotypical denouncements of women who pursued language studies, particularly classical languages, as superficial or pedantic: "Many people find fault with those who study languages, and say they study only words, and forget ideas." Eager to dismiss such criticism, she insisted that the reverse was true: "The truth is, those who learn languages to any purpose, study ideas *only*, through the medium of words their signs." Elizabeth asserted that such endeavors enabled an individual to deepen her understanding of various ideas, not "only words." She strongly defended the benefits of language studies as providing the ability "to feel the force of every expression, which a common reader passes over without observation."[77]

Harriet Bowdler later maintained that Elizabeth Smith engaged in her biblical translations primarily for her own spiritual benefit and "had no idea of ever offering them to the public."[78] Even if Elizabeth did not wish to publish her "Sunday work," her translation skills began to attract wider attention. Author Elizabeth Hamilton praised her "extraordinary talents," referring to her as "a most charming creature."[79] During her various travels, Elizabeth also made the acquaintance of several influential men. While visiting Bath in 1796, for example, she encountered James Losh, a lawyer and politician who was friends with Wordsworth, Coleridge, Southey, and other key literary figures. Southey was introduced to Elizabeth Smith by Losh, who "borrowed of her for me Carlyle's translations from the Arabic, then newly published."[80]

Through such contacts, word of Elizabeth Smith's extensive scholarly abilities, particularly in language studies, spread. In 1803, Harriet Bowdler discussed her protégé's talents with William Sotheby, translator of *Oberon* from the German. "He could scarcely credit what I said of the facility with which she translated from that difficult language," Harriet recalled. Sotheby picked a random passage from a German book "and requested me to ask her to translate it." Elizabeth completed the task the following day, initially unaware who had made the request. "Extremely pleased" with her work, Sotheby suggested that "Miss Smith's uncommon talents should be employed in something which might interest the public." With his "encouragement and kind assistance," Elizabeth began translating the writings of the German poet Frederick Klopstock and his wife, Margaret.[81]

Originally published in German, Frederick Klopstock's poem *The Messiah* was translated into several languages and praised in England as "the best epic poem which Germany ever produced."[82] Several Romantic-era poets were inspired by Klopstock's creative powers. "Till I heard these," Robert Southey wrote of Klopstock's odes, "I knew nothing of lyric poetry." According to Southey, Klopstock wrote with "the burst of feeling from one who has fed upon the scriptures."[83] In 1798, Samuel Coleridge and William Wordsworth traveled to Germany to meet Klopstock, eager to discuss poetry with him.[84] Romantic-era figures admired Klopstock's personal character as well as his poetic genius.

Shortly after Frederick Klopstock's death in 1803, further interest was inspired by his wife's letters to Samuel Richardson, several of which appeared in Anna Laetitia Barbauld's six-volume *The Correspondence of Samuel Richardson*.[85] Margaret Klopstock's letters to Richardson were singled out by the *Edinburgh Review* to have "pleased us infinitely beyond any thing else in the collection." Robert Southey agreed, musing, "How delightful are the letters of Klopstocks wife there!" Another review essay included a full transcription of one of Margaret Klopstock's letters, declaring, "All who read it must love her."[86] The popularity of Margaret Klopstock's letters, Harriet Bowdler recounted, "led me to suppose that authentic information with regard to that amiable woman would be well received by the public."[87] Eager to take advantage of the reading public's growing interest in Margaret Klopstock, Harriet directed Elizabeth to focus primarily on translating materials written by or about her. Elizabeth planned to translate all the relevant materials but informed her mentor that she "shall wait your orders to send what you choose."[88]

To help shepherd the project to print, Harriet Bowdler sought assistance from Dr. Jacob Mumssen of Altona, an "intimate friend" of Frederick Klopstock who "supplied me with many letters and other works in prose and verse, which Miss Smith translated."[89] Mumssen "very willingly" agreed to "look out for materials" written by Frederick and Margaret Klopstock. He expressed enthusiasm for the proposed work of translation, asserting that "Klopstock certainly deserves to be more known to the English, not only for his extraordinary genius as a sublime poet, but also for his private virtues and amiable character."[90] As the project progressed, Harriet Bowdler forwarded additional materials from Mumssen, including what Elizabeth Smith called a "parcel of great treasures"—several letters written by Margaret Klopstock to her husband, as well as a series of her "letters from the dead to the living."[91]

As she translated, Elizabeth developed warm admiration for Margaret Klopstock's "highly interesting" letters, confident these writings would "delight" Harriet.[92] Elizabeth also ardently defended Frederick Klopstock, whose writings apparently "disappointed" her friend. Elizabeth acknowledged that his prose was "in general dull" but maintained a high opinion of him. "In truth he is so great a favourite of mine," she informed Harriet, "that I would gladly excuse him at any rate."[93] Like her youthful defense of Ossian, Elizabeth had no trouble asserting her strong literary opinions to Harriet, despite her otherwise deferential tone regarding her mentor's editorial expertise. "I am so delighted with Klopstock," she mused, "that I feel very glad of an excuse to give up my whole time and thoughts to him."[94]

As Elizabeth Smith prepared various documents for publication, she found little need for the German dictionary that William Sotheby had provided for her use. Enthralled by Frederick and Margaret Klopstock's writings, the work of translation seemed to flow effortlessly. "The English often runs so naturally in the same course with the German," she explained, "that I have nothing to do but to write it down." Harriet Bowdler may have responded to these remarks by questioning her friend's seeming lack of modesty, for in a subsequent letter Elizabeth explained her translation process in more detail. "That you may not suspect me of arrogance in saying that I made no use of the Dictionary," she noted, "I must tell you that the difficulty of Klopstock's Odes (for difficult many of them certainly are) does not consist in hard words, but in the wide range of ideas, and the depth of thought," which contained "such obscurity as no dictionary has power to dissipate." In working with Frederick Klopstock's prose writings, Elizabeth occasionally found the translation of "some words" challenging but hoped her friend Mary Hunt—who had first encouraged Elizabeth to study German—could provide assistance.[95] On the whole, Elizabeth's translation work confirmed her belief that language studies provided a means to acquire ideas "through the medium of words."

Her biggest challenge, Elizabeth admitted, was scheduling the work around her duties and loyalty to her family. In November 1804, her mother left Coniston to visit friends, leaving Elizabeth with "a clear week between her going and my Sister's coming" to devote to her work without familial interruptions.[96] Weeks later, Elizabeth's productivity was disrupted by the arrival of her sisters and brother at home. "If you imagine me making rapid progress," she wrote to Harriet, "you are totally mistaken." With so many family members around, Elizabeth found "my perfect stillness is at an end." It was challenging to find the solitude she needed to work effectively. "My brains being of that kind which requires the aid of outward composure," she noted, "it is not without difficulty that I can now translate the prose, and the poetry I do not think of attempting."[97]

Familial disruptions to her work routines underscored how difficult it could be for learned women to balance domestic duties and literary ambitions. An unmarried woman living at home with her parents, Elizabeth certainly had fewer domestic responsibilities than a typical married woman with children. She was able to take long rambles in the countryside and devote hours to her scholarly pursuits. Yet Elizabeth's loyal, accommodating nature often led her to put other people's wishes ahead of her own aspirations. On one occasion, Juliet Smith had to decline Thomas Wilkinson's invitation to have Elizabeth visit: "I believe Terpin [a servant in the Smith household] would run away, if Bess was absent whilst I was—You know she is the steady Comfort and Anchor of the Family."[98] In scheduling her days around her family's needs, Elizabeth's time was often not fully her own.

With her translation efforts interrupted by a busy household, Elizabeth worried about the viability of the project: "I fear it will be so long before all our materials are collected, that the subject will be forgotten in the world."[99] Her concerns centered less on whether or not it was appropriate for her, as a woman, to engage in preparing a work of translation for publication, but rather about the importance of seizing the opportunity to publish a work about Frederick and Margaret Klopstock during a moment of heightened interest in their lives and writings. Elizabeth did not express any doubts about her scholarly abilities and capacities. She was ready and eager to put her talents to good use.

Despite interruptions to her schedule, Elizabeth Smith continued her efforts, while Harriet Bowdler used her literary and publishing connections to position her friend toward a career as a published translator. Harriet continued to search for materials written by the Klopstocks, including a "new edition" of writings recently published in German. "Let me have every thing written by Mrs. Klopstock," Harriet requested in March 1805. "We can determine on nothing till we have got *all* our treasures."[100] By mid-March 1805, Elizabeth fulfilled Harriet's request, sending her a "small box" of translated materials, along with a document that she referred to as a "preface to the whole" titled "'The Poem's complaint,' that you may see what poor Klopstock would say to me if he could."[101]

As she reflected on the work she did to prepare the Klopstock materials for publication, Elizabeth described the "employment" of translation as "very delightful to me." "I could not have got through the winter," she wrote in April 1805, "without something to engage my thoughts, to fix my attention." Elizabeth expressed gratitude to Harriet for providing "both the subject and the motive for action."[102] Excited to continue her scholarly activities, Elizabeth informed Harriet that she would be happy to translate "any thing else that you bid me do."[103]

The publication of the Klopstock project had the potential to take Elizabeth Smith's scholarly endeavors to new heights. It was one thing to write poetry and prose for close friends but quite another thing to have one's writings "put in the trumpet of fame, and blown to the four quarters of the world," as when Mary Hunt had shared Elizabeth's Snowdon travel narrative with a larger audience.[104] Most likely, Elizabeth Smith planned to publish the Klopstock work anonymously, following in the footsteps of her friends Harriet Bowdler, Mary Hunt, and Mary Ann Burges, who published their own works without author attribution. In any case, Elizabeth's work on the Klopstock project was clearly an "open secret" within her circle of acquaintances.[105] She was excited and enthusiastic about the work she was doing and ready for more scholarly opportunities.

As she delighted in the work of translation, Elizabeth Smith began to seek not only forgiveness for but also recognition of her talents. Perhaps she imagined herself as another Elizabeth Carter, the celebrated bluestocking whose translations of *Epictetus* from Greek earned her both fortune and fame.[106] Elizabeth completed work on the Klopstock project in spring 1805 but the last-minute arrival of additional materials from Dr. Mumssen, as Harriet Bowdler later explained, "delayed our intended publication." Unfortunately, by late 1805, Elizabeth became "too ill to attend to them."[107]

"If I Cannot Live *Here*"

Early one evening in July 1805, Elizabeth Smith "took a book, and walked about two miles from home, where I seated myself on a stone beside the Lake." Absorbed by the poetry she was reading, she lost track of time. The sun set and "was succeeded by a very heavy drew; till in a moment I felt struck on the chest as if with a sharp knife." Afterward, Elizabeth developed a "bad cough, with occasional loss of voice."[108] She experienced intermittent health issues for several weeks. By late summer, Elizabeth was well enough to make the thirty-mile trek to visit Thomas Wilkinson, stopping at the inn at Patterdale and almost meeting Walter Scott and William Wordsworth. Later that autumn, Elizabeth made plans to accompany her mother to Bath, but before they could begin their journey, her health declined. Her mother consulted a physician in Kendal, who agreed that relocation to a "warmer climate would be very desirable." During the journey, Elizabeth grew worse, and by the time they arrived in Bath in mid-October, Elizabeth was "unable to speak or stand." Under good medical care, Elizabeth began to recover, and her mother "had sanguine hopes of her being restored to health."[109]

Illness did not dampen her spirits. During her visit to Bath, according to Harriet Bowdler, Elizabeth "enjoyed society and expressed particular pleasure in meeting Mr. De Luc," a close friend of Mary Ann Burges who served as a reader in the royal household of Queen Charlotte. By the end of 1805, Elizabeth's health had improved, and family and friends were hopeful that she would make a full recovery. "She could then converse with ease and pleasure, and walk without difficulty," Harriet recalled.[110] Elizabeth had the energy to resume a variety of pursuits, including studying ancient history and visiting local attractions.[111] In late December 1805,

Elizabeth traveled to Sunbury, near London, to visit with family friends and reunite with her sister Kitty, who was about to be married and move to Scotland. As her mother later suggested, "the marriage of her sister had greatly agitated her spirits, as occasioning a separation from the favourite of the heart."[112]

In early 1806, friends and family reported with relief that "Bessy is better."[113] By March 1806, however, Elizabeth's health was again in decline. Despite her failing health, Elizabeth was stoic. "I want you, my Kitty," she wrote to her beloved sister, "to be as composed on this subject, as I am myself." Elizabeth hoped that the summer air might restore her health but did not want to offer "false hopes." As she admitted, "the constitution seems to be wearing out."[114] When Juliet reunited with Elizabeth at Sunbury after a visit to Bath, she was "thunderstruck" by her daughter's "confirmed decline" in appearance. Juliet took Elizabeth to London for a consultation with a physician, who "candidly told me it was a very bad case."[115] Juliet did not mention a specific medical diagnosis, but it is possible that Elizabeth was suffering from tuberculosis, one of the leading causes of death for much of the nineteenth century.

The doctor recommended a warmer climate, asserting "that the change of Air and of Scene will be beneficial." Juliet Smith confessed to Thomas Wilkinson that she was considering selling "my little property at Coniston, for if my precious Invalid should recover, it is not likely she should pass any further winters in it."[116] Despite the doctor's advice, Elizabeth "shewed a decided preference to Coniston." Back home in the Lake District, Juliet set up a tent near the house for Elizabeth's repose, where "she sat the chief part of the day." Elizabeth thought the tent's location would "be a good situation for a new cottage" to replace the family's current house. Juliet was reluctant to agree, thinking that the family would need to sell their land at Coniston and "settle in the south," where the climate would be more favorable to Elizabeth's condition. "She answered with more than usual quickness," her mother recalled, "'If I cannot live *here*, I am sure I can no where else.'" This observation, Juliet later reflected, was the only indication that her daughter gave "*to me* which implied an expectation of approaching death."[117]

Family and friends, including Elizabeth's beloved sister Kitty, continued to maintain "hopes of the summer restoring her."[118] But her mother sensed the truth about Elizabeth's health, even if "no one seemed to think her so ill as I did."[119] "Alas! I can send no good tidings," she lamented to Thomas Wilkinson in June 1806, concerned that her daughter "appears to me to grow weaker." Juliet feared that Elizabeth would be "a *confirmed Invalid* for the remainder of her Life."[120] Elizabeth's indeterminate diagnosis was accompanied by marked fluctuations in health. On sunny and warm days, as she informed a friend in July 1806, "I seem then to inhale new life at every pore; but if a northern blast springs up, (my original enemy,) I seem to shrink and wither like a blighted leaf."[121] With no real cure for her condition, Elizabeth continued to express calm resignation regarding her uncertain fate. She wrote to Harriet Bowdler ("my best of friends"), conveying gratitude for her mentor's support: "Thanks to you and your ever dear and respected mother, I have learnt to look on life and death with an equal eye."[122]

Even as her body weakened, Elizabeth maintained her strength of mind. She continued to take joy in literary and social pursuits. In early August, her mother read to her from James Thomson's *Seasons*, as Elizabeth "made many observations, and entered entirely into the subject." Her friend Mary Dixon visited, and after spending time "cheerfully" conversing with Elizabeth, "was of the opinion that she might last some time."[123] Yet early the next morning, on August 7, 1806, twenty-nine-year-old Elizabeth Smith succumbed to her illness.

Elizabeth Smith was buried in Hawkshead, near her Coniston home, her grave marked by "a small Tablet of White Marble" with the following inscription:

> She possessed great Talents,
> Exalted Virtues
> And humble Piety.[124]

These short, formulaic lines did little to capture her true spirit. "We have lately lost one of the most remarkable Young Women I ever knew for Power both of Body and Mind," Thomas Wilkinson wrote to a friend.[125]

Wilkinson offered a more fitting tribute, composing verses that fondly celebrated Elizabeth's adventurous spirit and intellectual abilities:

> Yet whilst to her sublimest scenes arise,
> Of mountains pil'd on mountains to the skies,
> The intellectual world still claim'd her care,—
> There she would range, amid the wise and fair,
> Untutor'd range;—her penetrating mind
> Left the dull track of school research behind;
> Rush'd on, and seiz'd the funds of Eastern lore,
> Arabia, Persia, adding to her store.[126]

Upon hearing the news of Elizabeth Smith's death, "I broke into such a passion of tears that I was ashamed," family friend Mary Leadbeater informed Thomas Wilkinson. Leadbeater considered that her strong response was not just a reflection of personal grief: "I seemed to meant her loss to the world, as well as to her family and friends."[127] Family and friends were determined that Elizabeth would not be forgotten by the world. A year later, Mary Leadbeater heard from Juliet Smith that "there is likely to be a publication relating to her sweet Bessy. I long for it."[128] Through private and public acts of remembrance, Elizabeth Smith began her enduring afterlife.

PART II

Literary Afterlife

5

※

"Thoughts of Publishing a Little Biographical Work"

TRANSITION TO THE AFTERLIFE

AFTER HER DEATH IN August 1806, Elizabeth Smith's surviving letters and compositions were a source of consolation to her family and friends. "I believe the overlooking my Elizabeth's papers has administered more comfort to me than I could have received from any other source," her mother reflected.[1] Juliet Smith found particular solace in sharing her daughter's writings with family friend Thomas Wilkinson. "She had a sincere regard for you," Juliet Smith wrote to Wilkinson, "but even *you* know not half her excellence! I wish you were here at this moment to overlook with me her papers, every line would increase your Esteem of the dear Writer."[2] She looked forward to sharing her daughter's writings with Wilkinson, including several items that she transcribed "purposely to show you."[3] Through these writings, Wilkinson discovered fresh insights into Elizabeth Smith's personality and character. "Her turn always appeared serious," Wilkinson mused in a December 1806 letter to a friend, "but from her Manuscripts I have seen since her Death, she appeared to have been thoughtful, humble, and truly Pious."[4]

Soon after her daughter's death, Juliet Smith "packed up a box, consigning all the papers I have found, written by my Angel."[5] The person Juliet Smith trusted to preserve her daughter's papers—and her legacy—was Harriet Bowdler. In November 1807, Bowdler wrote to the London publisher firm Cadell and Davies to describe her "thoughts of publishing a little biographical work."[6] In Bowdler's skillful editorial hands, Smith's personal papers were transformed from treasured family artifacts to printed memorialization. In spring 1808, the first edition of Elizabeth Smith's memoir, *Fragments, in Prose and Verse: By a Young Lady, Lately Deceased. With Some Account of Her Life and Character*, was published by Richard Cruttwell in Bath and sold by Cadell and Davies in London.[7]

The preparation and publication of *Fragments* offers a behind-the-scenes look at how Elizabeth Smith's posthumous legacy was shepherded into print. It was a collaborative effort on the part of family and friends, involving the work of collecting and curating Smith's papers for publication, along with a careful crafting of her public image. In consigning her daughter's papers to Harriet Bowdler, Juliet Smith helped assure that Elizabeth Smith was not just privately mourned but publicly celebrated. Smith's life story and writings would no longer be shared only among her close family and friends but with an admiring reading public.

The publication of *Fragments* reflected the continued influence of the social networks and literary aspirations that had inspired Elizabeth Smith during her lifetime. Harriet Bowdler enjoyed longstanding ties to Bath's vibrant community of women authors, while Juliet Smith benefited from her close proximity to a thriving literary culture in her Lake District home. Both women were eager to share Elizabeth Smith's talents with a larger audience, yet it is unclear whether they could have predicted that *Fragments* would be read widely not just in England but also in Ireland and America. With the publication of Elizabeth Smith's memoir in 1808, the young woman who lived from 1776 to 1806 began a long, enduring afterlife.

"The Partial Fondness of Surviving Friendship"

In publishing Elizabeth Smith's memoir, Harriet Bowdler expressed her hope that "the feeling heart will view with indulgence the partial fondness of surviving friendship, which endeavours to save from oblivion the object of its affection, and to strew a few flowers on the humble tomb of departed virtue."[8] In print, Bowdler presented *Fragments* as a personal tribute, motivated primarily by deep affection and a desire to ensure a friend's remembrance. Bowdler's extensive literary networks suggest that her motivations for publishing Elizabeth Smith's memoir went beyond the noble dictates of "surviving friendship." Yet friendship was certainly instrumental to the preparation of the *Fragments* manuscript. Behind the scenes, the publication of *Fragments* was a carefully orchestrated plan executed by Harriet Bowdler, Juliet Smith, and close family friends. This was a collective endeavor that involved both the emotional labor of transforming personal grief into remembrance as well as the more practical tasks of preparing a publishable manuscript.

As she readied the memoir for publication, Harriet Bowdler sought assistance from the same community of learned women who had supported Elizabeth Smith's intellectual pursuits during her lifetime. Such efforts reveal the various behind-the-scenes work done by learned women to navigate the male-dominated world of printers, publishers, and booksellers. Women's personal and literary networks were instrumental to the process of book making in ways that were less visible but still essential.

Juliet Smith was closely involved in the preparation of *Fragments,* reporting to Thomas Wilkinson that she was waiting for Harriet Bowdler to send her the manuscript "for my correction and opinion."[9] In addition to turning over her daughter's papers to Bowdler, Juliet Smith also sent a portrait of her daughter directly to Cadell and Davies to be used as an engraving in the memoir. Her letter to the publishers was brief and formal, noting, "By desire of Mrs. H. Bowdler I trouble you with a box containing a Picture and letter to Mr. Meadows the Engraver."[10] By stressing that she sent her daughter's picture at Bowdler's "desire," Juliet Smith seemingly minimized her role in the production process. This portrait, as Harriet Bowdler explained in a separate letter to the publishers, was to be forwarded to an engraver who had previously prepared an "admirable engraving" of Jane Bowdler for inclusion in her posthumously published *Poems and Essays*. Harriet Bowdler instructed Cadell and Davies to have the engraver "send me a line when he has seen the picture, mentioning the price of the Plate, and if that meets my Friend's ideas, I shall depend on his promise of executing the work within two months."[11] Work on the engraving depended on Juliet Smith's approval of the pricing and terms, yet she trusted Harriet Bowdler to engage in communications and negotiations with her publishing contacts.

While Juliet Smith provided essential content, Harriet Bowdler turned to her circle of friends for assistance with editing the manuscript. In

August 1807, Eliza Simcoe reported to Mary Hunt that she was helping Bowdler with the *Fragments* manuscript: "I have been looking over her little account of Miss Smith's and correcting some of the errors in the Subjunctive Mood, do not you think I am a person of great importance?"[12] Simcoe's remarks echoed Bowdler's use of language, demurely referring to the manuscript as a "little account," even as she proudly drew attention to her labor on its behalf. Bowdler had praised Simcoe's skills as "a most excellent Grammarian," underscoring the fact (as any author or editor knows) that careful editing and proofreading of a manuscript are crucial steps in the production process.[13] When Bowdler began to prepare Elizabeth Smith's translations of the writings of Frederick and Margaret Klopstock for publication, she also required Mary Hunt's particular expertise in the German language. "I am very sorry the publication is so long delayed," Bowdler explained to Eliza Simcoe, "but I want a little, and *but* a little assistance from Miss Hunt, and cannot send the book to the Printer till she can bestow a few hours on it."[14]

These brief examples reveal the various behind-the-scenes activities that enabled Harriet Bowdler's "little account of Miss Smith's" to become a published text. From the box of original papers that Juliet Smith gave her to the final proofreading of the manuscript, Bowdler received valuable assistance from the same individuals who had provided Elizabeth Smith with support and encouragement during her lifetime. While serving as an affectionate representation of "surviving friendship," the memoir was also a testament to the social and literary networks that had been so essential to Elizabeth Smith's ability to craft a learned life. It is not surprising that Smith's family and friends were eager to lend their support to a project that sought to preserve her memory. "The *example* my child has left me,—'tis a rich Legacy!" Juliet Smith mused to Thomas Wilkinson.[15]

In choosing to publish Elizabeth Smith's memoir, her family and friends engaged in a public form of posterity that went beyond the rituals of personal remembrance. In doing so, they conducted editorial work that was strategic and attentive to future readers. Included in *Fragments* was an elegy that Thomas Wilkinson had sent to Juliet Smith just weeks after her daughter's death. His verses celebrated Elizabeth Smith's virtue and modesty: "Yet unobtrusive, serious and meek, / The first to listen, and the last to speak." Wilkinson also referenced his friend's spirit of adventure and intellectual achievements:

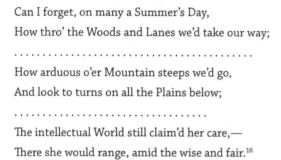

> Can I forget, on many a Summer's Day,
> How thro' the Woods and Lanes we'd take our way;
> . . . .
> How arduous o'er Mountain steeps we'd go,
> And look to turns on all the Plains below;
> . . . .
> The intellectual World still claim'd her care,—
> There she would range, amid the wise and fair.[16]

After thanking him for "the sweet lines of my beloved Daughter," Juliet informed her friend that she had shared his verses with Harriet Bowdler, "without your permission I own." A mother's desire to share a heartfelt tribute about her daughter is certainly understandable, but what is perhaps unexpected is that Juliet Smith then suggested edits to Thomas Wilkinson's poem, including "the alteration of a word or two, and the change of the tense in a few instances." It may have seemed presumptuous for Juliet Smith to ask Wilkinson to make changes to a poem that he wrote as a personal tribute, but she was confident that her friend would approve of her suggestions. "When I see you, and we read the copy together, I have little doubt but you will agree with me," she assured him.[17] Juliet Smith's edits to the poem seemed relatively minor. As she informed Wilkinson in a follow-up letter: "I took the liberty of placing the word *wise* instead of *just*, because as it related to Learning I thought it more appropriate." She also deleted "4 lines" that she felt were repetitive and thus "better omitted."[18]

With her edits to Thomas Wilkinson's poem, Juliet Smith may have already had her eye toward its inclusion in *Fragments*—or at the very least, to its broader circulation among her circle of family and friends. Wilkinson freely shared his elegy in manuscript form with several of his friends, so he was certainly open to a wider readership that may have also included eventual publication. Wilkinson's poem honoring Elizabeth Smith, as his friend Elihu Robinson reported, had "been much read and admired by several of my acquaintances."[19] Robinson transcribed a copy of the verses for one friend, who in turn commended the work for its "genuine, cultivated taste and real Poetic Genius."[20] These members of Thomas Wilkinson's social circle had never met Elizabeth Smith personally but greatly admired the poem—and its subject. Such praise may have strengthened the idea that the elegy was worthy of inclusion in Smith's memoir, thus assuring an even wider public readership.

The editorial revisions and manuscript circulation of Thomas Wilkinson's elegy indicate how Elizabeth Smith's family and friends actively worked to craft her posthumous legacy. In the process, Smith's personal papers, along with other individuals' writings about her, took on new life. In Wilkinson's case, what began as "sweet lines" written to honor the memory of a close friend became widely circulated verses celebrated for their "real Poetic Genius." The same could be said about Elizabeth Smith herself, as her personal character was crafted into what she would have considered a copperplate representation.

"Will Interest the Public"

When Harriet Bowdler wrote to publishers Cadell and Davies in November 1807 about her plans for a "little biographical work," she confidently noted, "I have reason to believe [it] will interest the public." Bowdler wrote not to pitch Elizabeth Smith's memoir but rather to let her publishers know of her intention "to place [it] in your hands," notifying them that the manuscript "might be ready in a few weeks." Her primary concern in writing to Cadell and Davies was to solicit their assistance with an engraving of Smith that she wished "to ornament" the memoir.[21]

With assistance from family and friends, Bowdler successfully produced "a little biographical work" that brought the private life of its subject into public view. When *Fragments* was published in 1808, Bowdler began the preface by acknowledging "the favour with which memoirs and letters are generally received by the public."[22] With this reference, she called to mind an emerging celebrity culture characterized by strong public interest in the lives and writings of notable literary figures. In the late eighteenth century, a number of "celebrated living ladies" from England had become well known across transatlantic cultures of print.[23] At the dawn of the nineteenth century, several of these women died, including Elizabeth Montagu (in 1800), Hester Chapone (in 1801), Elizabeth Carter (in 1806), and Anna Seward (in 1810). These celebrated women then became the subjects of posthumous "memoirs and letters" published between 1807 and 1811.[24] While Elizabeth Smith was not a famous bluestocking or salonnière, *Fragments* was published at the same time as works featuring these more well-known women.

Praised by many as a means of preserving "their memories beyond the grave," posthumous works sparked a variety of commentary about what type of life and legacy was worth commemorating in print.[25] An 1802 biographical sketch about French salonnière Madame De Staël acknowledged that some readers were skeptical as to whether women's lives should be "consigned with equal effect to the page of the biographer."[26] Sensitive to such critiques, posthumous works about women often contained formulaic disclaimers and apologies. *The Posthumous Works of Mrs. Chapone* asked for readers' understanding for their decision "to publish these volumes," which in turn was pointed out by a reviewer: "A modest preface ushers in this work, apologizing for troubling the world with particulars of a life so little varied."[27]

Those eager to celebrate accomplished women carefully considered how to claim space in the literary public sphere for their life stories and writings. "It can hardly be deemed necessary to say much by way of apology for offering to the Public the Memoirs of so high and excellent a character as that of Mrs. Carter," read the preface to her 1807 posthumous memoir, "though her life was so little diversified by incident, or marked by any events but such as happen to all."[28] Elizabeth Carter was a famous bluestocking and successful author who achieved a degree of celebrity within her own lifetime. Yet in publishing her posthumous memoir, her nephew Montagu Pennington attempted to frame Carter's life as unremarkable and "little diversified," perhaps in an effort to downplay the extent of her literary ambitions.

Memoirists engaged in a careful balancing act: they had to make a case for their subjects' importance while at the same time assuring potential critics that these women did not challenge gendered notions of respectable behavior. In preparing Elizabeth Smith's memoir for publication, Harriet Bowdler skillfully navigated these cultural and literary attitudes. In the preface to *Fragments,* Bowdler acknowledged that "the production of a great many biographical works" sparked a range of feelings, from "delight" to "disgust." She called for a sympathetic audience, particularly "when the character that is brought before the public is really deserving of esteem."[29] Both the explanatory tone of Harriet Bowdler's printed remarks as well as her confident assertion to Cadell and Davies that Smith's memoir "will interest the public" reflected her keen understanding of the literary marketplace and the reading sensibilities of her targeted audience.

A well-connected author from an accomplished literary family, Bowdler was no stranger to the world of publishing. By 1807, Cadell and Davies had already printed several editions of her anonymously published work, *Sermons on the Doctrines and Duties of Christianity,* as well as a volume of her late sister's poetry.[30] "I do not write for fame," Bowdler insisted in the preface to her *Sermons,* "but in the humble hope of being useful" by providing readers with sermons particularly suited to "family reading."[31] Such modest disclaimers, even for anonymously published texts, were common strategies employed by many women authors during this era. Portraying herself as a reluctant author with altruistic intentions, Bowdler entered the literary public sphere cloaked in the garb of modesty and respectability.

In her correspondence with publishers Cadell and Davies, Bowdler often employed polite and deferential language, but she was also candid about her literary aspirations. Writing in 1801, after the first edition of *Sermons* had appeared in print, she requested "that Mr. Cadell will favor her with some account of the success of the little Publication committed to his charge; and begs he will tell her whether it has been mentioned in any of the Reviews, and when she may look for it."[32] While Bowdler modestly downplayed her work as a "little Publication," she also revealed an acute understanding of literary markets, especially the importance of having her work positively reviewed in journals. She kept careful records of her sales, reminding her publishers that "I always am desirous to know the exact state of all my accounts."[33] Writing in early 1809 after the initial success of *Fragments,* she reminded her publishers: "I have received the

Balance on our account for 1807, but I have not yet rec'd the account for 1808, and should be much obliged to you for it."[34]

Bowdler actively collaborated with booksellers and publishers to encourage sales of her published works. Working with printers Richard Cruttwell in Bath and Stuart Cheyne in Edinburgh, Bowdler made sure that multiple editions of *Sermons* were printed and distributed in these key provincial markets. In 1803, Cheyne wrote to Cadell and Davies requesting "a copy of the advertisement as Mrs. B. wishes me to copy it exactly to advertise it in the Edinburgh papers."[35] Writing in 1805, she called on Cadell and Davies to "advertise the 8th Edition of the Sermons," and two years later she informed them that she "ordered a fresh supply of the Sermons to be sent to you, and a new edition to be printed."[36] Her efforts yielded impressive results. In 1810, the twenty-second edition of *Sermons* appeared, and the work remained popular for decades, with its forty-first edition published in 1828 and a "new edition" released in 1852, twenty-two years after Bowdler's death.[37]

Harriet Bowdler also worked closely with her brother Thomas on the publication of *The Family Shakespeare*, which first appeared in 1807 as she was preparing Elizabeth Smith's memoir for publication. The Bowdlers excised passages from Shakespeare in order to make his writings more appropriate to middle-class readers' sensibilities—thus, the origins of the term "bowdlerize." As Harriet Bowdler explained in a letter to an acquaintance, *The Family Shakespeare* included "all the Plays, with nothing added, but omitting such passages as would not be proper to be read aloud." The Bowdlers hoped that *The Family Shakespeare* would "be the means of placing this charming author in all the Houses," where he could "be read and admired as he deserves."[38] The bowdlerizing of Shakespeare is often regarded as a conservative, moralizing effort to dilute his writings. However, it is worth noting that the Bowdlers' efforts to create a family-friendly Shakespeare enabled women to engage with these works in a manner that was acceptable to the dominant culture. At the time, it would have been unlikely that a woman could enter the literary marketplace as a "scholarly expert" on Shakespeare. *The Family Shakespeare* gave women a safe, respectable way to participate in literary culture without sacrificing their claims to feminine virtue or moral standing.

Harriet Bowdler's publication history, particularly her contributions to *The Family Shakespeare*, surely influenced her approach to publishing Elizabeth Smith's memoir. With her savvy understanding of literary trends, Bowdler recognized how Smith's life and writings could be bowdlerized to present a carefully constructed tale of a modest, unassuming girl genius. Bowdler's editing of *Fragments* sought to present a learned woman's life to the public in a way that allowed readers of both sexes to celebrate Smith's scholarly accomplishments and unblemished character.

"Useful to All Her Sex"

As Harriet Bowdler acknowledged in the preface to *Fragments*, her friend and protégé seemed an unlikely candidate for traditional biography: "The Young Lady whose talents and virtues are here pointed out to the reader, was little known in the world. Her short life was spent in retirement, and it affords no incidents to awaken curiosity; but it offers an example, which may be useful to all her sex."[39] With this disclaimer, Bowdler staked a strategic claim for her friend in print. The key to appreciating Smith's life, Bowdler insisted, was through a careful exploration of the relationship between her scholarly capacities and feminine character.

Fragments offers a carefully shaped account of a learned woman's well-lived life. Yes, Elizabeth Smith possessed impressive intellectual abilities, but, as Harriet Bowdler stressed, it was the "use which she made of learning, and the effect which it produced on her conduct in life . . . [that] will prove that every acquisition in science only increased the humility of her natural character, . . . [and] added strength to her conviction of those great truths of revealed religion."[40] Smith was worthy of praise not merely because of her extensive learning but because that learning was never frivolous or affected. Rather, it was *useful*—serving primarily to augment, not detract from, her seemingly natural qualities of femininity, domesticity, and piety. Smith's well-lived, useful life could serve as a model of emulation for female readers.

The life story of Elizabeth Smith that Harriet Bowdler presented in *Fragments* was positive, celebratory, and inspirational, providing important life lessons to readers at every stage. Bowdler celebrated Smith's lifelong love of learning and deep appreciation for the picturesque scenes of nature that surrounded her. Smith was studious and serious but also pious and cheerful, even in the face of adversity. Smith experienced her share of challenges, including her father's financial crisis, which led to the loss of her beloved home at Piercefield. Such hardships, however, never discouraged her. The family's nomadic lifestyle before their eventual move to the Lake District, as Harriet Bowdler noted, created new opportunities for intellectual expression, as friends opened up not just their homes but also their libraries. Even Elizabeth Smith's illness and early death were framed as idealized depictions of stoic patience and resignation to the will of God. *Fragments* presents an inspiring life story; indeed, in many spots in the memoir, Elizabeth Smith comes across as almost too good to be true. Perhaps that is the nature of posthumous tribute, reflecting a desire to memorialize a dearly departed loved one in the best possible light. It was, indeed, a copperplate presentation, not a true likeness.

Careful attention to the content, form, and focus of *Fragments* reveals the extent of Harriet Bowdler's editorializing. She carefully curated selections from Elizabeth Smith's writings while also providing commentary that sought to shape readers' perceptions. It is worth noting that Bowdler included—rather than expunged—various writings from Smith that described her bold explorations at Snowdon and other travel adventures. Yet Bowdler often passed over such passages without comment, or deliberately took time to remind readers of Smith's modesty. In editing *Fragments*, Bowdler focused primarily on presenting a safe, appealing model of learned womanhood to the reading public.

Throughout *Fragments*, Harriet Bowdler repeatedly tempered Elizabeth Smith's extensive learning with feminine grace, continually reminding readers of her protégé's seemingly flawless character. After listing Smith's many scholarly accomplishments, particularly with respect to language studies, Bowdler reflected, "With all these acquirements she was perfectly feminine in her disposition; elegant, modest, gentle, and affectionate; nothing was neglected, which a woman ought to know; no duty was omitted."[41] Despite her rigorous devotion to her studies, Smith still found time to maintain what her mother called "a scrupulous attention to all the minutiae of her sex." Although some critics feared that extensive learning would cause women to shun domestic duties, commentary included throughout *Fragments* asserted the opposite was true about Elizabeth Smith: "Far from despising them, [she] considered them as part of that system of perfection at which she aimed."[42]

As Bowdler repeatedly reminded her readers, Smith never allowed her intellectual endeavors to interfere with her domestic duties. While recounting the unhospitable lodgings provided for the family while visiting George Smith's barracks in Ireland, Bowdler included Juliet Smith's account of how her daughter was able to find a "blessing" in their meager surroundings. Bowdler informed her readers that Juliet Smith often told the story of how "Elizabeth contrived to make a currant tart in this uncomfortable dwelling" as evidence of her daughter's "ingenuity, as well as good-humour." For Bowdler, such "trifling circumstances" served another important purpose. "I wish to convince my *young* readers," Bowdler wrote directly after describing these incidents, "that learning is not incompatible with the most minute attention to the peculiar duties, as well as to the elegant accomplishments, which belong to the female character." Bowdler then called readers' attention to Smith's "elegant simplicity" and modest disposition: "She made a gown or a cap, or any other article of dress, with as much *skill* as she displayed in explaining a problem in Euclid, or a difficult passage in Hebrew."[43]

With this particular comment about Elizabeth Smith's domestic and intellectual skills, Harriet Bowdler deliberately mimicked Samuel Johnson's published remarks about Elizabeth Carter, the famous bluestocking and translator who "could make a pudding as well as translate Epictetus from the Greek, and work a handkerchief as well as compose a poem."[44] The structure and content of the two comments bear a close resemblance to each other—suggesting a deliberate framing on Bowdler's part, rather than mere coincidence. Both comments served to remind readers that a learned woman's domestic skills were not compromised by her intellectual accomplishments. According to literary scholar Claudia Thomas, Samuel Johnson sought to idealize his friend Elizabeth Carter by emphasizing her "balanced" qualities of domesticity and learning, yet he often did so "at the expense of biographical accuracy." Johnson was determined to defend Carter from those who disliked excessive learning in women, and the best way to do so, he felt, was to reassure critics that Carter remained suitably domestic despite her intellectual acquirements. This framing was also evident in Carter's posthumous memoir, edited by her nephew, who insisted her life was "little diversified by incident." Such efforts, however, downplayed the complexity of Carter's personality, especially the fact that Carter never married. Johnson's assertions about Carter's balanced nature thus served to obscure the more troubling implications of her literary ambitions—as a successful author, Carter was able to remain single, set up her own household, and not rely on a man to support her.[45]

Like Samuel Johnson, Harriet Bowdler was eager to defend her friend's extensive intellectual achievements against prevailing criticisms that learned ladies would inevitably neglect their domestic duties. Bowdler presented an idealized representation of Elizabeth Smith in which she effectively—indeed, effortlessly—maintained a proper balance between learning and femininity. Bowdler's focus, however, offered a narrow view of Smith's life and writings. In framing Smith's character as a successful combination of intellect and domesticity, Bowdler sought to present Smith as a model of learned womanhood already made familiar to many transatlantic readers through writings such as Samuel Johnson's comments about Elizabeth Carter. But like Carter, Smith resisted simple classifications and sought more than to balance a pen in one hand and a needle in the other.

Elizabeth Smith and Elizabeth Carter shared significant traits: both women died in 1806, and both were the subject of posthumously published memoirs that garnered attention on both sides of the Atlantic. Elizabeth Smith bore another striking resemblance to Elizabeth Carter that received no attention in *Fragments*—both women remained single. Throughout the memoir, Bowdler cast Smith as a dutiful daughter, suspended in a state of perpetual youth. Smith was just sixteen when her family fortunes changed, and twenty-five when she settled in Coniston. Her prime "marriage market" years, then, were spent during a time of economic downturn and flux. Yet during these years, both her older brother, George-Thomas, and younger sister Kitty married, suggesting that the Smith family's social prospects were not irrevocably damaged by their financial constraints. There is no evidence that her family's economic status ever compelled Elizabeth Smith to remain single in order to support her parents. She never sought work as a governess, employment that would have been considered a respectable and logical choice for a young woman of her socioeconomic status—work that her close friend Mary Hunt pursued.[46]

Elizabeth Smith must have understood how challenging it would have been, as a wife and mother, to devote countless hours to her studies and works of translation. Marriage and motherhood typically led most women to abandon or curtail their youthful intellectual pursuits. Her close friends Harriet Bowdler, Mary Hunt, and Mary Ann Burges remained single, a factor that undoubtedly contributed to their ability to focus on their studies and become published authors. Other contemporary examples of unmarried women authors—including Elizabeth Carter—may have served to further reinforce the notion that a woman's literary productions depended, in significant measure, on the extent of her domestic and familial duties. Whatever her reasons, Smith remained single—and this was very likely a calculated choice that enabled her to craft a life devoted to her studies. Yet Bowdler never addressed whether Smith's singlehood was a choice rather than a matter of circumstance—in fact, she never addressed Smith's single status at all. Bowdler obscured the fact that by her late twenties, Smith "should" have married and begun raising a family, a change in status that most likely would have directed her energies away from her studies and toward domestic duties.

Although she remained silent on this matter in *Fragments*, Harriet Bowdler explored the theme of singlehood in *Pen Tamar; or, The History of an Old Maid*. Bowdler originally wrote the novel in 1801, but the work was not published until 1830, after her death. Set in the seventeenth century, *Pen Tamar* offers a spirited defense of women who remain single, either by choice or circumstance. When confronted with stereotypical opinions of the "sour, discontented, disagreeable old maid," her main character praises single women who "are engaged in the constant exertion of active benevolence" and "cultivate their minds by reading and reflection." The single women Bowdler extolled in her novel bore a strong resemblance to the learned women of her own social circle. "I could bring examples of single women, equal in talents and virtues to any of my married acquaintance," her character asserts, "and who deserve and possess, in the highest degree, the respect and esteem of all who know them." At this point in the novel, Bowdler breaks the narrative flow to remind her readers that her novel was set in the 1600s, when such "illiberal prejudice" against spinsters was commonplace. "Had Mrs. Heywood lived in a period adorned by the talents and virtues which *now* command universal admiration," Bowdler informed her readers, "it would not have been difficult to prove that single women *may* be an honour and a blessing to the world; and that when they are really contemptible and ridiculous, it is generally owing to defective education."[47]

Given Harriet Bowdler's views on single women as revealed in *Pen Tamar,* the absence of any discussion about Elizabeth Smith's unmarried status is a revealing silence in *Fragments.* In *Pen Tamar,* Bowdler was perhaps overly optimistic in declaring that she lived in an era where single women could "*now* command universal admiration." In the early nineteenth century, single and learned women were still subjected to scorn and stereotypical denouncements. An otherwise favorable review of Elizabeth Carter's memoir referred to her as "a social and conversible companion, although an Old Maid."[48] With such concerns in mind, Bowdler likely considered it a useful strategy to present Smith as a dutiful daughter, to divert attention from those who might have condemned her as an eccentric spinster.

Moreover, in its silence, Elizabeth Smith's single status could be read as proof of her virtue and purity. *Fragments* lacks any discussion whatsoever of Smith's sexuality—there are certainly no scandalous tales of her extramarital affairs, as Mary Wollstonecraft's posthumous memoir revealed. Bowdler's decision to avoid any discussion of her friend's singlehood or sexuality was part of a conscious crafting of a public reputation that would help make Smith's extensive learning seem acceptable to both admiring readers and potential critics. Presented as a modest, reserved daughter, Smith was presumed innocent of the questionable, disreputable behavior often associated with more notorious women. Instead, as Bowdler repeatedly emphasized throughout the memoir, Smith remained as committed to her femininity, domesticity, and piety as she was to her studies.

Close reading of *Fragments* demonstrates the various ways that Bowdler shaped the text, both through its silences as well as through careful editorial insertions at key moments throughout the text. As a bowdlerized text,

Fragments is significant not only for what was left out but also for the additional content and editorializing provided to help shape Smith's legacy.

"Valuable Records"

Throughout *Fragments,* Harriet Bowdler included excerpts from Elizabeth Smith's various writings, "to shew what were her studies and amusements" and to illustrate "the unstudied effusions of a grateful and affectionate heart."[49] *Fragments* serves as a representative example of the "life and letters" format typical of many posthumous memoirs published in the early nineteenth century. The memoir presents a brief, chronological summary of Elizabeth Smith's life, interspersed with lengthy extracts from her various writings, including poetry, prose, and correspondence.

In publishing Smith's literary remains, Bowdler gave the impression that she largely allowed her subject to speak for herself. In his now classic "communications circuit" outlining the complex web of individuals and processes involved in the making of books, historian Robert Darnton starts with the premise of the author as an autonomous unit.[50] But who should be considered *the* author of Elizabeth Smith's posthumous memoir? Although Smith authored much of the content included in *Fragments,* the book's format and structure were heavily mediated by Bowdler's role as editor.

In turning over her daughter's surviving papers to Bowdler, Juliet Smith also played an essential role in the process that transformed Elizabeth Smith's manuscript writings into printed text. Without access to these personal papers, the publication of *Fragments* would not have taken the same form. Bowdler still could have produced a biographical sketch in tribute to her friend, but it was the inclusion of Elizabeth Smith's writings that gave the memoir its authentic, autobiographical authority. Extracts from women's previously unpublished letters and other writings were considered especially valued content in posthumous memoirs, as they were believed to provide readers with an up-close sense of familiarity and intimacy with their subjects. The memoir depended on Smith's original compositions to provide effective, compelling evidence of her talents and character.

There does not appear to be any purposefulness on Elizabeth Smith's part to write an autobiography or to publish her own life story. Careful about how she presented herself in public, she was upset, for example, when her Snowdon travel writings were shared without permission. Given her self-conscious modesty in certain social settings, Smith may have objected to seeing her personal writings appear in print posthumously. Unlike other literary figures of the era, Smith did not methodically preserve or curate her personal papers with their future publication in mind. Indeed, Juliet Smith regretted that her daughter "destroyed many papers" shortly before her passing.[51] Ever protective of her reputation, perhaps Elizabeth Smith deliberately destroyed these writings, reluctant to have them circulated widely after her death.

As Harriet Bowdler acknowledged, many of Elizabeth Smith's letters and writings also had been lost or destroyed by friends who could not predict that her early death would raise both their literary and sentimental value. Often, there was no premeditation to such decisions; individuals might discard personal letters after a certain time passed, especially if they kept up voluminous correspondence with many friends and relatives. For example, although *Fragments* includes a few letters that Smith wrote to Bowdler, Harriet lamented that "I destroyed many others which I shall never cease to regret."[52] There is no telling how many documents written by Smith were not available for inclusion in the memoir because they were deliberately destroyed, inadvertently lost, or deemed unworthy of publication.

As its title implies, *Fragments, in Prose and Verse* provides a fragmented, incomplete account of Smith's life and writings. To help fill the gaps, Bowdler included, in an appendix, over fifty pages of various documents and excerpts written by family and friends. Rather than expunging text, this form of bowdlerizing added content. Some of these materials date from the weeks immediately following Elizabeth Smith's death and may not have been originally written with eventual publication in mind. For example, one of the appendix items is a letter that a Lake District resident wrote to Bowdler about a month after Elizabeth's death, describing "an affecting visit" to comfort Juliet Smith.[53] The appendix also included carefully crafted reminiscences by several individuals who knew and admired

Smith, including Elizabeth Hamilton, Thomas Wilkinson, and Dr. Francis Randolph. Several of these accounts were written several months after Smith's death, when Harriet Bowdler and Juliet Smith were actively engaged in the process of preparing the manuscript for print.

The first documents in the appendix consist of three lengthy letters that Juliet Smith wrote to Randolph, a Bath minister, in 1807. These letters were almost certainly composed to consider a wider audience. By this time, Juliet Smith had already entrusted her daughter's papers to Bowdler. Even if Juliet did not expect the letters themselves to be published, she must have known that their content would be mined for key biographical information about her daughter. While there is a certain formal quality present even in Juliet Smith's surviving letters to her friend Thomas Wilkinson (reflecting letter-writing conventions of the era), the format and composition of her letters to Francis Randolph are notably stylized. She self-consciously framed them as "complying with your wish" for a brief biographical sketch of her daughter's life, insisting that the task afforded her with a source of "melancholy pleasure in reflecting." At the same time, she noted that she hoped to "repress the feelings and partiality of a parent, and merely state a few simple facts."[54] Such a disclaimer, however, would hardly be necessary in a letter meant only to be shared between trusted friends (and indeed no such disclaimers appeared in her surviving letters to Thomas Wilkinson).

Juliet Smith's letters to Francis Randolph represent acts of selective remembrance that were clearly produced with an eye toward posterity and publication. Despite her insistence that she would focus on "simple facts," her letters are filled with moralizing reflections about her daughter's esteemed character and impressive talents. For example, after commenting on Elizabeth's language skills, Juliet Smith reflected, "This degree of information, so unusual in a woman, occasioned no confusion in her well-regulated mind." Juliet Smith also made decisions about what parts of her daughter's life to not write about: "I pass over in silence a time in which we had no home of our home," she noted, although it was during this time that Elizabeth was exploring old castles and climbing mountains.[55] Throughout her narrative, Juliet Smith conformed to the era's literary conventions, emphasizing her daughter's exemplary character and piety, rather than highlighting her fearless adventures and restless spirit. Her third letter in this series included a lengthy description of Elizabeth's illness and last months, reflecting the era's cultural fascination with sentimental narrations of deathbed scenes. "Perhaps my desire of fulfilling your wish, may have led me into a tedious detail of little matters," she wrote by way of apology, while explaining that her grief "may have occasioned my omitting some things of more importance."[56]

In reply to Juliet Smith's letters, Francis Randolph thanked her for sharing biographical details about her daughter, noting that "the most trifling incidents of her life are now become valuable records." His comments underscored the process by which personal remembrances of Elizabeth Smith were transformed into "valuable records" worthy of a public audience. As Randolph entreated, "It seems a duty you owe to society to mark the several points and stages of its advancement to such early maturity." Randolph insisted that Elizabeth Smith's life story and writings were worthy of "universal remembrance" for the inspiration they would inevitably evoke from readers. "The world, deprived by her death of one its brightest ornaments," he reflected, "has a claim to every memorial of her exalted worth and talent." Posthumously, Smith served as "an example of what *has been done* even in so short a space of time, by fulfilling the duties of a Christian life, and the purposes of rational existence."[57] Smith's worth was measured by her many talents, especially her piety and modesty. With the publication of *Fragments*, other readers, particularly young women, could be inspired to emulate Smith's exemplary character.

Such glowing accounts, Harriet Bowdler suggested, convinced Juliet Smith to share the "valuable records" of her daughter's life with the reading public. As Juliet Smith later recounted privately to Thomas Wilkinson, "[The bishop of Elphin] was the first Person who urged me to publish. He was particularly partial to Elizabeth and when I met with him at Bath I shew'd him her MSS papers." Although Juliet Smith had freely shared her daughter's papers with Bowdler, Wilkinson, and other family friends, she insisted that "I really had not the smallest idea of making them public, till his Lordship earnestly pressed me to do so—and on Dr. Randolph's seconding the request very strenuously, I consented."[58] Juliet Smith seemed to downplay her active role in the memoir's publication, even to her trusted friends. After all, Bowdler had access to Elizabeth Smith's writings because Juliet Smith collected and sent them to her shortly after her daughter's death. *Fragments* would not have been possible without Juliet Smith's active support of the project, yet she seemed reluctant to claim direct responsibility for the publication of her daughter's private writings. Perhaps she feared that her involvement would be seen as too opportunistic. Instead, she relied on Harriet Bowdler's more visible role as editor to account for the memoir's publication. Left unspoken, of course, was any indication of how Bowdler and Smith would benefit financially from sales of the memoir—a detail too materialistic and unsuitable for public discussion, particularly for a work produced by and about learned women.[59]

The various letters included in *Fragments'* appendix reinforced Juliet Smith's and Harriet Bowdler's assertions about the value in sharing Elizabeth Smith's impressive talents and modest disposition to admiring audiences. As part of this process, they carefully selected the facts and memories they saw as essential to Elizabeth Smith's legacy, which Harriet Bowdler shaped into a compelling narrative for readers.

"Such an Edition Is Loudly Call'd For"

Elizabeth Smith's *Fragments* was well received by an admiring reading public. By August 1808, as Juliet Smith reported to Thomas Wilkinson, the "3rd Edition of the little Book is nearly all sold," and plans for additional, expanded editions were underway.[60] In the book's first year in print, Bath publisher Richard Cruttwell issued five editions of *Fragments*, with key distribution networks in London and Edinburgh.[61] By October 1808, as a family friend reported, "E Smith's Fragments are printed in Dublin, & greatly admired."[62] Imported and reprint editions in America soon followed, contributing to Elizabeth Smith's growing fame within transatlantic cultures of print. As *Fragments* traveled to America, both Smith's character and Bowdler's editorial skills received praise. "To the affectionate compiler of these memoirs," one advertisement in Massachusetts enthused, "the world is indebted for the view of a character embracing the whole circle of virtues."[63] A reviewer in Philadelphia agreed, wishing "to thank the editor for the part she has acted, in erecting this durable mausoleum to her friend."[64]

In initially publishing *Fragments*, Bowdler insisted that she sought to "remove the veil which an excess of modest reserve threw over uncommon merit."[65] The memoir's original title reflected this deliberate sense of modesty: *Fragments, in Prose and Verse: By a Young Lady, Lately Deceased. With Some Account of Her Life and Character, by the Author of "Sermons on the Doctrines and Duties of Christianity"* (fig. 10). Elizabeth Smith first appeared in print only as "Miss Elizabeth S——," while friends and correspondents were referred to as "Miss H——" or "Miss B——." In early editions, Bowdler selectively removed some identifying details while keeping others. For example, she referred to the Smith family as "S——," but noted that they had lived at Piercefield and later settled in the Lake District—revealing clues, especially given the prominence of these places on the picturesque tourism scene. When Mary Leadbeater first heard from her friend Juliet Smith about "the rapid sale of her Daughter's work," she initially did not know the book's title. Writing from her home in Ballitore, Ireland, Leadbeater accurately speculated that "a Book advertised by one of our Printers as now in the Press I have thought might be hers. . . . It mentions, by a young Lady lately deceased, with some account of her life & character."[66] Leadbeater borrowed a copy of the book from a friend but was eager to learn "when the edition is published with her portrait" so that she could have "my bookseller get it for me."[67]

Harriet Bowdler's decision to partially conceal identities sparked commentary from early reviewers. In its September 1808 review of *Fragments*, the London *Eclectic Review* questioned Bowdler's "excess of delicacy," asserting that "it would be an appropriate punishment to disclose her own name." The *Eclectic Review* chose to "content ourselves" by identifying Elizabeth Smith as the memoir's subject but not Harriet Bowdler as editor.[68] As these comments suggest, critics and readers "in the know" would have recognized the key players and places referred to throughout *Fragments*.

Smith's identity was an open secret for many and desired information for others. "We see no cause for concealing it, nor can we admit the plea of modesty," the *Belfast Monthly Magazine* noted in its December 1808 review

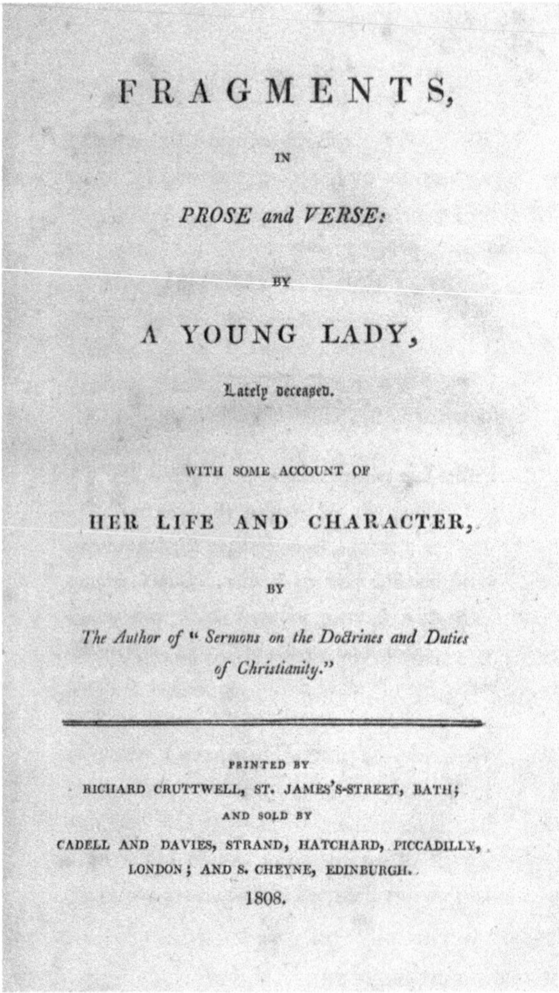

FRAGMENTS,

IN

PROSE and VERSE:

BY

A YOUNG LADY,

Lately Deceased.

WITH SOME ACCOUNT OF

HER LIFE AND CHARACTER,

BY

The Author of " Sermons on the Doctrines and Duties of Christianity."

PRINTED BY
RICHARD CRUTTWELL, ST. JAMES'S-STREET, BATH;
AND SOLD BY
CADELL AND DAVIES, STRAND, HATCHARD, PICCADILLY,
LONDON; AND S. CHEYNE, EDINBURGH.
1808.

FIGURE 10. Title page of *Fragments, in Prose and Verse: By a Young Lady, Lately Deceased*, first edition (1808), published without author or editor attribution. (Library Company of Philadelphia)

of *Fragments*. "When we read the pleasing memoirs of a virtuous character, we wish to know her name."[69] Beginning with editions published in 1809, the *Fragments* of "a Young Lady, Lately Deceased," became publicly known to be the writings of "Miss Elizabeth Smith" (fig. 11). Bowdler made the decision to identify Smith both on the book's title page as well as throughout the memoir. As Bowdler explained in an "Advertisement" included in subsequent editions, "In compliance with what appears to be the general wish" of the public, the memoir revealed the full names

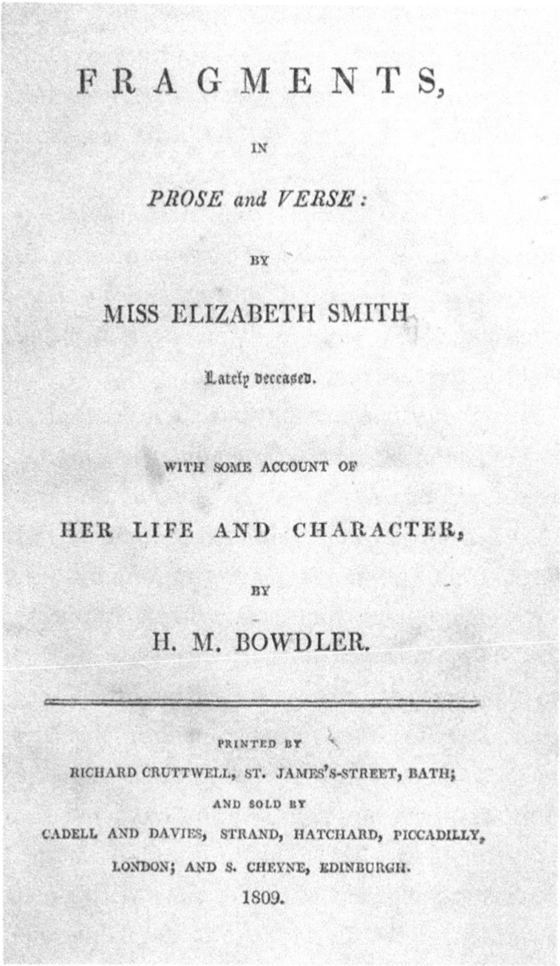

FRAGMENTS,

IN

PROSE and VERSE:

BY

MISS ELIZABETH SMITH

Lately deceased.

WITH SOME ACCOUNT OF

HER LIFE AND CHARACTER,

BY

H. M. BOWDLER.

PRINTED BY
RICHARD CRUTTWELL, ST. JAMES'S-STREET, BATH;
AND SOLD BY
CADELL AND DAVIES, STRAND, HATCHARD, PICCADILLY,
LONDON; AND S. CHEYNE, EDINBURGH.
1809.

FIGURE 11. Title page of *Fragments, in Prose and Verse: By Miss Elizabeth Smith*, revised edition (1809), identifying Elizabeth Smith and H. M. Bowdler. (Library Company of Philadelphia)

of Elizabeth Smith and her circle of friends, and published additional excerpts and new letters "which have hitherto been omitted."[70]

In a letter to a friend, Bowdler privately expressed concerns about her decision to remove the dashes and include full names. The new edition of "*Fragments* with all of our names at full length in compliance with innumerable solicitations" put more of a spotlight on the work and its editor. "I am afraid to think what I have done," she remarked. "I hope it will come out before I return to Bath; for I shall be ashamed to look any body in the face," Bowdler confessed. "Yet I tell nothing but what every body knew," acknowledging that Bath readers in particular had already figured out the thinly veiled secret of Elizabeth Smith's identity, as well as other individuals and places featured throughout the text.[71] Still, the decision to officially reveal Smith's identity also led to Bowdler's public identification as the book's editor, as well as her authorship of the previously anonymously published *Sermons*. As Bowdler's own literary reputation rested on the presumption of her modest, self-effacing nature, this decision was not without personal consequence. The continued success of *Fragments*, however, ultimately seemed to have outweighed her concerns.

As *Fragments* gained in popularity, Bowdler continued to make strategic editorial decisions about the memoir's contents, responding to strong public interest in Smith's life and writings. Along with revealing Smith's identity, new editions included her portrait and additional content. In early editions, only brief excerpts from Smith's various letters were included; later editions included expanded content from these writings. In the first editions, for example, Elizabeth Smith's October 15, 1793, letter to Mary Hunt consists of just two paragraphs describing her "well furnished" reading materials and her study of Algebra.[72] In revised editions of *Fragments*, the letter contains a previously unpublished paragraph discussing Mary Hunt's health, along with a passage in which Elizabeth Smith expressed her desire to become better acquainted with Mary Ann Burges. The additional content indicates the value that Smith placed on her supportive female friendships, but there is nothing especially intimate or deeply personal revealed. It is not clear why Bowdler initially edited out these excerpts. She may have felt that such details were too trivial or personal, or perhaps she felt that they distracted from her main focus to highlight Smith's intellectual talents and modest disposition.

Editions published after 1809 also included previously unpublished content that was not available when Harriet Bowdler first prepared the memoir for publication. As Juliet Smith reported to Thomas Wilkinson in June 1808: "I have got a great Treasure! Eleven letters of my dear Elizabeth's written to Lady Isabella King, which will be published in a future Edition."[73] When these letters appeared in subsequent editions of

Fragments, Bowdler explained that "Lady Isabella King . . . has favoured me with some extracts from her letters."[74] Juliet Smith's role in procuring these additional letters was not mentioned, and in Bowdler's telling, the "eleven letters" became "some extracts"—suggesting an editorial decision to publish only selections from, rather than the entirety of, Elizabeth Smith's letters to her friend.

Although she relied on Smith's family and friends for materials and assistance, it appears that Bowdler made the final editorial decisions concerning the format and content of *Fragments.* As Juliet Smith explained to Wilkinson after the expanded edition of *Fragments* was published, "I really was not aware that any more of your letters were to be published, or I should undoubtedly have first asked your permission." Juliet Smith implied that she had no control over what happened to content once she shared it with Bowdler, even though she was certainly aware that previously shared documents had appeared in earlier editions of the memoir: "The fact is, that being greatly pleased with your sketch of our inestimable Elizabeth's Character, I sent it to Mrs. Bowdler well knowing how highly it would gratify her, and she printed it without ever naming her intention to me."[75] Juliet Smith and Thomas Wilkinson enjoyed a warm friendship, and she often wrote candidly to him about a variety of matters, including her previous financial struggles. It is possible, then, that she was unaware of Bowdler's intentions on this particular matter. Yet in continually deferring to Bowdler's editorial decisions, Elizabeth Smith's mother repeatedly attempted to downplay the role she played in the publication process.

Hoping to further capitalize on the popularity of *Fragments,* Bowdler worked to publish the translations of Frederick and Margaret Klopstock's writings that Elizabeth Smith had been working on before her fatal illness. Juliet Smith expressed concerns about the Klopstock project, confessing to a friend that she found much of the work "rather too rhapsodical, and enthusiastic."[76] Fellow Lake District resident Dorothy Wordsworth agreed. Upon reading "Miss Smith's Translation of Klopstock's and Mrs. K's letters" in 1809, Wordsworth informed Thomas De Quincey that "I wish she had never translated them; for they disturb that beautiful image which you conceive of Mrs. K's character from the few letters to Richardson."

The Klopstocks' writings, Wordsworth complained, contained excessive "Godliness" and "exclamations without end."[77] Sensitive to such critiques, Juliet Smith wished to keep *Fragments* and the Klopstock translations as "perfectly distinct," but Bowdler insisted on publishing the works together in a two-volume set.[78]

Bowdler also made the decision to produce "a splendid Edition," consisting of "the Fragments & Klopstocks Memoirs, with an Engraving— fine paper & a large Type" marketed as a two-volume set. "I do not see the *reason* for this," Juliet Smith insisted, "but my excellent Friend Mrs. B. understands these matters better than I do, and she says it must be so,— for that such an Edition is loudly call'd for." While deferring to Bowdler's expertise, Juliet Smith also expressed her desire "that afterwards the Fragments may be published separately, with the additions and engraving, on the same sort of paper and using the same type as was originally used."[79] Bowdler's desire to promote a "splendid Edition" with higher-quality type and paper may have been to encourage purchase of the set for gift giving or for prominent display in family libraries. Writing to a friend in 1810, Hannah More, one of the most successful British women authors of the era, acknowledged how material matters such as paper size and type could influence book sales: "As you know, books do not sell in proportion to their intrinsic value, but to their size. I was vexed to see Miss Smith's Fragments, excellent as they are, and Mrs. Montagu's Letters, two shillings a set more than Coelebs, though there is not much above half the paper and letter-press."[80] As a growing number of works by women created competition in the literary marketplace, the form as well as the content of books could influence their sales and reception.

With key assistance from Juliet Smith and others, Harriet Bowdler engaged in extensive work to publish and promote *Fragments*. She bowdlerized selections from Elizabeth Smith's letters and compositions, decided which supplementary materials written by family and friends to include in the memoir's appendix, commissioned an engraving for the volume, and—after the success of the initial editions—provided additional content for future editions. This was considerable work, and it was done not just to memorialize a departed friend but to stake a claim for learned women in the literary marketplace.

"The Applause of the World"

Posthumous memoirs such as Elizabeth Smith's *Fragments, in Prose and Verse* helped inspire a particular form of literary celebrity—being memorialized in death—that offered an acceptable means of showcasing women's writings. Through the medium of posthumous tribute, women could enter the literary public sphere not as striving authors but as cherished remembrances. Such memoirs presented copperplate versions of learned women suitable for print.

The publication of *Fragments* in 1808, which occurred around the same time as memoirs about British bluestockings such as Elizabeth Carter and Elizabeth Montagu, led to a proliferation of publications venerating worthy women from both sides of the Atlantic. In the 1810s, posthumous memoirs featuring several American women, including Isabella Graham, Nancy Maria Hyde, Harriet Newell, and Martha Ramsay, were also published in local, national, and transatlantic cultures of print. By the mid-nineteenth century, individual memoirs as well as works of collective biography celebrated scores of British and American women for their piety, benevolence, teaching careers, missionary work, or literary talents.[81] Before their deaths, many of these women remained relatively unknown outside their own communities. The posthumous publications of their memoirs, however, led to the broad dissemination of their life stories and writings in print.[82]

Posthumous memoirs were often recommended to young women readers and praised for providing real-life models of conduct that could compete with novels and other works of fiction. "Biographical sketches of distinguished women afford more suitable lessons than fictitious characters," one Baltimore essayist insisted in 1811, "because they are far more interesting and more likely to excite emulation in youthful minds."[83] Of course, the key was to excite the right kind of emulation, to present young women with safe, acceptable models of accomplishment that did not challenge prescriptive gender roles. Posthumous memoirs offered a way to fulfill public interest in women's lives and writings while avoiding charges of female literary ambition. These publications, as Harriet Bowdler and other editors insisted, were typically presented to the reading public as affectionate representations of "surviving friendship," not as ambitious forays into print.

There was, of course, an obvious drawback to this form of literary fame. In death, a woman could not control or shape her own reputation, and she certainly could not materially benefit from the admiration she inspired. On the other hand, this may have been the key to success. Posthumously, Elizabeth Smith could be praised precisely because she no longer posed any threat as a living, embodied female author. It would be difficult for critics to accuse Smith of being ambitious, especially as she played no direct role in the publication of her memoir and did not actively seek fame. Indeed, according to her mother, Smith never sought "the applause of the world," noting that "the approbation of God and her own conscience were the only rewards she ever sought."[84] As Harriet Bowdler and Juliet Smith insisted, Elizabeth Smith's extensive scholarly pursuits were conducted for their own sake and to serve God, not out of any desire for literary acclaim. Smith's seeming lack of public ambition made her an especially safe model for other learned women to emulate.

Some critics, however, were unhappy with the idea of so many women cluttering up the literary public sphere from beyond the grave. One reviewer of Elizabeth Carter's memoir decried literary trends that "rake obscure characters from the ashes in which they sleep, and expose them to the public eye, with somewhat more of pomp and retinue than properly belongs to them."[85] By the 1820s, the proliferation of posthumous works prompted another essayist to complain, "The moderns have deluged us with letters."[86] Works by and about women were beginning to crowd the field of biography, a genre typically reserved for assessing the role of "great men" in history. Such cultural attitudes shaped the literary reception of Elizabeth Smith's *Fragments* within transatlantic cultures of print. In its review of Smith's memoir, for example, the London *Critical Review* griped about the "feelings of surviving friends, which induce publications like the present."[87]

Elizabeth Smith was just twenty-nine years old when she died in 1806. Had she lived, she almost certainly would have sought publication of her various works of translation—that was clearly her plan before her untimely fatal illness. As portrayed by Harriet Bowdler's skillful editorial hand, however, Smith was decidedly *unlike* those troubling examples of ambitious living women who willingly entered the literary marketplace. As a living, published author, Smith might have been found it much more challenging to maintain an unblemished reputation for successfully balancing learning, piety, and domesticity. But throughout her enduring literary afterlife, Elizabeth Smith succeeded where many living learned ladies had failed.

6

"A Lasting and Meritorious Monument"

THE LIFE OF *FRAGMENTS*

I
N JANUARY 1810, BOSTON publisher Samuel Parker announced that he
received, "by the hands of a gentleman just from England, a copy of
the Life and Fragments of Miss Elizabeth Smith." Imported copies of
Smith's memoir had been available for sale in America since the work's initial publication in 1808, but Parker planned to "put immediately to press"
his own edition of *Fragments*. To promote this first American edition,
Parker published a twenty-four-page pamphlet, including a reprinted
review of *Fragments* (originally published in the August 1808 issue of
the Boston *Christian Observer*), along with a positive reference to Smith
that appeared in Hannah More's widely popular novel *Coelebs in Search of
a Wife*. "The death of this young lady," Parker mused, "has deprived the
public of a brilliant example of the powers of the female mind, and the
present work is a lasting and meritorious monument of her acquisitions
in every science."[1]

The story of how Elizabeth Smith's memoir attracted the attention
of American publishers and readers is an important component in the
making of her posthumous reputation. The behind-the-scenes work conducted by Harriet Bowdler and Juliet Smith to edit and publish *Fragments*
represented the first stage in shaping Elizabeth Smith's literary afterlife.
The publication, dissemination, and review of *Fragments* across local,
national, and transatlantic print markets further contributed to her "lasting and meritorious" reputation.

By the early nineteenth century, significant connections and overlaps
between British and American print markets contributed to an emerging

transatlantic literary celebrity culture. The success of any book, along with the making of literary celebrity, depended on several interrelated factors, including trade routes, marketing strategies, and literary assessments. Booksellers and literary critics influenced what works were promoted, distributed, and reviewed, helping to launch the careers of Walter Scott, Lord Byron, Hannah More, Maria Edgeworth, and other celebrated writers.[2]

Both commercial trade networks and gendered concepts of authorship shepherded books such as Elizabeth Smith's *Fragments* through transatlantic cultures of print. Works by and about women largely followed the same trade routes and literary markets as those written by men, yet no matter how far or wide their works traveled, women's right to write remained culturally contested. Women authors were often subject not just to critiques about the quality of their literary works but to larger debates about whether and under what conditions it was appropriate for them to write. Women faced explicitly gendered assessments about their intellectual and literary capacities that inextricably informed how their books were published, disseminated, and received.

In explicitly calling attention to Elizabeth Smith's "powers of the female mind," Samuel Parker's pamphlet highlighted gendered aspects of print culture and celebrity literary culture. As *Fragments* traversed through literary markets on both sides of the Atlantic, the book and its contents conveyed the era's contested ideas about female authorship. Examining *Fragments'* printed circulation as well as its literary reception provides important insights into the making of Elizabeth Smith's posthumous reputation.

"Its Extensive Circulation and Celebrity"

As one London reviewer noted after the initial publication of *Fragments, in Prose and Verse,* "Before we had time to notice this very interesting little work, the first edition was sold off; and those who have had the pleasure of perusing it, will be at no loss to account for the earliness and extent of the demand." The success of *Fragments* served as a "pledge of its extensive circulation and celebrity."[3] In the decade after *Fragments* was first published,

Elizabeth Smith's memoir and other writings enjoyed "extensive circulation" on both sides of the Atlantic. Bath publisher Richard Cruttwell printed several editions of both *Fragments* and the *Memoirs of Frederick and Margaret Klopstock,* the work of German translation that Smith completed shortly before her death. In 1810, Cruttwell also published Elizabeth Smith's translation of the Book of Job, and in 1814 a London publisher printed a guide to Hebrew, Arabic, and Persian based on her various translation efforts.[4]

The publication of Smith's memoir, along with her various works of translation, served as "proof of her extraordinary attainments" and contributed to her literary fame within transatlantic cultures of print.[5] Extensive developments in the publishing, distribution, and selling of books, coupled with the strategic efforts of Harriet Bowdler's and Elizabeth Smith's circle of family and friends to promote *Fragments,* contributed to the work's widespread popularity in Great Britain.[6] Bowdler's savvy understanding of local and national markets assured that *Fragments* was distributed in Bath, London, Edinburgh, and Dublin. Just months after its initial 1808 publication, imported copies of Smith's memoir were also available for sale in America, soon followed by American reprint editions of both *Fragments* and *Klopstock.*[7] Between 1808 and 1818, over two dozen editions of Smith's works were published and sold in Bath, London, Dublin, and Edinburgh, as well as in Boston, Baltimore, Philadelphia, and Burlington, New Jersey.

The publication paths of *Fragments* and Smith's works of translation reflected larger trends in book history and were made possible by a number of interrelated developments. Improvements in transportation routes and commercial growth fostered the expansion of local, regional, national, and transnational literary markets. In England, the 1774 ruling against perpetual copyright and its impact on reprinting helped transform the book trade. After this ruling, publishers "were freer to reprint," leading to an expanding book trade, especially between London publishers and local print markets. London was the center of the British publishing industry, but as scholars have demonstrated, Edinburgh, Dublin, and key provincial markets represented an increasingly significant part of the British book trade.[8] Like other local publishers, Richard Cruttwell in Bath maintained ties with Cadell and Davies, a major London publishing firm. As we have seen, Bath's publishing market offered learned women such as Harriet Bowdler and Mary Hunt important entry points into local, national, and transnational cultures of print.

Fragments' journey to America followed paths traveled by numerous other material texts in the early national period. A substantial part of the American book trade during this era, as James N. Green notes, was "built on a foundation of British books."[9] American booksellers depended on imported works from England to help stock their shelves and made no secret of their sustained ties to the British book trade. In November 1809, for example, "Miss Smith's Works" were among the "large and valuable assortment of Books" that Mathew Carey marketed as "just received from London."[10] The importing of British publications remained key to many American booksellers' success.

While booksellers relied on British imports to help supply their customers with a variety of books, a "culture of reprinting" was also a central feature of the American book trade.[11] The limited nature of American copyright law, passed in 1790, offered protection only to American authors, so that publishers could reproduce books from England without incurring copyright costs. As a result, early national printers were free to reprint books from London "within a year or two of publication." This method could be cheaper than importing original London editions. American book traders developed an extensive system of mutually beneficial exchanges in which "a single imprint of an English title could circulate up and down the nation, free from competing editions."[12] American publishers and booksellers were instrumental to the continued and growing success of British books in the transatlantic literary marketplace.

Within this expanding book trade, demand for new works shaped the choices made by both local printers and large publishing firms. In England, these developments led to the widespread distribution of popular, bestselling books that were published in London while also enabling less well-known books that were produced in provincial markets to reach more dispersed reading publics than previously possible. Like their counterparts in Great Britain, American booksellers sold a combination of imported books, reprinted editions, and locally produced publications.

Through various means, early national American publishers and booksellers were determined "to provide the new nation with books." Given the uneven economic conditions of the book trade, however, the decision to publish any individual book carried "a distinct risk." A successful "steady seller" could keep a bookseller comfortably in business, while even one poor selling book "could cause enormous problems."[13] To offset risk, American publishers produced steady sellers like textbooks, almanacs, or primers to generate dependable income, which enabled them to invest in more niche market publications. Early national publishers and printers made strategic decisions about which British books to import or reprint, based in part on the reading public's diverse interests.

In 1810, Boston publisher Samuel Parker decided that an American reprint edition of Elizabeth Smith's *Fragments* was a risk worth taking. Throughout 1808 and 1809, copies of *Fragments* available for sale in America had been limited to editions originally published in England and shipped to American booksellers. Parker's decision to publish Smith's memoir was undoubtedly shaped by the widespread practices of importing and reprinting British works, particularly those written by notable women such as Elizabeth Carter, Hannah More, and Elizabeth Montagu. In an 1801 essay on Hannah More, the *New-York Missionary Magazine* noted, "It is highly satisfactory to observe, that her writings are beginning to be more known and read in the United States." A few years later, the Philadelphia *Port-Folio* praised the literary productions of British bluestocking Elizabeth Carter, recommending "that a cheap edition of her works, including her translation of Epictetus, ought to be undertaken in America."[14] Given the growing fame achieved by several British women writers, Parker surmised that Smith's *Fragments* might appeal to American readers. On both sides of the Atlantic, publishers and booksellers were increasingly open to selling and promoting books that showcased "the powers of the female mind."

"Deriving Both Pleasure and Profit"

When *Fragments* was published in 1808, the *Belfast Monthly Magazine* referred to Elizabeth Smith as "our female heroine," enthusiastically "recommending this material, or rather transcript of her amiable and virtuous mind to the perusal of our young Female readers."[15] In 1810, Baltimore bookseller Edward J. Coale ran a prominent advertisement for *Fragments*, confidently asserting, "It is not deemed presumptuous to assert that no lady can read this work illustrative of the life and mind of one of the most ingenious and most excellent women, without deriving both pleasure and profit from it."[16] Although *Fragments* was not marketed exclusively to women, they were certainly a key target audience. Both as readers and authors, women enjoyed expanded access to publications across transatlantic cultures of print.

On both sides of the Atlantic, increased access to education and improved literary rates for men and women sparked a "reading boom." A consumer culture flourished to promote the purchase and consumption of books, while the establishment of circulating libraries and book clubs enabled an increasing number of books to reach more and more readers.[17] In the process, particular types of publications—novels, periodicals, memoirs, and poetry—were marketed to various groups of readers, especially women. A review essay on *Mrs. Montagu's Letters* that was published in both London and Philadelphia described noticeable patterns which helped shape the literary marketplace: "Women read, and talk of what they have read, not out of affectation and pedantry, but as common amusement, and a natural subject of conversation."[18] This seemingly obvious observation underscored how women readers helped to increase the popularity and circulation of books.

By the early nineteenth century, booksellers and publishers on both sides of the Atlantic recognized the value of promoting works by and for women. Publishers sometimes strategically placed notices in their books, designed to appeal to readers' tastes and sensibilities (we might think of these paratexts as early versions of the complicated algorithms that provide targeted recommendations for music, reading, and consumer choices in the digital world). The fifth edition of *Fragments,* published in 1808 by Richard Cruttwell in Bath and sold by Cadell and Davies in London and Stuart Cheyne in Edinburgh, included an end-page advertisement for several works, including Harriet Bowdler's *Sermons on the Doctrines and Duties of Christianity*, Jane Bowdler's posthumously published *Poems and*

Essays, and Mary Hunt's anonymously published works.[19] In doing so, Cruttwell deliberately placed Smith's memoir within the same community of women writers that had played supportive roles during her lifetime. Even posthumously, then, Smith remained linked to her circle of learned friends, with her publishers recognizing that these women's literary productions would likely appeal to similar sets of readers. The connections forged among Smith's social circle thus informed the ways in which these women's books were marketed to other learned women.

With increased demand from and competition for readers, booksellers and publishers also relied on newspapers and other periodicals to promote books and encourage sales. In 1781, there were 76 newspapers and periodicals in England and Wales; by 1821, 267 papers were published in London, Edinburgh, Dublin, and numerous localities. Across the United States, the number of newspapers also grew dramatically—from 359 in 1810 to 861 in 1828—as the new nation expanded its population and borders. Notices of new publications and inventory listings of booksellers were common features in British and American newspapers: "The aim was to generate excitement in a new or controversial product and to encourage those already buying to buy more."[20]

When Samuel Parker published the first American edition of *Fragments* in March 1810, he placed advertisements in Boston newspapers, including the *Boston Gazette, Repertory,* and *New England Palladium.* Prominently titled "Miss Smith," these notices were designed to puff up interest in Parker's edition.[21] By early summer, *Fragments* was available for sale by local booksellers across the eastern seaboard, from Isaac Smith's shop in Portland, Maine, to James Kennedy's bookstore in Alexandria, Virginia.[22] The popularity of Parker's reprint edition inspired American publishers in Boston, Baltimore, and Philadelphia to issue their own editions of Smith's *Memoirs of Frederick and Margaret Klopstock.*[23] In Great Britain, these works were often sold as a two-volume set. One literary notice underscored the important connections between *Klopstock* and *Fragments:* "These two works have such a relation to each other, that no one can have read the latter [*Fragments*] without possessing a strong desire to peruse the former. The Translation of '*Klopstock*' was finished by Miss Smith in the year 1805, and is virtually a second volume of her '*Fragments.*'"[24]

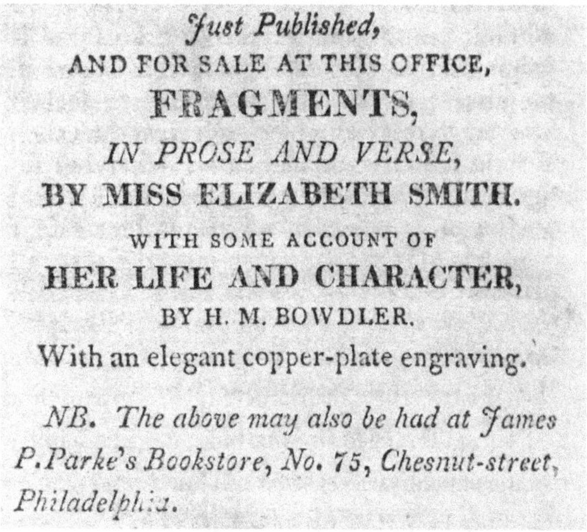

Just Published,
AND FOR SALE AT THIS OFFICE,
FRAGMENTS,
IN PROSE AND VERSE,
BY MISS ELIZABETH SMITH.
WITH SOME ACCOUNT OF
HER LIFE AND CHARACTER,
BY H. M. BOWDLER.
With an elegant copper-plate engraving.

NB. The above may also be had at James P. Parke's Bookstore, No. 75, Chesnut-street, Philadelphia.

FIGURE 12.
Newspaper advertisement for the 1811 edition of *Fragments* published in the *Rural Visiter* of Burlington, New Jersey. (Library Company of Philadelphia)

In 1811, a second American edition of *Fragments* was issued after David Allinson, a printer from Burlington, New Jersey, announced that he had purchased "the plate to their edition of 'Fragments in prose & verse" from Munroe and Francis, Samuel Parker's publishing partners. The publication of his "very handsome edition" would enable Allinson and his affiliated booksellers to "supply the repeated orders from their friends for this highly interesting little volume."[25] Advertisements placed in various northeast newspapers in Trenton, New York, Philadelphia, and New Haven informed readers where they could purchase Allinson's edition of *Fragments,* as well as copies of his *Rural Visiter* (fig. 12).[26]

Copies of Elizabeth Smith's works also reached American readers through personal channels. Deborah Logan of Philadelphia made the following inscription in her copy of a two-volume, "new edition" of *Fragments* and *Klopstock* published by Richard Cruttwell in Bath: "These volumes were brought from England soon after their publication in 1810 by my beloved Husband, they were a present to me from his friend Hannah Rathbone widow of Wm. Rathbone and daughter of Richard Reynolds."[27] While such individual transactions can be challenging to trace (not all readers were as careful as Logan to record the specific transatlantic paths that led a British book to make its way into an American reader's hands), individuals with personal or professional connections in

England continued to import copies of Smith's works even after American editions were available for sale.

Through various means, British and American editions of Elizabeth Smith's works found their way into bookstores, personal households, and library collections across the nation. For example, key repositories such as the Charleston Library Society and the Library Company of Philadelphia held British editions of Smith's works published in 1810 or later.[28] Copies of *Fragments* and/or *Klopstock* were listed in several library inventories in the early nineteenth century, including the New York Society Library; the Franklin Circulating Library in Boston; the Baltimore Library Company; and branches of the Union Circulating Library located in Boston, Philadelphia, and Washington, DC.[29] Circulating libraries gave both men and women increased access to a variety of books and print materials.

The extensive sale, distribution, and dissemination of Elizabeth Smith's memoir and her other posthumously published works reflected the growing presence of women authors and readers within transatlantic cultures of print. "Without flattering the sex," one Boston essayist on women's education declared in 1808, "we may observe, that some of the first literary characters of the present age and the last have been found among them."[30] As the number of books written by and about women grew, readers and reviewers took careful note.

"The Force of Miss Smith's Genius"

With several printings in circulation, "that much admired work, entitled *Fragments in Prose & Verse*, by Miss E. Smith" attracted the notice not only of booksellers and readers but of literary critics on both sides of the Atlantic.[31] "Indeed we have seldom met with a publication, of which the indirect influence seemed likely to be so effectual and beneficent," the London *Eclectic Review* remarked in its 1808 review of *Fragments*, "and we shall be happy if our recommendation should avail to extend the sphere of that probable influence to every school and juvenile library in the kingdom."[32] In promoting particular books, newspapers and periodicals sought to serve as arbiters of taste and culture. Prominent advertisements and review essays published in newspapers and periodicals helped to shape literary choices and sensibilities, designating particular books and authors as worthy of their readers' attention.

The publication of *Fragments* occurred during a significant historical moment, as expansions in the book trade helped inspire new forms of literary celebrity.[33] This emerging celebrity culture was characterized by strong public interest in both the literary outputs and inner lives of beloved figures. While men such as Walter Scott and Lord Byron were among the most renowned authors of the era, women such as Hannah More and Elizabeth Carter were also celebrated for their literary contributions. "This is the age of female authors," one reviewer of Elizabeth Carter's memoir asserted in 1810, "and as an evidence of the improvement of society, we rejoice that it is."[34] The age of female authors sparked celebration and critique. As women achieved a growing presence in the literary marketplace, some critics warned that women risked both their femininity and respectability by becoming published authors. In an otherwise generally favorable assessment of Elizabeth Montagu's published letters, for example, one reviewer noted that "an inkspot is no ornament to the finger or the apron of a female."[35]

Whatever the quality of their literary productions, women authors were subject to scrutiny about whether, and under what circumstances, it was appropriate for them to take up their pens. Even warm supporters of women's educational accomplishments expressed uncertainty toward women authors. An 1810 essay published in the *Port-Folio* declared, "The cultivation of knowledge is a very distinct thing from its publication; nor does it follow that a woman is to become an author, merely because she has talent enough for it." This *Port-Folio* essay was explicit in its attitudes about women authors: "We do not wish a lady to write books."[36] Such critics sought to serve as gendered gatekeepers. Women could be well-educated and accomplished but not published authors. Even when they acknowledged women's intellectual capacities and talents, prescriptive writers simultaneously insisted that women's authorship was unnatural and unfeminine and would inevitably lead to the neglect of their prescribed domestic duties.

The era's ambivalence toward women authors was reflected in literary reviews of *Fragments* published in transatlantic cultures of print. As

Elizabeth Smith's published works traveled through regional, national, and transatlantic literary markets, her life and writings were subject to numerous reviews and gendered assessments in both England and America. Cultural critics often used the publication of *Fragments* as a springboard for larger conversations about learned women.

The earliest published review of *Fragments* appeared in the August 1808 edition of the Boston *Christian Observer*, just months after the book's release in England. (This was the review that Samuel Parker reprinted in 1810 to help promote his edition.) Reviews published in London and Dublin papers followed soon after, but the quick attention that *Fragments* received in America indicates the close connections that existed within transatlantic literary markets. The *Christian Observer* warmly described Elizabeth Smith as "a young lady whose talents and attainments appear to have been of the very first class, and whose character was as interesting as her genius was extraordinary." Anticipating the skepticism of those who might wonder "by what magic such acquisitions could be gained, at so early an age," this lengthy, fourteen-page review excerpted several passages from *Fragments,* including Harriet Bowdler's glowing descriptions of Smith's extensive studies, as well as selections from her poetry and letters, to demonstrate "the force of Miss Smith's genius."[37]

In praising Elizabeth Smith, the *Christian Observer* acknowledged that it often took a more critical stance in evaluating works of biography: "Biographers complain that we are ill-natured."[38] Indeed, just one year earlier, a reader wrote in to take issue with the periodical's review of Elizabeth Carter's memoir: "I am not sure that you have so justly estimated her claims, or that, in speaking of her you have maintained that tone of respect and kindness."[39] This complaint was made in response to the *Christian Observer*'s October 1807 review, which chastised the editor of Carter's memoir for having "filled a great part of a quarto with a life, the main ingredients of which might easily be recounted in the space usually assigned to an epitaph." The "dull" and "tedious" aspects of Carter's memoir, the *Christian Observer* groused, "put our good humour, and the principles concerning biographical productions, which we already stated, to the severest test."[40] With this exchange in mind, the *Christian Observer* felt compelled to offer a lengthy explanation for its uncharacteristically effusive tone in reviewing Elizabeth Smith's memoir: "Our readers perhaps, knowing how little we are accustomed to flatter, may feel some surprise at the spirit of eulogy prevailing through this article. Let it be recollected, that she whom we have freely praised is deaf to our praises. We are slow to commend a living author, lest applause, however worthless, should feed or awaken vanity. . . . But to posthumous merit we can do justice without fear; and the office of commendation is delightful."[41] Posthumously, Elizabeth Smith could be enthusiastically applauded for her intellectual attainments, unsullied by charges of ambition or "vanity" that living women authors often faced. Such commendation was possible in part because Smith had remained unpublished before her death. By contrast, Elizabeth Carter, a famous bluestocking, was well known during her lifetime for her published works of translation. Perhaps the fame Carter received as a "living author" factored into the *Christian Observer*'s more critical assessments of her posthumous memoir.

On the whole, posthumous praise seemed safer than commendation directed at living learned ladies. Smith's literary afterlife depended on the willful obscuring of the ambitions she possessed while she was still alive. A close reading of *Fragments* illustrates the active work that Smith engaged in to shepherd the Klopstock memoir into print before her death. Had she lived to see the publication of her Klopstock translations, Smith might have been subject to more pronounced censure, particularly by a periodical that freely confessed its reluctance to praise authors during their lifetimes. From the safety of the grave, however, Smith could serve as a "striking example of the *general* advantages of intellectual improvement among women." Smith had devoted much of her time to scholarly pursuits, yet as the *Christian Observer* approvingly reported, "it is equally clear that she was amiable."[42] In other words, Smith earned posthumous praise not merely for her intellect talents (however impressive) but because she remained suitably pious, feminine, and modest *despite* her scholarly accomplishments.

A London review of *Fragments*, published in the September 1808 issue of the *Eclectic Review*, evoked similar themes, asserting that *Fragments* "describes a character few will be able to contemplate without the most tender and salutary emotions." This review praised Smith's memoir for providing proof of "her strong and acute understanding, of her determined and vigorous application, and of her many excellent moral qualities." While admiring Smith's extensive accomplishments, the reviewer was particularly pleased "to find that the young lady was neither 'a fright' nor 'a pedant.'" Her "female loveliness" was not sacrificed by her ardent intellectual interests.[43] Another London reviewer agreed, quoting from Smith's reflection that "the greatest misfortune in the world is to have more learning than good sense." This observation served as an important "check on pedantry," one that "cannot be too much valued: particularly, when the subject is the cultivation of the female mind."[44] Such comments praised Elizabeth Smith yet also reflected widespread ideas that tended to categorize most learned ladies and bluestockings as disagreeable and pedantic.

Smith's unblemished character was praiseworthy but demanded explanation, in part because it defied prevailing expectations that women's intellectual pursuits came at a cost that would inevitably lead to disorder. Reviewers who found themselves captivated by her extraordinary intellectual attainments and amiable character thus tended to display a defensive position—an indication that they were aware of and sensitive to the negative criticisms typically directed against learned women. Accordingly, even glowing reviews of *Fragments* made pointed attempts to diffuse potential critics who might question the warm admiration they extended to Smith: "Many of our readers, may probably start at the idea of such learned accomplishments, and shrink from the study necessary to acquire them." Smith, however, "well defended the cause of study against such as pronounce it unsuitable to the female character."[45]

Reviews of *Fragments* published on both sides of the Atlantic typically followed a similar pattern, offering positive assessments of Elizabeth Smith that stressed her seemingly rare combination of intellectual accomplishment, Christian virtue, and feminine modesty. To defend her against stereotypical denouncements of learned women, reviewers frequently quoted examples from *Fragments* "to justify the assertion, that this lady was no common character."[46] References to Smith as an "extraordinarily ingenious and most excellent young Lady," or "a female of uncommon talents and acquirements," repeatedly emphasized her "uncommon" character.[47] Such praise tended to reinforce the idea that Smith's achievements were singular or unique. In treating individual women like her as exceptional, cultural critics contributed to general misrepresentations about the nature and extent of women's intellectual accomplishments.

A particular tension was evident: even when Elizabeth Smith and other "extraordinary" women received commendation, reviewers expressed general discomfort with the potential forms, uses, and effects of female intellect, repeatedly insisting that most educated women would inevitably become pedantic, brash, and masculine. As one essayist declared, "It is a pity that females cannot oftener unite erudition with the elegancies of life, and the practice of that domestic qualification which is entitled good housewifery." Individual women who somehow managed this seemingly tenuous balancing act were singled out as "those rare exceptions to a rule which is become almost general."[48] Such "exceptions" were often explicitly highlighted in essays and reviews about accomplished women from the era. One reviewer referred to Elizabeth Carter as "a learned lady in the most honourable sense"—suggesting dishonorable forms were more common.[49] Describing author Elizabeth Hamilton (a Smith family friend), another essayist remarked that her "cheerfulness, good sense, and good humour, her obvious characteristics, soon reconciled every one to the 'literary lady.'"[50] The underlying notion implied that the typical 'literary lady' was *not* cheerful and good-humored—and often required a degree of societal forbearance and tolerance.

These tensions shaped the literary reception of *Fragments* within transatlantic cultures of print, as critics grappled with how to assess the seemingly extraordinary character of Elizabeth Smith. "Some rare examples, indeed, like that of Elizabeth Smith," may have succeeded in striking the right balance of feminine charm and intellectual accomplishment, but it was widely assumed that most learned ladies would fail in their efforts to combine scholarly pursuits with amiable femininity and proper attention to domestic duties.[51]

"The Peculiar Bent of Her Genius"

Writing to a friend in 1809, Harriet Bowdler was pleased, but wary, about *Fragments'* early literary reception: "I hope the Reviewers have done with us, and all that I have seen have been very warm in the praise of my friend." Bowdler was grateful for the "warm" assessments *Fragments* had received to date but understood that reviewers were often fickle and ambivalent, particularly when it came to works by and about accomplished women. Bowdler feared that *Fragments* might be subject to a change in critical assessments, citing the example of Hannah More's popular novel *Coelebs in Search of a Wife*. As Bowdler noted, *Coelebs* was "so much admired, and so much abused. Everybody was delighted at first, and now they have all found out that it requires more than they like to do, and they do not like it."[52] As Bowdler clearly understood, the shifting reception of books such as *Coelebs* reinforced how women's literary productions could attract criticism as they became more widely read, or as the implications of their contents came into sharper focus. That was especially true for works that presented inspiring models of female accomplishment. As *Fragments* gained in literary popularity in both England and America, Elizabeth Smith's extraordinary accomplishments and unblemished character signaled the possibility of a new prototype for learned womanhood. For some critics, facing the implications of this prodigy was perhaps, as Bowdler suggested, "more than they like to do."

As *Fragments* gained in popularity, reviewers in both England and America attempted to make sense of Elizabeth Smith's seemingly uncommon intellect and character in light of gendered assumptions about women's intellectual capacities. The *Monthly Anthology and Boston Review*, which reviewed *Fragments* in May 1810 (shortly after Parker's American edition was published), acknowledged Smith's intellectual attainments with a seemingly reluctant admiration: "The interesting subject of this memoir appears to have been peculiarly formed by nature and education for the character of a persevering student." The reviewer admitted that Smith was "equally amiable and intelligent," a quality that he (and many other cultural critics) found rare in learned women. However, this writer questioned the extent of her intellectual talents: "That she had genius, so far as it signifies an aptitude for peculiar studies, no one can deny; but in that other and higher sense, where it implies an uncommon originating faculty, we do not think her claim equally strong."[53]

Such assessments of Elizabeth Smith's intellect reflected cultural critiques of learned women, as well as emerging shifts in the forms and definitions of genius.[54] When genius was considered a characteristic that one *possessed,* commentators were perhaps more willing to praise talented women, often employing the designation "a lady of excellent genius."[55] Thus, even as it questioned Smith's literary genius, the *Monthly Anthology* conveyed appreciation for other women writers: "She does not evince the exquisite wit of Miss Edgeworth, the gorgeous imagination of Miss Owenson, nor the philosophical acuteness of Elizabeth Hamilton."[56] Such assessments acknowledged the talents of prominent women authors, some of whom were given credit for successfully cultivating traits such as wit and imagination.

By the early nineteenth century, as we have seen, genius became more associated with innate individual identity than with a trait one possessed. In other words, genius increasingly became a "who" rather than a "what." Over time, the idea prevailed that genius represented one's intrinsic quality of being, echoing Romanticism's privileging of unique individualism. This evolving definition of genius is what the *Monthly Anthology* referenced when it evoked an "uncommon" and "higher sense" type of genius. Such definitions, however, obscured the gendered constructs and material conditions that nourished this seemingly unique form of genius. During her lifetime, Smith had carefully considered the relationship between gender and genius that critics evoked to assess her literary legacy. She recognized "how many circumstances are necessary" to the "production" of genius, but critics tended to posit innate genius as the spontaneous flowing of (male) creativity.[57]

As the idea of innate genius developed, the notion that any individual (but especially a woman) was truly a genius was treated with heightened levels of scrutiny by literary gatekeepers. As the London *Monthly Review* asserted in its joint review of *Fragments* and *Klopstock,* most "early prodigies of genius" were falsely identified, as "such precocity generally ends in untimely barrenness."[58] The promise of seeming genius in a youth often failed to bear fruit—and critics assumed this was particularly true for learned women. Such assessments failed to acknowledge how the flourishing of creative genius required careful cultivation.

According to the *Monthly Review*, Elizabeth Smith was undoubtedly "accomplished," but she remained "deficient in genuine poetical taste"—one of the markers of true genius privileged during the Romantic era. The *Monthly Review* conceded that "the peculiar bent of her genius seems to have lain another way"—namely, in her "reasoning powers." This critique underscored the idea that Smith's claim to genius was not only "peculiar" but also not fully developed. Still, conceding that Smith possessed *some* genius was an implicit recognition of her intellectual capacity and a nod to earlier notions of genius as the product of hard work and individual effort. This was an important concession in an era that still considered women's study of logic as "a shocking proposition to many hearers."[59]

Admitting that Elizabeth Smith evinced *some* powers of genius raised the troubling possibility that other young women would emulate her in the wrong ways—finding inspiration in the endless hours she devoted to study, rather than in her piety or domesticity. As another reviewer acknowledged, "We would not wish to witness in our fair friends an emulation of that particular species of learning, in which she excelled." This is not because women were intellectually incapable of advanced language studies (Elizabeth Smith, Elizabeth Carter, and other women had clearly shown otherwise), but because such scholarly activity "generally requires a vast portion of time" and was thus incompatible with prescribed gender roles. Most women, critics assumed, would be unable to pursue such interests without sacrificing their "most important duties," such as housework and childcare.[60] The implication was that only a rare woman of uncommon character could learn as much as Smith without becoming unfeminine and pedantic.

By repeatedly asserting a false dichotomy between women's scholarly activities and their prescriptive duties, cultural critics attempted to preclude the possibility of true genius in *all* women. The era's understandings of gender roles and duties were predicated on the belief that sexual difference determined one's identity and place in society. Romanticism's understanding of "higher" genius was gendered male and primarily used to refer to particular men of uncommon abilities and imaginative powers. Positing a fundamental disconnect between seemingly innate gender differences and innate (male) genius, prescriptive ideas dismissed the possibility of such genius being embodied in a woman. While conceding that certain "extraordinary" women might possess impressive talents (that is, could be possessed "of" genius), the possibility that a woman could be *a* genius was more at odds with evolving constructions of both gender and genius. Both cultural constructions problematically set "lady" and "genius" as oppositional, rather than synonymous, terms, underscoring the prevailing cultural attitudes that cast all women's intellectual accomplishments as rare and potentially problematic. Yet to be considered a "lady *of* genius" was a less threatening idea, in part because it was notably less impressive than the idea of "a genius" who was also a lady. A woman genius challenged both the elusive, rare quality of genius as well as the prescriptive gender roles upon which this definition of genius was founded.

Even when cultural commentators expressed admiration for "exceptional" women, then, they tended to reiterate gendered constructions. These attitudes can be found in American and British reviews of *Fragments* and other works by accomplished women. In describing "extraordinary" instances of "gifted" and "distinguished" intellect, an 1809 British review of *Fragments* reprinted in a Philadelphia periodical proclaimed, "No one will presume to deny that this has happened more frequently in one sex than in the other; and though many females have appeared, whose claims to genius and learning also will never be denied, there have been no rivals to the illustrious names of Homer, Plato, . . . or Milton."[61] As such comments suggest, even individual women with strong "claims to genius" were still considered inferior to the most learned men. As another critic declared definitively, "Women are not profound scholars and philosophers: it is admitted."[62]

In underscoring the "peculiar bent" of Elizabeth Smith's genius, critics sought to discount the possibility that even the most exceptional learned woman could match the true genius associated with men. Writing in his journal in 1811, which was published shortly after his death in 1832, Scottish author and professor James Mackintosh noted that he was moved to "tears" after "reading the fragments of poor Miss Smith." He was impressed by Smith's "pure, mild, kind" character but concluded that she was "not of much genius."[63] Mackintosh's comments echoed critical assessments of gender and genius that informed several published literary reviews of *Fragments*.

Evolving understandings of genius as rare and exclusionary certainly informed the London *Critical Review*'s appraisal of Smith's *Fragments*, which it reviewed alongside the posthumous memoir of John Dawes Worgan, an aspiring young poet who had died in 1809. The reviewer began by bemoaning the publication of "the crude papers and unimportant biography of every young person of a literary turn, who should henceforth die in the bloom." While expressing its admiration for the posthumously published memoir of Henry Kirk White (edited by Robert Southey), the *Critical Review* feared that its publication had apparently set a "bad example" of imitation. While White's "genius was undoubted," the reviewer felt that neither Smith nor Worgan measured up. Both were "lovely in their lives" and "learned and well disposed," but neither, according to the *Critical Review*, met their exacting criteria for true genius.[64]

On the surface, the *Critical Review*'s skepticism was gender neutral—both Smith and Worgan failed to meet the increasingly elusive and rare definition of genius at the heart of Romanticism's cultural project. Yet while Worgan's literary deficiencies inspired just a couple of pages of patronizing critique ("there is no poetry in Mr. Worgan's poems"), the reviewer dedicated six pages to Smith. After quoting extensively from *Fragments,* the *Critical Review* proclaimed there was nothing of merit in Smith's poetry or prose. In contrast to nearly all other assessments of Smith's extraordinary or exceptional talents, the *Critical Review* insisted that Smith's writings revealed only "ordinary talents," lacking any "new or striking" insights. Her historical inquiries were dismissed as little more than "the results of a little antiquarian research into the subject, such as any young person of sixteen, of an active enquiring mind would have made." Her poetry was condemned as "irregular ode" and "rhymeless rubbish." The piece was equally unimpressed by Smith's letters to her circle of friends: "Miss Smith's letters are like those of other young ladies, excepting they talk of books instead of bonnets."[65] The gendered component

of this critique moved beyond an assessment of Smith's literary productions to reveal broader hostility toward learned women. This dismissive
commentary was directed not only at Smith as an individual but at any
learned women who dared to discuss "books instead of bonnets."

As such comments suggest, reviewers with less than favorable ideas
about women's intellectual accomplishments frequently offered gendered
assessments about what counted as appropriate subjects for letters or any
other writings deemed fit to appear in print. In the hands of cranky critics,
even the most talented women's lives and letters risked being characterized as unimportant and uninteresting. One reviewer derided the posthumously published letters of Elizabeth Montagu, a famous eighteenth-
century bluestocking, as "letters of mere idleness, friendship and flat-
tery. There are no events."[66] Yet such assessments were often uneven.
The Philadelphia *Port-Folio* approvingly noted that Montagu's letters "will
afford amusement, and excite admiration," while also taking the time to
dismiss the writings of Elizabeth Carter as "tiresome."[67] Any praise directed
at an individual woman seemed to demand the critique of another one, or
inspired broad critical assessments about learned ladies as a whole.

Such critiques are indicative of a general reluctance to concede the
broader possibility of women's intellectual parity with—or the more
unthinkable likelihood of women's intellectual superiority to—men. Thus,
the *Critical Review* concluded that Elizabeth Smith was no genius but
rather a more typical figure of the era: a learned lady with problematic literary ambitions. "If Miss Smith had lived," the *Critical Review* speculated,
"she might have published her memoirs and letters of the Klopstocks,
and nobody would have regarded them."[68] As a living woman author in a
crowded literary marketplace, Smith's career might have been dismissed
by male critics as unremarkable and mediocre—and thus unworthy of the
extensive praise she inspired posthumously.

The *Critical Review* was right in one crucial sense. Had she lived,
Elizabeth Smith certainly would have sought to publish her translations of
Frederick and Margaret Klopstock's writings. The "what ifs" surrounding
Smith's possibilities for a literary career raise important questions about
the status of women authors and translators within transatlantic cultures

of print. Would Smith have continued to employ her language skills to pursue a career as a translator, despite the criticisms often directed at learned women? Would she have followed her mentor Harriet Bowdler's lead and self-consciously crafted a public image for herself that emphasized not only her scholarly talents but also her piety, domesticity, and modesty? Would Smith have strategically decided to publish her works anonymously, like her friends Mary Hunt and Mary Ann Burges? Would she have been praised as another worthy example of British women authors—or subjected to what one commentator referred to as the "male horror of Bluestockings"?[69] Would her various writings have circulated widely within British and American literary markets, or would her works have remained obscured and unread, as the *Critical Review* implied? So much of Smith's literary celebrity was predicated on the fact that her publications appeared posthumously—a key factor that enabled her "brilliant example" to shine brightly without the persistent shadows often cast by actual living women authors.

Indeed, had she lived, the *Critical Review* speculated, Smith "might have become one of the members of the blue stocking club."[70] This was not meant as a compliment. The literary legacies of the British women originally known as the bluestockings—including Elizabeth Carter, Elizabeth Montagu, and Hannah More—illustrate the complex, often contradictory set of cultural attitudes that learned women inspired within transatlantic cultures of print. Throughout the eighteenth century, bluestockings enjoyed a degree of fame and celebrated status. By the early nineteenth century, however, the term *bluestocking* had become fraught with contested meanings and was increasingly used to discredit women's intellectual aspirations. As a growing number of women achieved literary success in transatlantic cultures of print, labels such as *bluestockings* or *learned ladies* were common shorthand to convey pejorative ideas. As one Boston essayist noted in 1808, "The unhappy being, who is at once characterized and condemned by the significant appellation of 'Blue-stocking,' meets hostility on every side."[71] On both sides of the Atlantic, quips about bluestockings signified the era's often negative and shrill reactions to female literary ambition. Critics presumed that *"learned ladies* must necessarily 'make sloppy tea,'"* reflecting widespread concerns that women would inevitably neglect their domestic duties in favor of their intellectual ambitions.[72]

As more women writers achieved success in the literary marketplace, gendered critiques grew increasingly sharp. In the process, definitions of genius became more exclusionary, and even the most exceptional women fell short. Yet how many seemingly exceptional women would it take to recognize women's extensive talents and capacities? "The mere existence of three or four extraordinary women in a country is of comparatively little value," one essayist reflected in 1813, before acknowledging that there were a "great and increasing number of educated, intelligent, accomplished women" on both sides of the Atlantic.[73] Despite their "great and increasing number," individual learned women were still treated as unusual, anomalous, and suspect. The notion of the "extraordinary" woman as a rare exception remained in effect, shaping broad assessments of all learned women's lives and writings. In focusing on the exceptional quality of particular women who were deemed worthy of commendation, critics reinforced negative, stereotypical assessments as the presumed norm. "It is the temper of the times to look on a learned woman with a kind of abhorrent awe," another essayist acknowledged, finding "the acquirement of knowledge in a female, as incompatible with that delicacy of sentiment."[74]

As a seemingly extraordinary woman, Elizabeth Smith embodied the fraught relationship between gender and genius. Any effort to determine whether she was actually a "true" genius is perhaps less important than interrogating the cultural conditions that sought to identify and regulate women's intellectual productions and capabilities. Debates about Smith's "peculiar" genius were never just assessments of her individual intellectual attainments but rather reflected the era's gendered gatekeeping of genius and authorship.

"Illustrative of the Life and Mind of Miss Smith"

Although Elizabeth Smith's potential literary career was cut short by her death in 1806, the 1808 publication of her memoir helped launch her posthumous reputation within transatlantic cultures of print. *Fragments* was, as Samuel Parker declared, "a lasting and meritorious monument" to a woman who possessed the seemingly rare combination of a strong intellect and an amiable disposition. As her memoir and other writings traveled through extensive local, national, and transnational book markets, Smith attracted attention from literary critics who offered everything from effusive praise of her extraordinary qualities to skeptical assessments of her genius.

What is striking is how most reviews focused on Smith's scholarly accomplishments and feminine character. Her daring mountain adventures and extensive travels received almost no commentary. At the end of its review of *Fragments,* one London essayist briefly noted, "but for its length, we should have substituted the account of her midnight expedition to the top of Snowdon."[75] In its fourteen-page review, the Boston *Christian Observer* commented, "Our limit forbids us to insert a letter . . . describing the ascent of Snowdon, which Miss Smith, though deserted by her fellow travellers, had the courage to undertake and accomplish alone." Despite describing this account as "the longest and best letter in the collection," the reviewer nonetheless chose not to include any excerpts.[76] Smith's Snowdon account could have drawn readers' attention to her bold explorations, or even been used purposefully by critics to make shrill, gendered critiques about her "unfeminine" behavior. Yet for unknown reasons, most reviewers largely ignored or failed to even mention her embodied experiences as an adventurer. Perhaps writers did not want to give her credit for achieving daring feats that were becoming closely identified with men's creative powers. For literary gatekeepers, what clearly mattered most was her identity as a learned lady. "Illustrative of the life and mind of Miss Smith," *Fragments* served as a symbol of learned women's powers of *mind*—and also highlighted the troubling implications embedded in evolving understandings of gender and genius.[77]

Writers on both sides of the Atlantic expressed deep ambivalence about learned women that shaped their perceptions of Smith's life and legacy. In this context, it is significant that she presented a model of female intellect which commanded a certain level of respect and admiration.

Even those reviewers who questioned the legitimacy of Smith's genius remained impressed (surprised? shocked?) that an intellectually accomplished woman remained so amiable in her disposition. Critics were astonished by her ability to balance extensive intellectual pursuits with a modest disposition and commitment to domestic duties. "In her character that harmony of all its qualities appears to have existed," one review conceded, "which blended and balanced the whole into something as near perfection as our nature admits to be realized at present."[78] Her perfectly balanced character confounded reviewers who assumed that most learned women would become shrill and unfeminine. Even those who doubted her genius, then, could not successfully accuse her of the pedantic, ostentatious, and brash behavior commonly used to discredit other learned ladies. She was seen as extraordinary, in part because she was more challenging to criticize than the stereotypical figure of the bluestocking or learned lady.

Smith may have indeed possessed impressive talents, but her *Fragments* was a representative, not exceptional, publication. In the early nineteenth century, a proliferation of works featuring the lives and writings of celebrated women from America, England, and across Europe were published. "It is, indeed, a glorious epoch of the triumph of female genius—an epoch, that will be contemplated with admiration by succeeding generations," Anna Maria Lee wrote with enthusiasm in the preface to her 1827 *Memoirs of Eminent Female Writers, of All Ages and Countries*. Lee's work of collective female biography compiled an impressive list of "illustrious females who have done honour to the intellectual character of their country," particularly in Great Britain and the United States. Elizabeth Smith was among the scores of women included in Lee's *Memoirs*. "The force of Miss Smith's genius," as Lee noted, was evident in her many scholarly achievements, as well as her exemplary character.[79]

Works such as *Memoirs of Eminent Female Writers* contributed to Smith's enduring literary legacy. As the nineteenth century progressed, readers encountered her life story and writings not only through *Fragments* but also through accounts of her that appeared in a variety of published writings, including tribute poetry, biographical sketches, and conduct literature. For decades after her death, diverse sources that referenced Smith circulated in local, national, and transnational networks. Over time, representations of "Miss Smith" as a symbolic *character*, rather than commentary on her *memoir* as a book, increasingly began to shape her literary reputation. This next phase of her enduring posthumous fame reveals how social, literary, and print cultures kept the memory and example of Elizabeth Smith alive, long after the initial reviews of *Fragments* faded from view.

7

※

"Lives in This Record"

AN AFTERLIFE, IN PROSE AND VERSE

I N 1812, FELICIA HEMANS, a popular English poet, included the tribute "Lines, Written in the Memoirs of Elizabeth Smith" in her published collection, *The Domestic Affections and Other Poems*. The poem's title suggests that Hemans initially composed her verses as handwritten marginalia directly *in* her individual copy of Smith's memoir, *Fragments, in Prose and Verse*. Once published, Hemans's seemingly personal response took new form, offering readers a public account of her high regard for Smith:

> Oh thou! whose pure, exalted mind,
> Lives in this record, fair and bright;
> Oh thou! whose blameless life combin'd
> Soft female charms and grace refin'd
> With science and with light![1]

Felicia Hemans's use of the phrase "lives in this record" suggests the power of texts to provide imaginative insights into their subjects' lives and minds. Nineteenth-century literary celebrity culture promoted an "intense personalization of literary figures," cultivated through "readers' sympathetic identification" with favorite authors and books.[2] Posthumously published memoirs such as Elizabeth Smith's *Fragments*, which typically contained previously unpublished letters, journal entries, and other writings, were believed to provide intimate portraits of departed literary figures. The growing popularity of such "life and letters" memoirs and biographies fueled literary celebrity, reflecting readers' ardent interest in the private, inner lives of beloved authors and other renowned figures.

Over time, the essence of Smith's character not only lived in *Fragments*, as Hemans's poem suggested, but was further disseminated through a wide range of manuscript and published source materials. In the years and decades following the publication of *Fragments,* numerous individuals contributed a variety of private and public accolades in Smith's honor, including tribute poems, conduct essays, travel narratives, biographical sketches, manuscript writings, and book marginalia. These diverse responses to Smith's life and writings helped create a fluid, expansive "record" of her posthumous legacy that extended well beyond the pages of her memoir.[3]

Taken together, these literary fragments helped define and expand Smith's enduring afterlife. The *forms* these tributes took in both published and manuscript sources enable us to trace how her posthumous reputation was created, disseminated, and transmitted across local and transatlantic cultures of print. Their *content* illustrates how Smith's character served as an ideal storyboard for larger cultural assessments about the promises and perils of women's intellectual ambitions. In expressing admiration for Smith's seemingly extraordinary combination of an "exalted mind" and "female charms," such tributes often reinforced the prevailing idea that it was rare for any woman to be so intellectually accomplished, and perhaps even more rare for an accomplished woman to be so charming and graceful. Posthumous representations and remembrances of Elizabeth Smith underscore how learned women's lives and legacies were shaped by gendered assessments, with transatlantic reach.[4]

"Hannah More Has Paid a Just and Noble Tribute"

British author Hannah More's popular novel *Coelebs in Search of a Wife* was published in 1808—the same year as the first editions of *Fragments*. In a chapter that referenced debates about whether it was appropriate for women to study Latin and other classical languages, More evoked

Elizabeth Smith's example to guide young women embarking on their own educational journeys:

> And let such women as are disposed to be vain of their comparatively petty attainments, look up with admiration to those two contemporary shining examples, the venerable Elizabeth Carter, and the blooming Elizabeth Smith. I knew them both, and to know them was to revere them. In *them*, let our young ladies contemplate profound and various learning chastised by true Christian humility. In *them*, let them venerate acquirements which would have been distinguished in a University, meekly softened, and beautifully shaded by the gentle exertion of every domestic virtue, the unaffected exercise of every feminine employment.[5]

More's published tribute played an influential role in shaping Smith's posthumous reputation. More praised Elizabeth Carter and Elizabeth Smith for their extensive learning—"which would have been distinguished in a University"—while expressing equal admiration for their piety and femininity. Women such as Smith and Carter possessed impressive intellectual capacities, but what truly inspired More's admiration was how their learning was properly "softened" to avoid vain, selfish, and unappealing behavior. More thus offered her readers a vision of learned womanhood in which intellect was tempered by meekness. Her celebration of Carter's and Smith's accomplishments contained a warning to young women not to let their own "petty" intellectual ambitions detract from their prescribed feminine roles and domestic duties. More's comments underscored a key aspect of literary celebrity: women rarely earned approval solely on the basis of their intellectual attainments but rather for how successfully they evaded criticism as they enacted learned lives.

Although there is no evidence that Elizabeth Smith and Elizabeth Carter knew each other, Hannah More's assertion "I knew them both" helped link them together in the cultural imagination. Carter and Smith shared several qualities that gave weight to More's association: both women were noted for their translation skills, both died in 1806, and both were the subjects of posthumous memoirs published shortly after their deaths. During her lifetime, Carter's published works of translation as well her active role in notable bluestocking circles earned her considerable fame in England and America.[6] More's joint tribute contributed to Smith's growing celebrity status by placing her in the same category of accomplishment and renown as the already well-known Carter.

Hannah More's *Coelebs* was a bestselling novel, read widely in England and America. In the decades following its publication, several authors who expressed their admiration for Smith explicitly referenced More's tribute. These references offer compelling evidence of the novel's impact in helping to disseminate Smith's literary reputation. When the *Monthly Anthology and Boston Review* reviewed Smith's memoir in 1810, the essayist began by noting, "Among the many readers of the popular romance of 'Coelebs,' there are probably few, at least on this side of the Atlantick, who have not inquired respecting that 'Elizabeth Smith,' whose name is there connected with the *time-honoured* celebrity of Mrs. Carter."[7] In 1814, Elizabeth Frank, author of *Classical English Letter-Writer*, noted that "Mrs. Hannah More has paid a just and noble, tribute to the great worth of Mrs. Carter, and of another lady [Elizabeth Smith], scarcely less celebrated, whose early removal has given peculiar interest to her example."[8] In *Select Female Biography*, an 1821 collective biography featuring "eminent British ladies," Mary Roberts began her entry on Elizabeth Smith with More's quotation from *Coelebs*.[9] Margaret Coxe's *The Young Lady's Companion*, published in Ohio three decades after *Coelebs*, included More's account of Smith in her chapter on women's study of languages and praised Smith as a worthy model of emulation: "Seek to imitate this exalted woman, my dear niece, in the beautiful features of her character as an affectionate, dutiful and sympathizing daughter, no less than in her intellectual habits."[10]

For several decades, conduct literature that praised Elizabeth Smith's life and character frequently included references to either or both Hannah More and Elizabeth Carter. "To Miss Carter we listen with respectful deference," an 1824 essay noted, "while our sympathies are yielded to the blooming Minerva of our own times; the meritorious Elizabeth Smith."[11] When U.S. Chief Justice Joseph Story wrote in support of women's education in 1826, he asserted, "Who is there that does not contemplate with enthusiasm the precious Fragments of Elizabeth Smith, the venerable learning of Elizabeth Carter, the elevated piety of Hannah More?"[12] In

1858, a memoir about the accomplished linguist Cardinal Giuseppe Caspar Mezzofanti briefly celebrated the achievements of "Lady-Linguists," calling particular attention to "the beautiful Mrs. Carter, translator of Epictetus . . . and the amiable and singularly gifted Elizabeth Smith."[13] Nearly a hundred years after *Coelebs* was first published, a history of the Lake District published in 1905 referred to "'the blooming Elizabeth Smith, whom to know was to revere,' writes the author of an ancient book called 'Coelebs in Search of a Wife.'"[14]

Over time, various references and tributes sparked something of a literary "chain reaction" that contributed to Smith's posthumous fame across transatlantic cultures of print. For decades after her death, Smith was a well-known literary figure who could be evoked without the need for an extended introduction—the presumption was that readers already knew and admired her. "I think you must have heard and read of Miss Smith," Dorothy Wordsworth wrote to a friend in 1828. "Mrs. Bowdler published a short account of her life, and early and lamented death, with some of her letters and translations from the German—and a few other compositions."[15] Although she provided a somewhat terse account of Smith's literary remains, Wordsworth was certain that her friend "must have heard and read" about Elizabeth Smith. *Fragments* was the initial source of Smith's fame, yet over time individuals both "read" and "heard" about her through a variety of printed, manuscript, and oral communications.

"I Am to Read Miss Smith's Life"

In July 1810, Rachel Van Dyke of New Brunswick, New Jersey, learned about Elizabeth Smith's *Fragments* after a friend from Burlington, New Jersey, "wrote me nearly a page about this wonderful book—or more properly this lady." For some readers, the "book" and "this lady" were seemingly interchangeable, affirming Felicia Hemans's idea that Elizabeth Smith "lives in this record." Van Dyke took note when another one of her Burlington friends also wrote and referred to Smith's memoir "in a most flattering manner." Both friends, Van Dyke remarked, assumed that "I must have read it."[16] Van Dyke's friends eagerly recommended

Fragments to her, presumably because they believed she would relate to Smith's scholarly interests. At the time, Van Dyke was studying chemistry and Latin, and her journal contained passionate defenses of women's intellectual capacities.

Burlington publisher David Allinson had recently printed his edition of *Fragments*, which helps explain why Rachel Van Dyke's friends from that town were so interested in Smith's memoir. Initially, Van Dyke assumed that her friends' interest reflected Burlington's provincialism. "I suppose it is a general topic of conversation in Burlington—thus it is in small towns," she wryly noted, without truly appreciating how a small town in New Jersey came to be interested in the memoir of a British woman in the first place.[17] That the small town in question was Burlington is significant to the publication history of *Fragments*. David Allinson's edition of Smith's memoir demonstrates that local, national, and transatlantic trends contributed to *Fragments'* continued success in the literary marketplace. Extensive networks of publishers, printers, and booksellers enabled an increasingly wide circulation of printed materials, making it possible for books such as *Fragments* to transverse multiple literary markets in both England and America.[18]

The success of any book was made possible by booksellers and publishers but also depended on reader interest and enthusiasm. It was her friends' recommendations, not a bookseller's advertisement, that drew Rachel Van Dyke's attention to Smith's memoir. Ultimately, it was up to the individual reader to decide if a book seemed worth her time and attention. Despite her own intellectual ambitions, Van Dyke was initially cynical about whether Smith merited the high praise she inspired in her friends. "I am very impatient to learn something more of this eighth wonder of the world," she quipped in her journal. As Van Dyke's curiosity outweighed her skepticism, she turned to local resources in search of *Fragments*. She began at her town's circulating library but "was sorry to find they did not possess" the book. Next, she visited her former teacher at a local boarding school, who had already lent out her copy of *Fragments* but "promised to lend it to me whenever Mrs. Boggs returns it." A few weeks later, Van Dyke learned that the circulating library had received *Fragments*, "which at my request had been sent for."[19] Such informal practices—individuals lending books out to friends and neighbors, or requesting that their circulating libraries purchase particular titles—are indicative of some of the behind-the-scenes ways in which books gained popularity in local markets.

After waiting weeks to get her hands on a copy of *Fragments,* Rachel Van Dyke was finally able to begin reading. The evening she picked up the book from the library, she "retired to my room as soon as I could and have been reading about Miss Smith." As she read, Van Dyke turned to writing in her journal to help process her response to Smith's life story and writings. After reading about half of *Fragments,* Van Dyke expressed admiration for Smith's "uncommon, astonishing character" but disagreed with those who asserted that Smith was able to achieve so much despite possessing "but few advantages." Smith's "advantages were certainly great," she countered, recognizing how Smith benefited from being "surrounded by the most amiable friends" who were themselves "blessed with wisdom and knowledge." Having such a social circle, Van Dyke mused, must have played a significant role in Smith's "happiness and improvement," especially when compared to her own experiences of being "surrounded by friends who are but little acquainted with your studies, [and] who think you waste your time in attending to them."[20] Despite significant gains in access to educational opportunities in both America and England, learned women were often subjected to skeptical or negative assessments regarding their scholarly endeavors.[21] Van Dyke envied Smith, who had been surrounded by a supportive network of like-minded friends.

When she finished reading *Fragments,* Van Dyke "intended to have written my opinion" of Smith's memoir in her journal but was surprised and distracted by out-of-town guests and did not have time to record her observations. It was clear that her initial skepticism was replaced by ardent admiration—noting that Smith's sentiments "agree so well with my own."[22] Inspired by Smith's life and writings, Van Dyke was eager to share the book with someone who would support and validate her interests and opinions.

After she finished reading, Van Dyke enthusiastically recommended *Fragments* to her teacher and friend Ebenezer Grosvenor, with whom she enjoyed a warm relationship characterized by shared intellectual pursuits both in and outside the classroom. Grosvenor eagerly began reading Smith's memoir, curious to learn what parts of the book Van Dyke found most inspiring. "I am to read Miss Smith's life," he noted, "and shall look for the mark of your pencil where an idea occurs which *on any account* is noticeable."[23] Van Dyke's penciled dashes served as personal signposts, designed to direct Grosvenor's attention to particular passages that she wanted him to notice. This practice, she noted, was one "we always do in books we read together." When Grosvenor returned the book to Van Dyke, she was happy to learn that he "was very, very much pleased with it." Van Dyke eagerly re-reviewed *Fragments,* this time focusing on Grosvenor's responses to the passages she had marked for him. While she had "only put strokes of the pencil" to highlight particular passages, "he has written sentences."[24] Grosvenor wrote detailed marginalia in the circulating library's copy of *Fragments,* providing personal commentary for Van Dyke's benefit that added another layer to their shared reading experiences.

One of the sentences that Van Dyke marked for Grosvenor's notice related to the time Elizabeth Smith called her friend Mary Hunt "a blab" for having shared her Snowdon mountain climbing adventure with mutual friends. Grosvenor had apparently engaged in a "thoughtless act" of sharing some of Van Dyke's writings, but he asserted that his actions were "as different from a *blab* as need be." Yet he clearly recognized that Van Dyke's "dash" in this instance was meant as a personal communication to him. "Do you think I am a *blab*? It is impossible."[25] The two friends' responses to *Fragments* resonated on a personal level that went beyond Smith's own life story and writings.

For Van Dyke and Grosvenor, the margins of *Fragments* served as a conduit for communication, as they literally created a set of "lines, written in the memoirs of Elizabeth Smith." Hemans's published tribute poem reached thousands of readers by evoking the idea of such marginalia. Grosvenor's and Van Dyke's lines written in *Fragments,* however, were only meant to be shared between the two of them. The pair deleted all of their dashes and written comments—Grosvenor noted his intention to "rub them out before he returned" the book to the library.[26] Although this practice kept the circulating library's copy of the book unmarked for other readers, it erased valuable evidence of their shared responses.

Rachel Van Dyke's experiences with Elizabeth Smith's *Fragments* reveal several interrelated aspects of nineteenth-century readers' engagement with authors, books, and literary celebrity culture. Her journal entries indicate a deeply personal response to Smith's life and writings, while also revealing how Smith's literary fame spread via unofficial channels. Individual readers shared their literary opinions by lending books, conversing about favorite authors, and circulating written commentary in the form of correspondence, journal writing, and marginalia. Along with published commentary found in various essays and books, these personal practices played important roles in the dissemination of books and the making of literary celebrity.

The habits and responses of readers, however, can be difficult for scholars to recover, often requiring a "needle in a haystack" methodological approach.[27] Without the preservation and eventual publication of Rachel Van Dyke's journal, the story of how she and Ebenezer Grosvenor read *Fragments* would be lost. Only fragments of how books were read—marginalia, written responses, shared reading habits—remain. Yet when available, such evidence can offer rich insights into nineteenth-century reading patterns and practices. Reading *Fragments,* Van Dyke and other learned women were pleased to discover that Smith's scholarly interests "agree so well with my own."

"We Shall Have an Elizabeth Smith"

Reflecting on the achievements of her new neighbors in 1810, Smith family friend Mary Leadbeater mused, "These young women often remind me of the Smiths, accomplished, classical, humble, modest, and pious." In particular, one of the daughters demonstrated impressive language skills: "I could scarcely enough admire the ease, unconsciousness and modesty with which Harriet translated Latin. I thought of dear Bess Smith."[28] Leadbeater had spent months with the Smith family during their stay in Ballitore, Ireland, so her comparisons were based on direct experience. Yet even readers without such personal connections drew similar associations between Elizabeth Smith and the accomplished women in their social circles.

In 1814, Mary Moody Emerson, Ralph Waldo Emerson's aunt, made the following observations about her friend Sarah Alden Bradford: "Society begins to find that we shall have an Elizabeth Smith. Did I ever tell you, I tho't there was a striking resemblance in character and acquisition? I have forgotten what I have told you about Sarah A. Bradford. She ascribes much to her Instructor—but the Greek she acquired alone. She solves a problem in Euclid, in astronomy, in mathematics, with as much ease as she uses her needle, and as much simplicity as she makes pultices for the sick."[29] Emerson's comments about Bradford unmistakably paraphrased Harriet Bowdler's remarks about Elizabeth Smith included in *Fragments:* "She made a gown or cap . . . with as much *skill* as she displayed in explaining a problem of Euclid."[30] Bowdler's comments, as we have seen, were modeled in turn after Samuel Johnson's remarks on Elizabeth Carter.[31] Such deliberate framing suggests a common standard was used to assess how well women successfully balanced their intellect and domesticity. With her phrase "we shall have an Elizabeth Smith," Emerson evoked Smith as an ideal model to measure the accomplishments of other learned women.

Throughout her enduring afterlife, Elizabeth Smith was a source of inspiration and emulation for women on both sides of the Atlantic. In an 1861 essay published in the influential *Atlantic Monthly,* British author Harriet Martineau reflected on Smith's legacy: "I do not know whether her name and fame have reached America; but in my young days she was the English school-girls' subject of admiration and emulation."[32] Accounts by Rachel Van Dyke, Mary Moody Emerson, and other women indicate that *Fragments* indeed reached American readers. As a growing number of American and British women benefited from expanded access to educational opportunities, Smith served as a recognizable symbol of women's achievements. "Within the circle of our own acquaintance," as one American essayist wrote in 1826, "we know of several examples that approximate to that of Elizabeth Smith."[33]

As they read, recommended, and discussed *Fragments,* learned women discovered a kindred spirit in Elizabeth Smith. In 1811, Martha Laurens Ramsay of South Carolina requested her friend Juliana Hazlehurst to "lend me the memoirs of miss Elizabeth Smith," after being unable to locate a copy of *Fragments* at her local library. Ramsay's daughter noted how Smith's character resonated with Hazlehurst: "You have known how to appreciate her merit; and I believe so sincere has been your admiration of it, that in the most valuable circumstances of her life, you are imitating her example."[34] Upon reading *Fragments* in 1817, Lusanna Richmond of Rhode Island remarked in her diary, "I scarcely ever read so much goodness, piety and knowledge being combined in any person. She confirms me in what I have already undertaken." In Smith's example, Richmond found validation for her own intellectual ambitions and expressed determination to "note down the most important periods and circumstances which happened during my life, and also to extract from books, such sentences as peculiarly strike me for piety, goodness, elegance, sublimity, &c. &c."[35] Richmond felt a strong sense of affinity with Smith, sharing with her a love of reading, writing, and reflecting. Around the same time, Lucinda Read of Massachusetts copied several passages from Smith's memoir into her commonplace book. Inspired by reading various women's memoirs as well as by her work as a teacher, Read "determined to improve every *inch* of time to gain useful knowledge."[36]

Smith's intellectual accomplishments and unblemished character inspired warm praise from women readers. After reading "the Memoir of Miss Smith," Mary Wilder White, a friend of Mary Moody Emerson, noted that the work "more than realized every expectation. She must, indeed, be considered the wonder of the age."[37] Smith may have been considered a "wonder," but her aspirations were not unique. Readers of *Fragments* used her accomplishments and character to create shared affinities and identities as learned women. Writing to her daughter Margaret Manigault in 1811, Alice Izard of South Carolina expressed high regard for Smith, after having "at last read" *Fragments:* "What an astonishing young woman! What attainments in learning; what an extent of talents! And with what meekness they were possessed! Lovely in virtues, as admirable in acquirements: How truly deserving was her character." Izard considered Smith a worthy model of womanhood. "It is really consoling to know that such characters exist," she mused. "It does one's heart good to think that there is still so much worth in the World."[38] Izard was pleased that Smith's example lived on as an inspiration to others.

Although relatively few in number, surviving fragments from manuscript diaries, letters, and other writings provide rich evidence of individual readers' responses to *Fragments*. Additional manuscript materials detailing how other readers from both America and England reacted
to Smith's life and writings may be waiting to be discovered in research
archives (although we must also consider that many such writings by "ordinary" women were not preserved). However compelling in content, individual readers' responses were often meant to remain private, or shared
with only a small circle of family and friends. Over time, personal accounts
highlighting Elizabeth Smith's accomplishments took on new forms,
reflecting larger trends that shaped nineteenth-century cultures of print.

"All Admiration at What I Read about Her"

In December 1808, Hannah More discussed Elizabeth Smith's life and
writings in a letter to her friend W. W. Pepys: "You have doubtless seen
and wondered at her life and fragments. I knew and admired her long
ago, before I suspected what knowledge lay concealed under that modest
countenance." More's private admiration for Smith echoed the published
comments she included in her popular novel *Coelebs*. More informed
Pepys that she was currently reading Smith's work on the Klopstocks and
was aware of the forthcoming publication of Smith's translations of Job,
"said to be the finest ever made." In his reply, Pepys remarked that he "was
all admiration at what I read about her" in *Fragments*.[39]

Hannah More personally knew both Elizabeth Smith and Harriet
Bowdler, so her opinion was rooted in direct knowledge unavailable to
most readers of *Fragments*. She was aware of the open secret of Smith's
identity as the "young lady, lately deceased" even before editions of
Fragments began using Smith's full name. Moreover, More was confident
that her friend had "doubtless" heard about the just-published memoir—
suggesting that well-connected literary figures helped each other to stay
informed about the publication of notable books.

As More's comments illustrate, both the form and content of individual responses expressing admiration of Smith reveal interconnected

aspects of readers' responses and literary culture. Friends were eager to recommend and lend favorite books to each other and used a variety of communications to convey their enthusiasm for reading. These informal practices helped create communities of readers that influenced the public reception and dissemination of books and authors' reputations.[40] Such personal recommendations were even more powerful when a particular reader was herself an admired literary figure.

Careful attention to More's letter as a primary source also provides insights into the dissemination and circulation of texts within transatlantic cultures of print. When first written in 1808, her letter to Pepys would have been what historians commonly consider a "private" or "personal" manuscript source—correspondence addressed to a particular friend, without a wider public audience in mind. More's recommendation resembled personal writings that women such as Rachel Van Dyke composed and received discussing *Fragments*. Yet in 1835, More's correspondence with Pepys and other literary figures was included in her posthumous memoir. The publication of this memoir made her response to Smith's life and writings, over and above her tribute in her novel, available to thousands of readers.

Personal writings have often been disseminated in ways that amplified their audience. Manuscript writings that remained unpublished were informally copied, shared, and circulated among select literary and social networks. Reading letters aloud in social circles or copying passages to mutual friends were common epistolary practices during this era.[41] Elizabeth Smith's mild annoyance when Mary Hunt shared her Snowdon travel narrative with her larger circle of friends (and how this example resonated with Rachel Van Dyke and Ebenezer Grosvenor) helps to illustrate these trends. While the informal sharing and circulation of manuscript writings was common practice, their dissemination typically remained limited to specific social and literary circles.

The expanding "life and letters" format of memoirs and biographies took the distribution of personal texts to new levels, creating overlapping categories and classifications of source materials. Presumably, famous writers such as More must have considered the possibility that they would someday be the subject of such memoirs. More was friendly with famous bluestockings such as Elizabeth Carter and Elizabeth Montagu—women whose correspondence had appeared in posthumous memoirs published around the same time as Smith's *Fragments*. The fact that both sides of More's correspondence with several key figures were preserved suggests that some attention was paid to curating her "literary remains." Given the growing popularity of "life and letters" memoirs during the nineteenth century, the safeguarding of an author's correspondence was often done with an eye toward possible publication. Once published, these sources took new forms and reached new readers.

Published accounts by literary figures describing their responses to Smith's life and writings represent another set of fragments that contributed to her enduring fame across time and place. From Scotland, author Anne Grant wrote a lengthy letter to a friend after reading Smith's memoir in 1814. "You cannot think how they and she rose upon me," Grant mused, deeply impressed by Smith's "soundness and purity." Although Grant did not personally know Smith, she was well acquainted with Elizabeth's sister Kitty, who had moved to Edinburgh after her marriage. "To resemble her in what is most important," Grant mused, "it is not necessary to emulate her attainments or to possess her abilities: we may all be as true, as pious, as charitable, and as indulgent to others."[42] Grant's reflections echoed those made by various women who recorded their responses to Smith's memoir in their personal journals and letters. Thirty years later, Grant's letter was included in the *Memoirs and Correspondence of Mrs. Grant of Laggan*. When such writings were published, readers encountered references to Elizabeth Smith in unexpected sources.

Through both personal and public channels, Smith's fame grew. In October 1808, Mary Leadbeater wrote to her friend Melesina Chenevix Trench about the publication of "my friend Juliet Smith's daughter's book," inspiring Trench to read *Fragments*: "What a character is drawn in that little volume of your angelic friend Elizabeth Smith, who shines a bright luminary amongst our brightest females."[43] These exchanges were later printed in *The Leadbeater Papers*, which also contained Leadbeater's descriptions of the Smith family's residence in Ireland.

Personal accounts that were transformed into printed references created multifaceted, interconnected, widely disseminated tributes. Having first learned of Smith from Leadbeater, Melesina Trench later enjoyed an "evening *tête-à-tête*" with a friend of Harriet Bowdler while visiting Bath in 1812: "She illuminated the past for me, and gave me an infinity of anecdotes from the fountain-head, relative to Mrs. Bowdler (her intimate friend), that prodigy, Miss Smith, the Edgeworths, who live near her daughter, and other equally interesting people."[44] The "infinity of anecdotes" illustrate how Smith's reputation lived on through exchanges that were initially forged by social and personal networks, and then later shared through the medium of published memoirs.

Manuscript and published sources played key roles in the dissemination of Elizabeth Smith's posthumous reputation—and in some cases, sources could be considered both manuscript and published materials. A personal letter subsequently printed in a posthumous memoir transformed from manuscript to published source. The once "private" writing was now available for "public" consumption. Informal discussions of Smith's life and writings that were initially shared within select social and literary circles became more visible when they appeared in posthumous memoirs and other publications. When readers encountered these previously personal letters and journals, they likely regarded them as authentic, "on the spot" records. The informal, conversational tone of such writings—even if they were actually carefully composed or later edited for publication—may have seemed particularly fresh, genuine, and moving.

The publicizing of previously private source materials fueled nineteenth-century literary celebrity, by offering readers new windows into the lives and minds of beloved literary figures. When a Belfast magazine printed Thomas Wilkinson's essay describing his Lake District adventures, a footnote identified "the celebrated Elizabeth Smith and her sisters" as his companions, noting, "Elizabeth Smith's 'Fragments in Prose and Verse,' and the account of her accomplishments, genius, and amiable disposition, are doubtless, familiar to the recollections of most of the readers of the *Belfast Monthly Magazine*."[45] Through Wilkinson's essay, readers presumed to be already "familiar" with *Fragments* discovered fresh details about Elizabeth Smith. Wilkinson's account had circulated informally in manuscript form for about a decade before its initial publication in 1812. The essay was later included in Wilkinson's 1824 book,

Tours to the British Mountains, potentially reaching even more readers in England and beyond.[46]

As a result of her residence in the region, Smith's reputation was particularly well-established among Lake District residents. In September 1808, Robert Southey received a copy of Smith's memoir from his friend John Neville White: "We are very much obliged to you for the Fragments of poor Miss Smith, which I had heard of and wished to see." Southey explained that he had been introduced to Smith in Bath in 1796 but "neither saw nor knew anything of her till about three years ago, when, hearing that one of Mrs. Smith's daughters, at Coniston, understood Hebrew, I knew that she must be the person to whom I had formerly been made known." During the years of Smith's residence in the Lake District, Southey "made no attempt at renewing the acquaintance," primarily, as he admitted, because he disliked Juliet Smith. Southey recalled passing Elizabeth Smith in a carriage shortly before her death, remarking that "the sight of her made me melancholy for the rest of the day."[47] In 1856, Southey's introspections were published in *Selections from the Letters of Robert Southey,* a posthumous work edited by his son-in-law. Nearly fifty years after her death, Smith's legacy reached a variety of new readers through such works.

These published personal writings served to highlight the extensive social connections and literary communities prevalent in the Romantic era and to make them visible to new generations of readers on both sides of the Atlantic. During her lifetime, Elizabeth Smith personally knew and spent time with respected women writers such as Hannah More, Mary Leadbeater, and Elizabeth Hamilton. Other notable literary figures such as Anne Grant, Robert Southey, Dorothy Wordsworth, and various Lake District writers had some form of personal associations with the Smith family. These authors all had some direct knowledge of Elizabeth Smith as an embodied being, rather than just as a posthumous literary figure. These connections, however fleeting, informed how these writers read and responded to *Fragments,* and also worked to sustain Smith's celebrated status for decades after her death.

Once published, writers' personal responses to *Fragments* enabled additional readers to create imaginative connections with Smith's life and legacy. Through both prose and poetry, tributes to Smith sought to convey shared affinities and sensibilities. Recall that Felicia Hemans framed her tribute to Smith as a personal form of response purportedly penned right within the margins of *Fragments*. Her poem "Lines, Written in the Memoirs of Elizabeth Smith" was meant to evoke Hemans's immediate, authentic reaction to reading *Fragments*. If Hemans had truly kept her poem in its supposed form as marginalia, only those individuals with physical access to her individual copy of *Fragments* would have ever read her tribute. Its full impact depended on a wider circulation through the medium of publication.

Individuals wished to share their written reflections about Smith with others who would appreciate their sentiments. In 1810, Elijah Waring of Alton, England, wrote to Thomas Wilkinson about a monody he wrote in Smith's honor "on the simple impulse of feelings awakened by reading H. Bowdler's publication of *Memoirs & Fragments*." Waring had an advantage that only select readers of *Fragments* enjoyed—he had met Harriet Bowdler, who recommended that he send his poem to Wilkinson to seek advice about the possibility of offering "it to the public as a tribute to the memory of the amiable Person whose merits it attempts to celebrate."[48] Wilkinson's own tribute poetry to Smith was published in *Fragments*, yet for unknown reasons he cautioned Waring about the "inexpediency of publishing this production." Waring accepted Wilkinson's advice to have his poem "remain MS." Reflecting on the matter, Waring explained that he had intended to publish his poem without having "printed my name." As a Quaker, Waring was reluctant to seek literary fame, "yet as ESmith's character is so well known and admired," he speculated, publishing his poem "might have been a degree of Publicity which I wish to shun."[49]

Waring's tribute was not published, but other individuals did not share his reservations about using published poetry as a means to honor Smith's "well-known and admired" character. In the years following the publication of *Fragments*, Elizabeth Smith was the subject of several works of published tribute poetry. These poems venerated her as a "gentle spirit pure / Sent on this earth to teach, exalt, allure. . . . / With modesty and learning, side by side." Smith was revered as larger than life—"More than mortal, Albion's fairest flow'r!"[50] Taken together, these tribute poems represented a distinctly public form of readers' response to Smith's life and writings. Several poems' titles directly referenced the act of reading *Fragments*, including John Wilson's "Lines Written on Reading the Memoirs of Miss Smith," William Lisle Bowles's "On Reading Fragments by a Young Lady Lately Deceased," and "On Reading the Fragments in Prose and Verse, by Elizabeth Smith" by "Cotswoldia."[51] These titles reflect how writers deliberately used the inspirational effects of readers' responses as the framework for their poetry.

Sometimes, the strong inspiration felt "on reading" Elizabeth Smith's memoir inspired writings "in" *Fragments*. The title of John Gwilliam's 1809 poem "Quatorzains: Written in the First Volume of Miss Elizabeth's Smith Fragments in Prose and Verse" suggests that he was inspired to compose his poem directly *within* his personal copy of *Fragments*.[52] In framing their stylized poems as marginalia, poets such as John Gwilliam and Felicia Hemans evoked a stylized literary device that was meant to capture their spontaneous, "on the spot" reactions to reading *Fragments*. These poems mirrored the experiences of readers such as Rachel Van Dyke and Ebenezer Grosvenor, who used marginalia in books and journals to record and share their responses with friends. In transforming their supposed marginalia into published, polished verses, poets self-consciously presented public accounts of their responses that were explicitly designed to be shared with others.[53] Like accounts penned in personal journals, letters, and book margins, tribute poems evoked a strong sense of affinity with Elizabeth Smith, praising her learned yet modest character as worthy of emulation.

Readers' responses to Elizabeth Smith's life and writings often blurred the boundaries between local and transnational, between manuscript and print, and between intellectual and imaginative. Whatever their form—poetry or prose, public or private, published or manuscript—these variety of responses created extensive literary exchanges that contributed to Smith's enduring afterlife. Through such records, her legacy lived on to inspire others.

"Read the Lives of Celebrated Females"

Writing in 1824, one essayist conveyed sentiments about Smith's *Fragments* that would have resonated with many readers on both sides of the Atlantic:

"We are irresistibly attracted to this little volume and its biographical elu-cidations."[54] Various personal and published accounts featuring admiring responses to *Fragments* reflected the growing popularity of memoirs and other biographical works featuring accomplished women. These works helped to create expanded notions about whose lives and writings were worthy of commemoration within transatlantic cultures of print.

In 1833, after hearing about a "new book" of collective biography fea-turing the lives of several distinguished men, Mary Greenville wondered, "Are there no histories of good and great women, mother?" Her mother was pleased by the query and assured her daughter that "there are many biographies of eminent women written and published." Mrs. Greenville also injected a note of caution, informing her daughter that "you need a mature judgment to point out such traits of character as are worthy of imitation." She decided to review and "read the lives of celebrated females for you," including *Fragments,* and then "select such parts as are most interesting, and calculated to benefit you."[55]

This account describing the "benefit" of reading about celebrated women such as Smith appeared not in an individual journal or post-humous memoir but in *Sketches of the Lives of Distinguished Females,* a collective biography first published in 1833 in New York. The work was framed as a series of biographical sketches carefully curated by the char-acter "Mrs. Greenville," which she then read aloud to her daughter and several other young women. Greenville presented accounts about several famous women from history, including Lady Jane Grey, Queen Elizabeth, and Queen Christina. She reserved special praise for "the incomparable Elizabeth Smith," expressing her wish that "you will be led to follow her example." After summarizing Smith's life, including lengthy extracts directly copied from *Fragments,* Mrs. Greenville instructed her young audience: "It is not as a linguist or a scholar that I hold her forth as a model, but I wish you to resemble her, my dear children, in her humble, unaffected piety, her cheerful submission to misfortune, . . . and her per-severance in the path of duty."[56] It was Smith's seemingly unblemished character, rather than her strong intellect, that earned the highest praise.

Sketches offered a fictionalized version of readers' responses that called explicit attention to the life lessons embedded within individual memoirs such as *Fragments* as well as collective biographies featuring scores of notable women. In its structure and content, then, this fictional work mirrored the actual reading experiences of many women who found models of affinity and emulation in *Fragments* and other works about learned women. *Sketches* helps illustrate how personal and public remembrances of Elizabeth Smith overlapped and informed each other over time.

A fictionalized account of readers' responses to Smith's life and writings also appeared in *The Two May-Days*, an 1844 short story that began as a rather formulaic, didactic tale about two schoolgirls. Despite stormy weather, the frivolous Laura Wilmot insists on going forward with the sparsely attended May Day ceremonies and catches a dreadful cold. Her classmate Emma Sydney makes the sensible decision to spend the day at home with her mother, "in such agreeable conversation, with books and works, [that] the hours flew swiftly by." The intended message was clear: "By indulging in ambition, bad temper, envy, or any other sin, we prepare for ourselves disappointment and misery." Laura learns her lesson and the next year spends May Day at Emma's cheerful home.[57]

This is where one might expect such a story to end, but for the last third of *The Two May-Days*, the literary representation and symbolic re-reading of Elizabeth Smith's memoir takes center stage. As they enjoy a quiet day together, Mrs. Sydney draws the girls' attention to a nearby book—"a Biography of Elizabeth Smith." *The Two May-Days* was published in 1844—nearly three decades after *Fragments* first appeared—yet Smith's memoir is presented as a work that Emma's mother had been "reading the other day." The girls are eager to learn more about Smith, and Emma's mother is happy to oblige: "You could scarcely have mentioned a subject of conversation more agreeable, profitable, or appropriate." As Mrs. Sydney reads selections from *Fragments* aloud, Laura and Emma learn how Elizabeth Smith devoted countless hours to her studies yet never sought the "applause of the world" or developed a conceited manner: "She never gave herself an air of consequence for genius, learning, or beauty; though she possessed them all." The girls are mesmerized and plead with Emma's mother to "tell us all you possibly can about this wonderful Elizabeth."[58]

Through this story-within-a-story-format, *The Two May-Days* provides a compelling exploration of the girls' growing admiration for Smith. As the hours fly by, Mrs. Sydney shares several stories from *Fragments*, including an account of George Smith's bankruptcy and subsequent loss of their family home. As Emma's mother describes how Elizabeth Smith cheerfully made a tart while her mother despaired at the meager state of their temporary lodgings in Ireland, she reminds the girls, "Should you make any attainment in learning, never scorn the allotted duties of woman's sphere." The lesson is again clear: no matter how accomplished, no woman should ever become *so* involved in her studies that she neglects her domestic duties. By the end of the story, the flighty Laura is converted and determines to "no longer waste my life in thoughtless follies."[59]

Works such as *Sketches of the Lives of Distinguished Females* and *The Two May-Days* present carefully curated, stylized accounts of seemingly personal responses to the act of reading *Fragments*. These works of conduct literature, which featured lengthy excerpts from *Fragments*, focused on fictional girls who were deeply moved by the real-life example of Elizabeth Smith, in stories clearly meant to guide actual readers embarking on their own educational journeys. Despite their obvious didactic tone, these fictional accounts of reading *Fragments* reflected the real-life experiences of learned women. Fact and fiction merged, creating strong affinities between female characters and their readers bound together by the era's contested ideas of learned womanhood. A portrait of Elizabeth Smith that appeared in a nineteenth-century periodical shows her with a stack of books nearby, suggesting the centrality of reading to her—and other women's—character formation (fig. 13).

In highlighting patterns of shared reading between mothers and daughters, these stories also suggest how generational transmissions of interest in *Fragments* contributed to Smith's enduring posthumous fame. Memoirs and biographies of accomplished women were purposefully shared by female family members. American educator Elizabeth Palmer Peabody recalled that when she was young, her mother "gave me the memoirs of many very learned women to read, such as Mrs. Elizabeth Carter, Madame Dacier, [and] Miss Elizabeth Smith."[60] In a family memoir

FIGURE 13. Portrait of Elizabeth Smith, shown reading with a pile of books on a nearby table, from the 1822 edition of London *Lady's Monthly Museum.* (© Trustees of the British Museum)

published in 1889, Anne Ogden Boyce described the reading habits of her relatives who came of age around the same time as Elizabeth Smith. As Boyce recalled, Smith's translations of Frederick and Margaret Klopstock's writings "excited great interest in Quaker circles," she explained, "not only on account of the attractive character of Meta Klopstock, but of the still more remarkable personality of the translator, Elizabeth Smith." Smith's posthumously published works had enduring appeal that helped create bonds between generations of learned women: "The 'Memoir of Frederick and Meta Klopstock,' and the 'Life of Elizabeth Smith,' by Miss Bowdler," Boyce noted, "were favourite books of the writer's mother, and are still treasured for her sake."[61] *Fragments* remained a "treasured" book even decades after her death, as Smith's legacy circulated in diverse forms of personal and printed remembrances.

The British author Margaret Gatty, as her daughter later recalled, developed "an early fit of hero-worship for Miss Elizabeth Smith." Gatty owned a copy of Smith's *Fragments*, in which she inscribed "the date 1820, with her name as Meta Scott; a form of her own Christian name which she probably adopted in honour of Margaretta—or Meta—Klopstock."[62] The sense of affinity that Gatty developed for Smith, as well as for Margaret Klopstock, the subject of Smith's work of German translation, illustrates the deep connections women forged through reading about other intellectually accomplished women. Gatty's youthful experience of "hero-worship" may have contributed to her decision to pursue a career as an author.

Both real and imagined examples of reading *Fragments* suggest that learned women's identities were shaped by compelling links between literary representations and lived experiences. Inspiring examples of Smith and other accomplished women lived in the various records circulating within transatlantic cultures of print. Early in her literary career, Harriet Martineau published an anonymous essay about the power of these literary role models, singling out the "well-known and universally-interesting Elizabeth Smith" as an illustrious example of "shining talents and humble virtue." Martineau highlighted the appeal of reading memoirs such as *Fragments*: "Eminent persons form the most interesting study. We love to observe in what respect we resemble them, and in what we differ from them, and to what their superiority is owing." Nineteenth-century readers were drawn to and inspired by biographical accounts of "eminent persons": "We make ourselves one with them, learn to enter into their feelings, to understand their motives of action." This desire to be "one with them" illustrates the strong connections forged between individual readers and the beloved literary figures they encountered in print.[63]

"The Admiration of the World"

As her posthumous fame grew, the celebrated Elizabeth Smith inspired numerous tributes from writers on both sides of the Atlantic. "It is very well to hold up such an extraordinary woman as Miss Smith to the admiration of the *world*," enthused a review of the *American Lady's Preceptor* published in the April 1811 issue of the *Baltimore Repertory*. Among the extensive conduct writings, poetry, and "biographical sketches of distinguished women" featured in the *American Lady's Preceptor*, the reviewer singled out the entry on Elizabeth Smith as worthy of particular commendation:

"Even in England, which abounds with distinguished females, her genius was contemplated with mingled emotions of astonishment and reverence." Smith's character offered "so illustrious an example" for young women "admirably calculated to excite their ambition and industry."[64]

In remarking that England "abounds with distinguished females," the *Baltimore Repertory* called to mind the transatlantic fame already achieved by several British women writers such as Hannah More and Elizabeth Montagu. The implication was that England was home to more learned women than America. Yet by the early nineteenth century, an increased number of American women were engaging in educational and literary pursuits on par with their British counterparts. As a result, conduct literature on both sides of the Atlantic often expressed similar concerns about the need for suitable role models to guide women's intellectual ambitions. For much of the nineteenth century, a wide array of poetry, essays, and books conveyed shared sensibilities about learned women, with many works reprinted and marketed in both England and America.

Works of collective female biography often linked together scores of notable women from across various times and places to promote idealized standards of womanhood. In several compilations, "the number of British names would be great and splendid," a point of British pride that some Americans could not help but notice.[65] In its 1829 review of Anna Maria Lee's *Eminent Female Writers, of All Ages and Countries,* the Boston *Ladies' Magazine* asserted American preferences for women worthy of commendation: "We do not, in our country, at least, want exhibitions of those talents and acquirements, which have fitted women to rule empires and manage state intrigues." The United States sought to discourage political ambitions in women, emphasizing their prescribed domestic and familial roles: "We want patterns of virtue, of intelligence, of piety and usefulness in private life." This reviewer particularly recommended the entry on Elizabeth Smith included in *Eminent Female Writers,* praising her "cultivated mind" coupled with "true piety of heart."[66] In highlighting Smith, a British woman, as an ideal example for American women to emulate, the *Ladies' Magazine* may have overstated its claims about the distinctiveness of prescriptive models of American womanhood. Despite a history of queens and noblewomen, British conduct writers also promoted feminine models of domesticity, rather than "state intrigues." As one London review essayist noted in 1814, "It is in England, and within the last thirty or forty years, that the progress of learning has been most extensive among women, and yet we see no reason to suppose they make worse wives, worse mothers, or less agreeable members of society."[67]

Elizabeth Smith's literary reputation was informed by—and helped reinforce—prevailing notions about women's intellectual capacities and prescriptive roles with transatlantic reach. Biographical sketches and other forms of conduct literature published in both America and England agreed that Elizabeth Smith was an "extraordinary and amiable character."[68] In many accounts, Smith was represented in idealized and exceptional terms: "As a model of self-culture Elizabeth Smith is unexcelled, if not unequalled, among women."[69] Many writings tended to follow similar conventions, describing Smith in glowing terms: an "extraordinarily ingenious and most excellent young lady," a "highly gifted and amiable young lady," "the celebrated Elizabeth Smith."[70]

There was a certain uniformity to these accounts, underscoring overlaps and connections within transatlantic cultures of print. Writers on both sides of the Atlantic repeatedly emphasized particular traits—intellect, piety, domesticity, and resignation—that Elizabeth Smith was thought to exemplify. In her works of conduct literature, including *Moral Pieces in Prose and Verse* and *Letters to Young Ladies*, American author Lydia Sigourney highlighted Smith's "invariable calmness, sweetness, and humility" in the face of adversity. "The celebrated Miss Elizabeth Smith," Sigourney noted, remained "still, unobtrusive, serious and meek" despite her impressive intellectual attainments. With these lines, Sigourney referenced Thomas Wilkinson's popular tribute poetry featured in *Fragments*, which reads, "Yet unobtrusive, serious, and meek."[71] In 1865, British conduct writer Charlotte Yonge expressed similar sentiments for the "well-known and charming Elizabeth Smith," who was "as pious and as humble, as she was learned and accomplished."[72] Recurring use of language and phrasing created nearly identical descriptions of Smith in works published in both America and England.

For decades after her death, admiring references to Elizabeth Smith appeared in conduct books, collective biographies, tribute poems, and periodical essays published in the United States and England.[73] Several collective biographies, including *Memoirs of Eminent Female Writers* by Anna Maria Lee, *Select Female Biography* by Mary Roberts, and Clara Lucas Balfour's *Women Worth Emulating,* featured Smith among their selections of worthy women.[74] At the nineteenth century's end, Smith was still considered significant enough to merit an entry in the 1898 edition of the *Dictionary of National Biography.*[75] Over time, then, even individuals who did not read *Fragments* may have encountered references to Smith in numerous published works.

These various tributes contributed to Smith's enduring fame while also offering broader insights into learned women's literary receptions within transatlantic cultures of print. Although literary celebrity was commonly associated with famous male authors such as Lord Byron and Walter Scott, by the early nineteenth century several British women in particular had "attained a high station in the temple of fame, by their literary accomplishments, such as Mrs. Elizabeth Carter, Miss Elizabeth Smith, Mrs. Montague, and many now living."[76] As a growing number of women achieved success in the literary marketplace, they often had to navigate ambivalent responses to their intellectual productions. Renowned literary lions such as William Wordsworth and Walter Scott were fêted as unique, creative geniuses worthy of admiration and fame, but even the most "exceptional" women authors faced scrutiny about whether and under what circumstances it was appropriate for them to participate in the literary public sphere.

Even commentators who expressed positive assessments of women's intellectual capacities warned about potential dangers. On both sides of the Atlantic, conduct writers expressed fears that learned women would abandon domestic duties and feminine charms in order to focus exclusively on their literary productions. One London essay praised the extent of "female talent" but asserted, "no female is justified in poring over the stores of learning, to the neglect of other more apparent duties."[77] To alleviate these concerns, commentators repeatedly stressed the need for women to balance learning with careful attention to femininity, piety, and humility. As one Boston commentator urged, "Let their attention be guided to those studies which will tend to make them wise, but not unassuming; useful, but not unamiable."[78] Such comments reflect deep-seated ambivalence about the forms, uses, and effects of women's educational achievements and literary productions.

Conduct writers explicitly appropriated Smith's example to make gendered claims about female intellect and identity. An 1821 essay published in Connecticut focused on Smith's successful balancing of learning and domesticity: "Miss Smith furnished an instance that it is possible for a woman to retain a fondness for literature, and even to become an adept in the sciences, without sacrificing the knowledge of domestic employments, or departing from those meek, humble, complying dispositions, which have a closer affinity with happiness than the possession of the most splendid talents."[79] Thirty years later, British author Clara Lucas Balfour celebrated "the good and learned Elizabeth Smith" not merely for her intellectual abilities but for her "gentle, industrious, unassuming, pious" nature. Smith deserved particular admiration for "neglecting no domestic duty, even while perfecting herself in a perfectly amazing knowledge of languages, ancient and modern."[80] Smith was repeatedly praised for offering a model of learned womanhood that was compatible with prescribed ideas about gender identity and roles.

For decades after her death, Elizabeth Smith represented the promise and potential of female genius, tempered by modesty and mildness and unsullied by problematic assertions of ambition and affectation. Conduct writers encouraged young women to view Smith as "an example eminently fitted to excite affectionate admiration and useful emulation."[81] She was deemed worthy of admiration and emulation not merely because of extensive scholarly acquirements but because she maintained her femininity, domesticity, and modesty *despite* her learned character.[82] As one author wrote, "In Elizabeth Smith, you find that the truly intelligent female is never fond of displaying her acquirements, and is as assiduous in the discharge of her domestic duties as in the pursuit of literature."[83] Young women were urged to follow Smith's example and warned against developing too much pride or ambition. As an 1841 essay on "What to Read" argued, "Some, who may have presumed too much on their own attainments, must have closed the memoirs of Elizabeth Smith with an amended self-appreciation."[84]

Tributes to Smith functioned as both celebratory and cautionary tales, highlighting the possibilities and limitations any woman faced in pursuit of a learned life. Her seemingly ideal character helped to question pejorative notions that "'a learned lady,' is the cant and sneer of barbarism." As an 1826 essayist insisted, "Were there no other example than that of Elizabeth Smith . . . it is enough to provide how false this opinion is." Smith's ability to balance intellectual pursuits with proper "female character" was within the reach of other learned women.[85] Even if other young women "fail to realize the heights to which she soared," an English writer mused in 1862, "her life may still to them be of the utmost value in prompting to fresh exertion and to renewed effort."[86]

Elizabeth Smith's posthumous fame highlights the literary practices and cultural attitudes that informed how learned women were represented within transatlantic cultures of print. For decades after her death, a series of interrelating references and representations served not only to celebrate Smith's individual accomplishments but also to promote an acceptable form of learned womanhood. Taken together, these various fragments—their forms, functions, and distribution patterns—underscore how transatlantic cultures of print sought to actively shape learned women's lives, writings, and reputations.

"None Have Done Greater Honour"

Writing in 1847, one London essayist enthusiastically declared, "Among the literary ladies of England—among the women of any time or country, whether literary or otherwise, we may say none, have done greater honour to their sex than Miss Elizabeth Smith."[87] Through a variety of manuscript and published tributes, Smith's legacy lived on long after her death, first in the pages of *Fragments* and then more expansively within transatlantic cultures of print. For decades after her death, both individual readers and conduct writers expressed their admiration for the celebrated Elizabeth Smith. Published works by well-known figures such as Hannah More, Felicia Hemans, Lydia Sigourney, and Joseph Story contributed to Smith's enduring afterlife, as did numerous individuals who shared their insights in personal letters, journals, and book margins. Stitched together, these fragments form a patchwork collage of her posthumous legacy across time and place.

The ardent and widespread admiration of Smith was possible in large part because individual readers and conduct writers alike rarely explicitly called attention to the more ambitious paths that learned women might have wished to explore. By repeatedly emphasizing the modest, domestic aspects of her character, tributes typically gave less space to Smith's bolder traits, such as her mountain climbing or restless desire for intellectual stimulation. Celebrations of Smith's seemingly ideal character drew attention away from her physical adventures and growing ambitions as a translator. Conduct writers often ignored or silenced those aspects of her life and writings that did not match their idealized representations. Through strategic retellings of Smith's lived experiences, many tributes attempted to shape the ways in which other learned women might emulate her example.

Over time, whether or not the "real" Elizabeth Smith matched the celebrated figure highlighted in letters, essays, and poems became less important than the stories told about her. Her legacy was crafted—and at times exploited—by writers seeking to present a safe, nonthreatening model of learned womanhood. In the afterlife, Smith's own fondness for rude, rocky precipices was often supplanted by carefully curated, flowery meadows. But not always. Despite efforts at narrowing her influence, Smith's life and writings took expansive forms and continued to inspire others. Writing in the 1861 *Atlantic Monthly*, Harriet Martineau referred to Elizabeth Smith as "an accomplished girl in all ways," highlighting her association with the Lake District's picturesque and sublime scenes of exploration: "We know from Mrs. Elizabeth Hamilton's and the Bowdlers' letters, how Elizabeth and her sister lived in the beauty about them, rambling, sketching, and rowing their guests on the lake."[88] The Lake District provided ideal landscapes for more compelling records of Smith's accomplishments. As her legacy spilled off pages and onto places, the celebrated Elizabeth Smith was able to maintain her preferred association with rocky precipices and rude mountains, even in the afterlife.

8

"To Tread in Thy Footsteps"

LITERARY TOURISM

IN THE SUMMER OF 1810, Marianne Fothergill of York conducted a tour of the Lake District, accompanied by her "amiable friend Thomas Wilkinson." After visiting William Wordsworth's home in Grasmere, Fothergill and Wilkinson traveled about ten miles to the church at Hawkshead. Fothergill "approached it with profound respect, as the remains of Elizabeth Smith lie within its hallowed walls." Upon viewing the inscription dedicated to Smith's "sainted memory," she "looked upon it till my eyes overflowed with tears, my heart was indescribably affected." The next day, Fothergill accompanied Wilkinson on a visit to the Smith family home in Coniston, where she was welcomed "with great politeness and warm cordiality." After visiting Smith's home and grave, Fothergill reflected, "Ah! How precious is her memory even to those who knew her only by her works, what then must it be to those who shared her friendship, and her affection." It was "some consolation," Fothergill noted, that even in death, Smith inspired "pilgrims in a reign of sorrow . . . to tread in thy footsteps."[1]

During her visit to the Lake District, Fothergill became friends with William Knight, another traveler. She recommended that he read *Fragments, in Prose and Verse.* Knight eagerly complied with her request, informing their mutual friend Thomas Wilkinson "how much I was delighted with 'Fragments of Miss Smith.'" Knight regretted not having visited Smith's grave before leaving the Lake District: "Had I known she was interred at Hawkshead I would have seen her Tomb.—I take great pleasure in visiting the Depositories of Genius."[2]

Marianne Fothergill and William Knight were among the growing number of nineteenth-century individuals in both England and America who engaged in physical and imaginative acts of "literary pilgrimage."[3] Literary tourism became an important element of the picturesque travel scene. Throughout the nineteenth century, men and women with sufficient leisure time, financial means, and well-read sensibilities added destinations associated with books and authors to their travel itineraries.[4] To achieve a heightened sense of connection with their favorite authors, some travelers sought, quite literally, to "tread in thy footsteps."

The practices of literary tourism represent a key aspect of Elizabeth Smith's enduring afterlife. By the early nineteenth century, both the Lake District and Smith's childhood home at Piercefield were considered renowned destinations on the picturesque travel map. After her death, Smith's association with these locations offered extra incentive for those seeking to pay homage to her. Of course, only a relatively small number of British and American travelers engaged in physical acts of literary pilgrimage, especially when compared to those who encountered Smith's legacy primarily through cultures of print. Yet such travels were symbolically significant, helping to enshrine her memory not only in the literary public sphere but in the physical locations most closely associated with her life and legacy.

"A Pilgrim to the Shrine of Worth and Departed Genius"

In 1827, Harriet Douglas of New York planned a visit to the Lake District. The Scottish author Anne Grant provided Douglas with letters of introduction to Robert Southey and Juliet Smith. Grant had only met Juliet Smith once, but they had "many mutual friends," including Elizabeth Smith's sister Kitty, who resided in Edinburgh after her marriage to Thomas Allan. Grant was confident that Juliet Smith "will be ready to honour my introduction" but provided Douglas with important advice. "The value of your introduction to Mrs. Smith at Coniston," Grant instructed Douglas, "depends on your having read the little Memoir and Letters of her daughter, the celebrated Elizabeth Smith, a creature of the highest attainments."

Grant assured Douglas that Juliet Smith "will, I think, be rather pleased with your pilgrimage to the shrine of her sainted daughter."[5] Once in the Lake District, Douglas willingly complied with Grant's instructions, eager to present herself as a worthy visitor. Upon meeting Juliet Smith, Douglas was described by a local resident "as a 'Pilgrim to the Shrine of Worth & *departed* Genius' (meaning Elizabeth Smith)."[6] Such comments reflected how Smith's reputation as a celebrated genius was a key component of her posthumous legacy, especially in the Lake District.

Harriet Douglas was the quintessential literary tourist, eager to tread in the footsteps of acclaimed authors. Her pilgrimage to the Smith family home was one of many visits that Douglas conducted to places associated with notable literary figures throughout England, Ireland, and Scotland. The American woman was explicit and unapologetic about her desire to meet, converse, and correspond with famous literary figures such as Scott and Wordsworth. "Her object in Traveling seems to be *Lions*," Sara Hutchinson, William Wordsworth's sister-in-law, noted. "As Southey says she [is] never happy except in a Lions Den."[7]

Hutchinson, Robert Southey, and other members of their social and literary circle poked fun at Douglas's keen interest in the literary lions. "She was so bewitched with all she saw," Hutchinson wrote to the poet Edward Quillinan, describing Douglas as "a most ingenuous and enthusiastic creature" with "the oddest manners."[8] After his meeting with Douglas, Walter Scott disparaged her as "a professed lion-huntress" full of "affectation."[9] Her friend Anne Grant acknowledged that Douglas was "quite a character" but focused on "her good qualities," including "sincerity, candour, a perfect sunshine of good humour." Grant recognized that Douglas's enthusiasm stemmed from "a profound admiration of talent."[10] Ultimately, the brash Douglas won the affections of many members of the literary circles that she so ardently admired. Hutchinson softened her earlier opinion, acknowledging that "she is really worthy of knowing—quite an oddity—but overflowing with kindness & generosity."[11] Wordsworth personally extended an invitation to Douglas if she returned to the Lake District: "Pray let us see you here—I have plenty of room in my house."[12]

A wealthy, well-read, and well-connected individual, Douglas was part of an elite, select group of nineteenth-century travelers from both Great

Britain and the United States who engaged in acts of literary tourism.[13] Her relationships with Anne Grant, Maria Edgeworth, and other notable authors provided her with letters of introduction that enabled her to meet Scott, Wordsworth, Southey, and other acclaimed literary lions. Such social connections, confirmed by letters of introduction, allowed privileged travelers to navigate literary circles and tourist scenes. Having access to influential personal and social networks literally opened doors to the most sought-after locations on the literary tourism map.

Harriet Douglas benefited from her socioeconomic privilege and connections, but her warm admiration and keen enthusiasm for literary celebrity was by no means unique. The growth of a transatlantic celebrity culture venerating distinguished authors, both living and dead, took root during the nineteenth century. Literary tourism privileged the power of texts, places, and objects to create a heightened sense of connection with beloved literary figures. Readers first developed imaginative bonds of affinity with authors and books "through intense and engaged private reading experience."[14] As they read, individuals imagined themselves in the settings and scenes that were central to their favorite authors and stories. Inspired by their reading habits, some enthusiasts sought out physical visits to key locations to experience "a kind of immediacy that reading alone at home could not supply."[15] Throughout the nineteenth century, a number of individuals sought to visit the "homes and haunts" of famous authors. The opportunity to conduct a pilgrimage to a location associated with a beloved author or book represented an ultimate form of tribute. Such ritualistic practices took readers' admiration to the next level, inscribing geographical places with meaning "far beyond the page."[16]

The Lake District was an ideal setting for the development of literary tourism. By the early nineteenth century, the region was a popular destination on the picturesque travel scene. Its inspiring landscapes resonated with visitors long after their return home. "Often do I lift up my eyes as if to behold, your mountains and beautiful scenery," Marianne Fothergill wrote to Thomas Wilkinson, "where I found so much to admire and love."[17] The region's enchanting vistas inspired an intense, deeply personal style of exploration that was distinct from seemingly formulaic, commercialized forms of tourism. Discerning travelers were encouraged to immerse themselves in the region's sublime settings. "Do not ride along the border of that region at the rate of forty a miles an hour on the railway, and then assert that you have seen it," one mid-nineteenth-century essayist implored. To truly appreciate the Lake District, one needed to "walk for hundreds of miles along the margins of the lakes and on the mountainsides."[18]

The desire for authentic, meaningful connections with sublime, picturesque landscapes readily translated into veneration of the notable poets and authors associated with the Lake District. As Anne Grant mused to Harriet Douglas: "These Lake poets are of the excellent of the earth; living peacefully in the bosom of nature."[19] William Wordsworth, Robert Southey, and other Lakers were celebrated for cultivating a "sanctuary of genius." Their way of living was "so talented, so pure, so every way amiable, enjoying in the beautiful bosom of nature so much of all that wealth cannot purchase."[20]

Over time, the Lake District became as renowned for its literary figures as for its sublime landscapes. Referred to as "the wildest, most romantic portion" of England, the Lake District was celebrated for its "charming" scenes of nature as well as "the conservation of genius." Inspirational spots were valued for having symbolic connections with notable individuals. As one essayist recalled after completing a tour of the Lake District in 1853: "I listened to the morning hymn of nature in the same place where William Wilberforce listened. . . . The rosebud planted by Mrs. Hemans I fondly bent over. . . . I worshipped during the hours of a long northern twilight, in the garden of Wordsworth. . . . I stood by the grave of Elizabeth Smith, at the sight of which the wild Byron's heart melted with him. . . . I paused by the dwelling-place of the immortal Coleridge."[21] Along with seeking to tread in the footsteps of famous male poets such as Wordsworth and Coleridge, nineteenth-century literary tourists to the Lake District venerated locations affiliated with Elizabeth Smith, Felicia Hemans, and other women.

Historical and cultural interest in the Lake District is now virtually synonymous with Wordsworth and other Romantic-era male poets. Yet for much of the nineteenth century, the area was associated with a number of literary women, including Smith, Hemans, and Harriet Martineau. In an essay published in the May 1861 issue of the *Atlantic Monthly*, Martineau reached elite American readers interested in acts of literary tourism. A longtime Lake District resident, Martineau gave Smith a place of honor in helping to develop the region's cultural and literary reputation: "Before the Lake poets began to give the public an interest in the District, some glimpses of it were opened by the well-known literary ladies of the last century who grouped themselves round their young favorite, Elizabeth Smith." Reflecting on Smith's legacy over fifty years after her death, Martineau asserted, "It was through her that a large proportion of the last generation of readers first had any definite associations with Coniston."[22]

Perhaps Martineau overstated Smith's influence in the Lake District, yet her sentiments accurately reflect women's strong contributions to celebrity culture and literary tourism. "Literary ladies" were among the many readers, writers, and travelers who engaged in the practices of literary tourism. Women openly traversed the same well-traveled paths as notable male Lake District visitors and residents. Accounts of their experiences can be found in unpublished letters and journals, as well as in published essays and travel guides, penned by both British and American tourists and guidebook authors. In some cases, women such as Harriet Douglas made their presence loudly known. Other women travelers, including Marianne Fothergill, drew less attention to themselves, yet their experiences and contributions can be seen and felt in many sources.

Through a close look at pages and places, we can find evidence of Elizabeth Smith's legacy, along with activities by other "literary ladies," hiding in plain sight against picturesque backgrounds.[23] Women's presence and influence is evident in various accounts of literary tourism, especially in the Lake District, a region particularly renowned for cultivating genius. With its enchanting landscapes and celebrated authors, the Lake District served as an ideal backdrop for the development of literary tourism. There was, perhaps, no more fitting location for a "Shrine of Worth and *departed* Genius" in Elizabeth Smith's honor.

"Localities Mentioned in the Beautiful Fragments"

In 1835, Harvard professor George Ticknor conducted an "excursion up Coniston Water." His guide was none other than William Wordsworth, by then the Lake District's most celebrated resident. As Ticknor recalled, "To show us the best points he carried us to the houses of two of his friends. The first was Mrs. Copley's. . . . The other place was that of the venerable Mrs. Smith,—the mother of the extraordinary Miss Smith." During his outing to Coniston, Ticknor visited "the site of the tent" where Smith spent her last days convalescing and "the other localities mentioned in the beautiful 'Fragments,' printed after her premature death."[24] Ticknor was accompanied by his daughter Anna, who fondly recalled how Smith's "early loveliness and talent made so great an impression on my mind and memory."[25]

In the years after her death, Elizabeth Smith's Lake District home served as both the family residence and a revered memorial. In 1808, the Smith family began renovations to their Coniston lodgings, replacing their damp "old Cottage" with a new home. "I mean to call this little favorite spot *Tent Lodge*," Juliet Smith informed Thomas Wilkinson, explaining that the family home's new name referred "to the circumstances in the Book, of my Elizabeth's sitting in the Tent" during her illness. While reflecting on the scenic vistas from her tent's location, Elizabeth Smith had suggested the spot would "be a desirable situation for the House."[26]

Through both its location and name, Tent Lodge served as a physical tribute to Elizabeth Smith. Tent Lodge also represented the Smith family's financial security and social status in the Lake District, hard-earned after years of dislocation. In 1810, Juliet Smith was "surprised by a Legacy of a thousand pounds, from an old Schoolfellow." This "unexpected" gift enabled her to "now finish, and furnish my House."[27] Unfortunately, the family also endured additional heartache and grief. Three more of Juliet Smith's adult children died between 1810 and 1817, before her husband's death in 1822. "Few have met with more repeated trials of various kinds," one family friend sadly noted.[28]

Despite her grief and loss, Juliet Smith made a home for herself in the Lake District. She became known as a "sort of a queen" of Lake District society, admired for her "kindness and hospitality."[29] Friends and neighbors referred to her with fondness. "Every time I see this admirable and interesting woman," one local resident wrote, "increases my love for her and my gratitude for her kindness."[30] Juliet Smith enjoyed warm and cordial relationships with notable Lake District residents, including

Wordsworth, who occasionally conducted his own "very agreeable visit at Tent Lodge."[31] While visiting Juliet Smith with Wordsworth, Anna Ticknor was impressed by "the respectful attention of his manner to her."[32]

Over time, Juliet Smith became renowned as "the mother of the excellent Elizabeth Smith."[33] Friends and acquaintances conducted ritualistic visits to Tent Lodge to pay respect to Juliet Smith and to honor her daughter's memory. In 1809, Harriet Bowdler learned that her protégé Eliza Simcoe—who had met and socialized with Elizabeth Smith in Bath—was traveling to the Lake District. Bowdler encouraged her young friend to visit Juliet Smith: "If you go to Coniston pray introduce yourself to my dear Mrs. Smith. You will look with interest on *Tent Lodge,* and on the humble Tomb of my angel friend in Hawkshead Church."[34] Of course, travelers to the area, even those with direct ties to the Smith family, did not visit the region merely to see Elizabeth Smith's home and grave. Yet for many visitors, Tent Lodge and other spots associated with Smith became notable features of the Lake District travel experience. As part of his tour in 1810, Louis Simond, a French-born American merchant, was "shewn the house of the parents of a young lady lately dead (Miss E. Smith), who has since become so justly celebrated, by the proofs she left behind her of an erudition uncommon for her age and her sex."[35]

In the decades after her death, Smith's connection to the region became an ever more firmly embedded point of interest for travelers. Her memory became enshrined within her family home, gravesite, and other locations in the Lake District. Tour books included "Tent Lodge, formerly the residence of Miss Elizabeth Smith, a lady of extraordinary acquirements" as a stop on their recommended travel itineraries.[36] Her family home and gravesite became key spots venerated by artists, residents, and tourists (fig. 14). Local artist and Smith family friend William Green recommended Tent Lodge in his 1819 *The Tourist's New Guide.* He praised Elizabeth Smith as "justly celebrated for her uncommon literary attainments" and lamented her early death: "What fruits might we not have expected from mental endowments like these, had time been permitted to mature the labours of her mind!"[37]

Travel writers offered romanticized accounts of Elizabeth Smith's family home as well as her explorations in the Lake District. "The

FIGURE 14. *Coniston Water with Tent Lodge*, by Joseph M. Turner (1818), showing the Smith family's Lake District home built after 1808. (© Fitzwilliam Museum, Cambridge)

low-roofed cottage at Coniston," an 1824 essay noted, "has become a classic spot to rambling tourists; the little fairy boat, which with nymph-life grace she so often navigated under the romantic cliffs, is now a sacred relic." The mountain near Smith's Coniston home "which had been her favourite haunt, is cherished for her sake."[38] Harriet Martineau's *Complete Guide to the English Lakes* recommended that travelers explore particular spots that were personally meaningful to Smith: "The boat-house is at the bottom of the slope, down which she used to take her mother's guests; and she and her sister were so well practiced at the oar that they could show the beauties of the scene from any point of the lake."[39] In *The Land We Live In*, British writer Charles Knight offered a similar account: "In these waters it was that Elizabeth Smith used to dip her oar, on those summer days when she left her study to show the beauty of Coniston to her mother's guests."[40]

Even Wordsworth wrote about Smith in an early draft of his guide to the region. He included detailed descriptions of Smith's character as well as specific locations associated with her memory. In his account of the church where Smith was buried, Wordsworth remarked, "Nor can I omit noticing that the Church contains a plain marble slab sacred to the memory of Eliz. Smith." Wordsworth referred to Smith as an "extraordinary young Person," expressing particular admiration for her "attachments to scenes of nature" and her adventurous explorations: "The loftiest peaks that were accessible to female feet had been trodden by her light steps, & the deepest dells were not unknown to her." Although Wordsworth omitted his remarks about Smith in his published guidebooks, he recognized her story's appeal to Lake District travelers.[41] Wordsworth was certainly familiar with Smith's life and legacy. He personally conducted visitors to her family home and wrote to Juliet Smith on behalf of "particular friends" wishing to see "charming views from the front of Tent Lodge."[42] Wordsworth's reasons for not including Smith in his published guide are unknown. He frequently explored the Lake District with his sister Dorothy and clearly understood the region's appeal to women travelers such as Harriet Douglas and Anna Ticknor. Perhaps he did not wish to draw attention to a woman who accomplished the same daring explorations presumed to be the inspiration for his own creative powers.

More than anyone else, the Lake District resident most responsible for Elizabeth Smith's enduring connection with the region was Thomas Wilkinson. He was known to readers of *Fragments, in Prose and Verse* for his tribute poetry highlighting Smith's fearless explorations of the Lake District's sublime landscapes: "How scal'd th' aerial cliffs th' adven'trous maid, / Whilst, far beneath, her foil'd companions staid?" Wilkinson's verses celebrated the many adventures and climbs they took together: "Can I forget, on many a summer's day, / How through the woods and lanes we wont to stray. . . . How arduous o'er the mountains steeps to go, / And look by turns on all the plains below."[43] He provided firsthand knowledge celebrating Smith's courageous and adventurous spirit. Wilkinson's tribute poetry, as well as his status as a trusted friend who had personally explored the region with Smith, earned him a reputation as a trusted caretaker of her legacy. Wilkinson played a unique role in sustaining Smith's enduring fame, especially for literary pilgrims to the Lake District.

"Your Affectionate Tribute to Her Memory"

Readers of *Fragments* were familiar with Wilkinson's tribute poetry and his letters about Smith, which were prominently featured in her memoir. As one friend noted, "Your name was not unknown to him as the friend of Miss E. Smith, in the posthumous account of which interesting character he has read with pleasure your affectionate tribute to her memory."[44] In addition to his verses published in *Fragments*, Wilkinson was admired for his poem "Emont Vale," which widely circulated in manuscript form among his friends and acquaintances for years before its publication in 1824. In the years before the poem was published, Wilkinson's friends, particularly those who had visited the Lake District, copied out the poem for others or "let him have mine to transcribe himself."[45] In urging Wilkinson "to print" his various writings, his friend Mary Leadbeater wrote admirably: "Thy Prose & Poetry have both the stamp of originality, and a something which we can feel but not describe."[46]

"Emont Vale" offered a sweeping homage to the inspiring landscapes and notable poets and reformers associated with the Lake District: "With eyes of poesy and breasts of flame, / Here Wordsworth, Southey, Scott, and Coleridge came." Wilkinson's poem also included affectionate references to the Smith family: "Through these lone wilds with female worth I've stray'd, / With virtuous mother, or with studious maid." Like his tribute poetry included in *Fragments*, "Emont Vale" emphasized Elizabeth Smith's affinity with Lake District landscapes:

Here modest Smith in blest retirement dwelt.
Though pious, she the charms of Nature felt:—
In these green vales she was a lovely light
Around our dwellings, innocently bright![47]

Through both his poetic talents and kind disposition, Wilkinson developed a reputation as a beloved resident of the Lake District. "His poetry & his letters have a peculiar character of native taste," Mary Leadbeater reflected.[48] His social and literary connections extended across wide-ranging networks, including William Wordsworth, Thomas Clarkson, and other notable figures from the region: "He is well known, & of consequence well esteemed by persons of high rank."[49]

Travelers to the area regularly called on Wilkinson for advice and guidance. "I know not whether the short acquaintance I have had with my frd Thomas Wilkinson is sufficient to authorize the liberty I am about to take," one woman wrote in 1810, seeking his assistance with her planned visit "to see the lakes."[50] Marianne Fothergill's friend William Knight sought Wilkinson's expertise on behalf of a traveling friend, who "has never yet seen a Mountain, nor a Waterfall." Knight offered suggestions based on his own recent visit to the region but called on Wilkinson's "kindness to direct him respecting Ullswater, the *Elysium Fields, Lowther Castle, &c.*"[51] Another acquaintance wrote to introduce Wilkinson to "three Ladies Aunts of mine who on their journey to the Lakes wish to gratify their taste for simple pleasures by a visit to his dwelling."[52]

For individuals specifically interested in conducting acts of literary pilgrimage in Elizabeth Smith's honor, Thomas Wilkinson was a particularly valuable resource. Travelers who wished to visit Tent Lodge hoped to benefit from Wilkinson's close connections with the Smith family. In 1819, Mary Leadbeater wrote to Wilkinson with a special request on behalf of a friend traveling to the Lake District: "I would wish her to be introduced to the notice of Juliet Smith." Leadbeater highlighted that her friend had "superior gifts of mind bestowed upon her," aware that such traits would be admired by her Lake District friends.[53] Leadbeater was an old family friend of Juliet Smith, yet she understood how an introduction from Wilkinson was certain to open doors to Tent Lodge and other sought-after locations. As individuals such as Marianne Fothergill discovered, exploring the Lake District with Thomas Wilkinson promised insider access far beyond what many travelers to the region might expect.

For Elizabeth Smith's most enthusiastic admirers, Thomas Wilkinson provided unmatched opportunities to tread in her footsteps. In 1815, a gentleman wrote to Wilkinson on behalf of his friend William Peter Lunnell, a Bristol merchant who was visiting the Lake District with his family. "Having thro' the writings of Elizth Smith, & probably by other means become acquainted with thy name," Lunnell "wishes very much to call upon thee."[54] With Wilkinson's assistance, Lunnell secured an invitation to visit Tent Lodge. Juliet Smith welcomed such pilgrimages. As she noted to Wilkinson, "I feel desirous of knowing those who esteem the memory of my Elizabeth." She was "particularly pleased" with Lunnell's visit. After their meeting, Lunnell asked Wilkinson to inquire if she would be willing to send him "some writing or drawing of dear Elizabeth's."[55] As Lunnell later informed Wilkinson, Juliet Smith complied with his request and "sent me, of dear Elizabeth's, several Sketches of the Scenery of the Lake." Lunnell was deeply moved by Juliet Smith's generosity: "These Sketches given me by Mrs. Smith are placed among my Treasures."[56] While Lunnell gained access to the Smith family home in part because of Wilkinson's introduction, he must have made a strong impression to inspire Juliet Smith to part with such "treasures."

The desire for some sort of relic or keepsake associated with a deceased literary figure was a particular feature of what scholar Paul Westover refers to as the era's "necromanticism." Relics served as tangible markers of remembrance that seemed to contain part of a departed individual's spirit. As Lunnell mused to Wilkinson, "So it is you and others are so fond of drawings and Autography—because there is so much Mind connected with them."[57] Those who treasured drawings and writings believed that some essence of an individual's unique character was inscribed onto the page. William Lunnell was not the only individual to express an interest in possessing a material remembrance related to Elizabeth Smith. After his visit to the Lake District, John Griscom, an educator from New York, asked Wilkinson for "any little relic of Elizabeth Smith," such as "a specimen of her handwriting."[58] One woman wrote to Wilkinson "on behalf of a friend of mine who is a collector of autographs and who is very desirous of obtaining one of E. Smith's." Despite being "unknown to thee personally," this correspondent was familiar with Wilkinson's strong connection to Smith and "cannot think of any one more likely to be in the possession of some of her writing than thyself."⁵⁹ Another admirer was reported to have "travelled to seek a relic of her, and at last procured a shoe."⁶⁰

A visit to a specific place, or a treasured relic, made the imaginative connections first formed by reading seem more real. Relics served as material embodiments of the strong bonds of affinity forged by acts of literary tourism. These practices mirrored and replicated the ritualistic forms of personal mourning and remembrance that were believed to enshrine a loved one's spirit in symbolic places and objects. "I somehow do not feel that she is dead to me," Juliet Smith mused. "I fancy that she accompanies me in solitary walks, and is a partaker in my best thoughts."⁶¹

Admirers who sought the experience of holding a scrap of Elizabeth Smith's writing or treading in her footsteps sought meaningful connections with places, objects, and pursuits most closely associated with her memory. "Were I to visit Cumberland again," Thomas Robinson mused to his friend Thomas Wilkinson, "how interested I should be in hearing thee speak of Elizth Smith, and in seeing some of thy, no doubt, treasured relics of that departed friend!"⁶² Through such physical and imaginative encounters, Smith's spirit lived on.

"Elizabeth Smith Also Delighted to Wander"

Reflecting on the time that the British poet Felicia Hemans spent in Wales during her youth, American writer Lydia Sigourney mused, "It is an interesting coincidence, that amid the romantic regions of Conway, which she visited with such rapture, the lovely and accomplished Elizabeth Smith also delighted to wander." Although Hemans and Smith never met, Sigourney imagined the sublime scenery of Wales acting as a conduit between these two like-minded women: "Though personally unknown to each other, it might have been on the margin of the same clear lake—in the depths of the same embosomed vale—that the 'beautiful came floating o'er their soul.'"⁶³ Sigourney envisioned Smith and Hemans as kindred spirits whose bonds of affinity stretched across time, print, and place. Indeed, such imaginative connections infused the tribute poetry that

Hemans wrote in Smith's honor: "E'en *now*, thy seraph-eyes, / Undimm'd by doubt, nor veil'd by fear, / Behold a chain of wonders rise; / Gaze on the noon-beam of the skies."[64]

The intellectual pursuits, picturesque landscapes, and imaginative musings that were so fulfilling to Elizabeth Smith during her lifetime resonated with individuals who sought to enshrine her sacred memory and follow in her footsteps. Along with visiting Smith's home and grave, Marianne Fothergill accompanied Thomas Wilkinson on a mountain-climbing expedition during her travels in the Lake District. "After much weary exertion having climbed a steep ascent of about three miles," Fothergill and Wilkinson found themselves "by the side of a steep precipice." Perhaps inspired by Smith's fearless adventures, Fothergill expressed "resolution and fortitude," but Wilkinson "declared it was unsafe to proceed any further."[65] In deference to Wilkinson's wishes, she reluctantly turned back but retained an adventurous spirit that resembled Smith's. During a "pedestrian tour" of Wales in 1815, Fothergill "ascended Snowdon" and "had a glimpse" of the Ladies of Llangollen.[66] Through her reading of *Fragments* and friendship with Wilkinson, Fothergill certainly would have been familiar with and inspired by Smith's explorations of these same locations.

Select readers of *Fragments* welcomed the opportunity to visit locations where Smith had once wandered. When "James Henry, a fine youth, an enthusiastic admirer of the character of Elizabeth Smith," visited Mary Leadbeater in Ireland, "he was delighted to see the spot she had once inhabited" before the Smith family moved to the Lake District.[67] Such acts of literary tourism underscored the belief, as one essayist noted, that "there is even something in local associations to endear her to remembrance."[68] Powerful bonds of affinity were forged through the intertwined practices of readers' responses and literary pilgrimage.

For some admirers of Elizabeth Smith, the chance to visit her childhood home at Piercefield and its celebrated walks was a particularly inspiring experience. In 1813, one traveler enthusiastically described her "excursion to Piercefield, once the residence of the lovely Elizabeth Smith." During her visit, "the interesting life of the former occupier, was the subject of my thoughts," she mused. "I again felt an earnest desire, that the influence of her example might have due weight on myself."[69]

Thirty years after Smith's death, Louisa Crawford published an essay in a London periodical describing her visit to Smith's childhood home. In praising Piercefield's "natural beauties," Crawford remarked that the location evoked "still deeper interest from its having been the abode of early piety and genius." Like other literary pilgrims, Crawford was inspired to visit a location so closely associated with Smith's "extraordinary attainments." Smith's legacy remained embedded in Crawford's mind: "Often have I stopped at the bookseller's at Clifton, to contemplate her sweet face, so different from the worldly ones passing around me."[70]

In her published essay, Crawford noted that tour guides capitalized on Piercefield's association with "the beautiful Miss Smith," pointing out locations such as "a summer-house in the pleasure-grounds where she used to write."[71] During her lifetime, Smith's childhood home at Piercefield was already well known as a must-see location for its scenic walkways and picturesque views. For example, William Coxe's *Historical Tour in Monmouthshire,* first published in 1801, referred to George Smith's renovations to Piercefield but made no mention of his daughter Elizabeth. At the time, the living Elizabeth Smith had not achieved celebrity status, and so her association with Piercefield would not have been considered remarkable.[72] After Smith's death in 1806, several guidebooks began to specifically highlight Piercefield as the former "residence of the family of the celebrated Elizabeth Smith."[73] As John Evans noted in *The Picture of Bristol,* "This is now classic ground for its association with the memory of Miss Smith." Smith's former residence "give an additional charm even to the beauties of Piercefield."[74] In his *Gazetteer of the Most Remarkable Places in the World,* Thomas Bourn mentioned Smith in his entries on the Smith family estate at Burn Hall, noting, "Miss Elizabeth Smith, an amiable and learned lady, was born here in 1776." He described Piercefield as "the residence of Miss Elizabeth Smith, an accomplished and learned young lady."[75]

For decades after her death, various locations associated with Elizabeth Smith captivated the imaginations of readers and travelers. In 1819, British resident Elizabeth Selwyn conducted a tour through Wales, visiting several locations mentioned by Smith in her memoir. While in Wales, Selwyn climbed Snowdon, proudly noting that she and her companions "were attended by the same guide, who formerly accompanied Miss Elizabeth Smith." Whether or not Selwyn's guide was actually the same individual who accompanied Smith on her climb twenty years earlier, Selwyn gave significance to this purported connection. Three years later, Selwyn traveled to the Lake District. There, she visited Hawkshead and "saw the tablet to the memory of the celebrated Miss Elizabeth Smith."[76] Selwyn gave meaning to her travel explorations by explicitly placing them in the context of Smith's lived adventures and posthumous legacy. When Selwyn's travel journals were published in 1824, her references to these locations may have encouraged other travelers to follow in her own footsteps.

The links between page and place also found expression through the medium of poetry. Romantic-era writers privileged poetry as a form of writing that could "enable vivid, imaginary contact with the dead."[77] Tribute poems written about Elizabeth Smith, such as Felicia Hemans's "Lines, Written in the Memoirs of Elizabeth Smith," emphasized the importance of *Fragments* as a material *text*. Hemans's poem rested on the notion that the act of reading Smith's memoir inspired her to compose her verses right in the margins of the book. Other poems composed in Smith's honor explicitly employed the power of *place* to evoke a heightened sense of connection with a literary figure. In his "Lines Written on Reading the Memoirs of Miss Smith," Scottish writer and literary critic John Wilson described the enthusiastic responses he experienced not only by *reading* Smith's memoir, as his poem's title suggests, but in *visiting* the Lake District. Wilson imagined that Smith's spirit haunted the landscapes and mountains where she used to wander during her residence there: "Oft 'mid the calm of mountain solitude, . . . / I feel thy influence on my heart descend." As Wilson roamed the region, he felt Smith's presence: "And every cloud in lovelier figures roll, / Shaped by the power of thy presiding soul!"[78] Wilson's poem vividly captured the Romantic-era notion that both texts and places could inspire a heightened sense of connection with literary figures, living and dead.

Gravesites were considered particularly inspiring locations for generating imaginative connections with deceased figures. "Lines on the Late Miss Elizabeth Smith," an anonymous poem published in 1816, evokes the powerful effects believed to be associated with a person's burial site: "But pensive oft shall virtues friend / Approach, in tears, her simple tomb, / And genius o'er her ashes bend, / To mourn a sister's early doom."[79] The grave was regarded as a physical and symbolic repository of a departed figure's genius, underscoring why visits to burial sites represented an important element in literary tourism.

In 1828, sixteen-year-old British poet Mary Ann Browne published *Ada, and Other Poems,* which included the poem "To the Memory of Elizabeth Smith: Supposed to be Written by Her Grave." That same year, Browne's poem about Smith was reprinted in the *Friend,* a Quaker magazine published out of Philadelphia. No further identifying information was provided, suggesting that Philadelphia readers would be familiar with Smith twenty years after *Fragments* was first published. Like other tribute poems, the framing and setting of Browne's poem reveal key aspects of nineteenth-century literary tourism:

> It is with a strange sympathy
> I look upon thy name,
> And not without a wish that I
> Might be the very same:
> So loved, so blessed in thy life—
> So soon set free from earthly strife![80]

Like other tribute poems, Browne's verses recounted the strong emotions evoked by a visit to a gravesite. The "supposed" in Browne's title may have been a literary device to signal an imagined setting, rather than an actual visit. The use of the term "supposed" may also have been in reference to the Romantic-era ideal that "on-the-spot" compositions at inspiring locations were highly valued as a means of capturing the authentic experiences privileged by picturesque travel. In reality, such seemingly immediate compositions were often heavily edited, stylized literary constructs written after the fact to conform to prevailing literary conventions. Whether she actually visited Smith's grave or conjured the scene as an imaginative tribute, Browne underscored the Romantic-era belief that particular locations could impart strong feelings of connection with departed literary figures.

The chance to physically visit and reflect on Smith's grave, poets such as Browne recognized, deepened the "strange sympathy" initially developed through reading *Fragments*. Whether or not Browne's poem was truly written graveside, she clearly identified with Smith's accomplishments. She ended her poem with a "wish, whilst gazing on thy shrine, / My life, my death, might be like thine![81] Browne's wish referenced her admiration of Smith's character and talents, as well as her enduring posthumous fame. As one review essay noted, Browne's tribute represented "the natural sentiment of one gifted girl, thinking of the untimely fate of another."[82]

As literary tourism developed, both real and imaginative encounters with significant locations were embedded into a variety of literary forms and textual sources. Readers and travelers experienced a heightened sense of connection to individuals, locations, and events first encountered on the page. The publication of Smith's memoir inspired readers to imagine themselves exploring the same scenic landscapes that she described. In the process, her legacy became rooted in specific geographical locations as well as widely disseminated within transatlantic cultures of print.

"Comes Forward Formidably with a Thousand Pages"

In 1819, John Griscom, a New York educator and Quaker, visited the Lake District as part of his tour of Scotland, England, and other parts of Europe. Griscom kept a detailed journal of his travels. He "comes forward formidably with a thousand Pages," Thomas Wilkinson reflected. "He has been an indefeatable observer."[83] Griscom's two-volume travel journal, *A Year in Europe*, was published in 1823, with a second edition appearing the following year. Its publication illustrates how the practices of literary tourism were rooted in both place and print. Travelers were encouraged to record and share the experiences of literary pilgrimage, whether penned in a personal letter to a trusted friend or shared widely in a published travel guide. The widespread dissemination of individuals' encounters at key locations shaped the development of celebrity culture and literary tourism on both sides of the Atlantic.

Griscom's published account of his travels reflected cultural sensibilities showcasing the appeal of literary tourism, particularly in the Lake District. During his time in the region, he met with leading literary figures, including Wordsworth and Southey. Like Harriet Douglas, George Ticknor, and other well-connected travelers, Griscom benefited from social and literary networks that opened doors to desired locations and invitations to converse with celebrated authors. He arrived at Wordsworth's home with a "letter of introduction" from a respected Lake District resident. As Griscom fondly recalled, Wordsworth "received me with as much affability and kindness, as if I had been an old acquaintance." Griscom enjoyed a brief but intimate visit with Wordsworth: "Finding my time was short he proposed a walk" to point out the "interesting scenery."[84]

After visiting with Wordsworth, Griscom continued his travels north to Patterdale to meet with Wilkinson. Griscom stopped at the same inn where, "as I afterward learned," Walter Scott and William Wordsworth were inadvertently kept out of their lodgings by Elizabeth Smith and her companions: "They separated from the inn, without seeing each other, much to the subsequent regret of the parties, when they respectively found who their inmates had been."[85] Griscom enjoyed relaying the coincidence of having visited the same spot where these two groups of travelers had unknowingly been in such close proximity to each other. Acts of literary tourism privileged the power of place to create imagined connections and affinities with admired figures.

Upon arriving in Patterdale, John Griscom was invited to spend the night at Thomas Wilkinson's home, where he enjoyed "unaffected hospitality." During his stay with Wilkinson, Griscom was especially eager to hear more about Elizabeth Smith, as her "literary attainments and moral excellence, have claimed the admiration of all who have perused the interesting narrative of her life." Griscom's comments reflected how the publication of *Fragments* contributed to Smith's posthumous fame. Many American and British audiences would have already been familiar with Smith through reading *Fragments* and other published tributes that celebrated her life and writings. Griscom's own interest in Smith was inspired not only from reading her memoir but from personal encounters. As part of his European tour, Griscom had spent time in Edinburgh, where he met Thomas Allan, the husband of Elizabeth's sister Kitty, along with other individuals who knew and admired Elizabeth Smith. After hearing so much about Smith's legacy, Griscom especially welcomed the opportunity to converse with Wilkinson. "He had been an intimate friend of the late Elizabeth Smith," Griscom informed his readers. "His account of her, confirms the published statements of her extraordinary attainments in literature and science, of the energy of her character, and the amiable simplicity and sweetness of her disposition."[86]

An ardent admirer of his departed friend, Wilkinson eagerly described Smith's fearless wanderings throughout the Lake District landscape: "Regardless of fatigue, she would climb to the top of a high mountain with her drawing implements, in search of a fine landscape, with as much zest as the most persevering hunter in the pursuit of game." Wilkinson proudly showed Griscom and other visitors several sketches that Smith had gifted him "as memorials of her friendship." These drawings highlighted Smith's "uncommon skill" as an artist as well as her daring sense of adventure: "One of them was taken in a place so precipitous," Griscom relayed, "that she could support herself only by his [Wilkinson's] assistance; for he had been fond of accompanying her in those mountain rambles, though he confessed that she was more adventurous than he."[87]

A Year in Europe provided readers with written access to Wilkinson's oral storytelling about Smith. The appeal of Wilkinson's anecdotes, even when relayed through Griscom as an intermediary, rested in their authentic, insider status. Wilkinson had personally explored the Lake District with Smith and could show visitors drawings she made from their adventures together, as well as other original pages in her own handwriting. Griscom offered his readers accounts of Smith's physical explorations and material artifacts that showcased the up-close-and-personal connections he cultivated during his own travels in the Lake District.

From Wilkinson, Griscom discovered and shared new details related to Smith's adventurous wanderings and scholarly pursuits. As a former educator at an academy for young women, Griscom may have particularly appreciated the following story, which highlighted "the strength, as well as delicacy of her mind." Griscom shared the account with his readers in detail:

Being on a visit at Bishop Watson's, the latter, who was a good mathemati-
cian, offered one evening to a gentleman present, an algebraical problem,
with a request that he would furnish a solution of it the next morning.
Elizabeth, from what passed between them, caught the conditions of the
problem, and learning from the gentleman in the morning, that he had not
been able to solve it, she presented him with a solution of her own, with a
request that he would show it to the bishop, without saying a word respecting herself. The bishop was highly pleased with the solution, and gave the
gentleman all the credit which he thought he deserved.[88]

This anecdote served as an illustrative example of Smith's accomplished
but reserved nature. She was able to solve a complex math problem but did
not want to flaunt her knowledge publicly. She was satisfied with knowing
that her answer was accurate, even if someone else got the credit. Indeed,
Griscom's telling of the story seemed to imply that Smith enjoyed having
the bishop praise her intellectual accomplishments without knowing that
he was commending a woman's work.

The account gives us a glimpse into Smith's copperplate self-
presentation, as well as showing how her legacy was transmitted over
time. Smith may have directly shared this story with her friend Wilkinson
during her lifetime, or perhaps Juliet Smith relayed the account to him
after her daughter's death. Through his storytelling to John Griscom and
other travelers, Thomas Wilkinson conveyed his close connections to
Elizabeth Smith and her family, revealing details and anecdotes that were
not included in *Fragments*. When Griscom transcribed and published
these stories in his travel narrative, local lore about Smith undertook its
own journey, traveling extensively across transatlantic cultures of print.

As local storytelling was transmitted into print, Smith's association
with the Lake District became an increasingly essential element of her
enduring fame. The English writer Thomas De Quincey, another notable
Lake District resident, was also a key contributor to Smith's legacy.
Through oral communications and printed publications, De Quincey
kept Smith's memory alive in local lore and print. Unlike Wilkinson, De
Quincey had never met Smith, having moved to the Lake District shortly
after her death. He cultivated relationships with family and friends who

"had been intimately connected with her." He was eager to learn all he could about Smith: "I have conversed with Mrs. Hannah More often about her; and I never failed to draw forth some fresh anecdote illustrating the vast extent of her knowledge, the simplicity of her character, the gentleness of her manners, and her unaffected humility." Through such connections, De Quincey "came to know more than the world knew."[89]

Inspired by what he learned about Smith, De Quincey published an essay about her in *Tait's Edinburgh Magazine,* which was later included in his *Literary Reminiscences.* He devoted nearly an entire chapter, titled "Society of the Lakes," to an account of Smith and "the splendor of her attainments." De Quincey acknowledged that when he first heard of Smith's scholarly accomplishments, he "regarded them with but little concern," as he believed that too many people who claimed expertise in language studies did so on "false" grounds. Yet the more he heard about her, the more De Quincey came to appreciate her "very extensive" talents. He was also impressed to learn that she seemed devoid "of all ostentation"—a common criticism directed at learned women.[90]

Like Thomas Wilkinson, Thomas De Quincey enjoyed telling stories about Elizabeth Smith, including the time she lost her way while exploring a waterfall. Smith had composed a poem describing this peculiar experience, which was published in *Fragments.* De Quincey's retelling of this event largely followed the narrative of Smith's verses, but his account of this "very remarkable incident" also included several details that expanded on Smith's published poem.[91]

De Quincey described for his readers the day Smith set off "quite unaccompanied" to sketch "some picturesque features" of a waterfall. As she explored, "the path had vanished altogether," but Smith was undeterred and "continued to pick out one for herself amongst the stones." When she suddenly "found herself in a little stony chamber," she felt "a panic from she knew not what." She attempted to find her way out "by steps so rapid and agitated," until she "found herself standing at the brink of a chasm, frightful to look down." Smith was surrounded by rocks, and "retreat seemed in every direction alike even more impossible." Smith "resolved to sit down and turn her thoughts quietly," when she was seized with the comforting idea that "she was in the hands of God, and that he would not forsake her." She began to look again for a way out, when "suddenly, . . . she saw clearly, about 200 yards beyond her own position, a lady, in a white muslin morning robe. . . . The lady beckoned . . . [and] gave her confidence to advance." Smith recognized the figure as "her own sister . . . whom she had left at home." With the assistance of her "guiding sister," Smith found her way out of the chasm. She turned to greet her sister but found that "all trace of her had vanished." When Smith returned home, she found her sister there, "and the whole family assured her that she had never stirred from the house."[92]

De Quincey noted that this tale was "often mentioned" among local residents, reflecting the ways in which oral storytelling and local memory contributed to Smith's legacy.[93] De Quincey's retelling of this encounter was packed with drama and anticipation, suggesting that such tales were often embellished the more often they were shared. The mystical, fantastical elements embedded in Smith's waterfall story undoubtedly added to its appeal, especially for readers who sought their own imaginative encounters with departed figures. As they made their way to print, these stories, however elaborated, remained infused with a sense of authenticity. Authors who could claim firsthand knowledge of and connections with local landscapes and residents conveyed heightened trust and credibility. Readers may have believed that they were learning something significant about the "real" Elizabeth Smith.

What began as local, behind-the-scenes storytelling by Lake District residents and visitors shaped Elizabeth Smith's literary reputation across transatlantic cultures of print. Individuals such as Thomas Wilkinson, Thomas De Quincey, and John Griscom translated personal stories into printed, public records. The process can be compared to the practices that transformed personal letters and diaries into published memoirs and other printed texts. In both cases, source materials pertaining to Smith changed classification—moving from informal, personal forms of communication into public, published cultures of print. Retracing Smith's literary reputation shows that the categories scholars use to label source materials can be fluid and dynamic. Through circulation across social and literary networks, a personal or private account can, sometimes over a relatively short time, become public and published.

As fireside chats became transatlantic texts, Elizabeth Smith's enduring fame took new forms. Lake District remembrances often gave more space to Smith's adventures and explorations, highlighting aspects of her fearless personality that were often ignored in collective biographies and other works of conduct literature. The Lake District's literary figures and inspiring landscapes offered readers and travelers unmatched encounters in print and place. An interwoven web of geographical encounters, imaginative musings, and recorded stories published in both Britain and America instilled Smith's legacy with heightened significance. Through various acts of literary tourism, Smith's powers of mind and body remained embedded on pages and places.

"To Measure Her by Her Powers"

Reflecting on Elizabeth Smith's legacy, Thomas De Quincey asserted that "the stir which was made after her death soon subsided." In commenting on the transitory nature of posthumous fame, De Quincey speculated about why he felt Smith was eventually forgotten and obscured in the historical record: "But the reason was—that she wrote but little! Had it been possible for the world to measure her by her powers, rather than her performances, she would have been placed, perhaps, in the estimate of posterity, at the head of learned women."[94] Without a large body of her published work, Smith's literary legacy rested primarily on reputation and memory. Of course, writers such as De Quincey were doing their part to keep her memory alive. By including a detailed account about her in his *Literary Reminiscences,* he helped introduce Smith's legacy to a new generation of readers and admirers in the 1840s and beyond. Over time, however, her story was primarily conveyed through other people's remembrances, rather than her own writings.

Literary tourism represented a key means of keeping Smith's memory alive. Select readers who first learned of her through her *Fragments* and other published sources were inspired to journey to the Lake District and other destinations associated with her life story. Travelers then recorded their experiences in a variety of textual sources, including personal letters, travel narratives, guide books, and tribute poetry. In the process, the practices of literary tourism traveled full circle from page to place and back to page.

The cultural and historical significance of literary tourism thus extended far beyond the experiences of the relatively small number of individuals with the financial resources and leisure time to conduct travel to visit the homes and graves of celebrated authors. Literary tourism developed through geographical visits to locations as well as through shared accounts of such activities. Travel guides, tribute poetry, and other accounts provided readers with imaginative connections among readers, authors, and places. One did not have to actually travel to the spots associated with beloved figures to envision the emotional responses such visits would inspire. A variety of travel writings enabled "armchair" literary tourism, as readers encountered accounts of people met and places visited, observations on local customs, and amusing anecdotes. This was especially true for American audiences, many of whom did not have the means or opportunity to travel abroad. The practices of literary tourism emphasized real and imagined connections that were transmitted through both place and print.

As the nineteenth century came to a close, enduring traces of Elizabeth Smith's legacy lingered. In 1894, *Literary Associations of the English Lakes* referred to the story of "that little inn in Patterdale" where "four lady travellers," including "Elizabeth Smith of Tent-Lodge fame," nearly encountered Walter Scott and William Wordsworth.[95] Long after her death, Smith's legacy lived on in the landscapes she loved to explore, as well as within transatlantic cultures of print. It is fitting that a learned woman who loved scholarly pursuits and physical adventures inspired such continued wanderings across time, space, and print.

"She Was No Blue-Stocking"

I N 1898, "AN OLD Scottish friend" gave the author Alexander H. Japp a copy of Elizabeth Smith's translation of the Book of Job, first published in 1810. Intrigued by this "old fashioned looking" book, Japp "took a day or two at the British Museum to learn more about this bold and remarkable young woman." Through his research into Smith's life and writings, he determined that she was "a genius born out of due time." His published tribute essay, "A Woman Learned and Wise," offered a generous assessment of Smith's intellect and character: "If the 'Book of Job' shows her as a fine scholar," her memoir, *Fragments, in Prose and Verse*, "reveals her as a keen observer, and as a true woman." In praising Smith as both a "fine scholar" and a "true woman," Japp assured his readers, "though she was learned, she was no blue-stocking."[1] One year earlier and across the Atlantic, Mary Davies Steele, a writer from Dayton, Ohio, also published a biographical account of Smith. Steele was impressed and inspired by Smith's extensive studies and works of translation, but like Japp she pointedly noted that "learning had not made her an awkward and pedantic bluestocking."[2]

Although Alexander Japp and Mary Davies Steele conveyed genuine admiration for Elizabeth Smith's intellectual powers, both felt the need to inform their readers that a woman who had died nearly a century earlier "was no blue-stocking." The figure of the bluestocking conveyed prevailing prejudices that helped shape learned women's place in the cultural imagination and historical record in the Anglophone world. Had she lived longer, as one critic surmised in 1811, Smith "might have become one of the members of the blue stocking club."[3] The original bluestockings—women such as Elizabeth Carter, Elizabeth Montagu, and Hannah More—were celebrated authors who often employed the term good-naturedly in reference to their gatherings of "persons of both sexes distinguished either for learning or genius."[4] By the early nineteenth century, however, negative uses of the term became the norm in both England and America, even as a growing number of women writers, educators, and scholars embraced the literary practices and intellectual ideals promoted by the original bluestockings. Pejorative representations of bluestockings typically depicted nineteenth-century women writers as shrill and unattractive: "If there e'er was a woman that frightened me quite / A Blue-stocking 'twould be, who had talent to write" (fig. 15).[5]

Derogatory uses of the term *bluestocking* came at a cultural cost, working to distance generations of learned women from a rich lineage and

LITERARY WOMAN.
If there e'er was a woman that frightened me quite,
A Blue-stocking 'twould be, who had talent to write,
Who'd much rather spend her time writing a yarn,
Than teaching her children, their stockings to darn.

FIGURE 15.
Literary Woman, a nineteenth-century caricature (circa 1850) of a woman writer portrayed as a bluestocking. (Library Company of Philadelphia)

usable past of women's intellectual achievements. Instead of evoking a long legacy of scholarly women, the term served as a powerful shorthand that reified negative characterizations of learned women. As British author Amelia Opie lamented in the 1830s, "The term *blue*, in the present day, means something so disagreeable, so disliked by women, and so sneered at by men." Opie reminded her readers that the term was once a badge of honor, recalling that "women at that period did not as now, shrink from the title of Blue-stocking."[6] When we consider the persistent ambivalence and even explicit hostility they often encountered, nineteenth-century women may have strategically chosen to "shrink" from association with the label in order to avoid criticism of their scholarly ambitions. As Edgar Allan Poe quipped, "When we think *very* ill of a woman, and wish to *blacken* her character, we merely call her 'a *blue-stocking*.'"[7]

The cultural transformation surrounding the figure of the bluestocking—from one of celebration to condemnation—illustrates the persistent challenges that learned women have confronted. By the late nineteenth century, even as tens of thousands of women gained greater access to both single-sex and coeducational colleges and other institutions of higher education, they faced continued scrutiny and debates about their intellectual ambitions.[8] When writers such as Alexander Japp or Mary Steele expressed admiration for Elizabeth Smith by deliberately distancing her from the bluestocking label, they reified norms that had long encouraged readers to view the general existence of learned women with skepticism and derision. References to Smith as *not* an "awkward and pedantic blue-stocking" still served to reinforce sweeping characterizations denigrating the very existence of any learned lady.

Enduring prejudices against bluestockings and learned ladies highlight why, nearly a century after Smith's death, commentators on both sides of the Atlantic were still searching for ways to assess her seemingly uncommon character. Smith was "no blue-stocking" but was she, as Japp suggested, "a genius born *out* of due time?" What if we instead consider her a genius born *in* a time that was deeply skeptical about women's intellectual capacities and scholarly potential? Romanticism privileged notions of innate genius embodied in *men* believed to possess creative, unique powers of mind. Men identified as geniuses were encouraged to explore the full expression of their intellects, yet the same aspirations in women were considered unacceptably selfish and overly ambitious. As Ralph Waldo Emerson argued, "A woman in our society finds her safety and happiness in exclusions and privacies. . . . Only the most extraordinary genius can make the career of an artist secure and agreeable to her." A woman's scholarly talents, no matter how impressive, were best employed in the service of others, rather than left free and unfettered. Even a woman as accomplished as Margaret Fuller, Emerson believed, accepted these gendered constraints. "Willingly she was confined to the usual circles and methods of female talent. . . . She could converse, and teach, and write."[9] Women who desired to move beyond the "usual circles and methods of female talent" represented a threat not only to their inherent femininity but to a social order predicated on prescriptive gender roles.[10] A male genius epitomized unique, creative powers, while the idea of female genius remained an unsettling anomaly.

For over a century, Elizabeth Smith's posthumous reputation was shaped by gendered concepts that simultaneously sought to celebrate and constrain the force of her genius. The strength of her intellect, coupled with her gentle, modest disposition, was regarded as a rare, extraordinary occurrence worthy of commendation. Impressed by Smith's achievements, Japp made a claim for her historical significance in 1898: "We regard it as a privilege to be enabled here to draw attention to a very remarkable Englishwoman, who did a remarkable work, and who well deserves a place in the supplementary volume of the Dictionary of National Biography."[11] Japp got his wish. The 1898 edition of the *Dictionary of National Biography* included an entry on Elizabeth Smith, along with a familiar, comforting disclaimer: "With her intellectual accomplishment went, we are assured, facility in women's work, like cooking and needlework."[12] Admirers who continued to assign equal weight to Smith's scholarship and domestic skills reinforced longstanding prescriptions that encouraged learned women to balance their intellectual accomplishments with proper notions of femininity.

As the twentieth century began, Smith's fame waned. Scattered references can be found in a handful of early twentieth-century sources, serving as scant remnants of her enduring afterlife across time, place, and print. In particular, the cultural practices of literary celebrity and literary tourism associated with the Lake District help keep her memory alive in that region. Published in 1905, *Literary Celebrities of the English Lake-District* by Frederick Sessions celebrated the "blooming Elizabeth Smith," although in somewhat antiquated terms: "Let it be remembered that she was born in the days previous to any thought of the 'emancipation' of woman, or her 'equality' with man, and when the only sphere it was considered proper for her to fill was that of wife and mother." In praising Smith's many accomplishments, Sessions mused, "It will be satisfactory to those, if any are left, who still hold old theories about the highest feminine virtues, that this talented young woman" successfully balanced scholarly pursuits with domestic skills. As the twentieth century progressed, new generations of ambitious, college-educated women eager to forge professional careers and public identities for themselves may not have related to Smith's seemingly old-fashioned virtues. Her fearless explorations faded from view, supplanted by quaint descriptions of her "retiring, even timid" character.[13]

Ultimately, Smith's story ends not with her death but with the slow vanishing of her afterlife. In his 1955 work *The Lakers: The Adventures of the First Tourists,* Norman Nicholson, a poet and resident of the Lake District, referred to Smith as "a picturesque figure" and "shadowy form." These descriptions serve to highlight the challenges of trying to reconstruct her biographical story, especially given the lack of surviving manuscript materials written by her. Instead, as Nicholson contemplated, we have only other people's accounts and representations: "We see her almost entirely through the eyes of friends, for of the fragments she left behind, the translations reveal nothing of herself, and the letters seem to have received the treatment one might have expected from an editor whose name was Bowdler." Known through mediated and fragmented sources, Smith was a ghost-like figure, remembered more for her "almost perfect picturesque death," rather than her lived experiences. "It was not her learning," Nicholson mused, "but her early death which aroused the interest of the literary Lakers."[14]

Beneath the shadowy surface, Elizabeth Smith's life and legacy reveal the persistent power of cultural prescriptions to shape both the lived experiences and cultural representations of accomplished women. Whether she was considered a "genius born out of time," "no blue-stocking," or a "shadowy form," Smith was repeatedly referred to as the exception that proved the rule. Throughout her enduring afterlife, Smith exemplified the ghost of female genius frozen in time—full of promise and potential but unsullied by problematic assertions of ambition and pedantry. Posthumously, Smith's reputation was able to rise precisely because she posed no threat as a living, learned woman.

The fragments of Smith's life story and writings that have survived indicate she was indeed a woman possessed with strong intellectual abilities, along with an adventurous spirit. Her scholarly talents, particularly with respect to language studies, were impressive and remarkable, as were her fearless explorations of mountainous terrains. Her desire for social acceptance and strong loyalty to her family were, at times, at odds with her aspirations and ambitions—but she was indeed aspiring and ambitious. Despite her advantages and accomplishments, Smith remained influenced by her era's gendered prescriptions and pejorative attitudes. She encountered repeated reminders that women should remain within their proper sphere and sublimate their own ambitions, factors that shaped how she presented herself in public. As she navigated her place in the world, she carefully developed a copperplate version of herself as pious, domestic, and modest. This identity often effectively shielded her from criticism, both during her lifetime and throughout her enduring afterlife.

I believe it is important to celebrate Smith's many accomplishments while also recognizing that she was not some anomaly. As scholars recover more women's life stories, we might consider that seemingly exceptional women—that is, women who do not appear to conform to gendered stereotypes about women's capacities—represent an important norm. Although terms such as "exceptional" or "extraordinary" have positive connotations, such labels may ultimately serve to diminish, rather than expand, any individual woman's place in the historical record. Whenever we label a woman as "extraordinary," she can be thought of as singular, unique, and rare. That framing does little to encourage us to revise our understandings of the past, or to place women at the center, rather than the margins, of larger historical narratives. A fuller recognition of women's lived experiences and literary contributions can help reframe our understandings of Romanticism, genius, travel, and other key developments of the long nineteenth century.

Elizabeth Smith came of age in an era marked by dramatic shifts in women's intellectual pursuits and cultural productions. Her social and literary circles reveal thriving communities of learned women with similar aspirations, as do the reactions of female readers of her memoir on both sides of the Atlantic. Smith benefited from extensive social and literary connections that she cultivated with like-minded individuals who shared, supported, and validated her scholarly endeavors and travel pursuits. The multigenerational and wide-ranging networks that nurtured Smith during her lifetime also worked to sustain her posthumous reputation. In turn, her enduring literary legacy helped to inspire generations of women in both England and America, who found in Smith a kindred spirit for their own learned lives. Retracing the extent and scope of these social connections and literary networks further underscores that she was not some solitary, exceptional figure. Her aspirations and ambitions are reflected in the experiences of numerous other learned women in her lifetime and beyond.

Inspired by the spirit of the age, women in both Great Britain and the United States eagerly crafted lives marked by intellectual achievements and physical explorations. Throughout the nineteenth century, women found ways to pursue their scholarly ambitions, despite exclusion from formal institutions of higher education, and despite widespread cultural antagonism toward learned women. Women also engaged in and found meaning in the same picturesque and sublime travel adventures privileged by William Wordsworth, Walter Scott, and other celebrated Romantic-era literary figures. The creative genius of male writers such as Wordsworth and Scott is often directly linked to their quest for adventure. Many scholars continue to regard these men's inspired endeavors as significant and noteworthy in helping to create new literary and cultural movements while continuing to confine "exceptional" women with similar experiences and aspirations to the margins of the historical record. Elizabeth Smith scaled the same mountains and traveled the same paths celebrated by renowned men in their poetry and other writings, yet her achievements remain in the shadows.

It is time that women's contributions were valued and recognized as emblematic and influential, not exceptional and thus less consequential. This is important recovery work, as gendered concepts have powerful resonance that continues to inform how we understand and define scholarly women's place in the world. According to a 2015 study, contemporary understandings of genius remain influenced by Romanticism's veneration of unique men of talent: "Cultural associations link men, but not women, with raw intellectual brilliance." In academic disciplines where "having a special inborn talent was seen as more important," women remain underrepresented.[15] For centuries, gendered definitions of genius have sought to disparage women's intellectual talents and limit their access to scholarly spaces. Such concepts are reinforced in literary and historical records that seem to categorize all women of talent and genius as uncommon and atypical. Individual women's life stories are presented as notable exceptions, rather than a continuous lineage of women's achievements. Yet as sociologist Tressie McMillan Cottom reflected on being named a 2020 MacArthur genius, "I am sure that there has been genius all along the way. If nothing else, I am proof of that."[16]

Despite many gains, women's intellectual and professional achievements remain subjected to gendered assessments with pernicious undertones. On social media sites such as Twitter, hashtags such as #womenalsoknowhistory, #womenwhowrite, and #womenwriters have signified twenty-first-century efforts to highlight how gendered norms continue to shape notions of scholarly expertise. These hashtags represent clever and compelling calls to action, but one concern is that they may inadvertently serve to reify our understandings of what is normal and exceptional. Elizabeth Smith's life and legacy challenges us to rethink the ways we categorize women's scholarly achievements.

In seeking to exercise the full powers of her mind and body, Elizabeth Smith was as emblematic and representative of her era as William Wordsworth or Walter Scott. Her residence in key picturesque spots such as Piercefield and the Lake District, along with the social and literary networks she cultivated in Bath and other local communities, literally place her at the center of key intellectual and cultural trends. Unafraid to wander, she conducted a relentless search for inspired vistas. As a scholar *and* a woman, she dared to pursue boundless knowledge and expansive spaces. With the continued recovery of their life stories, women of superior talents may no longer seem so extraordinary—and may no longer have to seek *forgiveness* for their ambitions.

NOTES

Abbreviations

ES	Elizabeth Smith
HMB	Henrietta Maria (Harriet) Bowdler
MAB	Mary Ann Burges
MH	Mary Hunt
LIK	Lady Isabella King
JS	Juliet Smith
TW	Thomas Wilkinson
Fragments	Elizabeth Smith, *Fragments, in Prose and Verse* (1809 Bath edition)
SFP-AO	Simcoe Family Papers, Archives of Ontario, Toronto
SFP-LAC	Simcoe Family Papers, Library and Archives Canada, Ottawa, Ontario
TWP	Thomas Wilkinson Papers, Library of Society of Friends, London
TWP-BL	Thomas Wilkinson Papers, British Library, London

Introduction

1. Thomas Wilkinson wrote about this account in at least two letters to friends; the details of the encounter are more or less the same in both letters. See TW to Martha Frances Smith, January 1, 1806, TWP, Folder 24; TW to Mary Leadbeater, August 31, 1809, TWP, Folder 20a. In his January 1, 1806, letter, Wilkinson noted that the visit took place the previous autumn, which is supported by other evidence. For accounts of Wordsworth's visit with Walter Scott, see Dorothy Wordsworth to Lady Beaumont, August 26, 1805, in De Selincourt et al., eds., *Letters of William and Dorothy Wordsworth,* vol. 1. For further evidence supporting that this trip took place in late

summer/early autumn of 1805, see Knight, ed., *Letters of the Wordsworth Family from 1787 to 1855*, vol. 1; and Lockhart, *Memoirs of the Life of Sir Walter Scott*, vol. 2.

2. Griscom, *Year in Europe*, 2:499–501. Griscom placed Humphry Davy and Robert Southey, other key members of Lake District literary society, at the inn with Walter Scott instead of William Wordsworth. This story was also featured in other published works about the Lake District, including Rawnsley, *Literary Association of the English Lakes*, 2:60–61.

3. Lockhart, *Memoirs of the Life of Sir Walter Scott*, 8:52.

4. TW, quoted in Carr, *Thomas Wilkinson*, 100–101.

5. "Female Authors," *New-England Galaxy and Masonic Magazine* (Boston), May 5, 1820, 134.

6. Elizabeth Smith receives almost no extensive treatment in most literary and historical studies. For a notable exception, see Brown, Clements, and Grundy, eds., "Elizabeth Smith, 1776–1806."

7. For efforts to reclaim women's literary contributions to Romanticism, see, for example, Behrendt, *British Women Poets;* Crisafulli and Pietropoli, eds., *Romantic Women Poets;* Lau, ed., *Fellow Romantics;* Mellor, *Romanticism and Gender;* and Wu, ed., *Companion to Romanticism.*

8. ES to HMB, April 16, [1805], in *Fragments*, 177. When possible, I have tried to identify the specific document information, including dates, from materials cited from Smith's memoir. Unless otherwise noted, I have used the 1809 Bath edition of *Fragments* for page reference consistency. Originally published in 1808, *Fragments* went through several editions in both England and America.

9. Leadbeater, "The Annals of Ballitore," *Leadbeater Papers*, 1:272.

10. JS to Dr. [Francis] Randolph, Letter II, 1807 (hereafter JS, Letter II), in *Fragments*, 228.

11. ES, Reflections, [circa 1800–1802], in *Fragments*, 151.

12. The first edition of Elizabeth Smith's memoir was published without attribution as *Fragments, in Prose and Verse: By a Young Lady, Lately Deceased. With Some Account of Her Life and Character, by the Author of "Sermons on the Doctrines and Duties of Christianity"* (Bath: Richard Cruttwell, 1808). By 1809, editions fully identified both Smith and Bowdler.

13. Wilkinson, "A Day's Tour," 1; "*Fragments in Prose and Verse,*" 553; "Review of New Publications," *Christian Observer*, 508; "Miss Elizabeth Smith," *Christian Disciple*, 257.

14. See Andrews, *Search for the Picturesque;* Buzard, *The Beaten Track;* and Kinsley, *Women Writing the Home Tour.*

15. For publishing practices and the history of the book, see Charvat, *Literary Publishing in America;* Darnton, *Great Cat Massacre;* Gross and Kelley, eds., *History of the Book in America,* especially the essay by James N. Green, "The Rise of Book Publishing," 75–127; Raven, *Business of Books;* Remer, *Printers and Men of Capital;* and Rezek, *London and the Making of Provincial Literature.*

16. For the rise of celebrity culture, especially literary celebrity culture, within transatlantic cultures of print, see Adams, *Performing Authorship;* Barry, "Celebrity, Cultural Production, and Public Life"; Eastman, *Strange Genius of Mr. O;* First, "The Mechanics of Renown"; Jackson, *Those Who Write for Immortality;* Looser, *Making of Jane Austen;*

Mole, *Byron's Romantic Celebrity;* Mole, ed., *Romanticism and Celebrity Culture;* O'Neill, "'The Best of Me Is There'"; Tillyard, "Celebrity in 18th-Century London"; and Wright, ed., *Cosmopolitan Lyceum.*

17. "Memoirs of Miss Hannah More," *New-York Missionary Magazine,* January 5, 1801, 357. For women authors and literary celebrity, see Brock, *Feminization of Fame;* Hawkins and Ives, eds., *Women Writers and the Artifacts of Celebrity;* and Teed, "A Passion for Distinction."

18. For overviews of women's educational achievements in this era, see Kelley, *Learning to Stand and Speak;* McMahon, *Mere Equals;* and Purvis, *History of Women's Education in England.*

19. "The Wanderer," "Hints on the State of American Literature," *Monthly Register, Magazine, and Review of the United States* (New York), December 1, 1807, 6.

20. The literature on nineteenth-century women writers in England and America is vast. For representative examples, see Clarke, *Rise and Fall of the Woman of Letters;* Guest, *Small Change;* Coultrap-McQuin, *Doing Literary Business;* Kelley, *Private Woman, Public Stage;* Rust, *Prodigal Daughters;* Stott, *Hannah More;* Tompkins, *Sensational Designs;* Turner, *Living by the Pen;* and Winckles and Rehbein, eds., *Women's Literary Networks and Romanticism.*

21. "Art. II. *The Letters of Mrs. Elizabeth Montagu. Part the Second,*" *Quarterly Review* (London), October 1813, 32–33. This review essay was reprinted in the *Analectic Magazine, Containing Selections from Foreign Reviews and Magazines* (Philadelphia), March 1814, 215–25.

22. "On Female Authorship," *Walker's Hibernian Magazine; or, Compendium of Entertaining Knowledge* (Dublin), August 1789, 421. This essay was reprinted in the *Weekly Entertainer; or, Agreeable and Instructive Repository* (Sherborne, England), October 19, 1793, 361–65, and also made its way to American print culture, appearing in *Ladies' Magazine and Repository of Entertaining Knowledge* (Philadelphia), January 1793, 68–72.

23. "Article 9. Memoirs of the Life of Mrs. Elizabeth Carter," *Monthly Anthology and Boston Review,* September 1, 1810, 195.

24. On Wollstonecraft, see especially Cayton, *Love in the Time of Revolution;* Barker-Benfield, *Culture of Sensibility;* Brown, "Mary Wollstonecraft, or the Female Illuminati"; Taylor, *Mary Wollstonecraft and the Feminist Imagination;* and Todd, *Mary Wollstonecraft.*

25. Richard Polwhele, *The Unsex'd Females; or, A Poem, Addressed to the Author of the Pursuits of Literature* (New York: William Cobbett, 1800), 19. Polwhele's poem was originally published in London in 1798.

26. In his classic study of eighteenth-century print culture, Michael Warner asserted that "printing constituted and distinguished a specifically white community" that was also implicitly male. See Warner, *Letters of the Republic,* especially 12–15. For important archival recoveries and interpretative interventions on race and ethnicity across transatlantic cultures of print, see Brooks, "The Early American Public Sphere"; Carretta, "Phillis Wheatley"; Chander, *Brown Romantics;* Cohen and Stein, eds., *Early African American Print Culture;* Jackson, "The Talking Book"; Jeffers, *Age of Phillis;* Peace, "Indigenous Intellectual Traditions"; and Rezek, "The Racialization of Print."

27. "Review of New Publications," *Christian Observer,* 508.

28. For discussions of women's posthumous fame during this era, see Cayton, "Canonizing Harriet Newell"; and Moreshead, "'Beyond All Ambitious Motives.'"

29. For influential scholarship on representations of women, gender, and print culture, see Bloch, "Changing Conceptions of Sexuality"; Dillon, *Gender of Freedom;* Mellor, *Romanticism and Gender;* and Mellor, ed., *Romanticism and Feminism.*

30. My analysis has been influenced by a number of biographical works that employ innovative methodological approaches to recovering women's lives and legacies. See, for example, Allgor, *A Perfect Union;* Anishanslin, *Portrait of a Woman in Silk;* Byrne, *Real Jane Austen;* Colley, *Ordeal of Elizabeth Marsh;* Foreman, *Georgiana, Duchess of Devonshire;* Glover, *Eliza Lucas Pinckney;* Godbeer, *World of Trouble;* Lewis, *Elizabeth Patterson Bonaparte;* Little, *Many Captivities of Esther Wheelwright;* Marshall, *Margaret Fuller;* and Skemp, *First Lady of Letters.*

31. Mellor, "Thoughts on *Romanticism and Gender,*" 345–46. For other useful accounts of recent efforts to recover previously understudied women writers, see Levy, "Do Women Have a Book History?"; Looser, "British Women Writers, Big Data and Big Biography"; and MacDonald, "Identifying Mrs. Meeke."

32. See "Distinguished Women," Evelyn Papers, British Library.

33. Henrietta Maria Bowdler worked with her brother Thomas on the publication of *Family Shakespeare,* excising and editing passages to make Shakespeare's writings more palatable to middle-class readers' sensibilities (thus, the origins of the term to "bowdlerize"). See Bowdler, *Family Shakespeare;* Perrin, *Dr. Bowdler's Legacy;* and Wolfson, "Shakespeare and the Romantic Girl Reader."

34. HMB, *Fragments,* 57. Any citation from *Fragments* designated as "HMB" represents Bowdler's direct writing/editorializing, as distinguished from Elizabeth Smith's or other individuals' writings also included in Smith's memoir.

35. For useful methodological discussions of archival fragments and the challenges of recovering women's lived experiences, see Brooks, *Our Beloved Kin;* Fuentes, *Dispossessed Lives;* and Knott, *Mother Is a Verb.*

36. For further discussion of how the making of celebrity depends on the interplay of individual talent, media culture, and audience reception, see Jenner, *Dead Famous.*

1. "Rocky Precipices"

1. ES to MH, July 7, 1792, in *Fragments,* 7–8. Throughout part 1, I typically use first (or full) names to refer to Elizabeth Smith and her family and friends, a stylistic choice reflective of this section's focus on her personal, day-to-day lived experiences.

2. For general overviews on Romanticism, see, for example, De Man, *Rhetoric of Romanticism;* Holsinger and Stauffer, "Romanticism, Now and Then"; Porter, ed., *Romanticism in National Context;* and Wu, ed., *Companion to Romanticism.*

3. See Andrews, *Search for the Picturesque;* and Buzard, *The Beaten Track.*

4. Genealogical information about the Smith family is compiled from "George Smith (1693–1756)" and "Sir Charles Felix Smith (1786–1858)," in Lee, ed., *Dictionary of National Biography,* 53:21, 36–37; and "Sir Charles-Felix Smith," in Burke, *Genealogical*

and Heraldic Dictionary of the Landed Gentry, 2:1251–52. Also see "The Venerable Bede and His Durham Editors."

5. Hutchinson, *History and Antiquities of the County Palatine of Durham,* 2:423.

6. The £400 rental income for Burn Hall is taken from George Smith's bankruptcy notices in 1793. See, for example, *Bath Chronicle and Weekly Gazette,* October 3, 1793, 2.

7. Jane Austen's characters in *Sense and Sensibility* illustrate the spectrum of wealth held by members of the gentry class during this era. The widowed Mrs. Dashwood and her daughters live on about £500 a year—sustaining a comfortable but not extravagant standard of living. Marianne Dashwood suggests that her standards and tastes require an annual income of approximately £2,000, an amount that her more sensible sister Elinor considers wealthy. See Heldman, "How Wealthy Is Mr. Darcy." For other sources on British income and socioeconomic status, see Boot, "Real Incomes of the British Middle Class"; Jackson, "British Incomes Circa 1800"; Mathias, *Transformation of England,* especially 171–89; and Toran, "Economics of Jane Austen's World."

8. "Sir Charles Felix Smith (1786–1858)," in Lee, ed., *Dictionary of National Biography,* 53:21.

9. TW to Elihu Robinson, June 7, 1801, TWP, Folder 27.

10. "The Grosvenor Exhibition," *Athenaeum: A Journal of English and Foreign Literature, Science, the Fine Arts, Music and the Drama* (London), January 17, 1885, 92. In the late nineteenth century, Gainsborough's portrait of young Juliet Mott was included in exhibitions held at the Royal Academy and Grosvenor Gallery. By 1934, the painting was part of the private collection of Mrs. J. Horace Harding of New York and exhibited at the Art Institute of Chicago. See *Catalogue of a Century of Progress: Exhibition of Paintings and Sculpture, 1934* (Chicago: Art Institute of Chicago, 1934), 25. For Gainsborough's career as an artist, see Susan Sloman, *Gainsborough in Bath* (New Haven, CT: Yale University Press, 2002).

11. See Evidence of Title of George Smith and Richard Mott, Suffolk Record Office.

12. Settlement Made by Thomas Mulliner Esq. on the Marriage of George Smith Esq. with Miss Juliet Mott, Suffolk Record Office.

13. See Davidoff and Hall, *Family Fortunes,* 450 (quotation); Guest, *Small Change;* Barker and Chalus, eds., *Women's History;* Vickery, *Gentleman's Daughter;* and Vickery, *Behind Closed Doors.*

14. Chapone, *Letters on the Improvement of the Mind,* 112.

15. For average number of servants, see Boot, "Real Incomes of the British Middle Class," and the other sources in note 7.

16. Bennett, *Letters to a Young Lady,* 2:206.

17. Vickery, *Behind Closed Doors,* especially chapter 6, 180 (quotation). For other useful accounts of eighteenth-century cultural values, especially material culture tastes common to England and America, see Boudreau and Lovell, eds., *Material World;* Dyer, *Material Lives;* Kelly, *Republic of Taste;* and Worsley, *Jane Austen at Home.* For transatlantic consumer market trends in the eighteenth century, see T. H. Breen, "Baubles of Britain: The American and Consumer Revolutions of the Eighteenth Century," *Past and Present* 119, no. 1 (1988): 73–104.

18. HMB to Eliza Simcoe, August 3, 1814, Simcoe Family Papers, Devon Archives.

19. For the importance of shared reading practices in eighteenth-century households, see Williams, *Social Life of Books.*

20. Bennett, *Letters to a Young Lady,* 2:224.

21. Chapone, *Letters on the Improvement of the Mind,* 132.

22. On British women's education, see Davidoff and Hall, *Family Fortunes;* Guest, *Small Change;* Hilton and Hirsh, ed., *Practical Visionaries;* Leranbaum, "Mistresses of Orthodoxy"; McDermid, "Conservative Feminism and Female Education"; Miller, "Women's Education"; and Purvis, *History of Women's Education in England.*

23. More, *Essays on Various Subjects,* 131–32.

24. Gisborne, *Enquiry into the Duties of the Female Sex,* 58.

25. More, *Essays on Various Subjects,* 23.

26. Bennett, *Letters to a Young Lady,* 1:164.

27. See McDermid, "Conservative Feminism and Female Education," and other sources on women's education in note 22 for the familial and social elements, rather than individual aspirations, stressed in prescriptive writings about women's education.

28. For educational history in the early American republic, see Kelley, *Learning to Stand and Speak;* McMahon, *Mere Equals;* and Nash, *Women's Education in the United States.*

29. Bennett, *Letters to a Young Lady,* 2:52.

30. See Davidoff and Hall, *Family Fortunes,* especially 289–93; and sources cited in note 22 above. As Miriam Leranbaum notes in "Mistresses of Orthodoxy," while some fathers took an active interest in the education of their daughters, ardent male support of daughters' education was considered relatively unconventional at the time.

31. JS to Dr. [Francis] Randolph, Letter I, 1807 (hereafter JS, Letter I), in *Fragments,* 216.

32. JS, Letter I, in *Fragments,* 216–17. The identity of this governess has not been determined.

33. See Will of Thomas Mulliner, National Archives (England). Mulliner's will upheld the "agreements" outlined in the settlement made upon Juliet Mott's 1774 marriage to George Smith.

34. For general histories and architectural overviews of Piercefield, see Newman, *Buildings of Wales;* Waters, *Piercefield on the Banks of the Wye;* and Elisabeth Whittle, "'All These Inchanting Scenes': Piercefield in the Wye Valley," *Garden History* 24, no. 1 (Summer 1996): 148–61.

35. Matheson, "'I Wanted Some Intelligent Guide,'" 140. Also see Andrews, *Search for the Picturesque;* and the online exhibit by C. S. Matheson, "Enchanting Ruin: Tintern Abbey and Romantic Tourism in Wales," Tintern Abbey and Romantic Tourism in Wales (2007), https://deepblue.lib.umich.edu/bitstream/handle/2027.42/144575/introduction.html.

36. Davies and Fulford, "Introduction: Romanticism's Wye," 115.

37. Ibbetson et al., *Picturesque Guide to Bath,* 227.

38. For the growth of the tourist industry in the region, see Buzard, *The Beaten Track;* and Davies and Fulford, "Introduction: Romanticism's Wye."

39. Gilpin, *Observations on the River Wye,* 39.

40. Ibbetson et al., *Picturesque Guide to Bath,* 227.

41. Coxe, *Historical Tour in Monmouthshire,* 2:400–402.

42. *New Bath Guide,* 60.

43. Ibbetson et al., *Picturesque Guide to Bath*, 259.

44. *The Cambrian Directory; or, Cursory Sketches of the Welsh Territories* (Salisbury, U.K.: J. Easton, 1800), 9.

45. George William Manby, *An Historic and Picturesque Guide from Clifton, through the Counties of Monmouth, Glamorgan, and Brecknock, with Representations of Ruins, Interesting Antiquities, &c. &c.* (Bristol, U.K.: Fenley and Baylis, 1802), 267.

46. "Sir Charles-Felix Smith," in Burke, *Genealogical and Heraldic Dictionary of the Landed Gentry*, 2:1252. See *St. James's Chronicle, or British Evening-Post* (London), November 10, 1787, 2; and *London Gazette*, February 5, 1788, 61, for notices of George Smith's term as sheriff of Monmouthshire. For banking as a profession, see Davidoff and Hall, *Family Fortunes*, 245–47.

47. As historian Amanda Vickery notes, some eighteenth-century families "lived their domestic life as if it were a cultural project." See Vickery, *Behind Closed Doors*, 152. Also see Lawrence Stone and Jeanne C. Fawther Stone, *An Open Elite? England, 1540–1880* (Oxford: Clarendon Press, 1984).

48. Coxe, *Historical Tour in Monmouthshire*, 2:398. These comments were made after the next owner of Piercefield "extended and improved the plan" of renovations begun by George Smith.

49. John Byng, "A Tour of South Wales, 1787," in Andrews, ed., *Torrington Diaries*, 273.

50. Coxe, *Historical Tour in Monmouthshire*, 2:399.

51. JS, Letter II, in *Fragments*, 228.

52. JS, Letter I, in *Fragments*, 217.

53. JS, Letter II, in *Fragments*, 228.

54. Chapone, *Letters on the Improvement of the Mind*, 174–75.

55. Bennett, *Letters to a Young Lady*, 1:163.

56. Fanny Burney, Journal, August 25, [1789], in Barrett, ed., *Diary and Letters of Madame d'Arblay*, 4:322.

57. [Bowdler], *Poems and Essays*, 5. Harriet Bowdler's literary productions are discussed further in chapters 2 and 5.

58. JS, Letter I, in *Fragments*, 218.

59. HMB, *Fragments*, 2.

60. Chapone, *Letters on the Improvement of the Mind*, 77.

61. Elizabeth Bowdler to ES, December 1791, in *Fragments*, 219–25.

62. ES to MH, August 13, 1792, in *Fragments*, 10.

63. ES to MH, July 27, 1792, in *Fragments*, 8–9.

64. HMB, *Fragments*, 11.

65. ES to MH, August 13, 1792, in *Fragments*, 10.

66. ES to MH, July 27, 1792, in *Fragments*, 9.

67. See especially Jenkins, ed., *Rattleskull Genius*; Jones, "Fictional Selves"; and Jones, "*The Bard Is a Very Singular Character*."

68. ES to MH, July 27, 1792, in *Fragments*, 9.

69. Iolo Morganwg to John Walters, February 24, 1791, in Jenkins, Jones, and Jones, eds., *Correspondence of Iolo Morganwg*, 1:375. Also see Mary-Ann Constantine, "This Wildernessed Business of Publication," in Jenkins, ed., *Rattleskull Genius*, 128.

70. For women's roles as patrons, see Eastman, *Strange Genius of Mr. O*.

71. Iolo Morganwg to John Walters, February 24, 1791, in Jenkins, Jones, and Jones, eds., *Correspondence of Iolo Morganwg*, 1:375.

72. HMB to Edward Williams, September 25, 1791, Letters of H. M. Bowdler to Iolo Morganwg, National Library of Wales.

73. HMB to Edward Williams, December 13, [1791], Letters of H. M. Bowdler to Iolo Morganwg, National Library of Wales. See letters in this collection dated August 17, 23, and September 25, 1791, for evidence of Bowdler's efforts to promote Williams's volume of poetry before her skepticism took over.

74. Williams, *Poems, Lyric and Pastoral,* vol. 1. For Williams's references to the Bowdlers and Smiths, see "Preface," xi–xiii, and "Subscribers Names," xxv–xxxix; for the reference to Piercefield, see his poem "The Line of Beauty," 160.

75. See [Hunt], "On Visiting the Ruins of an Ancient Abbey in Devonshire." Mary Hunt's poem also appeared anonymously in the *Universal Magazine of Knowledge and Pleasure* (London), November 1786, 259.

76. "H. T." [Mary Hunt], "Written on Visiting the Ruins of Dunkeswell-Abbey, in Devonshire, Sept. 1786," in Richard Polwhele, *Poems, Chiefly by Gentlemen of Devonshire and Cornwall* (Bath: R. Cruttwell, 1792), 1:134–36. In a preface entitled "Advertisement," Polwhele identified "Miss Hunt" as the poem's author: "The beautiful Elegy on *Dunkeswell Abbey* in *Devonshire,* signed H. T. is the production of Miss Hunt, daughter of the late Dr. Hunt, Rector of the *Stoke-Doyle* in *Northampshire*" (viii). This collection, and Hunt's poem, is briefly discussed in Dafydd Moore, "Patriotism, Politeness, and National Identity in the South West of England in the Late Eighteenth Century," *ELH* 76, no. 3 (Fall 2009): 739–62. For more information on Hunt's authorship of this poem, see "Mary Hunt (1764–1834)," in Ashfield, ed., *Romantic Women Poets,* 81–82. I also uncovered useful information and research leads about Mary Hunt from Julie Sampson, "Devon's 'Romantic Poet/s; Mary Hunt and Dunkeswell Abbey," Scrapblog: A Writer from the South-West, February 25, 2010, http://scrapblogfromthesouth-west .blogspot.com/2010/02/devons-romantic-poets-mary-hunt-and.html.

77. Elizabeth Simcoe to Richard Polwhele, October 13, 1790, in Polwhele, *Traditions and Recollections,* 1:240–41.

78. ES to MH, July 27, 1792, in *Fragments,* 9.

79. Jones, "Fictional Selves," 43.

80. ES to MH, December 12, 1792, in *Fragments,* 18.

81. ES, "A Supposed Translation from a Welsh Poem, Lately Dug up at Piercefield, in the Same Spot Where Llewellyn at Grynfyd Was Slain, Dec. 10th, 1281," in *Fragments,* 20–23.

82. ES to MH, December 12, 1792, in *Fragments,* 17.

83. Buzard, *The Beaten Track,* 16. For women's experiences as travelers, see Kinsley, *Women Writing the Home Tour;* and Imbarrato, *Traveling Women.*

84. Andrews, *Search for the Picturesque,* 49.

85. See Stafford, *Reading Romantic Poetry,* especially 123–26; also see Moore, "Patriotism, Politeness, and National Identity."

86. See Annette Gordon-Reed and Peter S. Onuf, *"Most Blessed of the Patriarchs": Thomas Jefferson and the Empire of the Imagination* (New York: Liveright, 2016), 228–229. Gordon-Reed and Onuf quote from Thomas Jefferson's letter to Charles McPherson,

25 February 1773, available at Founders Online, National Archives (U.S.), https://founders.archives.gov/documents/Jefferson/01-01-02-0071. For Ossian's popularity, see Haugen, "Ossian and the Invention of Textual History"; Laughlin, "The Lawless Language of Macpherson's Ossian"; DeLucia, "'Far Other Times Are These'"; and Stafford, *Sublime Savage.*

87. Walter Scott to Anna Seward, 1806, in Lockhart, *Memoirs of Sir Walter Scott,* 2:251–59.

88. More, *Strictures on the Modern System of Female Education,* 110.

89. See especially Looser, *British Women Writers;* and Lake, "Redecorating the Ruin."

90. Waters, *Piercefield on the Banks of the Wye,* 19. Also see H. J. Lloyd-Johnes, "A Tour in North and South Wales in the Year 1784 by George Cumberland," *National Library of Wales Journal* 19, no. 4 (1976): 330. Lloyd-Johnes asserted that Smith purchased the property for £20,000 but did not provide a citation for this figure.

91. For Soane's and Burdon's friendship, see Darley, *John Soane,* especially 38–46.

92. Du Prey, *John Soane,* 10; also see 259–60 for a brief discussion of the cowbarn's design.

93. See Notes on John Soane, "Designs for a Cow House for George Smith, June 1783," Sir John Soane's Museum Collection Online, http://collections.soane.org/home. Sir John Soane's Museum Collection Online features many scanned images of Soane's drawings for Burn Hall and Piercefield. Also see Soane, *Sketches in Architecture.*

94. For brief discussions of Soane's work on the Smith homes at Burn Hall and Piercefield, see Darley, *John Soane,* 65; and du Prey, *John Soane,* 281–83.

95. Darley, *John Soane,* 54.

96. See Notes on John Soane, "Variant Scheme A, 1785," Sir John Soane's Museum Collection Online.

97. See Wilson and Mackley, "How Much Did the English Country House Cost to Build."

98. "A Tour through Wales and the Central Parts of England," 1037. Although published in 1799, this source lists George Smith as the owner of Piercefield, so presumably it was originally written sometime between 1785 and 1793 when the Smiths lived at Piercefield.

99. Baker, *Picturesque Guide through Wales,* 1:32.

100. "E.M.," *Gentleman's Magazine* (London), April 1800, 331. The writer was responding to the previously quoted essay published in the December 1799 issue of the periodical (see note 98). That account, which presumably was written while the Smiths lived at Piercefield, indicated that "Mr. Smith is the present proprietor of Piercefield." By 1800, however, as this writer noted, ownership had transferred to a Colonel Wood.

101. *New Bath Guide,* 59. Another travel account, published in 1797, referred to a "professed improver" of Piercefield. It is unclear whether he meant George Smith or the subsequent owner. See Ireland, *Picturesque Views on the River Wye,* 145.

102. See John Soane, Journal No. 1, entries for March 4, September 30, October 1, 1790; June 2, 19, 1792, John Soane Papers, Sir John Soane's Museum; and Notes on John Soane, "Revised Design, 6 May 1792," Sir John Soane's Museum Collection Online. All quotations and references from Soane's archival collections are cited courtesy of the Trustees of Sir John Soane's Museum.

103. ES to MH, August 13, 1792, in *Fragments,* 10.

104. ES to MH, September 27, 1792, in *Fragments,* 15. Juliet Smith was pregnant at the time; in October she gave birth to another son (Richard).

105. HMB, *Fragments*, 24.

106. ES to MH, February 27, 1793, in *Fragments*, 25.

107. John Soane, Journal No. 2, February 20, 1793, John Soane Papers, Sir John Soane's Museum.

108. The number of bankruptcies in 1793 was over 1,200, more than double the previous year. See Hoppit, *Risk and Failure in English Business,* especially the chart on 182–83; and James, "Panics, Payments, Disruptions and the Bank of England."

109. ES to MH, March 3, 1793, in *Fragments*, 26.

110. For George Smith bankruptcy notices, see *London Gazette,* July 23, 1793, 629; August 17, 1793, 706; August 27, 1793, 745; and March 8, 1794, 217. For a description of bankruptcy proceedings in the eighteenth century, including the publication of notices in the *London Gazette,* see Hoppit, *Risk and Failure in English Business,* 35–37. Various notices of the auction of Smith's properties appeared in several London newspapers throughout the fall of 1793, including the *Universal Magazine of Knowledge and Pleasure* (London), August 1793, 157. Even after the sale of Piercefield, portions of George Smith's bankruptcy settlement were still being decided several years later. See various issues of the *London Gazette,* including July 12, 1796, 676; January 6, 1798, 29; June 12, 1798, 533; June 19, 1798, 563; and November 20, 1798, 1118–19. The 1796 notice related to the sale of Smith family holdings in Suffolk (presumably property that Juliet Mott Smith had brought to the marriage). As late as 1809, the case was still ongoing. See *London Gazette,* February 15, 1803, 194; August 15, 1809, 1308.

111. "Draft of Bond from George Smith Esq. to John Curre Esq.," 1791; John Scott, "Copy of a Case Relative to Smith and Curre," July 5, 1793, both John Soane Papers, Sir John Soane's Museum. This collection includes various correspondence and documentation related to the Smith bankruptcy case kept by Soane.

112. John Soane, Copy of Letter Sent to Mrs. Smith, November 4, 1793, Letterbook, John Soane Papers, Sir John Soane's Museum.

113. "Sale Catalogue No. 48," *Particulars and Conditions of Sale of Piercefield, by Mr. Christie, on Tuesday December 10, 1793,* John Soane Papers, Sir John Soane's Museum. Also see bankruptcy notices, such as *Bath Chronicle and Weekly Gazette,* October 3, 1793, 2.

114. Leadbeater, "The Annals of Ballitore," *Leadbeater Papers,* 1:271.

115. See Waters, *Piercefield on the Banks of the Wye,* 19.

116. See John Soane, Journal No. 1, September 30, 1790, John Soane Papers, Sir John Soane's Museum.

117. Davidoff and Hall, *Family Fortunes,* 20.

118. HMB, *Fragments,* 28.

119. JS, Letter II, in *Fragments,* 229.

120. Joseph Cottle, *Reminiscences of Samuel Taylor Coleridge and Robert Southey,* 2nd edition (London: Houlston and Stoneman, 1848), 27–28. For an account of their travels, see Vardy, "Joseph Cottle and Reminiscence."

121. Samuel Coleridge, "Reflections on Having Left a Place of Retirement," quoted in *The Stranger's Illustrated Guide to Chepstow and Its Neighbourhood; With Copious Notices of Tintern Abbey, Wyndcliff, and the Districts of Chepstow, Caldicot, Rhaglan, Monmouth, Goodrich, and Ross* (London: J. Newman, 1843), 19.

122. William Wordsworth, "Lines Written a Few Miles above Tintern Abbey," in Wordsworth, *Lyrical Ballads*, 201. Also see Fairer, "Revisiting 'Tintern Abbey.'"

2. "Well Furnished at Present"

1. HMB, *Fragments*, 30.
2. ES to MH, October 15, 1793, in *Fragments*, 36.
3. JS, Letter II, in *Fragments*, 230.
4. HMB, *Fragments*, 30.
5. Ibbetson et al., *Picturesque Guide to Bath*, 35.
6. *New Bath Guide*, 43. For historical accounts of eighteenth-century Bath, see Borsay, "Visitors and Residents"; Corfield, "Georgian Bath"; and Neale, *Bath, 1680–1850*.
7. Fanny Burney to Mrs. [Frederica] Locke, May 10, 1816, in Derry, ed., *Journals and Letters of Fanny Burney*, 9:125–26. Any quotations from the various editions comprising the published writings of Fanny Burney cited retain the spelling and punctuation of the transcriptions provided. A successful author and friend of Harriet Bowdler who made several visits to Bath, Fanny Burney's various writings provide important evidence of Bath's community of learned women in the late eighteenth century.
8. Plymley, Journal, October 27, 1794, in Wilson, "A Shropshire Lady in Bath," 101–2. This source presents the journals of Katherine Plymley, who made several visits to Bath between 1794 and 1807. Plymley made brief references to Harriet Bowdler and Mary Hunt in her journal entries, providing good supporting evidence of the social circles that Elizabeth Smith would have encountered in Bath.
9. For the community of women in Bath, see Bannet, "The Bluestocking Sisters"; Child, "'To Sing the Town'"; Hill, "A Tale of Two Sisters"; Rizzo, "Two Versions of Community"; and Rizzo, *Companions without Vows*.
10. Samuel Crisp to Fanny Burney, April 27, 1780, in Rizzo, ed., *Early Journals and Letters of Fanny Burney*, 4:73.
11. *New Bath Guide*, 23–27.
12. Plymley, Journal, October 21, 1794, in Wilson, "A Shropshire Lady in Bath," 100.
13. Plymley, Journal, October 27, 1794, in Wilson, "A Shropshire Lady in Bath," 102.
14. Plymley, Journal, October 27, 1794, in Wilson, "A Shropshire Lady in Bath," 101.
15. Burney, Journal, September 4, 1786, in Barrett, ed., *Diary and Letters of Madame d'Arblay*, 3:20–21.
16. Plymley, Journal, October 13, 1794, in Wilson, "A Shropshire Lady in Bath," 97.
17. Burney, Journal, June 1780, in Rizzo, ed., *Early Journals and Letters of Fanny Burney*, 4:154.
18. Fanny Burney to General [Alexandre] d'Arblay, September 17, 1817, in Barrett, ed., *Diary and Letters of Madame d'Arblay*, 6:328.
19. "Florio: A Tale, for Fine Gentlemen and Fine Ladies: and, the Bas Bleu; or, Conversation. Two Poems," *Critical Review; or, Annals of Literature* (London), April 1786, 267.
20. See Eger, *Bluestockings;* Eger and Peltz, *Brilliant Women;* Haslett, "Bluestocking Feminism Revisited"; Haslett, "Becoming Bluestockings"; Heller, "Bluestocking Salons and

the Public Sphere"; Myers, *Bluestocking Circle;* and Pohl and Schellenberg, *Reconsidering the Bluestockings.*

21. Eger, *Bluestockings,* 3.

22. "Memoirs of Miss Hannah More," *New-York Missionary Magazine,* 357–58.

23. See Guest, *Small Change,* 50; also see Chernock, *Men and the Making of Modern British Feminism;* Colley, *Britons;* and Major, *Madam Britannia.*

24. For an analysis of changing literary representations of the bluestockings, see especially Haslett, "Bluestocking Feminism Revisited," and the sources in note 20.

25. "*Nubilia in Search of a Husband,*" *Select Reviews, and Spirit of the Foreign Magazines* (Philadelphia), December 1809, 398.

26. Sir Gilbert Elliot to Lady Elliot, March 31, 1787, in *Life and Letters of Sir Gilbert Elliot, First Earl of Minto, from 1751 to 1806, When His Public Life in Europe Was Closed by His Appointment to the Vice-Royalty of India* (London: Longmans, Green, 1874), 1:146.

27. "Richard Brinsley Sheridan," in *Lives of the Illustrious (The Biographical Magazine)* (London: Partridge and Oakey, 1853), 3:180.

28. HMB to Eliza Simcoe, September 14, 1818, SFP-LAC, Reel A607, File 33/1.

29. Burney, Journal, June 28, 1817, in Barrett, ed., *Diary and Letters of Madame d'Arblay,* 6:311.

30. See for example, Clarke, *Rise and Fall of the Woman of Letters;* Kelley, *Learning to Stand and Speak;* and McMahon, *Mere Equals.*

31. "On Female Authorship," 421.

32. Hannah More to Mrs. [Ann] Kennicott, 1813, in Roberts, ed., *Memoirs of the Life and Correspondence of Hannah More,* 2:197.

33. Hannah More to Sir W. W. Pepys, December 19, 1808, in Roberts, ed., *Memoirs of the Life and Correspondence of Hannah More,* 2:140. In this same letter, More also noted, "Her mother has just sent me a beautiful engraving of her, which I much value as a striking resemblance." See chapter 7 for discussion of Hannah More's role in crafting Elizabeth Smith's posthumous reputation.

34. JS, Letter II, in *Fragments,* 228.

35. HMB, *Fragments,* 5.

36. Thomas Badcock to Mr. [John] Nichols, September 26, 1786, quoted in Polwhele, *Traditions and Recollections,* 1:241.

37. See George Streynsham Master, *Notices of the Family of Hunt, of Lyndon, Co. Rutland; Stoke Daubeny and Wadenhoe, Co. Northampton; Longnor and Boreatton, Co. Salop; and Lanhydrock, Co. Cornwall* (London: Mitchell and Hughes, 1880), 15. For women working as governesses, see Hill, *Women Alone,* especially chapter 5.

38. Elizabeth Simcoe to Mrs. [Ann] Hunt, April 1, 1793, Simcoe Family Papers, Devon Archives. For background information on members of the Simcoe family, see Arnold, "Genteel Widows of Bath"; and Fryer, *Elizabeth Postuma Simcoe.*

39. According to Mary Ann Burges, Mary wanted to stay with Harriet during this visit, but she did not have room in her house, presumably because she was hosting Elizabeth and perhaps other members of the Smith family. See MAB to Elizabeth Simcoe, March 1793, SFP-LAC, Reel A606, File 29/2.

40. HMB, *Fragments,* 32.

41. ES to MH, December 12, 1792, in *Fragments,* 19.

42. ES to MH, April 7, 1794, in *Fragments,* 38.

43. Eliza Simcoe to MH, June 1797, SFP-LAC, Reel A607, File 32/2. Weston was a village located near Bath.

44. Eliza Simcoe to MH, July 1807, SFP-LAC, Reel A607, File 32/12.

45. For Mary Ann Burges's visit to Bath in 1793, see MAB to Elizabeth Simcoe, September 15, 1793, SFP-AO, Reel 16, F47-9-0-3. Also see Fryer, *Elizabeth Postuma Simcoe,* 97–98.

46. MAB to Elizabeth Simcoe, March 14, 1794, SFP-AO, Reel 16, F47-9-0-3.

47. ES to MH, October 15, 1793, in *Fragments,* 35–36.

48. ES to MH, October 15, 1793, in *Fragments,* 35–36.

49. MAB to Elizabeth Simcoe, June 17, 1792, SFP-LAC, Reel A606, File 29/2.

50. MAB to Elizabeth Simcoe, October 12, 1793, SFP-AO, Reel 16, F47-9-0-3.

51. Eliza Simcoe to MH, April 17 1808, SFP-LAC, Reel A607, File 32/16.

52. HMB to Eliza Simcoe, May 24 [undated, circa 1807], SFP-LAC, Reel A607, File 33/16.

53. In their classic study *The Madwoman in the Attic,* Sandra M. Gilbert and Susan Gubar discussed how prevailing cultural and literary stereotypes cast the woman writer as eccentric, solitary, and isolated. Such conditions certainly were not the norm within the worlds that Elizabeth Smith inhabited, particularly in Bath. For other useful works describing the variety of women's literary practices, see Ezell, *Writing Women's Literary History;* Levy, "Do Women Have a Book History?"; and Winckles and Rehbein, eds., *Women's Literary Networks and Romanticism.*

54. MAB to Elizabeth Simcoe, April 1793, SFP-LAC, Reel A606, File 29/2.

55. MAB to Elizabeth Simcoe, June 1792, SFP-LAC, Reel A606, File 29/2.

56. "On the Literary Education of Women," *Universal Magazine of Knowledge and Pleasure* (London), January 1781, 42.

57. MAB to Elizabeth Simcoe, September 7, 1793, SFP-AO, Reel 16, F47-9-0-3.

58. See James Bland Burges, "Introduction," in Mary Ann Burges, *Progress of the Pilgrim Good-Intent,* 9th edition (London: John Hatchard, 1814), iv–vi. This edition was published after Burges's death in 1813 and includes a brief biographical sketch written by her brother.

59. MAB to Elizabeth Simcoe, April 1793, SFP-LAC, Reel A606, File 29/2.

60. MAB to Elizabeth Simcoe, September 5, 1793, SFP-AO, Reel 16, F47-9-0-3.

61. MAB to Elizabeth Simcoe, April 1793, SFP-LAC, Reel A606, File 29/2.

62. ES to MH, July 7, 1792, in *Fragments,* 6–7.

63. ES to MH, October 15, 1793, in *Fragments,* 36.

64. For the importance of letter writing as a site of intellectual exchange for women, see Halsey, "'Tell Me of Some *Booklings*'"; Linkin, "Mary Tighe's Newly Discovered Letters"; and McMahon, *Mere Equals,* especially chapter 2.

65. ES to MH, November 17, 1793, in *Fragments,* 37.

66. For classic interpretations of female friendship, see especially Smith-Rosenberg, "The Female World of Love and Ritual"; Cott, *Bonds of Womanhood;* Karlsen and Crumpacker, "Introduction"; and Lasser, "Let Us Be Sisters Forever."

67. Elizabeth Simcoe to MH, April 26, 1792, SFP-AO, Reel 16, F 47-9-0-1.

68. ES to MH, August 18, 1793, in *Fragments,* 34.

69. ES to MH, July 27, 1792, in *Fragments,* 9.

70. [Scott], *Description of Millenium Hall*. For a useful analysis of Scott's novel, see Kelly, "Introduction"; and Lake, "Redecorating the Ruin."

71. See Hesselgrave, *Lady Miller*. I am unaware of a more recent full-length biographical account of Miller; however, brief references to her Bath Easton gatherings appear in several recent sources. See Paula R. Backscheider, *Eighteenth Century Women Poets and Their Poetry: Inventing Agency, Inventing Genre* (Baltimore: Johns Hopkins University Press, 2010), 31–32; Brewer, *Pleasures of the Imagination*, 601–4; Child, "'To Sing the Town,'" 162; Prendergast, *Literary Salons across Britain and Ireland*, 143–47; White, "But Who Was the Queen of Bath?" 43–61; and Gillen D'Arcy Wood, *Romanticism and Music Culture in Britain, 1770–1840: Virtue and Virtuosity* (Cambridge: Cambridge University Press, 2010), 30–33.

72. [Philip Thicknesse], *The New Prose Bath Guide for the Year 1778* (London: Printed for the Author, 1778), 85. Also see Hesselgrave, *Lady Miller*, 22–23.

73. Burney, Journal, May 27, 1780, in Rizzo, ed., *Early Journals and Letters of Fanny Burney*, 4:127.

74. Anna Seward to Thomas Sedgwick Whalley, October 1, 1781, in Hill Wickham, ed., *Journals and Correspondence of Thomas Sedgwick Whalley* (London: Richard Bentley, 1863), 1:335.

75. Horace Walpole to H. S. Conway and Lady Aylesbury, January 15, 1775, in Peter Cunningham, ed., *The Letters of Horace Walpole, Fourth Earl of Orford* (Edinburgh: John Grant, 1906), 6:172; Boswell, *Life of Samuel Johnson*, 2:350.

76. Miller, *Poetical Amusements*, 1st edition.

77. Miller, *Poetical Amusements*, 2nd edition, 2:v.

78. Miller, *Poetical Amusements*, 2nd edition, 1:iv, vi–vii.

79. Miller, *Poetical Amusements*, 2nd edition, 1:4–6. As H. J. Jackson argues, Romantic-era readers enjoyed "filling in the blanks" and guessing the identities of names that were partially revealed/obscured through the use of dashes. See Jackson, *Romantic Readers*, especially 218–22.

80. Miller, *Poetical Amusements*, 2nd edition, 1:iv–v. For manuscript circulation as a key element of literary culture during this era, especially for women writers, see Ezell, *Social Authorship and the Advent of Print*; and Levy, *Literary Manuscript Culture*.

81. See Miller, *Poetical Amusements*, 2nd edition, 1:38–41; also see Hesselgrave, *Lady Miller*, 60.

82. In *Poems and Essays*, the poem appears under the title "Subject Love. For the Vase at Bath-Easton Villa." See [Bowdler], *Poems and Essays*, 23–26.

83. See Jane Bowdler, *Poems and Essays, by the Late Miss Bowdler*, 3rd edition (Bath: Richard Cruttwell, 1787); 7th edition (Bath: Richard Cruttwell, 1793); and 10th edition (Bath: Richard Cruttwell, 1798). The quoted text appears on p. ix of the 10th edition.

84. Anna Seward to F. N. C. Mundy, October 10, 1787, in Constable, ed., *Letters of Anna Seward*, 1:341.

85. Fanny Burney to Susanna Elizabeth Burney, April 29, 1780, in Rizzo, ed., *Early Journals and Letters of Fanny Burney*, 4:82.

86. ES to LIK, September 19, 1798, in *Fragments*, 109.

87. Child, "'To Sing the Town,'" 163.

88. For provincial print markets, see Rezek, *London and the Making of Provincial Literature*.

89. Randle Wilbraham Falconer and Anthony Beaufort Brabazon, *History of the Royal Mineral Water Hospital Bath,* (Bath, U.K.: Charles Halleti, 1888), 48–49.

90. See [Bowdler], *Sermons on the Doctrines and Duties of Christianity.*

91. Fanny Burney to Princess Elizabeth, December 21, 1815, in Derry, ed., *Journals and Letters of Fanny Burney,* 9:35.

92. See Bowdler, *Family Shakespeare.* For the bowdlerization of Shakespeare, see Perrin, *Dr. Bowdler's Legacy.*

93. "H. T." [Mary Hunt], "Written on Visiting the Ruins of Dunkeswell-Abbey." See chapter 1 for more discussion of this poem.

94. Mary Hunt's works—which to this day remain unattributed to her directly—include *Essay on the Happiness of the Life to Come;* and *Lectures on Astronomy, and Natural Philosophy.* See ES to MH, April 7, 1794, in *Fragments,* 38, for a reference to Hunt's *Essay on the Happiness;* and ES to MH, September 27 1794, in *Fragments,* 41, for reference to what Smith referred to as Hunt's "little book of Astronomy." Also see MAB to Elizabeth Simcoe, SFP-AO, Reel 16, F47-9-0-3.

95. MAB to Elizabeth Simcoe, March 10, 1795, SFP-AO, Reel 16, F47-9-0-3.

96. See [Burges], *Cavern of Death;* and [Burges], *Progress of the Pilgrim Good-Intent.* For a brief overview of Burges' literary career, see Humphreys, "Burges, Mary Anne (1763–1813)."

97. MAB to Elizabeth Simcoe, February 28, 1794, SFP-AO, Reel 16, F47-9-0-3.

98. MAB to Elizabeth Simcoe, April 26, 1794, SFP-AO, Reel 16, F47-9-0-3. For additional evidence that Burges was the author of this anonymously published work, see various references in her February 28, April 15, 26, 1794, writings to Elizabeth Simcoe, SFP-AO, Reel 16, F47-9-0-3; and Fryer, *Elizabeth Posthuma Simcoe,* 100.

99. "Art. 20. *The Cavern of Death, a Moral Tale,*" *British Critic* (London), April 1794, 444.

100. MAB to Elizabeth Simcoe, May 4, 1794, SFP-AO, Reel 16, F47-9-0-3.

101. "On Female Authorship," 421.

102. Bannet, "The Bluestocking Sisters," especially 45–46.

103. See Hill, "A Tale of Two Sisters," and other sources in note 9.

104. Stephanie Eckroth, "Celebrity and Anonymity in the *Monthly Review's* Notices of Nineteenth-Century Novels," in Hawkins and Ives, eds., *Women Writers and the Artifacts of Celebrity,* 13. For other accounts of British women's success as authors, see Cayton, *Love in the Time of Revolution;* Clarke, *Rise and Fall of the Woman of Letters;* Guest, *Small Change;* Mellor, *Mothers of the Nation;* and Turner, *Living by the Pen.*

105. "Art. II. *The Letters of Mrs. Elizabeth Montagu,*" 31.

106. "Female Authors," *Polyanthos* (Boston), November 1, 1813, 100.

107. More, *Strictures on the Modern System of Female Education,* 52, 123. For analysis of More's writings and influence, see Pearson, *Women's Reading in Britain,* especially 69–90; and Stott, *Hannah More.*

108. HMB to Eliza Simcoe, September 12, [undated, circa 1808], Simcoe Family Papers, Devon Archives.

109. ES to MH, September 27, 1794, in *Fragments,* 40.

110. ES to MH, April 7, 1794, in *Fragments,* 38.

111. ES to MH, February 1795, in *Fragments,* 43.

112. ES to MH April 7, 1794, in *Fragments,* 39.

113. ES to MH April 7, 1794, in *Fragments,* 39.

114. HMB, *Fragments*, 67.

115. ES, "Reflections," 1796–97, in *Fragments*, 71, 75.

3. "At the Foot of the Tower"

1. ES to MH, May 26, [1798], in *Fragments*, 97–99.

2. ES to MH, May 26, [1798], in *Fragments*, 97–99.

3. See Andrews, *Search for the Picturesque;* and Ousby, *Englishman's England.*

4. Buzard, *The Beaten Track*, 16, 130 (quotations); also see Bainbridge, *Mountaineering and British Romanticism;* and Pratt, *Imperial Eyes.*

5. Women did travel during this era, but in the cultural imagination they were more typically considered to be readers of travel narratives, rather than direct participants in such adventures. See De Ritter, "Reading 'Voyages and Travels'"; Kinsley, *Women Writing the Home Tour;* Imbarrato, *Traveling Women;* and Perkins, "'News from Scotland.'" According to Michael Freeman, who has conducted extensive research into travel accounts in Wales, "Of about 200 known accounts of tours of Wales by women between 1700 and 1900, only 20 were published during, or very soon after, the life of the authors." See Freeman, "Women Tourists."

6. MAB to Elizabeth Simcoe, March 14, 1794, SFP-AO, Reel 16, F47-9-0-3.

7. MAB to Elizabeth Simcoe, March 26, 1794, SFP-AO, Reel 16, F47-9-0-3.

8. ES to MH, April 7, 1794, in *Fragments*, 39–40.

9. For army commissions, see Allen, "Compatible Incentives and the Purchase of Military Commissions"; and Glover, "The Purchase of Commissions."

10. ES to MH, April 7, 1794, in *Fragments*, 38.

11. ES to MH, July 28, 1795, in *Fragments*, 45.

12. ES to MH, October 5, 1795, in *Fragments*, 46–47.

13. For summaries of reading patterns popular in transatlantic cultures of print, see Darnton, "First Steps toward a History of Reading"; Jackson, "Approaches to the History of Readers"; and Williams, *Social Life of Books.*

14. ES to MH, October 5, 1795, in *Fragments*, 45–46. For "testing" of affections, see Lystra, *Searching the Heart;* and McMahon, *Mere Equals.*

15. ES to MH, May 21, 1796, in *Fragments*, 50.

16. ES to MH, May 21, 1796, in *Fragments*, 49–51.

17. ES to MH, May 21, 1796, in *Fragments*, 49–51.

18. For travel experiences in late eighteenth-century Ireland, see Colbert, ed., *Travel Writing and Tourism in Britain and Ireland;* Schudds, "Old Coach Roads from Dublin"; and Williams, *Creating Irish Tourism.*

19. ES to MH, May 21, 1796, in *Fragments*, 49.

20. The term "romantic friendship" has been used to describe Eleanor Butler and Sarah Ponsonby's relationship. See especially Mavor, *Ladies of Llangollen;* and Mavor, ed., *Life with the Ladies of Llangollen.* Also see Bradbrook, "The Elegant Eccentrics"; Brideoake, *Ladies of Llangollen;* Crowell, "Ghosting the Llangollen Ladies"; and Faderman, *Surpassing the Love of Men.*

21. Anna Seward to Mary Powys, November 17, 1795, in Constable, ed., *Letters of Anna Seward*, 4:120.
22. Eleanor Butler, Journal, March 11, 1791, in Bell, ed., *Hamwood Papers*, 271.
23. Hutton, "Letters Written during a Tour in North Wales," 206.
24. Warner, *Walk through Wales*, 173.
25. Lockhart, *Memoirs of the Life of Sir Walter Scott*, 8:48–50.
26. William Wordsworth, "To the Lady E. B. and the Hon. Miss P," in Wordsworth, *Sonnets*, 91.
27. Anna Seward to Henry White, September 7, 1795, in Constable, ed., *Letters of Anna Seward*, 4:100.
28. Butler, Journal, April 16, 1789, in Bell, ed., *Hamwood Papers*, 197.
29. Butler, Journal, July 5, 1788, in Bell, ed., *Hamwood Papers*, 110.
30. Mavor, *Ladies of Llangollen*, 67.
31. Anna Seward to Lady Eleanor Butler, June 4, 1798, in Constable, ed., *Letters of Anna Seward*, 5:111.
32. HMB, *Fragments*, 51. There are several references in Eleanor Butler's journal to her correspondence with Harriet Bowdler and also references to corresponding with and visits from a "Mrs. Smith." This almost certainly refers to Juliet Smith, based on references that correspond to the Smith family's travels in Wales and Ireland at that time. See Eleanor Butler, Journal, 1799, Ladies of Llangollen Papers, Microfilm Reel 3, New York Public Library.
33. For evidence that Elizabeth Smith and Eliza Simcoe knew each other socially, see, for example, Eliza Simcoe to MH, June 1797, SFP-LAC, Reel A607, File 32/2. In *Fragments*, Bowdler noted that she "had a letter from Miss Smith on this subject" but it was "destroyed" (51–52).
34. Eliza Simcoe to MH, October 1809, Simcoe Family Papers, Devon Archives.
35. Eliza Simcoe to MH, October 1809, Simcoe Family Papers, Devon Archives.
36. ES to MH, May 26, [1798], in *Fragments*, 97–99.
37. JS, quoted in *Fragments*, 56.
38. ES to LIK, "Sligo, 1796," in *Fragments*, 54.
39. For an overview of women's purposes and experiences as travelers, see Imbarrato, *Traveling Women*; and Kinsley, *Women Writing the Home Tour*.
40. ES to LIK, September 13, 1796, in *Fragments*, 60. For an overview of Irish travel experiences, see Colbert, ed., *Travel Writing and Tourism in Britain and Ireland*.
41. ES to MH, August 8, 1796, in *Fragments*, 52–53.
42. ES to LIK, "Sligo, 1796," in *Fragments*, 55.
43. ES to LIK, January 13, 1797, in *Fragments*, 63–65.
44. Morgan, *Tour to Milford Haven*, 112–13.
45. ES to LIK, January 13, 1797, in *Fragments*, 62–64.
46. ES, "Reflections," circa 1796–97, in *Fragments*, 70.
47. ES to MH, July 10, 1798, in *Fragments*, 99–100.
48. ES to MH, May 26, [1798], in *Fragments*, 99.
49. Gilpin, "Observations on Several Parts of North Wales, Relative Chiefly to Picturesque Beauty; Made in the Summer of the Year 1773," in Gilpin, *Observations on Several Parts*

of the Counties, 161. For the development of tourism in Wales, see Freeman, "Perceptions of Welshness."

50. ES to MH, July 10, 1798, in *Fragments*, 101–2. At the time, Thomas Pennant was considered the foremost authority on Welsh travel; most travel guides published in the late eighteenth and early nineteenth centuries referenced his work. See Pennant, *Tour in Wales, 1770*; and Evans, "Thomas Pennant."

51. Andrews, *Search for the Picturesque*, 67.

52. See Kinsley, *Women Writing the Home Tour*, especially 38–39. For similar developments in nineteenth-century American tourism, see Mackintosh, *Selling the Sights*.

53. On the conventions of travel writing, see Andrews, *Search for the Picturesque*, especially 73–81; Austin, "Aesthetic Embarrassment"; Guentner, "The Sketch as Literary Metaphor"; and Kinsley, *Women Writing the Home Tour*.

54. John Byng, "A Tour to North Wales, 1784," in Andrews, ed., *Torrington Diaries*, 1:116.

55. Morgan, *Tour to Milford Haven*, ix.

56. Warner, *Walk through Wales*, 43.

57. Sotheby, *Poetical Epistle to Sir George Beaumont*, 15. This excerpt from Sotheby's poem is cited to illustrate the main locations on the scenic tour in Andrews, *Search for the Picturesque*, 35.

58. ES, "A Supposed Translation from a Welsh Poem," in *Fragments*, 20.

59. On Snowdon's appeal, see Andrews, *Search for the Picturesque*, chapter 6; Bainbridge, *Mountaineering and British Romanticism*; and Stempel, "Revelation on Mount Snowdon."

60. Warner, *Walk through Wales*, 121.

61. Hutton, *Remarks upon North Wales*, 154.

62. William Sotheby, "A Tour through Parts of South and North Wales, Book the Second," in Sotheby, *Tour through Parts of Wales*, 33.

63. Bainbridge, "Romantic Writers and Mountaineering," 2; also see Bainbridge, "Writing from 'The Perilous Ridge'"; and Bainbridge, *Mountaineering and British Romanticism*. Bainbridge's works contain brief references to Elizabeth Smith's mountain climbing at Snowdon as well as in the Lake District.

64. Wordsworth, *The Prelude*, 356. Wordsworth climbed Snowdon in 1791 but did not begin work on *The Prelude* until 1799; the work was completed in 1805 and first published in 1812.

65. Hutton, "Letters Written during a Second Tour in North Wales," 323. Accounts of Catherine Hutton's 1790s tours of Wales were subsequently published as a series of letters in the London *Monthly Magazine* between 1815 and 1818. She also later wrote works of fiction that incorporated travel motifs informed by her tours of Wales. See Constantine, "'The Bounds of Female Reach'"; Hill, "Catherine Hutton"; and Wilson, "'Something Like Mine.'"

66. Gilpin, "Observations on Several Parts of North Wales," 146–47.

67. Warner, *Walk through Wales*, 122–28.

68. Byng, "A Tour to North Wales, 1784," 164–65.

69. ES to MH, July 10, 1798, in *Fragments*, 100–102.

70. ES to MH, July 10, 1798, in *Fragments*, 102–3.

71. Wordsworth, *The Prelude*, 354.

72. ES to MH, July 10, 1798, in *Fragments*, 102–4.

73. ES to MH, July 10, 1798, in *Fragments*, 104–5.

74. Gilpin, "Observations on Several Parts of North Wales," 145.

75. ES to MH, July 10, 1798, in *Fragments*, 106.

76. ES to MH, July 10, 1798, in *Fragments*, 106–7.

77. Hutton, "Letters Written during a Third Tour in North Wales," 397.

78. Hutton, *Remarks upon North Wales*, 157–58.

79. For discussions of how both cultural understandings and personal experiences of travel were often gendered, see Hagglund, "Gendering the Scottish Guidebook"; and Kinsley, *Women Writing the Home Tour*, especially chapter 4. Both Hagglund and Kinsley note the experiences of Sarah Murray, who traveled throughout Scotland in the 1790s and referred to one of her own hikes as "a bold adventure (for a woman)." See Murray, *Companion, and Useful Guide*, especially 243.

80. In *Mountaineering and British Romanticism*, Simon Bainbridge provides ample evidence of women's mountain climbing throughout Wales, Scotland, and the Lake District during the Romantic era. His chapter on "Women and Mountaineering" includes discussions of Elizabeth Smith, Dorothy Wordsworth, Ann Radcliffe, and other women who recorded their climbing experiences. Citing William Hutton's account, Bainbridge recognizes how gendered constructs informed the era's perceptions of women's achievements: "For several male climbers and writers, the presence of women on the mountain was challenging because it potentially undermined their own sense of achievement, which they frequently registered in gendered terms" (221). This astute observation, however, does not fully inform the rest of the book's overarching themes. Throughout seven other chapters, Bainbridge repeatedly links mountaineering, masculinity, and creative expression with key Romantic-era male writers such as William Wordsworth, Samuel Coleridge, and John Keats. There is little explicit analysis, for example, of how these men's self-conscious, repeated touting of connections between their creative poetic powers and masculine strength of body might be reframed in light of women's similar adventures and experiences. As a result, despite his clear respect for women climbers, Bainbridge's study implicitly reifies gendered constructs from the Romantic era by continuing to privilege the seemingly unique characteristics of how men such as Wordsworth and Keats developed embodied ideas of poetic genius rooted in culturally constructed notions of masculinity.

81. ES to MH, July 10, 1798, in *Fragments*, 108.

82. See Andrews, *Search for the Picturesque*, 139; and Bainbridge, *Mountaineering and British Romanticism*, 68–69.

83. ES to MH, July 10, 1798, in *Fragments*, 102–8. See Linkin, "Mary Tighe's Newly Discovered Letters"; and Halsey, "'Tell Me of Some *Booklings*.'"

84. ES, "Observations in North-Wales, Probably Written at Conway," in *Fragments*, 129–30. For a discussion of women's scientific writing about the sublime, see Speese, "'Our Feelings Become Impressed.'" For a historical overview of women's scientific studies, see Fara, *Pandora's Breeches*.

85. Morgan, *Tour to Milford Haven*, v–viii. For Morgan's travel writings, see Prescott, "Women Travellers in Wales"; and Spunaugle, "A Travel Writer Reconsidered."

86. "L.A.," "Journal of a Welsh Tour," 227, 231. For other accounts of women's travels in Wales, see Freeman, "Women Tourists."
87. Mary Leslie to Vernor and Hood, August 24, 1803, Evelyn Papers.
88. ES to MH, March 29, 1799, in *Fragments,* 111–12.
89. Eliza Simcoe to MH, August 30 1811, SFP-LAC, Reel A607, File 32/23.
90. ES to LIK, September 19, 1798, in *Fragments,* 110. Isabella King seems to have taken Elizabeth Smith's advice to heart. By 1802, she had moved to Bath, becoming active in philanthropy and later establishing a charitable institute to benefit women. See Collier, "The Truly Benevolent Lady Isabella King."
91. ES to MH, May 7, 1799, in *Fragments,* 113–14.
92. ES to LIK, September 6, 1797, in *Fragments,* 88.
93. ES to LIK, September 6, 1797, in *Fragments,* 88.
94. HMB, *Fragments,* 114.
95. Leadbeater, "The Annals of Ballitore," in *Leadbeater Papers,* 1:273. Leadbeater, a Quaker, was a respected Irish poet and author. See Stephen C. Behrendt, "The Letter and the Literary Circle: Mary Leadbeater, Melesina Trench, and the Epistolary Salon," in Callaghan and Howe, eds., *Romanticism and the Letter,* 29–44.
96. Abraham Shackleton to TW, April 12, 1800, TWP, Folder 20.
97. Leadbeater, "The Annals of Ballitore," in *Leadbeater Papers,* 1:289.
98. ES to MH, March 22, 1801, in *Fragments,* 137.

4. "Rejoice in Their Own Energy"

1. ES, Reflections, circa 1800–1802, in *Fragments,* 149. Throughout this chapter, I quote from various reflections/writings that Elizabeth Smith composed and that were subsequently published in *Fragments.* The approximate dates for these writings are based on Harriet Bowdler's editorial comments throughout the memoir. On the sublime, see Edmund Burke, *A Philosophical Enquiry into the Origin of Our Ideas of the Sublime and Beautiful,* 5th edition (London: J. Dodsley, 1767). Burke argued that "terror is in all cases whatsoever, either more openly or latently, the ruling principle of the sublime" (97).
2. ES, Reflections, circa 1800–1802, in *Fragments,* 150.
3. Bennett, *Letters to a Young Lady,* 2:13–14. For cultural attitudes toward exercise during this era, see Batchelor, "Thinking about the Gym"; and Noel, "No Wonder They Are Sick."
4. West, *Guide to the Lakes,* 1–3.
5. JS to TW, June 2, [circa 1801], TWP, Folder 13.
6. See Account Book of Princess Charlotte of Wales, 1801–5, Papers of Princess Charlotte of Wales, Georgian Papers Online, GEO/MAIN/50134–50176. Mary Hunt earned an annual salary of three hundred pounds as sub-governess; the main governess at the time earned double that amount.
7. JS to TW, September 7, [circa 1801–2], TWP, Folder 13.
8. George Smith to TW, September 18, 1800, TWP, Folder 20.
9. TW to Elihu Robinson, June 7, 1801, TWP, Folder 27.
10. JS to TW, July 18, [circa 1801], TWP, Folder 13. While the exact details of how George Smith disposed of his commission are not known, Juliet Smith's comments suggest

that he did not receive the amount he hoped. According to military historian Michael Glover, a retiring officer "could sell his commission and, with the proceeds, buy an annuity" that would in essence serve as a retirement pension. During wartime, however, commissions became more challenging to sell, especially as so many officers had died in the Caribbean, creating opportunities for promotion without the need to purchase a commission. After 1795, renewed attempts to reform the system resulted in many officers being relegated to half-pay. See Glover, "The Purchase of Commissions."

11. Portions of George Smith's 1793 bankruptcy were still being settled several years later. See *London Gazette,* July 12, 1796, 676; January 6, 1798, 29; June 12, 1798, 533; June 19, 1798, 563; November 20, 1798, 1118–19; February 15, 1803, 194; August 15, 1809, 1308.

12. TW to Elihu Robinson, June 7, 1801, TWP, Folder 27.

13. ES to MH, March 22, 1801, in *Fragments,* 137.

14. JS to TW, June 2, [circa 1801], TWP, Folder 13.

15. Elizabeth Hamilton to HMB, August 8, September 2, October 25, [1802], in *Fragments,* 158–60.

16. JS to TW, September 20, [circa 1801–2], TWP, Folder 13.

17. JS to TW, September 20, [circa 1801–2], TWP, Folder 13.

18. Abraham Shackleton to TW, April 12, 1800, TWP, Folder, 20.

19. Elizabeth Hamilton to HMB, October 25, [1802], in *Fragments,* 159–60.

20. JS to TW, September 20, [circa 1801–2], TWP, Folder 13.

21. JS to TW, June 21, [circa 1802], TWP, Folder 13. Hamilton was the author of several books, including *Translation of the Letters of a Hindoo Rajah* (London: G. G. and J. Robinson, 1796); and *Letters on Education* (Bath: R. Cruttwell, 1801). See Joyce Goodman, "Undermining or Building Up the Nation? Elizabeth Hamilton (1758–1816), National Identities and an Authoritative Role for Women Educationists," *History of Education* 28, no. 3 (1999): 279–96; and Jane Rendall, "Correspondence and Community: Maria Edgeworth's Scottish Friends," *European Romantic Review* 31, no. 6 (2020): 681–98.

22. Elizabeth Hamilton to "Miss B——," October 10, 1803, in Benger, *Memoirs of the Late Mrs. Elizabeth Hamilton,* 2:59. This memoir contains several letters that reference Hamilton's friendship with the Smith family.

23. William Smith, ed., *Old Yorkshire* (London: Longmans, Green, 1889), 291.

24. On Wilkinson, see Carr, *Thomas Wilkinson;* Helliher, "Thomas Wilkinson of Yanwath"; and Percy, "Thomas Wilkinson."

25. William Wordsworth's "To the Spade of a Friend" was originally composed in 1804 and first published in 1807. A later edition of Wordsworth's poetry identified Wilkinson as "honoured also by the friendship of Elizabeth Smith, and of Thomas Clarkson and his excellent wife." See Knight, ed., *Poetical Works of William Wordsworth,* 3:24.

26. TW to Mary Leadbeater, February 15, 1801, TWP, Folder 21.

27. TW to Elihu Robinson, June 7, 1801, TWP, Folder 27.

28. JS to TW, November 8, 1802, TWP, Folder 13.

29. JS to TW, June 21, [circa 1802], TWP, Folder 13. In this same letter, Juliet Smith asked Thomas Wilkinson to "remember us very kindly to the Clarksons." Dorothy Wordsworth's journal from 1800 to 1802 contains at least two references to the Smith family. See Woof, ed., *Dorothy Wordsworth,* especially 22, 106.

30. TW to Mary Leadbeater, December 27, 1801, TWP, Folder 21.

31. Wilkinson's account was first published in 1812 in the *Belfast Monthly Magazine*. A slightly edited version was included in a travel book of prose and poetry that Wilkinson published in 1824. See Wilkinson, "A Day's Tour"; and Wilkinson, *Tours to the British Mountains*. The day's events inspired Wilkinson to compose his poem "Cottage Sorrow," which was also included in these published narratives. His writings from this adventure circulated in manuscript form for several years before being published in 1812.

32. Green, *Tourist's New Guide*, 251.

33. Dorothy Wordsworth to Lady Beaumont, October 27, 1805, in De Selincourt et al., eds., *Letters of Dorothy and William Wordsworth*, vol. 1.

34. Wilkinson, "A Day's Tour," 3–4.

35. Wilkinson, "A Day's Tour," 4.

36. Wilkinson, "A Day's Tour," 4–5.

37. Mary Leadbeater to TW, [undated, circa 1801–2], TWP, Folder 20.

38. See Andrews, *Wanderers*, especially chapters 2 and 5; and Susan J. Wolfson, "Two Wordsworths: Mountain-Climbing, Letter-Writing," in Callaghan and Howe, eds., *Romanticism and the Letter*, 61–82. For William Wordsworth's use of his sister's writings, see Levy, *Literary Manuscript Culture*; and Wordsworth, *Description of the Scenery of the Lakes*, 129–36.

39. See Bainbridge, *Mountaineering and British Romanticism*, for discussions of Elizabeth Smith's, Dorothy Wordsworth's, and other women's climbing experiences in the Lake District. Despite such evidence, the privileging of a male subject as normative is evident in many scholarly accounts, including in Jarvis, *Romantic Writing and Pedestrian Travel*. Citing "the relative scarcity of women's travel writing," Jarvis defines pedestrian travel as an almost exclusively masculine activity (158). Jarvis actually identifies and cites several published travel narratives written by women but dismisses them all as exceptional, rather than fully exploring these sources as providing recurring, collective, and compelling evidence of women's widespread participation in travel trends, including pedestrianism. As discussed in chapter 3 of this study, women produced hundreds of accounts detailing their travel experiences during this era. Although many accounts written by women remained in manuscript form during their lifetimes, these sources provide extensive evidence, indicating the need to rethink prevailing narratives that continue to downplay or obscure women's explorations in order to privilege the seemingly unique sources and characteristics of Romantic-era men's poetic genius.

40. JS to TW, September 7, [circa 1801–2], TWP, Folder 13.

41. JS to TW, February 20, [circa 1802], TWP, Folder 13.

42. JS, Letter II, in *Fragments*, 231.

43. Wordsworth, *Description of the Scenery of the Lakes*, 7.

44. Radcliffe, *Journey Made in the Summer of 1794*, 2:203.

45. Hutchinson, *Excursion to the Lakes*, 164.

46. Radcliffe, *Journey Made in the Summer of 1794*, 2:303.

47. Hutchinson, *Excursion to the Lakes*, 130.

48. West, *Guide to the Lakes*, 286.

49. ES to MH, March 22, 1801, in *Fragments*, 137–38.

50. ES, Poem, "Patterdale, February 1801," in *Fragments*, 138–39.

51. ES, Poem, "Patterdale, February 1801," in *Fragments*, 139–40.
52. ES, Poem, "Patterdale, January 1801," in *Fragments*, 140–41.
53. ES, Reflections, January 1, 1798, in *Fragments*, 85–86.
54. HMB, *Fragments*, 142.
55. For accounts of women's self-fashioning through journal and diary writing, see Beattie, "Where Narratives Meet"; Blauvelt, *Work of the Heart;* Bunkers and Huff, eds., *Inscribing the Daily;* Huff, "Reading as Re-Vision"; Russell, "An Improper Education?"; and Wink, *She Left Nothing in Particular.*
56. ES, Reflections, circa 1796–97, in *Fragments*, 73.
57. ES, Reflections, circa 1800–1802, in *Fragments*, 151–52.
58. ES, Reflections, circa 1800–1802, in *Fragments*, 151–52.
59. ES, Reflections, circa 1796–97, in *Fragments*, 74.
60. MAB to Elizabeth Simcoe, April 1793, SFP-LAC, Reel A606, File 29/2.
61. For a discussion of how shifting understandings of genius were reflected in the Romantic era's veneration of Isaac Newton as a genius, see Fara, *Newton*. For discussions of gender and genius, see Battersby, *Gender and Genius;* Fraisse, *Reason's Muse;* Kelley, "'The Need of Their Genius'"; and Olwell, "'It Spoke Itself.'"
62. ES, Reflections, circa 1796–97, in *Fragments*, 76–77.
63. See Marshall, *Peabody Sisters;* and Marshall, *Margaret Fuller.*
64. ES, Reflections, circa 1796–97, in *Fragments*, 76–77.
65. "Thoughts on the Proposed Improvement of Female Education," *Christian Observer, Conducted by the Members of the Established Church* (Boston), May 1808, 301.
66. "Art. VI. *Reasons for the Classical Education of Children of Both Sexes. By John Morell,*" *Augustan Review* (London), May 1815, 33.
67. ES, Reflections, circa 1800–1802, in *Fragments*, 151.
68. ES, Reflections, circa 1796–97, in *Fragments*, 74.
69. ES, Reflections, circa 1790s, in *Fragments*, 131–32.
70. ES, Reflections, circa 1796–97, in *Fragments*, 83–84.
71. TW, excerpted in *Fragments*, 58.
72. JS to TW, August 20, [circa 1802–5], TWP, Folder 13.
73. ES, Reflections, circa 1800–1802, in *Fragments*, 145.
74. ES to HMB, March 22, 1805, in *Fragments*, 175; HMB, *Fragments*, 180. For Smith's work on the *Book of Job*, see DeWispelare, "An Amateur's Devotion"; and O'Sullivan, "Introduction," 5–23.
75. JS to TW, June 15, 1810, TWP, Folder 13. In this letter, Juliet Smith specifically referenced a published work by the bishop of St. David that offered praise for Elizabeth Smith's Hebrew translations. See Thomas Burgess, *Motives to the Study of Hebrew*, 2nd edition (London: W. Calvert, 1814).
76. ES to HMB, April 16, [1805], in *Fragments*, 178. The dictionary Elizabeth Smith consulted was John Parkhurst, *An Hebrew and English Lexicon, without Points, to Which Are Prefixed (Also without Points) a Methodical Hebrew Grammar, and a Short Chaldee Grammar* (London: W. Faden, 1762).
77. ES, Reflections, circa 1796–97, in *Fragments*, 78–79.
78. HMB, *Fragments*, 180.
79. Elizabeth Hamilton to HMB, December 13, [1802], in *Fragments*, 160.

80. Robert Southey to John Neville White, September 30, 1808, Romantic Circles, http://www.rc.umd.edu/editions/southey_letters/Part_Three/HTML/letterEEd.26 .1515.html. The book referenced by Southey was Joseph Carlyle, *Specimens of Arabian Poetry: From the Earliest Time to the Extinction of the Khaliphat, with Some Account of the Authors* (Cambridge: John Burges, 1796). The work included original compositions in Arabic, along with translations and commentary in English.

81. HMB, *Fragments*, 162–68. See William Sotheby, *Oberon: A Poem, from the German of Wieland* (London: Cadell and Davies, 1798).

82. "Original Anecdotes and Remains of Eminent Persons," *Monthly Magazine and British Register* (London), April 1798, 280. See Frederick Klopstock, *The Messiah: Attempted from the German of Mr. Klopstock: To Which Is Prefix'd His Introduction on Divine Poetry* (London: R. and J. Dodsley; T. Durham; T. Field; and J. Collyer, 1763).

83. Robert Southey to John May, June 6, 1798, Romantic Circles, https://www.rc.umd .edu/editions/southey_letters/Part_Two/HTML/letterEEd.26.323.html.

84. See Ernest Bernhardt-Kabisch, "'When Klopstock England Defied': Coleridge, Southey, and the German/English Hexameter Author(s)," *Comparative Literature* 55, no. 2 (Spring 2003): 130–63; and Alan G. Hill, "Wordsworth's Reception in Germany: Some Unfamiliar Episodes and Contacts, 1789–1849," *Review of English Studies* 59, no. 241 (September 2008): 568–81.

85. For Margaret Klopstock's letters to Samuel Richardson, see Barbauld, *Correspondence of Samuel Richardson*, 3:139–58; and Peter Sabor, "'The Job I Have Perhaps Rashly Undertaken': Publishing the Complete Correspondence of Samuel Richardson," *Eighteenth-Century Life* 35, no. 1 (Winter 2011): 9–28.

86. "Art. II. *The Correspondence of Samuel Richardson*," *Edinburgh Review*, October 1804, 39; Robert Southey to Charles Danvers, January 15, 1805, Romantic Circles, https:// romantic-circles.org/editions/southey_letters/Part_Three/HTML/letterEEd.26.1021 .html; "Art. IV: *The Correspondence of Samuel Richardson*," *Monthly Review; or, Literary Journal* (London), January 1805, 40.

87. HMB, *Fragments*, 168.

88. ES to HMB, November 9, 1804, in *Fragments*, 169–71.

89. HMB, *Fragments*, 168; also see ES to HMB, November 9, 1804, in *Fragments*, 169. These materials included a book of odes by Klopstock published in 1798 and another book provided by Sotheby that had been originally published in 1771, both in German.

90. Dr. [Jacob] Mumssen to HMB, September 7, 1804, in Smith, *Memoirs of Frederick and Margaret Klopstock*, 43. Several letters written by Dr. Mumssen to Harriet Bowdler as the project progressed were included in this work.

91. ES to HMB, December 22, [1804], in *Fragments*, 173.

92. ES to HMB, December 22, [1804], in *Fragments*, 173.

93. ES to HMB, April 16, [1805], in *Fragments*, 178.

94. ES to HMB, November 9, 1804, in *Fragments*, 171.

95. ES to HMB, November 9, 1804, and November 25, [1804], in *Fragments*, 171–72.

96. ES to HMB, November 9, 1804, in *Fragments*, 169.

97. ES to HMB, November 25, [1804], in *Fragments*, 172–73.

98. JS to TW, October 18, [circa 1801–2], TWP, Folder 13.

99. ES to HMB, November 25, [1804], in *Fragments*, 172–73.

100. HMB to ES, March 1805, quoted in JS, Letter II, in *Fragments*, 233.

101. ES to HMB, March 22, 1805, in *Fragments*, 175.

102. ES to HMB, April 16, [1805], in *Fragments*, 177.

103. ES to HMB, March 22, 1805, in *Fragments*, 175.

104. ES to MH, March 29, 1799, in *Fragments*, 111.

105. See chapter 2 for further discussion of women's publishing practices.

106. Elizabeth Carter, *All the Works of Epictetus, Which Are Now Extant; Consisting of His Discourses, Preserved by Arrian, in Four Books, the Enchiridion, and Fragments* (London: S. Richardson, 1758). See part 2 for further discussions of comparisons between Elizabeth Smith and Elizabeth Carter.

107. HMB, *Fragments*, 179. Harriet Bowdler's use of the pronoun "our" is suggestive, indicating that she viewed the project as a collaborative effort. Although Elizabeth Smith was doing the actual work of translating, Bowdler considered her own literary connections and editorial guidance as instrumental in securing publication for the Klopstock project.

108. ES, quoted in JS to Dr. [Francis] Randolph, [1807], Letter III (hereafter JS, Letter III), in *Fragments*, 236–37.

109. JS, Letter III, in *Fragments*, 238; for the timeline, also see HMB, *Fragments*, 203.

110. HMB, *Fragments*, 204.

111. ES to Mrs. Claxton, December 28, 1805, in *Fragments*, 205–6.

112. JS, Letter III, in *Fragments*, 239.

113. Mary Dixon to TW, 1806, TWP-BL, Volume 2; also see TW to Mary Leadbeater, March 18, 1806, TWP, Folder 21.

114. ES to Kitty Smith Allan, March 28, [1806], in *Fragments*, 206–7.

115. JS, Letter III, in *Fragments*, 240.

116. JS to TW, April 10, 1806, TWP, Folder 13.

117. JS, Letter III, in *Fragments*, 241–43.

118. Kitty Smith Allan to TW, April 23, 1806, TWP, Folder 13.

119. JS, Letter III, in *Fragments*, 245.

120. JS to TW, June 12, [1806], TWP, Folder 13.

121. ES to "Mrs. Wilmot," July 4, 1806, in *Fragments*, 208–9.

122. ES to HMB, [July 1806], in *Fragments*, 210.

123. JS to HMB, August 1806, Letter IV, in *Fragments*, 247–48.

124. HMB, *Fragments*, 212.

125. TW to Elihu Robinson, December 20, 1806, TWP, Folder 27.

126. TW, "Lines Inclosed," in *Fragments*, 261.

127. Mary Leadbeater to TW, November 8, 1806, TWP, Folder 20.

128. Mary Leadbeater to TW, November 2, 1807, TWP, Folder 20.

5. "Thoughts of Publishing a Little Biographical Work"

1. JS to HMB, August 1806, Letter IV, in *Fragments*, 250–51. In part 2, I have made the decision to refer to Elizabeth Smith and Harriet Bowdler primarily using their full or last names, as this part of the book focuses largely on their status as published authors within transatlantic cultures of print. The use of their first names in part 1,

by contrast, reflects that section's emphasis on the biographical components of Elizabeth Smith's life story.

2. JS to TW, undated letter [circa August–September 1806], TWP, Folder 13.

3. JS to TW, September 4, [1806], TWP, Folder 13.

4. TW to Elihu Robinson, December 20, 1806, TWP, Folder 27.

5. JS to TW, September 4, [1806], TWP, Folder 13.

6. HMB to Cadell and Davies, November 13, 1807, H. M. Bowdler Correspondence, Special Collections Library, Pennsylvania State University.

7. *Fragments, in Prose and Verse: By a Young Lady, Lately Deceased. With Some Account of Her Life and Character, by the Author of "Sermons on the Doctrines and Duties of Christianity"* (Bath: Richard Cruttwell, 1808). The early editions of *Fragments* were originally published without direct attribution to Smith or Bowdler. Beginning in 1809, the work's title and content were amended to identify both Smith and Bowdler, appearing as *Fragments, in Prose and Verse: By Miss Elizabeth Smith Lately Deceased. With Some Account of Her Life and Character, by H. M. Bowdler* (Bath: Richard Cruttwell, 1809).

8. HMB, Preface, in *Fragments*, x.

9. JS to TW, March 3, 1809, TWP, Folder 13. While this comment referred to a revised edition of *Fragments* published in 1809, Juliet Smith was clearly involved in the preparation of the first edition of the text, particularly since she composed letters in 1807 that were included as part of the book's appendix.

10. See JS to Cadell and Davies, November 27, 1807, Cadell and Davies Records, Box 1, Folder 9, Beinecke Rare Book and Manuscript Library, Yale University. This letter was sent just two weeks after Harriet Bowdler wrote to the publishers about her plan to publish *Fragments*.

11. HMB to Cadell and Davies, [undated, circa November/December 1807], Cadell and Davies Records, Box 1, Folder 9.

12. Eliza Simcoe to MH, August 30, 1807, SFP-LAC, Reel A607, File 32/15.

13. Eliza Simcoe to MH, March 18, 1808, SFP-LAC, Reel A607, unnumbered file.

14. HMB to Eliza Simcoe, September 12, [circa 1808], Simcoe Family Papers, Devon Archives.

15. JS to TW, September 4, [1806], TWP, Folder 13.

16. For a manuscript copy of this elegy, see TW to Elihu Robinson, December 20, 1806, TWP, Folder 27. An almost identical version of the elegy was printed with very minor edits in *Fragments*, 260–63. I quote from this manuscript copy to corroborate Wilkinson's authorship and the revision process. The original copy of the verses that Wilkinson sent to Juliet Smith is not extant.

17. JS to TW, September 4, [1806], TWP, Folder 13.

18. JS to TW, October 6, [1806], TWP, Folder 13.

19. Elihu Robinson to TW, February 2, 1807, TWP, Folder 27.

20. Elihu Robinson to TW, April 12, 1807, TWP, Volume 3.

21. HMB to Cadell and Davies, November 13, 1807, H. M. Bowdler Correspondence. For an overview of women authors who worked with Cadell and Davies that briefly mentions Bowdler, see Michelle Levy and Reese Irwin, "The Female Authors of Cadell and Davies," in Winckles and Rehbein, eds., *Women's Literary Networks and Romanticism*,

99–136. For more on women's communications with Cadell and Davies and other publishers, see Levy, "Do Women Have a Book History?"

22. HMB, Preface, in *Fragments*, ix.

23. "Memoirs of Miss Hannah More," *Monthly Magazine and American Review* (New York), December 1800, 465. For key overviews of literary celebrity culture, see Eastman, *Strange Genius of Mr. O*, especially chapter 7; and Mole, ed., *Romanticism and Celebrity Culture*. For women authors and literary celebrity, see Brock, *Feminization of Fame;* Hawkins and Ives, eds., *Women Writers and the Artifacts of Celebrity;* and Teed, "A Passion for Distinction."

24. See Pennington, ed., *Memoirs of the Life of Mrs. Elizabeth Carter;* Chapone, *Posthumous Works of Mrs. Chapone;* Montagu, *Letters of Mrs. Elizabeth Montagu;* and Constable, ed., *Letters of Anna Seward.*

25. "Memoirs of Eminent Women of Great Britain: Mrs. Elizabeth Carter," *New British Lady's Magazine; or, Monthly Mirror of Literature and Fashion* (London), February 1816, 113. See Booth, *How to Make it as a Woman;* and Casper, *Constructing American Lives,* especially chapter 2.

26. "Sketch of the Life of Madam De Staël," *New England Quarterly Magazine* (Boston), July–September 1802, 82–86.

27. Chapone, *Posthumous Works of Mrs. Chapone,* vi; "From Aikin's Annual Review: The Posthumous Works of Mrs. Chapone," *Select Reviews, and Spirit of the Foreign Magazines* (Philadelphia), March 1801, 158.

28. Preface, in Pennington, ed., *Memoirs of the Life of Mrs. Elizabeth Carter.*

29. HMB, Preface, in *Fragments*, ix–x.

30. See [Bowdler], *Sermons on the Doctrines and Duties of Christianity;* and [Bowdler], *Poems and Essays.*

31. HMB, Preface, in [Bowdler], *Sermons on the Doctrines and Duties of Christianity,* iv–v.

32. HMB to Cadell and Davies, December 21, 1801, Cadell and Davies Records, Box 1, Folder 9. I have found a review of an 1801 title published by Cadell and Davies that most likely refers to Bowdler's first edition of *Sermons.* See "Art. 27—*Sermons on the Doctrines and Duties of Christianity, Addressed to a Country Congregation,*" *British Critic* (London), September 1801, 318–19.

33. HMB to Cadell and Davies, November 20, 1805, Cadell and Davies Records, Box 1, Folder 9.

34. HMB to "Sir" [presumably Cadell and Davies], March 3, [1809], Evelyn Papers.

35. Stuart Cheyne to Cadell and Davies, April 9, 1803, Cadell and Davies Records, Box 1, Folder 9.

36. HMB to Cadell and Davies, January 26, 1805, and undated letter [circa November/ December 1807], Cadell and Davies Records, Box 1, Folder 9.

37. See Henrietta Maria Bowdler, *Sermons on the Doctrines and Duties of Christianity,* 22nd edition (Bath: Richard Cruttwell, 1810); and "A New Edition" (London: Simpkin Marshall, 1852).

38. HMB to "Miss Gorman," July 17, 1818, H. M. Bowdler Correspondence, Folger Shakespeare Library.

39. HMB, Preface, in *Fragments*, vii.

40. HMB, Preface, in *Fragments*, xi–xii.

41. HMB, "Extract from a Letter from Mrs. H. Bowdler to Dr. [Jacob] Mumssen," Letter X, September 1806, in *Fragments*, 265.

42. JS, Letter II, in *Fragments*, 232.

43. HMB, *Fragments*, 56–57.

44. Johnson, quoted in "Apophthegms, Sentiments, Opinions, etc.," in Hawkins, ed., *Works of Samuel Johnson*, 11:205.

45. Thomas, "Samuel Johnson and Elizabeth Carter," 27; Preface, in Pennington, ed., *Memoirs of the Life of Mrs. Elizabeth Carter*. Also see Clarke, *Dr. Johnson's Women*.

46. For discussions of single women—often referred to as "spinsters" or "old maids"— see Hill, *Women Alone;* Hufton, "Women Without Men"; and Rizzo, *Companions without Vows*.

47. HMB, *Pen Tamar*, 197–200. Originally written by Bowdler in 1801, *Pen Tamar* was published in 1830, just months after her death. Bowdler "at length decided on deferring it during her life" but agreed before her death "that it should finally be offered to the public." See "Preface by the Editor," July 17, 1830; and "Preface by the Author," December 21, 1819, in HMB, *Pen Tamar*, v, vii.

48. "From the Literary Panorama," *Select Reviews, and Spirit of the Foreign Magazines* (Philadelphia), February 1809, 91.

49. HMB, *Fragments*, 5, 54.

50. Darnton, *Kiss of Lamourette*, especially chapter 7 and figure 7.1.

51. JS to HMB, August 1806, Letter IV, in *Fragments*, 251.

52. HMB, *Fragments*, 25.

53. Mrs. [Anne] Green to HMB, September 9, 1806, Letter VII, in *Fragments*, 256.

54. JS, Letter I, in *Fragments*, 215.

55. JS, Letter II, in *Fragments*, 228, 230.

56. JS, Letter III, in *Fragments*, 245. For cultures of mourning, see Seeman, *Speaking with the Dead;* and Simonds and Rothman, *Centuries of Solace*.

57. Dr. [Francis] Randolph to JS, [1807], Letter XII, in *Fragments*, 268–69.

58. JS to TW, December 13, [circa 1808–10], TWP, Folder 13.

59. See Will of Juliet Smith, National Archives (England). Juliet Smith "bequeath[ed] to my Grandson Thomas Allan my copyright and interest in [all?] work of my late daughter Elizabeth Smith published by Mr. Cadell in London." Thomas Allan was the son of Elizabeth's beloved sister Kitty (who died in 1817).

60. JS to TW, August 3, [1808], TWP, Folder 13.

61. The first newspaper advertisements for *Fragments* that I have located to date appeared in May 1808. See *Bath Chronicle and Weekly Gazette*, May 5, 1808, 3; *The Star* (London), May 23, 1808, 1; and *St. James's Chronicle, or British Evening-Post*, May 24, 1808, 1. Notices announcing the publication of the second edition of *Fragments* appeared throughout the summer of 1808. For example, see *Bath Chronicle and Weekly Gazette*, June 23, 1808, 3; *British Press* (London), July 1, 1808, 1; and *Morning Herald* (London), August 9, 1808, 1. For publication of the third edition, see *Bath Chronicle and Weekly Gazette*, July 21, 1808, 3; for the fourth edition, see *Bath Chronicle and Weekly Gazette*, September 29, 1808, 3; and for the fifth edition, see *Bath Chronicle and Weekly Gazette*, November 3, 1808, 3. These 1808 editions were

printed in Bath by R. Cruttwell, to be sold by Cadell and Davies and J. Hatchard in London and S. Cheyne in Edinburgh.

62. Mary Leadbeater to TW, October 4, 1808, TWP, Folder 20. For the Dublin edition, see *Fragments, in Prose and Verse: By a Young Lady, Lately Deceased, with Some Account of Her Life and Character, by the Author of "Sermons on the Doctrines and Duties of Christianity"* (Dublin: Graisberry and Campbell, 1808).

63. "Miss Smith's Fragments," *Salem Gazette*, July 10, 1810, 4.

64. "From the British Critick," 106.

65. HMB, Preface, in *Fragments*, x.

66. Mary Leadbeater to TW, August 17, 1808, TWP, Folder 20.

67. Mary Leadbeater to TW, October 4, 1808, TWP, Folder 20.

68. "Art. IX. *Fragments in Prose and Verse*," 827.

69. "Review of New Publications," *Belfast Monthly Magazine*, December 1, 1808, 291.

70. HMB, Advertisement, in *Fragments*, v. This explanation was included in editions of *Fragments* published in 1809 and later, once the book's title explicitly identified Smith and Bowdler.

71. HMB to Eliza Simcoe, July 8, 1809, SFP-LAC, Reel A607, File 33/24. Advertisements identifying Smith as the author appeared in British newspapers in the following months. See *Bath Chronicle and Weekly Gazette*, August 10, 1809, 3; and August 17, 1809, 3; *St. James's Chronicle, and London Evening-Post*, September 16, 1809, 1; and *Hull Advertiser and Exchange Gazette* (Yorkshire), September 30, 1809, 2.

72. See chapter 2 for further details on this letter.

73. JS to TW, June 17, 1808, TWP, Folder 13.

74. HMB, *Fragments*, 53.

75. JS to TW, December 13, [circa 1808–10], TWP, Folder 13.

76. JS to TW, March 3, 1809, TWP, Folder 13.

77. Dorothy Wordsworth to Thomas De Quincey, April 5, 1809, in De Selincourt et al., eds., *Letters of William and Dorothy Wordsworth*, vol. 2.

78. JS to TW, January 22, 1809, TWP, Folder 13.

79. JS to TW, March 3, 1809, TWP, Folder 13.

80. Hannah More to Mrs. [Ann] Kennicott, 1810, in Roberts, ed., *Memoirs of the Life and Correspondence of Hannah More*, 2:170.

81. For posthumously published works featuring American women that appeared in the 1810s, see Joseph Emerson, ed., *Writings of Miss Fanny Woodbury: Who Died at Beverly, Nov. 15, 1814, Aged 23 Years* (Boston: Samuel T. Armstrong, 1815); Isabella Graham, *The Power of Faith Exemplified in the Life and Writings of the Late Mrs. Isabella Graham* (New York: J. Seymour, 1816); Ramsay, ed., *Memoirs of the Life of Martha Laurens Ramsay*; Sigourney, ed., *Writings of Nancy Maria Hyde;* and Leonard Woods, *A Sermon Preached at Haverhill, in Remembrance of Mrs. Harriet Newell, Wife of the Rev. Samuel Newell, Missionary to India. Who Died at the Isle of France, November 30, 1812, Aged 19 Years. To Which Are Added Memoirs of Her Life*, 2nd edition (Boston: Samuel T. Armstrong, 1814).

82. For compelling analysis of posthumous fame in early nineteenth-century cultures of print, see Cayton, "Canonizing Harriet Newell"; and Moreshead, "'Beyond All Ambitious Motives.'"

83. "The Lady's Preceptor," 198.

84. JS, Letter II, in *Fragments*, 232.

85. "Review of New Publications—*Memoirs of the Life of Mrs. Elizabeth Carter*," *Christian Observer, Conducted by Members of the Established Church* (Boston), October 1807, 662–63.

86. "Art. XXII.—*The Letters of Mrs. Elizabeth Montague*," *Port-Folio* (Philadelphia), March 1821, 151.

87. "Art. IV—*Fragments in Prose and Verse*," 141.

6. "A Lasting and Meritorious Monument"

1. Preface, in Parker, *Review of the Life and Fragments;* advertisement placed by "Mr. Samuel H. Parker," *Boston Commercial Gazette,* February 1, 1810, 2; also see More, *Coelebs.* More's endorsement of Elizabeth Smith is discussed further in chapter 7. For the first American edition, see *Fragments, in Prose and Verse* (Boston: Munroe and Francis, and Samuel H. Parker, 1810).

2. As history of book scholars have noted, early nineteenth-century printers and booksellers often had interchangeable roles; as the book trade developed, these roles would become more distinct. This chapter's discussion of book history and cultures of print was informed by several key works, including Charvat, *Literary Publishing in America;* Darnton, *Kiss of Lamourette;* Gross and Kelley, eds., *History of the Book in America;* Loughran, *Republic in Print;* McGill, *American Literature and the Culture of Reprinting;* Raven, *Business of Books;* Remer, *Printers and Men of Capital;* and Rezek, *London and the Making of Provincial Literature.*

3. "Art. IX. *Fragments in Prose and Verse*," 827.

4. Elizabeth Smith's posthumously published works of translation include *Memoirs of Frederick and Margaret Klopstock* and *A Vocabulary, Hebrew, Arabic, and Persian.* Note: Throughout this chapter, I often refer to Smith's *Memoirs of Frederick and Margaret Klopstock* using the shorthand reference *Klopstock.*

5. Thomas Burgess, Preface, in Smith, *A Vocabulary, Hebrew, Arabic, and Persian,* v.

6. Between 1808 and 1818, advertisements for various editions of Smith's works appeared in British newspapers. See, for example, *The Star* (London), January 6, 1809, 1; *Bath Chronicle and Weekly Gazette,* August 17, 1809, 3; *Dublin Evening Post,* May 19, 1810, 1; *The Sun* (London), February 19, 1810, 1; *The Star* (London), July 13, 1811, 1; *The Globe* (London), March 23, 1812, 1; *Bath Chronicle and Weekly Gazette,* March 18, 1813, 2; *The Globe* (London), November 3, 1818, 1; and *British Press* (London), December 12, 1818, 1.

7. For early advertisements of *Fragments* in America, see "New Books," *New York Commercial Advertiser,* October 26, 1808, 3; "Inskeep and Bradford," *American Citizen* (New York), October 29, 1808, 3; "Just Received, via New York," *Political and Commercial Register* (Philadelphia), November 7, 1808, 3; "New Books," *New-York Spectator,* November 23, 1808, 4; "New Books," *New Jersey Telescope* (Trenton), December 23, 1808, 4; "Inskeep and Bradford," *New York Commercial Advertiser,* November 14, 1808, 4; and "New Books," *National Intelligencer and Washington Advertiser,* January 13, 1809, 1.

8. See Raven, *Business of Books*, 238 (quotation); and Rezek, *London and the Making of Provincial Literature*.

9. Green, "The Rise of Book Publishing," 75.

10. "New Books, M. Carey," *Democratic Press* (Philadelphia), November 15, 1809, 1.

11. See McGill, *American Literature and the Culture of Reprinting;* and other sources in note 2.

12. Robert A. Gross and Mary Kelly, "Introduction," in Gross and Kelly, eds., *History of the Book in America*, 25–27.

13. Remer, *Printers and Men of Capital*, 1–4. For further evidence of booksellers' strategic business practices, see Smith, "'Elements of Useful Knowledge.'"

14. "Memoirs of Miss Hannah More," *New-York Missionary Magazine*, 357; "Literary Intelligence," *Port-Folio* (Philadelphia), November 14, 1807, 307.

15. "Review of New Publications," *Belfast Monthly Magazine*, December 1, 1808, 291.

16. "An Interesting Work," *Federal Republican and Commercial Gazette* (Baltimore), May 22, 1810, 2. Coale's advertisement ran repeatedly in this newspaper throughout May and June 1810. See, for example, May 28, 1810, 1; May 30, 1810, 1; June 5, 1810, 1; June 18, 1810, 1; June 30, 1810, 1. Like Parker's pamphlet, this advertisement also included the commendation of Elizabeth Smith that appeared in Hannah More's novel *Coelebs in Search of a Wife*.

17. Jackson, *Romantic Readers*, 9. Also see Raven, *Business of Books*, especially 231–41.

18. "Art. II. *The Letters of Mrs. Elizabeth Montagu*," 35. This review was reprinted in the *Analectic Magazine, Containing Selections from Foreign Reviews and Magazines* (Philadelphia), March 1814, 215–25. As its title indicates, this American periodical contained reprints from reviews published in London, Edinburgh, and other foreign publications, demonstrating close transatlantic literary connections.

19. *Fragments*, 5th edition (Bath: Richard Cruttwell, 1808), unpaginated advertisement at end of work.

20. See Raven, *Business of Books*, especially 257–58, 280; and Gross and Kelley, eds., *History of the Book in America*, especially chart on p. 393.

21. See "Miss Smith" advertisements published in *Boston Gazette*, March 19, 1810, 3; *The Repertory* (Boston), March 20, 1810, 3; March 27, 1810, 1; and *New-England Palladium* (Boston), March 27, 1810, 2. Samuel Parker partnered with the Boston publishing firm of Munroe and Francis, and as a result some announcements listed Munroe and Francis, rather than Parker, as the main publisher. See "New Editions," *Panoplist, and Missionary Magazine United* (Boston), March 1810, 478; and "Books Lately Published by Munroe and Francis," *Christian Monitor* (Boston), July 14, 1810, 167.

22. See "Books and Stationary—Isaac Adams," *Portland Gazette, and Maine Advertiser,* August 6, 1810, 1; and "New Publications," *Alexandria [VA] Daily Gazette, Commercial and Political,* June 29, 1810, 4.

23. In 1810, Baltimore publisher Philip H. Nicklin and Co. issued the first American edition of *Klopstock;* that same year, Boston publishers Farrand, Mallory, and Co. and Philadelphia booksellers Edward Earle and B. B. Hopkins and Co. also released editions. See "Published This Day, by Philip H. Nicklin & Co.," *Federal Republican, and Commercial Gazette* (Baltimore), April 19, 1810, 2; "List of New Publications," *Christian's Magazine* (New York), May 1810, 303; "Late Publications, by Philip H. Nicklin &

Co.," *Federal Republican and Commercial Gazette* (Baltimore), June 4, 1810, 1; "Klopstock's Memoirs, Farrand, Mallory & Co.," *Boston Gazette, Commercial and Political,* May 3, 1810, 2; and "Literary Intelligence," *Select Reviews and Spirit of the Foreign Magazines* (Philadelphia), May 1810, 358.

24. "Klopstock's Memoirs," *Panoplist, and Missionary Magazine United* (Boston), April 1810, 536. In England, publishers sold individual volumes of *Fragments* and *Klopstock* but also issued two-volume sets of these works. See, for example, "This Day Are Published, in Two Vols.," *Bath Chronicle and Weekly Gazette,* August 17, 1809, 3; and *Morning Post* (London), September 7, 1809, 2; and "The Works of Miss Elizabeth Smith," *Saint James's Chronicle, and London Evening-Post,* July 20, 1811, 1; *The Globe* (London), March 23, 1812, 1; and *Bath Chronicle and Weekly Gazette,* September 3, 1812, 3. In America, the volumes were published and sold separately. Parker did not publish *Klopstock* to accompany his edition of *Fragments,* and American publishers who issued *Klopstock* did not reprint *Fragments.*

25. "David Allinson & Co.," *Poulson's American Daily Advertiser* (Philadelphia), March 21, 1811, 1. An advertisement for this new edition of *Fragments* was also printed at the end of a pamphlet published by David Allinson in 1811. See *Considerations on the Customary Use of Spirituous Liquors, by a Philanthropist. Also, a Treatise on Their Manufactory, &c., by Mentor* (Burlington, NJ: David Allinson, 1811). For Allinson's edition, see *Fragments* (Burlington, NJ: D. Allinson, 1811).

26. For advertisements of Allinson's edition of *Fragments,* see "Just Published, and for Sale at This Office," *Rural Visiter* (Burlington, NJ), June 10, 1811, 242; June 17, 1811, 246; July 8, 1811, 258; September 17, 1811, 32; "Just Received, and for Sale, by James P. Parke," *Philadelphia Gazette,* June 17, 1811, 2; "Just Received, and for Sale by Collins & Co.," *Commercial Advertiser* (New York), July 9, 1811, 3; "Just Received, and for Sale by D. Fenton, Trenton," *Trenton Federalist,* September 23, 1811, 3; "Just Received and for Sale by I. Cooke & Co.," *Connecticut Journal* (New Haven), November 21, 1811, 1; "New Spelling Book," *Berkshire Reporter* (Pittsfield, MA), November 21, 1811, 1; and "This Day Received and for Sale at the Haverhill Bookstore," *Merrimack Intelligencer* (Haverhill, MA), May 2, 1812, 4.

27. See inscriptions in copies of *Fragments* and *Klopstock,* Loganian Library Collection, Library Company of Philadelphia.

28. *A Catalogue of the Books Belonging to the Charleston Library Society* (Charleston: A. E. Miller, 1826), 67; *A Catalogue of Books Belonging to the Library Company of Philadelphia* (Philadelphia: Thomas T. Stiles, 1813), vol. 2, part 1, p. 79. In 1813, the Library Company also held a copy of *Fragments* published by Parker in 1810, listed as the "gift of Joseph Dennie," editor of the *Port-Folio.*

29. This evidence was drawn largely from an examination of circulating library catalogues held at the American Antiquarian Society in Worcester, MA. Works consulted include *A Catalogue of the Books Belonging to the New York Society Library, Together with the Charter and By-Laws of the Same* (New York: C. S. Van Winkle, 1813); *Catalogue of Books: Goodrich and Co.'s New-York Circulating Library and Reading-Room, No. 124 Broadway, Corner of Cedar-Street, Opposite the City Hotel* (New York: A. T. Goodrich, 1813); *Catalogue of the Boston Union Circulating Library, and Reading Room, No. 4 Cornhill, Corner of Water-Street* (Boston: Munroe, Francis, and Parker, 1815); *A Catalogue of the Union Circulating Library, for 1815, Kept by Joseph Milligan* (Georgetown, DC: W. A. Rind, 1815–[1816]);

Catalogue of Books, &c., Belonging to the Maryland Circulating Library, Corner of North Charles and Conewago-Streets, Baltimore (Baltimore: Frederick G. Schaeffer, 1822); *Catalogue of the Norfolk Circulating Library* (Dedham, MA: H and W. H. Mann, 1823); and *Catalogue of the Union Circulating Library, No. 16, South Seventh Street, Opposite Carpenter Street, Philadelphia* (Philadelphia: Mifflin and Parry, 1832).

30. "Thoughts on the Proposed Improvement of Female Education," 301.

31. "Fragments, Just Received and for Sale, by John & Thos. Vance," *Baltimore Patriot,* July 29, 1814, 3.

32. "Art. IX. *Fragments in Prose and Verse,*" 827–29.

33. For the rise of literary celebrity culture, see Brock, *Feminization of Fame;* Hawkins and Ives, eds., *Women Writers and the Artifacts of Celebrity;* First, "The Mechanics of Renown"; Jackson, *Those Who Write for Immortality;* Mole, *Byron's Romantic Celebrity;* Mole, ed., *Romanticism and Celebrity Culture;* O'Neill, "The Best of Me Is There"; and Teed, "A Passion for Distinction."

34. "Article 9. *Memoirs of the Life of Mrs. Elizabeth Carter,*" 194.

35. "Art. XXII.—*The Letters of Mrs. Elizabeth Montague,*" 152.

36. "Criticism—Advice to Young Ladies on the Improvement of the Mind. By Thomas Broadhurst," *Port-Folio* (Philadelphia), July 1810, 110.

37. "Review of New Publications," *Christian Observer,* 508–10.

38. "Review of New Publications," *Christian Observer,* 508–10.

39. "Review of Reviews, &c. &c.," *Christian Observer, Conducted by the Members of the Established Church* (Boston), November 1807, 745.

40. "Review of New Publications—*Memoirs of the Life of Mrs. Elizabeth Carter,*" *Christian Observer,* 663.

41. "Review of New Publications," *Christian Observer,* 508, 519.

42. "Review of New Publications," *Christian Observer,* 521.

43. "Art. IX. *Fragments in Prose and Verse,*" 827–29.

44. "Art. X. *Fragments in Prose and Verse*"; "Art. XI. *Memoirs of Frederick and Margaret Klopstock,*" *Monthly Review,* 71.

45. "Review of New Publications," *Belfast Monthly Magazine,* December 1, 1808, 292.

46. "From the British Critick," 109.

47. "Memoirs of the Late Miss Elizabeth Smith," 323; "*Fragments in Prose and Verse,*" 553.

48. "From the Ladies' Monthly Museum—Mrs. Elizabeth Carter," *Saturday Magazine: Being in Great Part a Compilation from the British Reviews, Magazines, and Scientific Journals* (Philadelphia, Trenton, and New York), October 6, 1821, 321.

49. "Memoirs of Eminent Women of Great Britain: Mrs. Elizabeth Carter," 104.

50. "Art. X. *Memoirs of the Late Mrs. Elizabeth Hamilton,*" *Port-Folio* (Philadelphia), September 1820, 110–11.

51. "Article 9. *Memoirs of the Life of Mrs. Elizabeth Carter,*" 195.

52. HMB to Eliza Simcoe, July 8, 1809, SFP-LAC, Reel A607, File 33/24.

53. "Article 13. *Fragments in Prose and Verse,*" 335–37.

54. For discussions of gender and genius, see Battersby, *Gender and Genius;* and Fraisse, *Reason's Muse.*

55. See for example, "Biographical Sketch of Anna Laetitia Barbauld," *Philadelphia Repository and Weekly Register,* December 15, 1804, 397.

56. "Article 13. *Fragments in Prose and Verse,*" 337.

57. ES, Reflections, circa 1796–97, in *Fragments,* 76–77. See chapter 4 for further discussion of Smith's evolving understanding of genius.

58. "Art. X. *Fragments in Prose and Verse*"; "Art. XI. *Memoirs of Frederick and Margaret Klopstock,*" *Monthly Review,* 67–72.

59. "Art. X. *Fragments in Prose and Verse*"; "Art. XI. *Memoirs of Frederick and Margaret Klopstock,*" *Monthly Review,* 67–72.

60. "Article 13. *Fragments in Prose and Verse,*" 337.

61. "From the British Critick," 106.

62. "For the Christian Observer: Cursory Remarks on the Assertion That Female Improvement Is Inimical to Domestic Happiness," *Christian Observer* (Boston), March 1808, 299.

63. James Mackintosh, Journal, July 1, 1811, in Mackintosh, ed., *Memoirs of the Life of Sir James Mackintosh,* 2:106.

64. "Art. IV—*Fragments in Prose and Verse*"; "Art. V—*Select Poems,*" 141. See Robert Southey, ed., *The Remains of Henry Kirk White: With an Account of His Life* (London: Vernon, Hood, and Sharpe, 1808).

65. "Art. IV—*Fragments in Prose and Verse*"; "Art. V—*Select Poems,*" 144–49.

66. "From the Edinburgh Review: *The Letters of Mrs. Montagu,*" *Select Reviews, and Spirit of the Foreign Magazines* (Philadelphia), April 1810, 229.

67. "Art. XXII—*The Letters of Mrs. Elizabeth Montague,*" 152.

68. "Art. IV—*Fragments in Prose and Verse*"; "Art. V—*Select Poems,*" 141.

69. "Satirists of Women—Chances of Female Happiness," *New Monthly Magazine and Literary Journal* (Boston), July 1822, 287.

70. "Art. IV—*Fragments in Prose and Verse*"; "Art. V—*Select Poems,*" 141–42.

71. "For the Christian Observer: Cursory Remarks," 156. See chapter 2 for further discussion of bluestockings.

72. "Satirists of Women," 287.

73. "Art. II. *The Letters of Mrs. Elizabeth Montagu,*" 32.

74. "On the Rights of Woman," *National Magazine; or, A Political, Historical, Biographical, and Literary Repository* (Richmond, VA), September 1800, 204–7.

75. "Art. IX. *Fragments in Prose and Verse,*" 831.

76. "Review of New Publications," *Christian Observer,* 515.

77. "Memoirs of the Late Miss Elizabeth Smith," 323.

78. "Art. X. *Fragments in Prose and Verse*"; "Art. XI. *Memoirs of Frederick and Margaret Klopstock,*" *Monthly Review,* 71.

79. Lee, *Memoirs of Eminent Female Writers,* iv, 169.

7. "Lives in This Record"

1. Hemans, "Lines, Written in the Memoirs of Elizabeth Smith," 57. Hemans's poem was later included in a biographical sketch of Elizabeth Smith featured in Kendrick and Child, *Gift Book of Biography,* 105–20.

2. O'Neill, "The Best of Me Is There," 747–48. For other works on nineteenth-century literary celebrity, see First, "The Mechanics of Renown"; Higgins, *Romantic Genius and*

the Literary Magazine; Jackson, *Those Who Write for Immortality;* Mole, *Byron's Roman-tic Celebrity;* Mole, ed., *Romanticism and Celebrity Culture;* and North, *Domestication of Genius.*

3. On posthumous literary celebrity, see Fara, *Newton;* Looser, *Making of Jane Austen;* and Vardy, *Constructing Coleridge.*

4. For recent scholarship that explores women, gender, and literary celebrity culture, see Booth, *How to Make It as a Woman;* Brock, *Feminization of Fame;* Easley, *Literary Celebrity, Gender, and Victorian Authorship;* Hawkins and Ives, eds., *Women Writers and the Artifacts of Celebrity;* and Teed, "A Passion for Distinction."

5. More, *Coelebs,* 2:250–51. Originally published in 1808, *Coelebs* went through several editions in both America and Great Britain. See Stott, *Hannah More.*

6. For recent scholarship on Elizabeth Carter and British bluestocking circles, see Clarke, *Dr. Johnson's Women;* Eger, *Bluestockings;* and Eger and Peltz, *Brilliant Women.*

7. "Article 13. *Fragments in Prose and Verse,*" 335.

8. Frank, *Classical English Letter-Writer,* 318.

9. Roberts, *Select Female Biography,* 264.

10. Coxe, *Young Lady's Companion,* 228.

11. "Authoresses and Autographs," 223–24.

12. Joseph Story, "Characteristics of the Age," in *The Miscellaneous Writings of Joseph Story,* ed. William Story (Boston: Little and Brown, 1852), 3:350.

13. C. W. Russell, *The Life of Cardinal Mezzofanti: With an Introductory Memoir of Eminent Linguists, Ancient and Modern* (London: Longman, Brown, 1858), 114–16.

14. Sessions, *Literary Celebrities of the English Lake-District,* 195. In addition to the exam-ples quoted, I have found a number of joint references to Elizabeth Smith, Elizabeth Carter, and/or Hannah More in a variety of both American and British periodical essays. See [Martineau], "On Female Education," 77–81; "Review of the Cultivation of Female Intellect in the United States—Continued," *Literary and Evangelical Magazine* (Richmond, VA), June 1827, 291–307; "On the Female Character, with Especial Refer-ence to the Powers of the Mind," *Imperial Magazine* (London), October 1830, 892–96; "[Review]: *Female Biography; Containing Sketches of the Life and Character of Twelve American Women,*" *American Sunday School Magazine* (Philadelphia), February 1830, 49; "What to Read," *Christian Register and Boston Observer,* August 7, 1841, 128; Joseph Matthews, "Original Substance of a Report on 'Female Education,' Presented to the 'College of Teachers,' in Cincinnati, Oct., 1840," *Ladies Repository, and Gathering of the West* (Cincinnati), February 1841, 50–53; and "Noble Deeds of English Women," *Lei-sure Hour: An Illustrated Magazine for Home Reading* (London), April 27, 1854, 266–70; reprinted as "From the Leisure Hour—English Women," *Eclectic Magazine of Foreign Literature, Science, and Art* (New York), August 1854, 493–98.

15. Dorothy Wordsworth to Mary Laing, January 21, 1828, in De Selincourt et al., eds., *Letters of William and Dorothy Wordsworth,* vol. 4. Wordsworth, who knew Smith from her residence in the Lake District, also "read Miss Smith's Translation of Klopstock's and Mrs. K's Letters." See Dorothy Wordsworth to Thomas De Quincey, April 5, 1809, in De Selincourt et al., eds., *Letters of William and Dorothy Wordsworth,* vol. 2.

16. Van Dyke, Journal, July 11, 1810, in McMahon and Schriver, eds., *To Read My Heart,* 75.

17. Van Dyke, Journal, July 11, 1810, in McMahon and Schriver, eds., *To Read My Heart,* 75.

18. See chapter 6 for publishing practices and book history trends that led to the distribution and sale of *Fragments* in England and America.

19. Van Dyke, Journal, July 11, July 13, and July 25, 1810, in McMahon and Schriver, eds., *To Read My Heart*, 75, 77, 87.

20. Van Dyke, Journal, July 26, 1810, in McMahon and Schriver, eds., *To Read My Heart*, 88–89.

21. For overviews of women's educational achievements in this era, see Kelley, *Learning to Stand and Speak*; McMahon, *Mere Equals*; and Purvis, *History of Women's Education in England*.

22. Van Dyke, Journal, July 31, 1810, in McMahon and Schriver, eds., *To Read My Heart*, 94–95.

23. Ebenezer Grosvenor, marginalia added in Rachel Van Dyke's Journal, Book 3 Cover [journal dated June 10, 1810; marginalia added July 1810], in McMahon and Schriver, eds., *To Read My Heart*, 41. For more on Grosvenor and Van Dyke's relationship, which included many instances of shared reading practices as sources of emotional and intellectual affinity, see McMahon, "'We Would Share Equally': Gender, Education, and Romance in the Journal of Rachel Van Dyke," in McMahon and Schriver, eds., *To Read My Heart*, 309–37.

24. Van Dyke Journal, August 2, 1810, in McMahon and Schriver, eds., *To Read My Heart*, 97. On marginalia writing, see Jackson, *Romantic Readers*.

25. Van Dyke Journal, August 2, 1810, in McMahon and Schriver, eds., *To Read My Heart*, 97. See chapter 3 of this study for a discussion of Elizabeth Smith's account of her Snowdon adventures.

26. Van Dyke Journal, August 2, 1810, in McMahon and Schriver, eds., *To Read My Heart*, 97.

27. On readers' responses, see Darnton, *Great Cat Massacre*, 215–56; Hackel and Kelly, eds., *Literacy, Authorship, and Culture in the Atlantic World*; David D. Hall, "The Uses of Literacy in New England, 1600–1850," in Joyce et al., eds., *Printing and Society in Early America*, 1–47; and Todd, "Walter Scott and the Nineteenth-Century American Literary Marketplace."

28. Mary Leadbeater to TW, April 29, 1810, and January 15, 1810, TWP, Folder 20.

29. Mary Moody Emerson to Anne Brewer, October 12, 1814, Gage Family Papers—Additional Papers, Series 1, American Antiquarian Society. See Noelle Baker, "'Let Me Do Nothing Smale': Mary Moody Emerson and Women's 'Talking' Manuscripts," *ESQ: A Journal of the American Renaissance* 57, nos. 1–2 (2011): 21–48; Goodwin, *Remarkable Mrs. Ripley*; and Simmons, ed., *Selected Letters of Mary Moody Emerson*.

30. HMB, *Fragments*, 56–57. See chapter 5 for further discussion of these remarks.

31. Thomas, "Samuel Johnson and Elizabeth Carter," 27; also see Clarke, *Dr. Johnson's Women*.

32. [Martineau], "Lights of the English Lake District," 542.

33. Review Essay, *The Evangelical Witness* (Newburgh, NY), September 1, 1826, 400.

34. Martha Laurens Ramsay to Juliana Hazlehurst, April 1811; Patty Ramsay to Juliana Hazlehurst, April 9, 1811, in Ramsay, ed., *Memoirs of the Life of Martha Laurens Ramsay*, 229–30.

35. Lusanna Richmond, Diary, March 6, 1817, in Lancaster, "'By the Pens of Females,'" 98–99.

36. Lucinda Read, Journal, December 31, 1817, Massachusetts Historical Society. See undated entries in Read's commonplace book for excerpted writings from Elizabeth Smith's memoir.

37. Mary Wilder White, March 1810, in Elizabeth Amelia Dwight, *Memorials of Mary Wilder White* (Boston: Everett Press, 1903), 342.

38. Alice Izard to Margaret Manigault, March 31, 1811, Manigault Family Papers, Princeton University Library.

39. Hannah More to Sir W. W. Pepys, December 19, 1808; Pepys to More, March 14, 1809, in Roberts, ed., *Memoirs of the Life and Correspondence of Hannah More,* 2:140, 159.

40. See Halsey, "'Tell Me of Some *Booklings*'"; and Linkin, "Mary Tighe's Newly Discovered Letters."

41. For works that examine the practices of circulating manuscript texts and letter writing forms, see Bigold, *Women of Letters;* Callaghan and Howe, eds., *Romanticism and the Letter;* Ezell, *Writing Women's Literary History;* Mulford, ed., *Only For the Eye of a Friend;* Shields, *Civil Tongues and Polite Letters;* and Stabile, *Memory's Daughters.*

42. Anne Grant to Mrs. D. H. Rucker, July 11, 1814, in Grant, ed., *Memoirs and Correspondence of Mrs. Grant,* 2:36–37.

43. Mary Leadbeater to Melesina Chenevix St. George Trench, October 2, 1808; Trench to Leadbeater, October 3, 1809, in Leadbeater, *Leadbeater Papers,* 2:160, 173. Through her correspondence with Thomas Wilkinson, Mary Leadbeater was kept informed of Juliet Smith and Harriet Bowdler's publication plans for various editions of *Fragments.* See various letters between Thomas Wilkinson and Mary Leadbeater in TWP, Folder 20.

44. Melesina Chenevix St. George Trench to Richard Trench, March 1, 1812, in Trench, ed., *Remains of the Late Mrs. Richard Trench,* 258.

45. Wilkinson, "A Day's Tour," 1. See chapter 4 for more information on Wilkinson's account.

46. See Wilkinson, *Tours to the British Mountains.*

47. Robert Southey to John Neville White, September 30, 1808, in Warter, ed., *Selections from the Letters of Robert Southey,* 2:89–90. This letter is also available online at Romantic Circles, http://www.rc.umd.edu/editions/southey_letters/Part_Three/HTML/letterEEd.26.1515.html.

48. Elijah Waring to TW, April 6, 1810, TWP-BL, Volume 3. Unfortunately, Waring's poem was not saved as part of this collection and has not been located.

49. Elijah Waring to TW, December 18, 1810, TWP-BL, Volume 3.

50. Bowles, "On Reading Fragments," 133; "Cotswoldia," "On Reading the Fragments," 519.

51. Bowles, "On Reading Fragments"; "Cotswoldia," "On Reading the Fragments"; and Wilson, "Lines Written on Reading the Memoirs of Miss Smith." These tribute poems to Elizabeth Smith can be found on the website Spenser and the Tradition: English Poetry, 1759–1830, compiled by David Hill Radcliffe. See http://spenserians.cath.vt.edu. My research also uncovered additional poems with similar titles, published in American periodicals. See "Lines on Reading the Memoirs of Miss Smith"; and "Lines Written after Reading Elizabeth Smith's Fragments."

52. Gwilliam, "Quatorzains."

53. For discussion of how Romantic-era poetry sought to convey imaginative connections with readers, see Stafford, *Reading Romantic Poetry.*

54. "Authoresses and Autographs," 223.

55. "An American Lady," *Sketches of the Lives of Distinguished Females*, xiii–xv.

56. "An American Lady," *Sketches of the Lives of Distinguished Females*, 84, 116–17.

57. *Two May-Days*, 18, 46.

58. *Two May-Days*, 49–50, 62–67.

59. *Two May-Days*, 66, 71.

60. "Mrs. Elizabeth Palmer Peabody," 586. See Marshall, *Peabody Sisters*.

61. Boyce, *Records of a Quaker Family*, 41–42. Boyce noted that her family knew fellow Quaker Thomas Wilkinson; this personal connection may have directly inspired the Richardson sisters' interest in Elizabeth Smith's life and writings.

62. Ewing, ed., *Parables from Nature*, xiii.

63. [Martineau], "Female Writers on Practical Divinity," 746–50. See Florence Fenwick Miller, *Harriet Martineau* (London: W. H. Allen, 1884); and Easley, *Literary Celebrity, Gender, and Victorian Authorship*.

64. "The Lady's Preceptor," 198.

65. "Memoir of Anna Letitia Barbauld," *Imperial Magazine; or, Compendium of Religious, Moral, and Philosophical Knowledge* (London), May 1825, 398.

66. "Eminent Female Writers," *Ladies' Magazine* (Boston), September 1829, 395–400. For attitudes toward women and politics in early national America, see, for example, Allgor, *Party Politics;* and Zagarri, *Revolutionary Backlash.*

67. "Art. II. *The Letters of Mrs. Elizabeth Montagu,*" 33.

68. "Noble Deeds of English Women," 268.

69. Balfour, *Working Women of the Last Half Century,* 117. Originally published in 1854, the 1869 revised edition also featured an entry on Smith. Balfour similarly included Smith in another work of collective biography published in 1877. See Clara Lucas Balfour, *Working Women of this Century,* 3rd edition (London: Cassell, Petter, and Galpin, 1869); and Balfour, *Women Worth Emulating.*

70. *American Lady's Preceptor,* 162; "Meta," "Anecdotes of Celebrated Women," 260; Coxe, *Young Lady's Companion,* 228. As several examples quoted illustrate, the phrase "the celebrated Elizabeth Smith" was commonly used, inspiring this book's title.

71. [Sigourney], *Moral Pieces, in Prose and Verse,* 90; Sigourney, ed., *Writings of Nancy Maria Hyde,* 8. Sigourney included this same reference to Elizabeth Smith in her *Letters to Young Ladies.* For Wilkinson's poem, see Wilkinson, "Lines Inclosed," in *Fragments,* 261.

72. Yonge, *Biographies of Good Women,* 492.

73. For examples of biographical sketches of Elizabeth Smith that appeared in British and American periodicals, see "Account of the Extraordinary Literary Endowments of Miss Elizabeth Smith"; "Miss Elizabeth Smith," *Christian Disciple;* "Biography of Miss Elizabeth Smith," *Churchman's Magazine;* "Miss Elizabeth Smith," *Ladies' Monthly Museum;* "Biography: Miss Elizabeth Smith," *Saturday Magazine;* "Biography: Miss Elizabeth Smith," *Minerviad;* "Meta," "Anecdotes of Celebrated Women"; and "Biographical Sketches of Celebrated Women."

74. Lee, *Memoirs of Eminent Female Writers;* Roberts, *Select Female Biography;* Balfour, *Women Worth Emulating.* Other nineteenth-century collective biographies that

featured entries on Smith include American Sunday-School Union, *Memoirs of Pious Women;* Burder, *Memoirs of Eminently Pious Women;* Elwood, *Memoirs of the Literary Ladies of England;* Johnson, *Clever Girls of Our Time;* Kendrick and Child, *Gift Book of Biography;* Timpson, *British Female Biography;* and Yonge, *Biographies of Good Women.*

75. "Elizabeth Smith (1776–1806)," in Lee, ed., *Dictionary of National Biography,* 53:32–33.
76. "Memoir of Anna Laetitia Barbauld," 398.
77. "On the Female Character, with Especial Reference to the Powers of the Mind," 895.
78. "For the Christian Observer: Cursory Remarks," 161.
79. "Biography of Miss Elizabeth Smith," *Churchman's Magazine,* 130.
80. Balfour, *Happy Evenings,* 259–60.
81. "Biographical Sketches of Celebrated Women," 321.
82. For an account of how representations of women in literary and historical records reflected the prevailing values of the era memorializing them, see Ezell, *Writing Women's Literary History,* especially chapter 3.
83. "An American Lady," *Sketches of the Lives of Distinguished Females,* 224.
84. "What to Read," 128.
85. Review Essay, *The Evangelical Witness* (Newburgh, NY), September 1, 1826, 400.
86. Johnson, *Clever Girls of Our Time,* 40.
87. Review of *The Pursuit of Knowledge under Difficulties, Illustrated by Female Examples, Critic* (London), September 25, 1847, 200. The work under review included a chapter on Elizabeth Smith. See G. L. Craik, *The Pursuit of Knowledge under Difficulties, Illustrated by Female Examples* (London: C. Cox, 1847), 189–228.
88. [Martineau], "Lights of the English Lake District," 542.

8. "To Tread in Thy Footsteps"

1. Marianne Fothergill, "A Sketch of a Little Tour with T. W. in the Summer of . . . ," TWP, Folder 6. Fothergill's journal is undated, but several letters in this folder dated 1810 describe her travel plans to the Lake District that year.
2. William Knight to TW, September 6, 1810, TWP, Folder 7; also see Knight to TW, August 26, 1810, TWP, Folder 7.
3. Westover, *Necromanticism,* 4.
4. For scholarly explorations of the development of literary tourism, see Booth, *Homes and Haunts;* Harris and Lowe, eds., *From Page to Place;* Watson, *Literary Tourist;* Watson, ed., *Literary Tourism and Nineteenth-Century Culture;* and Westover, *Necromanticism.*
5. Anne Grant to Harriet Douglas, August 15, 1827, in Grant, ed., *Memoirs and Correspondence of Mrs. Grant,* 3:98. For information on Harriet Douglas, see Angus Davidson, *Miss Douglas of New York: A Biography* (New York: Viking Press, 1953).
6. Sara Hutchinson to Edward Quillinan, September 12, [1827], in Coburn, ed., *Letters of Sara Hutchinson,* 351.
7. Sara Hutchinson to Edward Quillinan, September 12, [1827], in Coburn, ed., *Letters of Sara Hutchinson,* 351.

8. Sara Hutchinson to Edward Quillinan, September 12, [1827], in Coburn, ed., *Letters of Sara Hutchinson*, 351.

9. Walter Scott, Journal, July 1 and 2, 1828, in Scott, *Journal*, 2:210–11.

10. Anne Grant to Isabella Ewing Smith, July 18, 1828, in *Memoirs and Correspondence of Mrs. Grant*, 3:122–23.

11. Sara Hutchinson to Edward Quillinan, January 27, [1828], in Coburn, ed., *Letters of Sara Hutchinson*, 358.

12. William Wordsworth to Harriet Douglas, February 29, 1828, in Davidson, *Miss Douglas of New York*, 239.

13. For an overview of the experiences of nineteenth-century American travelers to England and Europe, see Kilbride, *Being American in Europe*.

14. Samantha Matthews, "The Poet's Grave," in Watson, ed., *Literary Tourism and Nineteenth-Century Culture*, 28.

15. Westover, *Necromanticism*, 17.

16. Jennifer Harris and Hilary Iris Lowe, "Introduction," in Harris and Lowe, eds., *From Page to Place*, 2.

17. Marianne Fothergill to TW, [undated month] 21, 1810, TWP, Folder 6.

18. "The Lake District in England," *Literary World* (New York), December 17, 1853, 332.

19. Anne Grant to Harriet Douglas, August 15, 1827, in Grant, ed., *Memoirs and Correspondence of Mrs. Grant*, 3:99.

20. Anne Grant to Harriet Douglas, September 20, 1827, in Grant, ed., *Memoirs and Correspondence of Mrs. Grant*, 3:103.

21. "The Lake District in England," 331.

22. [Martineau], "Lights of the English Lake District," 541–58.

23. For a biography of another nineteenth-century Lake District woman who was locally known but subsequently "forgotten," see Jenny Uglow, *The Pinecone: The Story of Sarah Losh, Forgotten Romantic Heroine—Antiquarian, Architect, and Visionary* (New York: Farrar, Straus, and Giroux, 2012).

24. George Ticknor, Journal, September 2, 1835, in Hillard, ed., *Life, Letters, and Journals of George Ticknor*, 1:433.

25. Anna Eliot Ticknor, Journal, September 2, 1835, in Allaback and Medlicott, "A Visit with Wordsworth," 89.

26. JS to TW, June 17, 1808, TWP, Folder 13. For more information about the tent set up for Elizabeth Smith during her fatal illness, see JS, Letter III, in *Fragments*, 242–43.

27. JS to TW, April 3, 1810, TWP, Folder 13.

28. Mary Leadbeater to George Crabbe, May 27, 1824, Egerton Manuscripts, British Library.

29. Fletcher, *Autobiography of Mrs. Fletcher*, 144, 148.

30. Sarah Hustler to TW, October 22, 1822, TWP, Folder 9.

31. William Wordsworth to Juliet Smith, November 28, 1832, in De Selincourt et al., eds., *Letters of William and Dorothy Wordsworth*, vol. 5.

32. Anna Eliot Ticknor, Journal, September 2, 1835, in Allaback and Medlicott, "A Visit with Wordsworth," 89.

33. Mary Leadbeater to George Crabbe, May 27, 1824, Egerton Manuscripts, British Library.

34. HMB to Eliza Simcoe, July 8, 1809, SFP-LAC, Reel A607, File 33/24.

35. Louis Simond, October 6, [1810], in *Journal of a Tour and Residence in Great Britain during the Years 1810 and 1811* (Edinburgh: George Ramsay, 1815), 1:341.

36. John Phillips, *Black's Picturesque Guide to the English Lakes: Including the Geology of the District*, 3rd edition (Edinburgh: Adam and Charles Black, 1846), 66; also see John Phillips, *Black's Picturesque Tourist and Road-Book of England and Wales* (Edinburgh: Adam and Charles Black, 1846), 263.

37. Green, *Tourist's New Guide*, 80.

38. "Authoresses and Autographs," 224. This article also appeared in the Boston edition of the *New Monthly Magazine and Literary Journal* (Boston: Cummings, Hilliard, 1824), 217–24.

39. Martineau, *Complete Guide to the English Lakes*, 28.

40. Charles Knight, *The Land We Live In: A Pictorial and Literary Sketch-Book of the British Empire* (London: Charles Knight, 1847–50), 2:255.

41. Wordsworth, ["An Unpublished Tour"], 330–32. Wordsworth's published *Guide to the Lakes* went through five editions between 1810 and 1835. See "William Wordsworth's Guide to the Lakes, A Romantic Circle Digital Edition," Romantic Circles, https://romantic-circles.org/editions/guide_lakes.

42. William Wordsworth to JS, [September 1835], in De Selincourt et al., eds., *Letters of William and Dorothy Wordsworth*, vol. 6.

43. Wilkinson, "Lines Inclosed," in *Fragments*, 261.

44. John Percival to TW, September 2, 1815, TWP, Folder 22/4.

45. Marianne Fothergill to TW, April 23, 1811, TWP, Folder 6.

46. Mary Leadbeater to TW, November 8, 1806, TWP, Folder 20.

47. Thomas Wilkinson, "Emont Vale," in Wilkinson, *Tours to the British Mountains*, 307–10.

48. Mary Leadbeater to George Crabbe, December 12, 1817, Egerton Manuscripts, British Library.

49. Mary Leadbeater to George Crabbe, May 27, 1824, Egerton Manuscripts, British Library.

50. Eliza Everett to TW, February 15, 1810, TWP, Folder 6.

51. William Knight to TW, March 8, 1813, TWP, Folder 7.

52. Eliza Fletcher to TW, June 17, 1807, TWP-BL, Volume 3.

53. Mary Leadbeater to TW, August 26, 1819, TWP, Folder 20.

54. H. Fisher to TW, June 15, 1817, TWP, Folder 22/5.

55. JS to TW, October 17, [1817], TWP, Folder 13.

56. William Peter Lunnell to TW, April 17, 1818, TWP, Folder 22/5.

57. William Peter Lunnell to TW, April 17, 1818, TWP, Folder 22/5. See Westover, *Necromanticism*.

58. John Griscom to TW, June 9, 1819, TWP-BL, Volume 3.

59. Eliza Beck to TW, July 22, 1827, TWP, Folder 22/4.

60. This anecdote appears in a footnote in Arthur St. John's poem *Weft of the Wye*, which refers to Smith as "Piercefield's pious, soul-illumined maid!" (139).

61. JS to TW, April 3, 1810, TWP, Folder 13. For imaginative connections with deceased figures, see Mole, *What the Victorians Made of Romanticism;* and Seeman, *Speaking with the Dead*.

62. Thomas Robinson Jr. to TW, October 29, 1829, TWP, Folder 22/3.

63. Lydia Sigourney, "Essay on the Genius of Mrs. Hemans," in Hughes, ed., *Works of Mrs. Hemans*, 1:x.

64. Hemans, "Lines, Written in the Memoirs of Elizabeth Smith," 57–59. See chapter 7 for further discussion of this tribute poem.

65. Fothergill, "A Sketch," TWP, Folder 6.

66. Marianne Fothergill to TW, October 15, 1815, TWP, Folder 6.

67. Leadbeater, "The Annals of Ballitore," in Leadbeater, *Leadbeater Papers*, 1:377.

68. "Authoresses and Autographs," 224.

69. Anna Maria Allis to TW, October 25, 1813, TWP, Folder 22/5.

70. Crawford, "Autobiographical Sketches," 280. It should be noted that Crawford's account contained some minor inaccuracies. For example, she mistakenly informed her readers that Smith "died at the early age of eighteen" from "excessive grief at leaving the delightful and endeared home of her childhood."

71. Crawford, "Autobiographical Sketches," 280.

72. See Coxe, *Historical Tour in Monmouthshire*, 2:397–402; and "A Lady," *A Picture of Monmouthshire; or, An Abridgement of Mr. Coxe's Historical Tour in Monmouthshire* (London: T. Cadell Jr. and W. Davies, 1802), 162–68.

73. *England and Wales; or, The County Album; Containing Four Hundred Topographical Hieroglyphics, Indicative of the Products, Staple Commodities, Manufactures, and Objects of Interest, in Every County. For the Amusement and Instruction of Fireside Tourists* (London: A. K. Newman, 1841), 138.

74. John Evans, *The Picture of Bristol; or, A Guide to Objects of Curiosity and Interest, in Bristol, Clifton, the Hotwells, and Their Vicinity; Including Biographical Notices of Eminent Natives* (Bristol: W. Sheppard, 1814), 138.

75. Thomas Bourn, *A Gazetteer of the Most Remarkable Places in the World; with Brief Notices of the Principal Historical Events, and of the Most Celebrated Persons Connected with Them*, 3rd edition (London: Printed for the Author, 1822), 112, 633.

76. Selwyn, Journal, July 17, 1819; September 5, 1822, in Selwyn, *Journal of Excursions*, 32, 158.

77. Westover, *Necromanticism*, 85; also see Stafford, *Reading Romantic Poetry*.

78. Wilson, "Lines Written on Reading the Memoirs of Miss Smith," 241.

79. "D," "Lines on the Late Miss Elizabeth Smith," 260.

80. Browne, "To the Memory of Elizabeth Smith," *The Friend* (Philadelphia), August 2, 1828, 332. Browne (1812–1844) was a British poet who published her first volume of poems at age fifteen.

81. Browne, "To the Memory of Elizabeth Smith," 332.

82. "The Editor's Room, No. III," *London Magazine*, June 1828, 468.

83. TW to Dorothy Parker, January 30, 1824, TWP, Folder 18.

84. Griscom, *Year in Europe*, 2:330–31. All citations in this chapter from Griscom's *Year in Europe* are from volume 2 of the second edition, published in 1824. For information on Griscom's travels, see Sinkankas, "John Griscom in Europe."

85. Griscom, *Year in Europe*, 2:332–33.

86. Griscom, *Year in Europe*, 2:333–34, 230.

87. Griscom, *Year in Europe*, 2:334.

88. Griscom, *Year in Europe*, 2:334.

89. Thomas De Quincey, "Chapter XIX. Society of the Lakes," in De Quincey, *Literary Reminiscences,* 2:169–70, 186. All references to De Quincey's essay on Elizabeth Smith are from this volume of *Literary Reminiscences.* De Quincey's essay was first published in 1840 in *Tait's Edinburgh Magazine.*

90. De Quincey, "Chapter XIX. Society of the Lakes," in De Quincey, *Literary Reminiscences,* 2:169–70. For De Quincey's complex, often contradictory views toward women, see North, "De Quincey and the Inferiority of Women."

91. De Quincey, "Chapter XIX. Society of the Lakes," in De Quincey, *Literary Reminiscences,* 2:180.

92. De Quincey, "Chapter XIX. Society of the Lakes," in De Quincey, *Literary Reminiscences,* 2:180–83. Also see chapter 4 for Smith's account of this experience and the poem she composed about it.

93. De Quincey, "Chapter XIX. Society of the Lakes," in De Quincey, *Literary Reminiscences,* 2:180.

94. De Quincey, "Chapter XIX. Society of the Lakes," in De Quincey, *Literary Reminiscences,* 2:186.

95. Rawnsley, *Literary Association of the English Lakes,* 2:60–61. Note that Rawnsley lists the date of this encounter as 1803 instead of 1805.

Conclusion

1. Japp, "A Woman Learned and Wise," 109–18. Originally published in London, Japp's essay was reprinted in the *Living Age* (New York), February 5, 1898, 400–406.

2. Steele, "Elizabeth Smith: A Self-Taught Linguist," 413.

3. "Art. IV—*Fragments in Prose and Verse,*" 142.

4. Pennington, ed., *Memoirs of the Life of Mrs. Elizabeth Carter,* 315.

5. *Literary Woman,* print, circa 1850, Library Company of Philadelphia Digital Collections, https://digital.librarycompany.org/islandora/object/digitool%3A5889.

6. Amelia Opie, *A Cure for Scandal; or, Detraction Displayed* (Boston: James Loring, 1839), 135–57.

7. Edgar A. Poe, "Fifty Suggestions," *Graham's American Monthly Magazine* (Philadelphia), May 1849, 317.

8. See Nash, ed., *Women's Higher Education in the United States;* and Solomon, *In the Company of Educated Women.*

9. Ralph Waldo Emerson, "Conversations in Boston," in Ralph Waldo Emerson, William Henry Channing, and James Freeman Clarke, *Memoirs of Margaret Fuller Ossoli* (London: Richard Bentley, 1852), 2:124–25. Also see Marshall, *Margaret Fuller.* This gendered understanding of genius may help explain why we often find examples of intellectually gifted women—such as Lydia Jackson Emerson and Dorothy Wordsworth—whose domestic and intellectual labor helped provide the material conditions that enabled male genius to flourish, and/or who gave up their own ambitions in the service of their genius husbands or brothers.

10. See especially Kelley, "'The Need of Their Genius'"; Battersby, *Gender and Genius;* Fraisse, *Reason's Muse;* and Olwell, "'It Spoke Itself.'"

11. Japp, "A Woman Learned and Wise," 118.
12. "Elizabeth Smith (1776–1806)," in Lee, ed., *Dictionary of National Biography*, 53:32–33. A brief entry on Elizabeth Smith appears in the current online edition. See Hawley, "Smith, Elizabeth (1776–1806)."
13. Sessions, *Literary Celebrities of the English Lake-District*, 195–96.
14. Nicholson, *The Lakers*, 127–28.
15. See Bahar Gholipour, "Women Can't Be Geniuses? Stereotypes May Explain Gender Gap," Live Science, January 15, 2015, http://www.livescience.com/49473-gender-gap -genius.html.
16. Tressie McMillan Cottom, "Metaphor, Mobility and 'Genius,'" Medium, October 7, 2020, https://medium.com/@tressiemcphd/metaphor-mobility-and-genius -52d8688b7acf.

SELECTED BIBLIOGRAPHY

Manuscript Collections

American Antiquarian Society, Worcester, MA

Circulating Library Catalogues
Gage Family Papers

Archives of Ontario, Toronto, Ontario

Simcoe Family Papers (microfilm)

Beinecke Rare Book and Manuscript Library, Yale University, New Haven, CT

Cadell and Davies Records

British Library, London

Egerton Manuscripts
Evelyn Papers: Original Letters Collected by William Upcott of the London Institution
Thomas Wilkinson Papers

Devon Archives and Local Studies, Devon Heritage Centre, Exeter, U.K.

Simcoe Family Papers

Folger Shakespeare Library, Washington, DC

H. M. Bowdler Correspondence

Georgian Papers Online, https://gpp.rct.uk/

Account Book of Princess Charlotte of Wales, 1801–1805
Correspondence between Princess Charlotte of Wales and Miss Mary Hunt
Papers of Princess Charlotte of Wales, 1796–1830

Library and Archives Canada, Ottawa, Ontario

Simcoe Family Papers (microfilm)

Library of the Society of Friends, London

Thomas Wilkinson Papers

Massachusetts Historical Society, Boston

Lucinda Read Journal and Commonplace Book

National Archives (England), Kew

Will of Thomas Mulliner, Gentleman of Stratford, Suffolk, 28 August 1784
Will of Juliet Smith, Widow of Coniston, Lancashire, 29 June 1839

National Library of Wales, Aberystwyth

Letters of H. M. Bowdler to Iolo Morganwg

New York Public Library

Ladies of Llangollen Papers (microfilm)
Original Letters Collected by William Upcott

Pennsylvania State University, Special Collections Library, University Park

H. M. Bowdler Correspondence to Cadell and Davies

Princeton University Library, Princeton, NJ

Manigault Family Papers (microfiche series, from South Carolina Historical Society)

Sir John Soane's Museum, Archives, London

Drawings and Notes for Piercefield and Burn Hall
John Soane Papers, Journals, and Letterbook

Suffolk Record Office, Ipswich, U.K.

Evidence of Title of George Smith and Richard Mott, 1774
Settlement Made by Thomas Mulliner Esq. on the Marriage of George Smith Esq. with Miss Juliet Mott, 14 March 1774

Published Primary Sources

"Account of the Extraordinary Literary Endowments of Miss Elizabeth Smith." *La Belle Assemblee; or, Bell's Court and Fashionable Magazine* (London), January 1809, 5–9.

Allaback, Steven, and Alexander Medlicott Jr. "A Visit with Wordsworth: From the Unpublished Journals of Anna Eliot Ticknor." *Wordsworth Circle* 9, no. 1 (Winter 1978): 88–91.

"An American Lady." *Sketches of the Lives of Distinguished Females: Written for Girls, with a View to Their Mental and Moral Improvement.* New York: J. and J. Harper, 1833.

American Lady's Preceptor: A Compilation of Observations, Essays, and Poetical Effusions Designed to Direct the Female Mind in a Course of Pleasing and Instructive Reading. 2nd edition. Baltimore: Edward J. Coale, 1811.

American Sunday-School Union. *Memoirs of Pious Women: Margaret Walker, Elizabeth Smith, Frances Cunningham.* Philadelphia: American Sunday-School Union, [1837].

Andrews, C. Bruyn, ed. *The Torrington Diaries, Containing the Tours through England and Wales of the Hon. John Byng (Later Fifth Viscount Torrington) between the Years 1781 and 1794.* New York: Henry Holt, 1935.

"Authoresses and Autographs—No. 1." *New Monthly Magazine and Literary Journal* (Boston), July 1824, 217–24.

Baker, James. *A Picturesque Guide through Wales and the Marches; Interspersed with the Most Interesting Subjects of Antiquity in that Principality.* Worcester, U.K.: J. Tymbs, 1795.

Balfour, Clara Lucas. *Happy Evenings; or, The Literary Institution at Home.* London: Houlston and Stoneman, 1851.

Balfour, Clara Lucas. *Women Worth Emulating.* London: Sunday School Union, 1877.

Balfour, Clara Lucas. *Working Women of the Last Half Century: The Lesson of Their Lives.* London: W. and F. G. Cash, 1854.

Barbauld, Anna Laetitia. *The Correspondence of Samuel Richardson: Selected from the Original Manuscripts, Bequeathed by Him to His Family, to Which Are Prefixed, a Biographical Account of That Author, and Observations on His Writings.* London: Richard Phillips, 1804.

Barrett, Charlotte, ed. *Diary and Letters of Madame d'Arblay, 1778–1840*. London: Macmillan, 1905.

Bell, G. H., ed. *The Hamwood Papers of the Ladies of Llangollen and Caroline Hamilton*. London: Macmillan, 1930.

Benger, Elizabeth. *Memoirs of the Late Mrs. Elizabeth Hamilton, with a Selection of Her Correspondence, and Other Unpublished Writings*. 2nd edition. London: Longman, Hunt, Orme, and Brown, 1819.

Bennett, John. *Letters to a Young Lady, on a Variety of Useful and Interesting Subjects, Calculated to Improve the Heart, to Form the Manners, and Enlighten the Understanding*. 3rd edition. London: Cadell and Davies, 1803.

"Biographical Sketches of Celebrated Women. No IV: Elizabeth Smith." *Englishwoman's Magazine and Christian Mother's Miscellany* (London), June 1846, 321–31.

"Biography: Miss Elizabeth Smith." *Minerviad* (Boston), March 30, 1822, 2–3.

"Biography: Miss Elizabeth Smith." *Saturday Magazine* (Philadelphia, Trenton, and New York), March 22, 1822, 273–75.

"Biography of Miss Elizabeth Smith." *Churchman's Magazine* (Hartford, CT), May 1821, 129–33.

Boswell, James. *The Life of Samuel Johnson: Comprehending an Account of His Studies and Numerous Works, in Chronological Order, a Series of His Epistolary Correspondence and Conversations with Many Eminent Persons, and Various Original Pieces of His Composition, Never Before Published: The Whole Exhibiting a View of Literature and Literary Men in Great-Britain, for Near Half a Century, during Which He Flourished*. 5th edition. London: Cadell and Davies, 1807.

Bowdler, Henrietta Maria. *Pen Tamar; or, The History of the Old Maid*. London: Longman, Rees, Orme, Brown, and Green, 1830.

[Bowdler, Henrietta Maria]. *Sermons on the Doctrines and Duties of Christianity*. 4th edition. Bath, U.K.: Richard Cruttwell, 1803.

[Bowdler, Jane]. *Poems and Essays, by a Lady Lately Deceased*. 2nd edition. Bath, U.K.: R. Cruttwell, 1786.

Bowdler, Thomas. *The Family Shakespeare*. Bath, U.K.: Richard Cruttwell, 1807.

Bowles, William Lisle. "On Reading Fragments by a Young Lady Lately Deceased." In *Poems (Never before Published), Written Chiefly at Bremhill, in Wiltshire*, 133–34. London: Cadell and Davies, 1809.

Boyce, Anne Ogden. *Records of a Quaker Family: The Richardsons of Cleveland*. London: Samuel Harris, 1889.

Browne, Mary Ann. "To the Memory of Elizabeth Smith: Supposed to Be Written by her Grave." In *Ada, and Other Poems*, 228–32. London: Longman, Rees, Orme, Browne, and Green, 1828.

Burder, Samuel. *Memoirs of Eminently Pious Women by Thomas Gibbon, a New Edition*. London: Duncan, Longman, 1827.

[Burges, Mary Ann]. *The Cavern of Death: A Moral Tale*. 2nd edition. London: J. Bell, 1794.

[Burges, Mary Ann]. *The Progress of the Pilgrim Good-Intent, in Jacobinical Times*. London: John Hatchard, 1800.

Burke, John. *A Genealogical and Heraldic Dictionary of the Landed Gentry of Great Britain and Ireland*. London: Henry Colburn, 1847.

Carr, Mary. *Thomas Wilkinson: A Friend of Wordsworth*. London: Headley Brothers, 1905.

Chapone, Hester. *Letters on the Improvement of the Mind, Addressed to a Young Lady*. London: J. Walter, 1790.

Chapone, Hester. *The Posthumous Works of Mrs. Chapone: Containing Her Correspondence with Mr. Richardson; a Series of Letters to Mrs. Elizabeth Carter, and Some Fugitive Pieces, Never before Published*. London: John Murray, 1807.

Coburn, Kathleen, ed. *The Letters of Sara Hutchinson from 1800 to 1835*. Toronto: University of Toronto Press, 1954.

Constable, Archibald, ed. *Letters of Anna Seward: Written between the Years 1784 and 1807, in Six Volumes*. Edinburgh: George Ramsay, 1811.

"Cotswoldia." "On Reading the *Fragments in Prose and Verse, By Elizabeth Smith*." *New Monthly Magazine* (London), January 1816, 519.

Coxe, Margaret. *The Young Lady's Companion: In a Series of Letters*. Columbus, OH: I. N. Whiting, 1839.

Coxe, William. *An Historical Tour in Monmouthshire; Illustrated with Views by Sir R. C. Hoare, Bart., a New Map of the County, and Other Engravings*. London: Cadell and Davies, 1801.

Crawford, Mrs. [Louisa]. "Autobiographical Sketches." *The Metropolitan* (London), November 1836, 273–282.

"D." "Lines on the Late Miss Elizabeth Smith, Written at Night, Dec. 20th, 1815." *The Portico, a Repository of Science and Literature* (Baltimore), March 1816, 260.

Derry, Warren, ed. *The Journals and Letters of Fanny Burney*. Oxford: Clarendon Press, 1982.

De Quincey, Thomas. *Literary Reminiscences; from the Autobiography of an English Opium-Eater*. Boston: Ticknor, Reed, and Field, 1851.

De Quincey, Thomas. "Sketches of the Life and Manners; from the Autobiography of an English Opium-Eater." *Tait's Edinburgh Magazine*, June 1840, 346–52.

De Selincourt, Ernest, et al., eds. *The Letters of William and Dorothy Wordsworth*. Revised 2nd edition (online), 1967–93; Oxford: Oxford University Press, 2015. https://www.oxfordscholarlyeditions.com/view/10.1093/actrade/9780198114642.book.1/actrade-9780198114642-book.1.

"Elizabeth Smith, Linguist, Etc." *Monthly Chronicle of North-Country Lore and Legend* (Newcastle-on-Tyne, U.K.), December 1891, 535–37.

Elwood, Anne Katharine. *Memoirs of the Literary Ladies of England: From the Commencement of the Last Century*. London: Henry Colburn, 1843.

Ewing, Juliana Horatia, ed. *Parables from Nature by Margaret Gatty, with a Memoir by Her Daughter, Juliana Horatia Ewing*. 1st series. London: George Bell and Sons, 1885.

Fletcher, Eliza. *Autobiography of Mrs. Fletcher, with Letters and Other Family Memorials*. 3rd edition. Edinburgh: Edmonston and Douglass, 1876.

Frank, Elizabeth. *Classical English Letter-Writer; or, Epistolary Selections; Designed to Improve Young Persons in the Art of Letter-Writing, and in the Principles of Virtue and Piety*. York, U.K.: Thomas Wilson, 1814.

Gilpin, William. *Observations on Several Parts of the Counties of Cambridge, Norfolk, Suffolk, and Essex. Also on Several Parts of North Wales; Relative Chiefly to Picturesque Beauty, in Two Tours, the Former Made in the Year 1769, the Latter in the Year 1773*. London: Cadell and Davies, 1809.

Gilpin, William. *Observations on the River Wye, and Several Parts of South Wales, &c., Relative Chiefly to Picturesque Beauty; Made in the Summer of the Year 1770*. London: R. Blamire, 1782.

Gisborne, Thomas. *An Enquiry into the Duties of the Female Sex*. London: Cadell and Davies, 1797.

Grant, J. P., ed. *Memoirs and Correspondence of Mrs. Grant of Laggan*. 2nd edition. London: Longman, Brown, Green, and Longmans, 1845.

Green, William. *The Tourist's New Guide: Containing a Description of the Lakes, Mountains, and Scenery in Cumberland, Westmorland, and Lancashire*. Kendal, U.K.: R. Lough, 1819.

Griscom, John. *A Year in Europe: Comprising a Journal of Observations in England, Scotland, Ireland, France, Switzerland, the North of Italy, and Holland, in 1818 and 1819*. 2nd edition. New York: Collins, 1824.

Gwilliam, John. "Quatorzains. Written in the First Volume of Miss Elizabeth Smith's *Fragments in Prose and Verse*." *Universal Magazine* (London), September 1809, 223–24.

Hawkins, Sir John, ed. *The Works of Samuel Johnson: Together with His Life, and Notes on His Lives of the Poets*. London: J. Buckland, 1787.

Hemans, Felicia Dorothea Browne. "Lines, Written in the Memoirs of Elizabeth Smith." In *The Domestic Affections and Other Poems*, 57–59. London: Cadell and Davies, 1812.

Hillard, George S., ed. *The Life, Letters, and Journals of George Ticknor*. Boston: Houghton Mifflin, 1909.

Hughes, Harriet, ed. *The Works of Mrs. Hemans, with a Memoir by Her Sister, and an Essay on Her Genius, by Mrs. Sigourney*. Philadelphia: Lea and Blanchard, 1840.

[Hunt, Mary]. *Essay on the Happiness of the Life to Come*. Bath, U.K.: R. Cruttwell, 1793.

[Hunt, Mary]. *Lectures on Astronomy, and Natural Philosophy, for the Use of Children*. Bath, U.K.: R. Cruttwell, 1794.

[Hunt, Mary]. "On Visiting the Ruins of an Ancient Abbey in Devonshire, September 1786, by a Young Lady." *Gentleman's Magazine* (London), October 1786, 885.

Hutchinson, William. *An Excursion to the Lakes, in Westmoreland and Cumberland, August 1773*. London: J. Wilkie, 1774.

Hutchinson, William. *The History and Antiquities of the County Palatine of Durham*. Durham, U.K.: G. Walker, 1823.

Hutton, Catherine. "Letters Written during a Tour in North Wales; by Miss Hutton, of Bennett's Hill, near Birmingham. Letter XVIII—Sept. 3, 1796." *Monthly Magazine; or, British Register* (London), April 1816, 205–7.

Hutton, Catherine. "Letters Written during a Second Tour in North Wales; by Miss Hutton, of Bennett's Hill, near Birmingham. Letter XII—October 7, 1797." *Monthly Magazine; or, British Register* (London), November 1816, 323–25.

Hutton, Catherine. "Letters Written during a Third Tour in North Wales; by Miss Hutton, of Bennett's Hill, near Birmingham. Letter XV—September 16, 1799." *Monthly Magazine; or, British Register* (London), June 1818, 397–99.

Hutton, William. *Remarks upon North Wales, Being the Result of Sixteen Tours through That Part of the Principality*. Birmingham, U.K.: Knott and Lloyd, 1803.

Ibbetson, Julius Caesar, et. al. *A Picturesque Guide to Bath, Bristol, Hot-Wells, the River Avon, and the Adjacent Country: Illustrated with a Set of Views, Taken in the Summer of 1792 by Mess. Ibbetson, Laporte, and J. Hassell, and Engraved in Aquatinta*. London: Hookham and Carpenter, 1793.

Ireland, Samuel. *Picturesque Views on the River Wye.* London: R. Faulder, 1797.

Japp, Alexander H. "A Woman Learned and Wise." *Temple Bar* (London), January 1898, 109–18.

Jenkins, Geraint H., Ffion Mair Jones, and David Ceri Jones, eds. *Correspondence of Iolo Morganwg.* Cardiff: University of Wales Press, 2007.

Johnson, Joseph. *Clever Girls of Our Time: And How They Became Famous Women.* London: Darton, 1862.

Kendrick, M., and L. M. Child. *The Gift Book of Biography, for Young Ladies.* London: Thomas Nelson, 1849.

Knight, William, ed. *The Letters of the Wordsworth Family from 1787 to 1855.* Boston: Ginn, 1907.

Knight, William, ed. *The Poetical Works of William Wordsworth.* Edinburgh: William Paterson, 1883.

"L.A." "Journal of a Welsh Tour." *Monthly Magazine* (London), October 1802, 227–32.

The Lady's Monitor: Selected from the Writings of Lady Jane Grey, Queen Catharine Parr, Lady Elizabeth Brooke, Elizabeth Smith, Sir Thomas More, Sir John Cheeke, and William Penn. London: John Taylor, 1828.

"The Lady's Preceptor." *Baltimore Repertory,* April 1, 1811, 198–99.

Lancaster, Jane. "'By the Pens of Females': Girls' Diaries from Rhode Island, 1788–1821." *Rhode Island History* 57, nos. 3–4 (August–November 1999): 59–113.

Leadbeater, Mary. *The Leadbeater Papers: The Annals of Ballitore, by Mary Leadbeater, with a Memoir of the Author; Letters from Edmund Burke Heretofore Unpublished: and the Correspondence of Mrs. R. Trench and Rev. George Crabbe with Mary Leadbeater.* London: Bell and Daldy, 1862.

Lee, Anna Maria. *Memoirs of Eminent Female Writers, of All Ages and Countries.* Philadelphia: John Grigg, 1827.

Lee, Sidney, ed. *Dictionary of National Biography,* vol. 53, *Smith—Stanger.* London: Smith, Elder, 1898.

"Lines on Reading the Memoirs of Miss Smith, the Translator of Klopstock's *Messiah.*" *Boston Pearl, and Literary Gazette,* July 11, 1835, 356.

"Lines Written after Reading Elizabeth Smith's Fragments." *Ladies' Garland and Family Wreath* (Philadelphia), July 1, 1838, 32.

Lockhart, John Gibson. *Memoirs of the Life of Sir Walter Scott.* 2nd edition. Edinburgh: Robert Cadell, 1839.

Mackintosh, Robert James, ed. *Memoirs of the Life of Sir James Mackintosh.* 2nd edition. London: Edward Moxon, 1836.

Martineau, Harriet. *A Complete Guide to the English Lakes.* Windermere, U.K.: John Garnett, 1855.

[Martineau, Harriet]. "Lights of the English Lake District." *Atlantic Monthly* (Boston), May 1861, 541–58.

[Martineau, Harriet (writing as "Discipulus")]. "Female Writers on Practical Divinity. No. II. Mrs. More and Mrs. Barbauld." *Monthly Repository of Theology and General Literature* (London), December 1822, 746–50.

[Martineau, Harriet (writing as "Discipulus")]. "On Female Education." *Monthly Repository of Theology and General Literature* (London), February 1823, 77–81.

McMahon, Lucia, and Deborah Schriver, eds. *To Read My Heart: The Journal of Rachel Van Dyke, 1810–1811*. Philadelphia: University of Pennsylvania Press, 2000.

"Meta." "Anecdotes of Celebrated Women, No. XIV. Miss E. Smith." *The Portfolio: Comprising the Flowers of Literature, the Spirit of the Magazines, the Wonders of Nature and Art, the Family Physician and Domestic Guide* (London), December 4, 1824, 206–7.

Miller, Lady Anna. *Poetical Amusements at a Villa Near Bath*. Bath: L. Bull, 1775.

Miller, Lady Anna. *Poetical Amusements at a Villa Near Bath*. 2nd edition. London: Edward and Charles Dilly, 1776–81.

"Miss Elizabeth Smith." *Christian Disciple* (Boston), September 1818, 257–58.

"Miss Elizabeth Smith." *Ladies' Monthly Museum* (London), December 1821, 301–2.

Montagu, Elizabeth. *The Letters of Mrs. Elizabeth Montagu: Containing Some of the Letters of Her Correspondents*. London: Cadell and Davies, 1809.

More, Hannah. *Coelebs in Search of a Wife*. 6th edition. London: Cadell and Davies, 1809.

More, Hannah. *Essays on Various Subjects, Principally Designed for Young Ladies*. London: Wilkie and Cadell, 1777.

More, Hannah. *Strictures on the Modern System of Female Education, with a View of the Principles and Conduct Prevalent among Women of Rank and Fortune*. 4th edition. Dublin: William Porter, 1799.

Morgan, [Mary]. *A Tour to Milford Haven, in the Year 1791*. London: John Stockdale, 1795.

"Mrs. Elizabeth Palmer Peabody—1800–1818." In *American Journal of Education*, ed. Henry Barnard, 5:584–87. Hartford, CT: Office of American Journal of Education, 1880.

Murray, Sarah. *A Companion, and Useful Guide to the Beauties of Scotland: To the Lakes of Westmoreland, Cumberland, and Lancashire; and to the Curiosities in the District of Craven, in the West Riding of Yorkshire*. London: Printed for the Author, 1799.

New Bath Guide. Bath: R. Cruttwell, 1791.

Pennant, Thomas. *A Tour in Wales, 1770*. London: H. Hughes, 1778–81.

Pennington, Montagu, ed. *Memoirs of the Life of Mrs. Elizabeth Carter*. London: F. C. and J. Rivington, 1807.

Polwhele, Richard. *Traditions and Recollections; Domestic, Clerical, and Literary*. London: John Nichols and Son, 1826.

Radcliffe, Ann. *A Journey Made in the Summer of 1794, through Holland and the Western Frontier of Germany, with a Return Down the Rhine; to Which Are Added, Observations during a Tour to the Lakes of Lancashire, Westmoreland, and Cumberland*. London: G. G. and J. Robinson, 1795.

Ramsay, David, ed. *Memoirs of the Life of Martha Laurens Ramsay, Who Died in Charleston, S.C., on the 10th of June, 1811, in the 52d Year of Her Age*. Charlestown, SC: Samuel Etheridge, 1812.

Rawnsley, Hardwicke Drummond. *Literary Association of the English Lakes: Westmoreland, Windermere and the Haunts of Wordsworth*. New York: Macmillan, 1894.

Rizzo, Betty, ed. *Early Journals and Letters of Fanny Burney*. Montreal: McGill-Queen's University Press, 2003.

Roberts, Mary. *Select Female Biography; Comprising Memoirs of Eminent British Ladies, Derived from Original and Other Authentic Sources*. London: John and Arthur Arch, 1821.

Roberts, William, ed. *Memoirs of the Life and Correspondence of Hannah More*. New York: Harper and Brothers, 1835.

St. John, Arthur. *The Weft of the Wye: A Poem, Descriptive of the Scenery of That River.* London: G. B. Whittaker, 1826.

[Scott, Sarah]. *A Description of Millenium Hall, and the Country Adjacent: Together with the Characters of the Inhabitants, and Such Historical Anecdotes and Reflections, as May Excite in the Reader Proper Sentiments of Humanity, and Lead the Mind to the Love of Virtue.* London: J. Newbery, 1762.

Scott, Walter. *The Journal of Sir Walter Scott: From the Original Manuscript at Abbotsford.* Edinburgh: David Douglas, 1890.

Selwyn, Elizabeth. *Journal of Excursions through the Most Interesting Parts of England, Wales, and Scotland, during the Summers and Autumns of 1819, 1820, 1821, 1822, and 1823.* London: Plummer and Brewis, 1824.

Sessions, Frederick. *Literary Celebrities of the English Lake-District.* London: Elliot Stock, 1905.

Sigourney, Lydia. *Letters to Young Ladies, by a Lady.* Hartford, CT: P. Canfield, 1833.

Sigourney, Lydia, ed. *The Writings of Nancy Maria Hyde, of Norwich, Conn., Connected with a Sketch of Her Life.* Norwich, CT: Russell Hubbard, 1816.

[Sigourney], Lydia Huntley. *Moral Pieces, in Prose and Verse.* Hartford, CT: Sheldon and Goodwin, 1815.

Simmons, Nancy Craig, ed. *Selected Letters of Mary Moody Emerson.* Athens: University of Georgia Press, 1993.

Smith, Elizabeth. *The Book of Job: Translated from the Hebrew by Elizabeth Smith; with a Preface and Annotations, by Rev. F. Randolph, D.D.* Bath, U.K.: Richard Cruttwell, 1810.

Smith, Elizabeth. *Fragments, in Prose and Verse: By a Young Lady, Lately Deceased. With Some Account of Her Life and Character, by the Author of "Sermons on the Doctrines and Duties of Christianity."* Bath, U.K.: Richard Cruttwell, 1808.

Smith, Elizabeth. *Fragments, in Prose and Verse: By Miss Elizabeth Smith Lately Deceased. With Some Account of Her Life and Character, by H. M. Bowdler.* Bath, U.K.: Richard Cruttwell, 1809.

Smith, Elizabeth. *Memoirs of Frederick and Margaret Klopstock, Translated from the German.* Bath, U.K.: Richard Cruttwell, 1809.

Smith, Elizabeth. *A Vocabulary, Hebrew, Arabic, and Persian, by the Late Miss E. Smith.* London: A. J. Valpy, 1814.

Soane, John. *Sketches in Architecture: Containing Plans and Elevations of Cottages, Villas, and Other Useful Buildings with Characteristic Scenery.* London: Taylor and Holborn, 1793.

Sotheby, William. *A Poetical Epistle to Sir George Beaumont, Bart. on the Encouragement of the British School of Painting.* London: John Wright, 1801.

Sotheby, William. *A Tour through Parts of Wales, Sonnets, Odes, and Other Poems. With Engravings from Drawings Taken on the Spot, by J. Smith.* London: J. Smeeton, 1794.

Steele, Mary Davies. "Elizabeth Smith: A Self-Taught Linguist." *Education* (Boston), March 1897, 411–17.

Timpson, Thomas. *British Female Biography; Being Select Memoirs of Pious Ladies, in Various Ranks of Public and Private Life.* London: Aylott, 1854.

"A Tour through Wales and the Central Parts of England." *Gentleman's Magazine* (London), December 1799, 1036–40.

Trench, Richard Chenevix, ed. *The Remains of the Late Mrs. Richard Trench, Being Selections from Her Journals, Letters, and Other Papers. Trench.* 2nd edition. London: Parker, Son and Bourn, 1862.

The Two May-Days. 2nd edition. Boston: Massachusetts Sabbath School Society, 1844.

"The Venerable Bede and His Durham Editors, Dr. John Smith and His Son, Bishop George Smith." *Durham University Journal,* November 12, 1883, 132–33.

Warner, Richard. *A Walk through Wales, in August 1797, by the Rev. Richard Warner, of Bath.* Bath, U.K.: R. Cruttwell, 1798.

Warter, John Wood, ed. *Selections from the Letters of Robert Southey.* London: Longman, Brown, Green, Longmans, and Roberts, 1856.

West, Thomas. *A Guide to the Lakes, in Cumberland, Westmorland, and Lancashire.* 2nd edition. London: Richardson and Urquhart, 1780.

Wilkinson, Thomas. "A Day's Tour in the North of England." *Belfast Monthly Magazine,* July 31, 1812, 1–5.

Wilkinson, Thomas. *Tours to the British Mountains, with the Descriptive Poems of Lowther, and Emont Vale.* London: Taylor and Hessey, 1824.

Williams, Edward, *Poems, Lyric and Pastoral.* London: J. Nichols, 1794.

Wilson, Ellen. "A Shropshire Lady in Bath, 1794–1807." *Bath History* 4 (1992): 95–123.

Wilson, John. "Lines Written on Reading the Memoirs of Miss Smith." In *Isle of Palms and Other Poems,* 234–45. Edinburgh: Longman, Hurst, Rees, Orme, and Brown, 1812.

Woof, Pamela, ed. *Dorothy Wordsworth: The Grasmere and Alfoxden Journals.* New York: Oxford University Press, 2002.

Wordsworth, William. *A Description of the Scenery of the Lakes in the North of England.* 3rd edition. London: Longman, Hurst, Rees, Orme, and Brown, 1822.

Wordsworth, William. *Lyrical Ballads.* London: J. and A. Arch, 1798.

Wordsworth, William. *The Prelude; or, Growth of a Poet's Mind: An Autobiographical Poem.* London: Edward Moxon, 1850.

Wordsworth, William. *The Sonnets of William Wordsworth, Collected in One Volume, with a Few Additional Ones, Now First Published.* London: Edward Moxon, 1838.

Wordsworth, William. ["An Unpublished Tour"]. In *The Prose Works of William Wordsworth,* ed. W. J. B. Owen and Jane Worthington Smyser, 2:287–348. Oxford: Clarendon Press, 1974.

Yonge, Charlotte M. *Biographies of Good Women.* 2nd series. London: J. and C. Mozley, 1865.

Reviews of *Fragments*

"Art II. *Fragments in Prose and Verse.*" *British Critic* (London), March 1809, 217–23.

"Art. IV—*Fragments in Prose and Verse*" and "Art. V—*Select Poems, &c. by the Late John Dawes Worgan.*" *Critical Review; or, Annals of Literature* (London), June 1811, 140–50.

"Art. IX. *Fragments in Prose and Verse.*" *Eclectic Review* (London), September 1808, 827–32.

"Art. X. *Fragments in Prose and Verse*" and "Art. XI. *Memoirs of Frederick and Margaret Klopstock.*" *Monthly Review; or, Literary Journal* (London), January 1811, 67–79.

"Art. XI. *Memoirs of Frederick and Margaret Klopstock.*" *British Critic* (London), July 1809, 59–63.

"Article 13. *Fragments in Prose and Verse.*" *Monthly Anthology and Boston Review,* May 1810, 335–38.

"*Fragments in Prose and Verse.*" *Poetical Register and Repository of Fugitive Poetry* (London), January 1812, 553–54.

"From the British Critick." *Select Reviews, and Spirit of the Foreign Magazines* (Philadelphia), August 1809, 106–9.

"From the *European Magazine.* Memoirs of the Late Miss Elizabeth Smith." *Select Reviews, and Spirit of the Foreign Magazines* (Philadelphia), April 1810, 269–73.

"Memoir of Miss Smith." *Monthly Panorama* (Dublin), March 1810, 144–52.

"Memoirs of the Late Miss Elizabeth Smith." *European Magazine and London Review,* November 1809, 323–26.

"Miss Elizabeth Smith." *Christian Disciple* (Boston), September 1818, 257–58.

Parker, Samuel H. *Review of the Life and Fragments of Miss Elizabeth Smith* (Boston: Samuel H. Parker, 1810).

"Review of New Publications." *Belfast Monthly Magazine,* December 1, 1808, 291–93.

"Review of New Publications." *Belfast Monthly Magazine,* September 30, 1809, 222–25.

"Review of New Publications." *Christian Observer, Conducted by Members of the Established Church* (Boston), August 1808, 508–21.

Secondary Sources

Adams, Amanda. *Performing Authorship in the Nineteenth-Century Transatlantic Lecture Tour.* Burlington, VT: Ashgate, 2014.

Allen, Douglas W. "Compatible Incentives and the Purchase of Military Commissions." *Journal of Legal Studies* 21, no. 1 (January 1998): 45–66.

Allgor, Catherine. *Party Politics: In Which the Ladies of Washington Help Build a City and a Government.* Charlottesville: University Press of Virginia, 2000.

Allgor, Catherine. *A Perfect Union: Dolley Madison and the Creation of the American Nation.* New York: Henry Holt, 2006.

Andrews, Kerri. *Wanderers: A History of Women Walking.* London: Reaktion Books, 2020.

Andrews, Malcom. *The Search for the Picturesque: Landscape Aesthetics and Tourism in Britain, 1760–1800.* Stanford, CA: Stanford University Press, 1989.

Anishanslin, Zara. *Portrait of a Woman in Silk: Hidden Histories of the British Atlantic World.* New Haven, CT: Yale University Press, 2016.

Arnold, Hilary. "Genteel Widows of Bath: Mrs. Margaret Graves and Her Letters from Bath, 1793–1807." *Bath History* 7 (1998): 78–91.

Ashfield, Andrew, ed. *Romantic Women Poets, 1770–1838: An Anthology.* Manchester, U.K.: Manchester University Press, 1995.

Austin, Linda M. "Aesthetic Embarrassment: The Reversion to the Picturesque in Nineteenth-Century English Tourism." *ELH* 74, no. 3 (Fall 2007): 629–53.

Bainbridge, Simon. *Mountaineering and British Romanticism: The Literary Cultures of Climbing, 1770–1836.* New York: Oxford University Press, 2020.

Bainbridge, Simon. "Romantic Writers and Mountaineering." *Romanticism* 18, no. 1 (2012): 1–15.

Bainbridge, Simon. "Writing from 'The Perilous Ridge': Romanticism and the Invention of Rock Climbing." *Romanticism* 19, no. 3 (2013): 246–60.

Bannet, Eve Tavor. "The Bluestocking Sisters: Women's Patronage, Millenium Hall, and 'The Visible Providence of a Country.'" *Eighteenth-Century Life* 30, no. 1 (2005): 25–55.

Barker, Hannah, and Elaine Chalus, eds. *Women's History: Britain, 1700–1850—An Introduction.* New York: Routledge, 2005.

Barker-Benfield, G. J. *The Culture of Sensibility: Sex and Society in Eighteenth-Century Britain.* Chicago: University of Chicago Press, 1996.

Barry, Elizabeth. "Celebrity, Cultural Production, and Public Life." *International Journal of Culture Studies* 11, no. 3 (2008): 251–58.

Batchelor, Robert. "Thinking about the Gym: Greek Ideals, Newtonian Bodies and Exercise in Early Eighteenth-Century Britain." *Journal for Eighteenth-Century Studies* 35, no. 2 (2012): 185–97.

Battersby, Christine. *Gender and Genius: Towards a Feminist Aesthetics.* Bloomington: Indiana University Press, 1989.

Beattie, Heather. "Where Narratives Meet: Archival Description, Provenance, and Women's Diaries." *Libraries and the Cultural Record* 44, no. 1 (February 2009): 82–100.

Behrendt, Stephen C. *British Women Poets and the Romantic Writing Community.* Baltimore: Johns Hopkins University Press, 2008.

Bigold, Melanie. *Women of Letters, Manuscript Circulation, and Print Afterlives in the Eighteenth Century: Elizabeth Rowe, Catharine Cockburn, and Elizabeth Carter.* Basingstoke, U.K.: Palgrave Macmillan UK, 2013.

Blauvelt, Martha Tomhave. *The Work of the Heart: Young Women and Emotion.* Charlottesville: University of Virginia Press, 2007.

Bloch, Ruth H. "Changing Conceptions of Sexuality and Romance in Eighteenth-Century America." *William and Mary Quarterly,* 60, no. 1 (January 2003): 13–42.

Boot, H. M. "Real Incomes of the British Middle Class, 1760–1850: The Experience of Clerks at the East India Company." *Economic History Review* 52, no. 4 (November 1999): 638–68.

Booth, Alison. *Homes and Haunts: Touring Writers' Shrines and Countries.* New York: Oxford University Press, 2016.

Booth, Alison. *How to Make It as a Woman: Collective Biographical History from Victoria to the Present.* Chicago: University of Chicago Press, 2004.

Borsay, Ann. "Visitors and Residents: The Dynamics of Charity in Eighteenth-Century Bath." *Journal of Tourism History* 4, no. 2 (August 2012): 171–80.

Boudreau, George W., and Margaretta Markle Lovell, eds. *A Material World: Culture, Society, and the Life of Things in Early Anglo-America.* University Park: Pennsylvania State University Press, 2019.

Bradbrook, M. C. "The Elegant Eccentrics." *Modern Language Review* 44, no. 2 (April 1949): 184–98.

Brewer, John. *The Pleasures of the Imagination: English Culture in the Eighteenth Century.* New York: Farrar, Straus, Giroux, 1997.

Brideoake, Fiona. *The Ladies of Llangollen: Desire, Indeterminacy, and the Legacies of Criticism.* Lewisburg, PA: Bucknell University Press, 2017.

Brock, Claire. *The Feminization of Fame, 1750–1830.* New York: Palgrave Macmillan, 2006.

Brooks, Joanna. "The Early American Public Sphere and the Emergence of a Black Print Counterpublic." *William and Mary Quarterly*, 62, no. 1 (January 2005): 67–92.

Brooks, Lisa. *Our Beloved Kin: A New History of King Philip's War*. New Haven, CT: Yale University Press, 2018.

Brown, Chandos. "Mary Wollstonecraft, or the Female Illuminati: The Campaign against Women and 'Modern Philosophy' in the Early Republic." *Journal of the Early Republic* 15, no. 3 (Fall 1995): 389–424.

Brown, Susan, Patricia Clements, and Isobel Grundy, eds. "Elizabeth Smith, 1776–1806." In *Orlando: Women's Writing in the British Isles from the Beginnings to the Present*, edited by Susan Brown, Patricia Clements, and Isobel Grundy. Cambridge: Cambridge University Press Online, 2006. https://orlando.cambridge.org/.

Bunkers, Susanne L., and Cynthia A. Huff, eds. *Inscribing the Daily: Critical Essays on Women's Diaries*. Amherst: University of Massachusetts Press, 1996.

Buzard, James. *The Beaten Track: European Tourism, Literature, and the Ways to "Culture," 1800–1918*. Oxford: Clarendon Press, 1993.

Byrne, Paula. *The Real Jane Austen: A Life in Small Things*. New York: Harper Perennial, 2013.

Callaghan, Madeleine, and Anthony Howe, eds. *Romanticism and the Letter*. London: Palgrave Macmillan, 2020.

Carretta, Vincent. "Phillis Wheatley: Researching a Life." *Historical Journal of Massachusetts* 43, no. 2 (Summer 2015): 64–89.

Casper, Scott. *Constructing American Lives: Biography and Culture in Nineteenth-Century America*. Chapel Hill: University of North Carolina Press, 1999.

Cayton, Andrew. *Love in the Time of Revolution: Transatlantic Literary Radicalism and Historical Change, 1793–1818*. Chapel Hill: University of North Carolina Press, 2013.

Cayton, Mary Kupiec. "Canonizing Harriet Newell: Women, the Evangelical Press, and the Foreign Mission Movement in New England, 1740–1840." In *Competing Kingdoms: Women, Mission, Nation, and the American Protestant Empire, 1812–1960*, edited by Barbara Reeves-Ellington, Kathryn Kish Sklar, and Connie A. Shemo, 69–93. Durham, NC: Duke University Press, 2010.

Chander, Manu Samriti. *Brown Romantics: Poetry and Nationalism in the Global Nineteenth Century*. Lewisburg, PA: Bucknell University Press, 2017.

Charvat, William. *Literary Publishing in America, 1750–1850*. Philadelphia: University of Pennsylvania Press, 1959.

Chernock, Arianne. *Men and the Making of Modern British Feminism*. Stanford, CA: Stanford University Press, 2010.

Child, Elizabeth. "'To Sing the Town': Women, Place, and Print Culture in Eighteenth-Century Bath." *Studies in Eighteen-Century Culture* 28 (1999): 155–72.

Clarke, Norma. *Dr. Johnson's Women*. London: Hambledon and London, 2000.

Clarke, Norma. *The Rise and Fall of the Woman of Letters*. London: Pimlico, 2004.

Cohen, Lara Langer, and Jordan Alexander Stein, eds. *Early African American Print Culture*. Philadelphia: University of Pennsylvania Press, 2012.

Colbert, Benjamin, ed. *Travel Writing and Tourism in Britain and Ireland*. London: Palgrave Macmillan, 2012.

Colley, Linda. *Britons: Forging the Nation, 1707–1837*. New Haven, CT: Yale University Press, 1992.

Colley, Linda. *The Ordeal of Elizabeth Marsh: A Woman in World History.* New York: Anchor Books, 2008.

Collier, Jackie. "The Truly Benevolent Lady Isabella King, 1772–1845." *Bath History* 11 (2009): 63–77.

Constantine, Mary-Ann. "'The Bounds of Female Reach': Catherine Hutton's Fiction and Her Tours in Wales." *Romantic Textualities: Literature and Print Culture, 1780–1840* 22 (Spring 2017): 89–103.

Corfield, Penelope J. "Georgian Bath: Matrix and Meeting Place." *Connecticut Review* 12, no. 1 (Spring 1990): 69–79.

Cott, Nancy. *The Bonds of Womanhood: "Woman's Sphere" in New England, 1780–1835.* New Haven, CT: Yale University Press, 1977.

Coultrap-McQuin, Susan. *Doing Literary Business: American Women Writers in the Nineteenth Century.* Chapel Hill: University of North Carolina Press, 1990.

Crisafulli, Lilla Maria, and Cecilia Pietropoli, eds. *Romantic Women Poets: Genre and Gender.* Amsterdam: Rodopi, 2007.

Crowell, Ellen. "Ghosting the Llangollen Ladies: Female Intimacies, Ascendancy Exiles, and the Anglo-Irish Novel." *Eire-Irel* 39, nos. 3–4 (Fall–Winter 2004): 203–27.

Darley, Gillian. *John Soane: An Accidental Romantic.* New Haven, CT: Yale University Press, 1999.

Darnton, Robert. "First Steps toward a History of Reading." *Australian Journal of French Studies* 23, no. 1 (1986): 5–30.

Darnton, Robert. *The Great Cat Massacre and Other Episodes in French Cultural History.* New York: Basic Books, 1984.

Darnton, Robert. *The Kiss of Lamourette: Reflections in Cultural History.* New York: Norton, 1991.

Davidoff, Leonore, and Catherine Hall. *Family Fortunes: Men and Women of the English Middle Class, 1780–1850.* Chicago: University of Chicago Press, 1987.

Davies, Damian Walford, and Tim Fulford. "Introduction: Romanticism's Wye." *Romanticism* 19, no. 2 (2013): 115–25.

DeLucia, JoEllen M. "'Far Other Times Are These': The Bluestockings in the Time of Ossian." *Tulsa Studies in Women's Literature* 27, no. 1 (Spring 2008): 39–62.

De Man, Paul. *The Rhetoric of Romanticism.* New York: Columbia University Press, 1984.

De Ritter, Richard. "Reading 'Voyages and Travels': Jane West, Patriotism and the Reformation of Female Sensibility." *Romanticism* 17, no. 2 (2011): 240–50.

DeWispelare, Daniel. "An Amateur's Devotion: Elizabeth Smith's Translation of the *Book of Job*." *Literature and Theology* 25, no. 2 (June 2011): 141–46.

Dillon, Elizabeth Maddock. *The Gender of Freedom: Fictions of Liberalism and the Literary Public Sphere.* Stanford, CT: Stanford University Press, 2004.

Du Prey, Pierre de la Ruffinière. *John Soane: The Making of an Architect.* Chicago: University of Chicago Press, 1982.

Dyer, Serena. *Material Lives: Women Makers and Consumer Culture in the 18th Century.* London: Bloomsbury Visual Arts, 2021.

Easley, Alexis. *Literary Celebrity, Gender, and Victorian Authorship, 1850–1914.* Newark: University of Delaware Press, 2011.

Eastman, Carolyn. *The Strange Genius of Mr. O: The World of the United States' First Forgotten Celebrity.* Chapel Hill: University of North Carolina Press, 2021.

Eger, Elizabeth. *Bluestockings: Women of Reason from Enlightenment to Romanticism.* New York: Palgrave Macmillan, 2010.

Eger, Elizabeth, and Lucy Peltz. *Brilliant Women: Eighteenth-Century Bluestockings.* New Haven, CT: Yale University Press, 2008.

Evans, R. Paul. "Thomas Pennant (1726–1798): 'The Father of Cambrian Tourists.'" *Welsh History Review* 13, no. 4 (December 1987): 395–417.

Ezell, Margaret J. M. *Social Authorship and the Advent of Print.* Baltimore: Johns Hopkins University Press, 1999.

Ezell, Margaret J. M. *Writing Women's Literary History.* Baltimore: Johns Hopkins University Press, 1993.

Faderman, Lillian. *Surpassing the Love of Men: Romantic Friendship and Love between Women from the Renaissance to the Present.* New York: William Morrow, 1981.

Fairer, David. "Revisiting 'Tintern Abbey': The Challenge of the Familiar." *Romanticism* 19, no. 2 (2013): 179–87.

Fara, Patricia. *Newton: The Making of Genius.* New York: Columbia University Press, 2002.

Fara, Patricia. *Pandora's Breeches: Women, Science, and Power in the Enlightenment.* London: Pimlico, 2004.

First, Sara Babcox. "The Mechanics of Renown; or, The Rise of a Celebrity Culture in Early America." Ph.D. dissertation, University of Michigan, 2009.

Foreman, Amanda. *Georgiana, Duchess of Devonshire.* New York: Modern Library, 2001.

Fraisse, Genevieve. *Reason's Muse: Sexual Difference and the Birth of Democracy,* Translated by Jane Marie Todd. Chicago: University of Chicago Press, 1994.

Freeman, Michael. "Perceptions of Welshness: Tourists' Impressions of the Material and Traditional Culture of Wales, 1770–1840." *Folk Life* 53, no. 1 (2015): 57–71.

Freeman, Michael. "Women Tourists." Early Tourists in Wales. 2015. https://sublimewales .wordpress.com/introduction/types-of-tourist/women/.

Fryer, Mary Beacock. *Elizabeth Postuma Simcoe, 1762–1850: A Biography.* Toronto: Dundurn Press, 1989.

Fuentes, Marisa J. *Dispossessed Lives: Enslaved Women, Violence, and the Archive.* Philadelphia: University of Pennsylvania Press, 2016.

Gilbert, Sandra M., and Susan Gubar. *The Madwoman in the Attic: The Woman Writer and the Nineteenth-Century Literary Imagination.* New Haven, CT: Yale University Press, 1979.

Glover, Lorri. *Eliza Lucas Pinckney: An Independent Woman in the Age of Revolution.* New Haven, CT: Yale University Press, 2020.

Glover, Michael. "The Purchase of Commissions: A Reappraisal." *Journal for the Society for Army Historical Research* 58, no. 236 (Winter 1980): 223–35.

Godbeer, Richard. *World of Trouble: A Philadelphia Quaker Family's Journey through the American Revolution.* New Haven, CT: Yale University Press, 2019.

Goodwin, Joan W. *The Remarkable Mrs. Ripley: The Life of Sarah Alden Bradford Ripley.* Boston: Northeastern University Press, 1998.

Gross, Robert A., and Mary Kelley, eds. *A History of the Book in America.* Volume 2, *An Extensive Republic: Print, Culture, and Society in the New Nation, 1790–1840.* Chapel Hill: University of North Carolina Press, 2010.

Guentner, Wendelin. "The Sketch as Literary Metaphor: The British Romantic Travel Narrative." *European Romantic Review* 7, no. 2 (December 1996): 125–33.

Guest, Harriet. *Small Change: Women, Learning, Patriotism, 1750–1810.* Chicago: University of Chicago Press, 2000.

Hackel, Heidi Brayman, and Catherine E. Kelly, eds. *Literacy, Authorship, and Culture in the Atlantic World, 1500–1800.* Philadelphia: University of Pennsylvania Press, 2008.

Hagglund, Betty. "Gendering the Scottish Guidebook: Sarah Murray's *Companion and Useful Guide.*" *Women's Writing* 17, no. 1 (May 2010): 129–46.

Halsey, Katie. "'Tell Me of Some *Booklings*': Mary Russell Mitford's Female Literary Networks." *Women's Writing* 18, no. 1 (February 2011): 121–36.

Harris, Jennifer, and Hilary Iris Lowe, eds. *From Page to Place: American Literary Tourism and the Afterlives of Authors.* Amherst: University of Massachusetts Press, 2017.

Haslett, Moyra. "Becoming Bluestockings: Contextualising Hannah More's 'The Bas Bleu.'" *Journal of Eighteenth-Century Studies* 33, no. 1 (2010): 89–114.

Haslett, Moyra. "Bluestocking Feminism Revisited: The Satirical Figure of the Bluestocking." *Women's Writing* 17, no. 3 (December 2010): 432–51.

Haugen, Kristine Louise. "Ossian and the Invention of Textual History." *Journal of the History of Ideas* 59, no. 2 (April 1998): 309–27.

Hawkins, Ann R., and Maura Ives, eds. *Women Writers and the Artifacts of Celebrity in the Long 19th Century.* New York: Ashgate, 2012.

Hawley, Judith. "Smith, Elizabeth (1776–1806), Scholar and Translator." In *Oxford Dictionary of National Biography.* Online edition. Oxford: Oxford University Press, 2004. https://doi .org/10.1093/ref:odnb/37978.

Heldman, James. "How Wealthy Is Mr. Darcy—Really? Pounds and Dollars in the World of *Pride and Prejudice.*" *Persuasions* 12 (1990): 38–49.

Heller, Deborah. "Bluestocking Salons and the Public Sphere." *Eighteenth-Century Life* 22, no. 2 (May 1998): 59–82.

Helliher, Hilton. "Thomas Wilkinson of Yanwath, Friend of Wordsworth and Coleridge." *British Library Journal* 8 (August 1982): 147–67.

Hesselgrave, Ruth Avaline. *Lady Miller and the Batheaston Literary Circle.* New Haven, CT: Yale University Press, 1927.

Higgins, David. *Romantic Genius and the Literary Magazine: Biography, Celebrity, and Politics.* New York: Routledge, 2005.

Hill, Bridget. "Catherine Hutton (1756–1846): A Forgotten Letter-Writer." *Women's Writing* 1, no. 1 (1994): 35–50.

Hill, Bridget. "A Tale of Two Sisters: The Contrasting Careers and Ambitions of Elizabeth Montagu and Sarah Scott." *Women's History Review* 19, no. 2 (April 2010): 215–29.

Hill, Bridget. *Women Alone: Spinsters in England, 1660–1850.* New Haven, CT: Yale University Press, 2001.

Hilton, Mary, and Pam Hirsh, ed. *Practical Visionaries: Women, Education, and Social Progress, 1790–1930.* New York: Longman/Pearson Education, 1990.

Holsinger, Bruce, and Andrew Stauffer. "Romanticism, Now and Then: An Introduction." *New Literary History* 49 (2018): v–xi.

Hoppit, Julian. *Risk and Failure in English Business, 1700–1800.* New York: Cambridge University Press, 1987.

Huff, Cynthia A. "Reading as Re-Vision: Approaches to Reading Manuscript Diaries." *Biography* 23, no. 3 (Summer 2000): 504–23.

Hufton, Olwen. "Women without Men: Widows and Spinsters in Britain and France in the Eighteenth-Century." *Journal of Family History* 9, no. 4 (Winter 1984): 355–76.

Humphreys, Jennett. "Burges, Mary Anne (1763–1813)." In *Oxford Dictionary of National Biography*. Online edition, revised by Rebecca Mills. Oxford: Oxford University Press, 2004. https://doi.org/10.1093/ref:odnb/3971.

Imbarrato, Susan Clair. *Traveling Women: Narrative Visions of Early America*. Athens: Ohio University Press, 2006.

Jackson, H. J. *Romantic Readers: The Evidence of Marginalia*. New Haven, CT: Yale University Press, 2005.

Jackson, H. J. *Those Who Write for Immortality: Romantic Reputations and the Dream of Lasting Fame*. New Haven, CT: Yale University Press, 2015.

Jackson, Ian. "Approaches to the History of Readers and Reading in Eighteenth-Century Britain." *Historical Journal* 47, no. 4 (December 2004): 1041–54.

Jackson, Leon. "The Talking Book and the Talking Book Historian: African American Cultures of Print—The State of the Discipline." *Book History* 13 (2010): 251–308.

Jackson, T. V. "British Incomes Circa 1800." *Economic History Review* 52, no. 2 (May 1999): 257–83.

James, John A. "Panics, Payments, Disruptions and the Bank of England before 1826." *Financial History Review* 19, no. 3 (December 2012): 289–309.

Jarvis, Robin. *Romantic Writing and Pedestrian Travel*. New York: St. Martin's Press, 1997.

Jeffers, Honorée Fanonne. *The Age of Phillis*. Middletown, CT: Wesleyan University Press, 2020.

Jenkins, Geraint, ed. *A Rattleskull Genius: The Many Faces of Iolo Morganwg*. Cardiff: University of Wales Press, 2005.

Jenner, Greg. *Dead Famous: An Unexpected History of Celebrity, from Bronze Age to Silver Screen*. London: Weidenfeld and Nicolson, 2020.

Jones, David Ceri. "Fictional Selves in the Life and Writings of Edward Williams ('Iolo Morganwg,' 1747–1826)." *Welsh History Review* 24, no. 1 (June 2008): 29–51.

Jones, Ffion Mair. *"The Bard Is a Very Singular Character": Iolo Morganwg, Marginalia and Print Culture*. Cardiff: University of Wales Press, 2010.

Joyce, William L., et. al, eds. *Printing and Society in Early America*. Worcester, MA: American Antiquarian Society, 1983.

Karlsen, Carol F., and Laurie Crumpacker. "Introduction." In *The Journal of Esther Edwards Burr, 1754–1757*, edited by Carol F. Karlsen and Laurie Crumpacker, 3–42. New Haven, CT: Yale University Press, 1984.

Kelley, Mary. *Learning to Stand and Speak: Women, Education, and Public Life in America's Republic*. Chapel Hill: University of North Carolina Press, 2006.

Kelley, Mary. "'The Need of Their Genius': Women's Reading and Writing Practices in Early America." *Journal of the Early Republic* 28, no. 1 (Spring 2008): 1–22.

Kelley, Mary. *Private Woman, Public Stage: Literary Domesticity in Nineteenth-Century America*. New York: Oxford University Press, 1984.

Kelly, Catherine E. *Republic of Taste: Arts, Politics, and Everyday Life in Early America*. Philadelphia: University of Pennsylvania Press, 2016.

Kelly, Gary. "Introduction." In Sarah Scott, *A Description of Millenium Hall,* 11–46. Orchard Park, NY: Broadview Press, 1999.

Kilbride, Daniel. *Being American in Europe, 1750–1860.* Baltimore: Johns Hopkins University Press, 2013.

Kinsley, Zoë. *Women Writing the Home Tour, 1682–1812.* Burlington, VT: Ashgate, 2008.

Knott, Sarah. *Mother Is a Verb: An Unconventional History.* New York: Sarah Crichton Books, 2019.

Lake, Crystal B. "Redecorating the Ruin: Women and Antiquarianism in Sarah Scott's 'Millenium Hall.'" *ELH* 76, no. 3 (Fall 2009): 661–86.

Lasser, Carol. "Let Us Be Sisters Forever: The Sororal Model of Nineteenth-Century Female Friendships." *Signs* 14, no. 1 (Autumn 1988): 158–81.

Lau, Beth, ed. *Fellow Romantics: Male and Female British Writers, 1790–1835.* Burlington, VT: Ashgate, 2009.

Laughlin, Corinna. "The Lawless Language of Macpherson's Ossian." *SEL: Studies in English Literature* 40, no. 3 (Summer 2000): 511–37.

Leranbaum, Miriam. "'Mistresses of Orthodoxy': Education in the Lives and Writings of Late Eighteenth-Century Women Writers." *Proceedings of the American Philosophical Society* 121, no. 4 (August 1977): 281–301.

Levy, Michelle. "Do Women Have a Book History?" *Studies in Romanticism* 53, no. 3 (Fall 2014): 296–317.

Levy, Michelle. *Literary Manuscript Culture in Romantic Britain.* Edinburgh: Edinburgh University Press, 2020.

Lewis, Charlene M. Boyer. *Elizabeth Patterson Bonaparte: An American Aristocrat in the Early Republic.* Philadelphia: University of Pennsylvania Press, 2012.

Linkin, Harriet Kramer. "Mary Tighe's Newly Discovered Letters and Journals to Caroline Hamilton." *Romanticism* 21, no. 3 (2015): 207–27.

Little, Ann M. *The Many Captivities of Esther Wheelwright.* New Haven, CT: Yale University Press, 2016.

Looser, Devoney. *British Women Writers and the Writing of History, 1670–1820.* Baltimore: Johns Hopkins University Press, 2000.

Looser, Devoney. "British Women Writers, Big Data and Big Biography, 1780–1830." *Women's Writing* 22, no. 2 (April 2015): 165–71.

Looser, Devoney. *The Making of Jane Austen.* Baltimore: Johns Hopkins University Press, 2017.

Loughran, Trish. *The Republic in Print: Print Culture in the Age of U.S. Nation Building, 1770–1870.* New York: Columbia University Press, 2007.

Lystra, Karen. *Searching the Heart: Women, Men, and Romantic Love in Nineteenth-Century America.* New York: Oxford University Press, 1989.

MacDonald, Simon. "Identifying Mrs. Meeke: Another Burney Family Novelist." *Review of English Studies* 64, no. 265 (June 2013): 367–85.

Mackintosh, Will B. *Selling the Sights: The Invention of the Tourist in American Culture.* New York: New York University Press, 2019.

Major, Emma. *Madam Britannia: Women, Church, and Nation 1712–1812.* New York: Oxford University Press, 2012.

Marshall, Megan. *Margaret Fuller: A New American Life.* New York: Houghton Mifflin, 2013.

Marshall, Megan. *The Peabody Sisters: Three Women Who Ignited American Romanticism.* New York: Houghton Mifflin, 2005.

Matheson, C. S. "'I Wanted Some Intelligent Guide': Charles Heath and the *Historical and Descriptive Accounts of the Ancient and Present State of Tintern Abbey.*" *Romanticism* 19, no. 2 (2013): 138–52.

Mathias, Peter. *The Transformation of England: Essays in the Economic and Social History of England in the Eighteenth Century.* Reprint Edition. 1979; New York: Routledge, 2011.

Mavor, Elizabeth. *The Ladies of Llangollen: A Study in Romantic Friendship.* London: Redwood Press, 1971.

Mavor, Elizabeth, ed. *Life with the Ladies of Llangollen.* New York: Viking Books, 1984.

McDermid, Jane. "Conservative Feminism and Female Education in the Eighteenth Century." *History of Education* 18, no. 4 (1989): 309–22.

McGill, Meredith L. *American Literature and the Culture of Reprinting.* Philadelphia: University of Pennsylvania Press, 2003.

McMahon, Lucia. *Mere Equals: The Paradox of Educated Women in the Early American Republic.* Ithaca, NY: Cornell University Press, 2012.

Mellor, Anne K. "Thoughts on *Romanticism and Gender.*" *European Romantic Review* 23, no. 3 (June 2012): 343–348.

Mellor, Anne K. *Mothers of the Nation: Women's Political Writing in England, 1780–1830.* Bloomington: Indiana University Press, 2000.

Mellor, Anne K., ed. *Romanticism and Feminism.* Bloomington: Indiana University Press, 1988.

Mellor, Anne K. *Romanticism and Gender.* New York: Routledge, 1993.

Miller, P. J. "Women's Education, 'Self-Improvement' and Social Mobility—A Late Eighteenth Century Debate." *British Journal of Educational Studies* 20, no. 3 (October 1972): 302–14.

Mole, Tom. *Byron's Romantic Celebrity: Industrial Culture and the Hermeneutic of Intimacy.* New York: Palgrave Macmillan, 2007.

Mole, Tom, ed. *Romanticism and Celebrity Culture, 1750–1850.* New York: Cambridge University Press, 2012.

Mole, Tom. *What the Victorians Made of Romanticism: Material Artifacts, Cultural Practices, and Reception History.* Princeton, NJ: Princeton University Press, 2017.

Moreshead, Ashley E. "'Beyond All Ambitious Motives': Missionary Memoirs and the Cultivation of Early American Heroines." *Journal of the Early Republic* 38, no. 1 (Spring 2018): 37–60.

Mulford, Carla, ed. *Only For the Eye of a Friend: The Poems of Annis Boudinot Stockton.* Charlottesville: University Press of Virginia, 1995.

Myers, Sylvia Harcstark. *The Bluestocking Circle: Women, Friendship, and the Life of the Mind in Eighteenth-Century England.* Oxford: Clarendon Press, 1990.

Nash, Margaret. *Women's Education in the United States, 1780–1840.* New York: Palgrave Macmillan, 2005.

Nash, Margaret, ed. *Women's Higher Education in the United States: New Historical Perspectives.* New York: Palgrave Macmillan, 2018.

Neale, R. S. *Bath, 1680–1850, A Social History; or, A Valley of Pleasure, Yet a Sink of Iniquity.* London: Routledge and Kegan Paul, 1981.

Newman, John. *The Buildings of Wales: Gwent/Monmouthshire*. New York: Penguin, 2000.

Nicholson, Norman. *The Lakers: The Adventures of the First Tourists*. Milnorpe, Cumbria, U.K.: Cicerone Press, 1955.

Noel, Rebecca. "'No Wonder They Are Sick, and Die of Study': European Fears for the Scholarly Body and Health in New England Schools before Horace Mann." *Pedagogica Historica* 54, nos. 1–2 (2018): 134–53.

North. Julian. "De Quincey and the Inferiority of Women." *Romanticism* 17, no. 3 (2011): 327–39.

North, Julian. *The Domestication of Genius: Biography and the Romantic Poet*. New York: Oxford University Press, 2009.

O'Neill, Bonnie Carr. "'The Best of Me Is There': Emerson as Lecturer and Celebrity." *American Literature* 80, no. 4 (December 2008): 739–67.

O'Sullivan, Maurice. "Introduction." In *The Book of Job: Translated by Elizabeth Smith*, 5–25. Delmar, NY: Scholars' Facsimiles and Reprints, 1996.

Olwell, Victoria. "'It Spoke Itself': Women's Genius and Eccentric Politics." *American Literature* 77, no. 1 (March 2005): 33–63.

Ousby, Ian. *The Englishman's England: Taste, Travel, and the Rise of Tourism*. New York: Cambridge University Press, 1990.

Peace, Thomas. "Indigenous Intellectual Traditions and Biography in the Northeast: A Historiographical Reflection." *History Compass* 16, no. 4 (April 2018): 1–10.

Pearson, Jacqueline. *Women's Reading in Britain, 1750–1835: A Dangerous Recreation*. New York: Cambridge University Press, 1999.

Percy, Joan. "Thomas Wilkinson (1751–1836): Cumbrian Landscaper." *Garden History* 21, no. 2 (Winter 1993): 217–26.

Perkins, Pam. "'News from Scotland': Female Networks in the Travel Narratives of Elizabeth Isabella Spence." *Women's Writing* 24, no. 2 (2017): 170–84.

Perrin, Noel. *Dr. Bowdler's Legacy: A History of Expurgated Books in England and America*. New York: Atheneum, 1969.

Pohl, Nicole, and Betty A. Schellenberg. *Reconsidering the Bluestockings*. San Marino, CA: Huntington Library, 2003.

Porter, Roy, ed. *Romanticism in National Context*. Cambridge: Cambridge University Press, 1988.

Pratt, Mary Louise. *Imperial Eyes: Travel Writing and Transculturation*. New York: Routledge, 1992.

Prendergast, Amy. *Literary Salons across Britain and Ireland in the Long Eighteenth Century*. New York: Palgrave Macmillan, 2015.

Prescott, Sarah. "Women Travellers in Wales: Hester Lynch Thrale Piozzi, Mary Morgan, and Elizabeth Isabella Spence." *Studies in Travel Writing* 18, no 2 (2014): 107–21.

Purvis, June. *A History of Women's Education in England*. Milton Keynes, U.K.: Open University Press, 1991.

Raven, James. *The Business of Books: Booksellers and the English Book Trade, 1450–1850*. New Haven, CT: Yale University Press, 2007.

Remer, Rosalind. *Printers and Men of Capital: Philadelphia Book Publishers in the New Republic*. Philadelphia: University of Pennsylvania Press, 1996.

Rezek, Joseph. *London and the Making of Provincial Literature: Aesthetics and the Transatlantic Book Trade, 1800–1850*. Philadelphia: University of Pennsylvania Press, 2015.

Rezek, Joseph. "The Racialization of Print." *American Literary History* 32, no. 3 (2020): 417–45.

Rizzo, Betty. *Companions without Vows: Relationships among Eighteenth-Century British Women*. Athens: University of Georgia Press, 1994.

Rizzo, Betty. "Two Versions of Community: Montagu and Scott." *Huntington Library Quarterly* 65, nos. 1–2 (2002): 193–214.

Russell, Penny. "An Improper Education? Jane Griffin's Pursuit of Self-Improvement and 'Truth,' 1811–12." *History of Education* 33, no. 3 (May 2004): 249–65.

Rust, Marion. *Prodigal Daughters: Susanna Rowson's Early American Women*. Chapel Hill: University of North Carolina Press, 2008.

Schudds, Colm. "Old Coach Roads from Dublin, 1745–1821." *Dublin Historical Record* 54, no. 1 (Spring 2001): 4–15.

Seeman, Erik R. *Speaking with the Dead in Early America*. Philadelphia: University of Pennsylvania Press, 2019.

Shields, David S. *Civil Tongues and Polite Letters in British America*. Chapel Hill: University of North Carolina Press, 1997.

Simonds, Wendy, and Barbara Katz Rothman. *Centuries of Solace: Expressions of Maternal Grief in Popular Literature*. Philadelphia: Temple University Press, 1992.

Sinkankas, John. "John Griscom in Europe, 1818–1819: An Early American View of Mineralogy Abroad." *Earth Sciences History* 17, no. 1 (1993): 3–21.

Skemp, Sheila L. *First Lady of Letters: Judith Sargent Murray and the Struggle for Female Independence*. Philadelphia: University of Pennsylvania Press, 2009.

Smith, Steven Carl. "'Elements of Useful Knowledge': New York and the National Book Trade in the Early Republic." *Papers of the Bibliographical Society of America* 106, no. 4 (December 2012): 487–538.

Smith-Rosenberg, Carroll. "The Female World of Love and Ritual: Relations between Women in Nineteenth-Century America." *Signs* 1, no. 1 (Autumn 1975): 1–29.

Solomon, Barbara Miller. *In the Company of Educated Women: A History of Women and Higher Education in America*. New Haven, CT: Yale University Press, 1985.

Speese, Erin K. Johns. "'Our Feelings Become Impressed with the Grandeur of Omnipotence': Mary Somerville's Feminine Scientific Sublime." *Prose Studies* 35, no. 2 (2013): 171–88.

Spunaugle, Emily D. "A Travel Writer Reconsidered: Recovering Mary Morgan's Mary, the Osier-Peeler." *ABO: Interactive Journal for Women in the Arts, 1640–1830* 10, no. 2 (Fall 2020): 1–18.

Stabile, Susan M. *Memory's Daughters: The Material Culture of Remembrance in Eighteenth-Century America*. Ithaca, NY: Cornell University Press, 2004.

Stafford, Fiona. *Reading Romantic Poetry*. Hoboken, NJ: Wiley-Blackwell, 2012.

Stafford, Fiona. *The Sublime Savage: A Study of James Macpherson and the Poems of Ossian*. Edinburgh: Edinburgh University Press, 1988.

Stempel, Daniel. "Revelation on Mount Snowdon: Wordsworth, Coleridge, and the Fichtean Imagination." *Journal of Aesthetics and Art Criticism* 29, no. 3 (Spring 1971): 371–84.

Stott, Anne. *Hannah More: The First Victorian*. New York: Oxford University Press, 2003.

Taylor, Barbara. *Mary Wollstonecraft and the Feminist Imagination.* New York: Cambridge University Press, 2003.

Teed, Melissa Ladd. "A Passion for Distinction: Lydia Huntley Sigourney and the Creation of a Literary Reputation." *New England Quarterly* 77, no. 1 (March 2004): 51–69.

Thomas, Claudia. "Samuel Johnson and Elizabeth Carter: Pudding, Epictetus, and the Accomplished Woman." *South Central Review* 9, no. 4 (Winter 1992): 18–30.

Tillyard, Stella. "Celebrity in 18th-Century London." *History Today* 55, no. 6 (June 2005): 20–27.

Todd, Emily B. "Walter Scott and the Nineteenth-Century American Literary Marketplace: Antebellum Richmond Readers and the Collected Editions of the Waverley Novels." *Papers of the Bibliographical Society of America* 93, no. 4 (December 1999): 495–517.

Todd, Janet. *Mary Wollstonecraft: A Revolutionary Life.* New York: Columbia University Press, 2000.

Tomalin, Claire. *Jane Austen: A Life.* New York: Vintage Books, 1999.

Tompkins, Jane. *Sensational Designs: The Cultural Work of America Fiction, 1790–1865.* New York: Oxford University Press, 1985.

Toran, Katherine. "The Economics of Jane Austen's World." *Persuasions On-Line* 36, no. 1 (Winter 2015). https://www.jasna.org/publications-2/persuasions-online/vol36no1/toran/.

Turner, Cheryl. *Living by the Pen: Women Writers in the Eighteenth Century.* New York: Routledge, 1994.

Vardy, Alan D. *Constructing Coleridge: The Posthumous Life of the Author.* New York: Palgrave Macmillan, 2010.

Vardy, Alan. "Joseph Cottle and Reminiscence: The Picturesque Gone Awry." *Romanticism* 19, no. 2 (2013): 188–96.

Vickery, Amanda. *Behind Closed Doors: At Home in Georgian England.* New Haven, CT: Yale University Press, 2009.

Vickery, Amanda. *The Gentleman's Daughter: Women's Lives in Georgian England.* New Haven, CT: Yale University Press, 1998.

Warner, Michael. *The Letters of the Republic: Publication and the Public Sphere in Eighteenth Century America.* Cambridge, MA: Harvard University Press, 1990.

Waters, Ivon. *Piercefield on the Banks of the Wye.* Chepstow, U.K.: F. G. Comber, 1975.

Watson, Nicola J., ed. *Literary Tourism and Nineteenth-Century Culture.* New York: Palgrave Macmillan, 2009.

Watson, Nicola J. *The Literary Tourist: Readers and Places in Romantic and Victorian Britain.* New York: Palgrave Macmillan, 2006.

Westover, Paul. *Necromanticism: Travelling to Meet the Dead, 1750–1860.* New York: Palgrave Macmillan, 2012.

White, Barbara. "But Who Was the Queen of Bath?" *Bath History* 12 (2011): 43–61.

Williams, Abigail. *The Social Life of Books: Reading Together in the Eighteenth-Century Home.* New Haven, CT: Yale University Press, 2017.

Williams, William H. A. *Creating Irish Tourism: The First Century, 1750–1850.* London: Anthem Press, 2010.

Wilson, Cheryl A. "'Something Like Mine': Catherine Hutton, Jane Austen, and Feminist Recovery Work." *Eighteenth Century* 56, no. 2 (2015): 151–64.

Wilson, R. G., and A. L. Mackley. "How Much Did the English Country House Cost to Build, 1660–1880?" *Economic History Review* 52, no. 3 (August 1999): 436–68.

Winckles, Andrew O., and Angela Rehbein, eds. *Women's Literary Networks and Romanticism: "A Tribe of Authoresses."* Liverpool: Liverpool University Press, 2017.

Wink, Amy L. *She Left Nothing in Particular: The Autobiographical Legacy of Nineteenth-Century Women's Diaries.* Knoxville: University of Tennessee Press, 2001.

Wolfson, Susan J. "Shakespeare and the Romantic Girl Reader." *Nineteenth-Century Contexts* 21, no. 2 (September 1999): 191–234.

Worsley, Lucy. *Jane Austen at Home.* London: Hodder and Stoughton, 2017.

Wright, Tom F., ed. *The Cosmopolitan Lyceum: Lecture Culture and the Globe in Nineteenth-Century America.* Amherst: University of Massachusetts Press, 2013.

Wu, Duncan, ed. *A Companion to Romanticism.* Hoboken, NJ: Wiley-Blackwell, 1999.

Zagarri, Rosemarie. *Revolutionary Backlash: Women and Politics in the Early American Republic.* Philadelphia: University of Pennsylvania Press, 2008.

INDEX

References to illustrations are indicated by italicized page numbers.

adventure: ES's predilection for, 5–6, 17, 23, 43, 49–50, 77, 79, 81, 84, 90, 98–99, 109–10, 115–18, 190, 221, 231, 242; landscapes as inspiration for, 50, 79, 90, 110, 143; mountain climbing and, 96–106, 116–17; women adventurers, male opinion of, 101–2. *See also* Snowdon

advice writers. *See* conduct literature

Alken, Samuel, 97

Allan, Thomas (brother-in-law), 223, 242

Allinson, David, 175, 198

America: biographies and memoirs of accomplished women, popularity of, 145, 165, 172, 210–15, 287n81; conduct literature using ES as role model in, 217, 219; family life in, 26–27; feminine ideals in, 216–17; *Fragments* in, 140, 158–59, 168, 170–72, 174–76, 178, 182, 185, 197–98, 202, 289nn23–24; literary reputation of ES in, 245–47; literary tourism and, 223, 227; more learned women in Britain than in America, 216; women's political ambitions discouraged in, 216, 296n66. *See also* transatlantic shared culture

American Lady's Preceptor on ES as role model, 215

anonymity of women authors, 33, 37, 69, 71–73, 75, 132, 146, 162, 188; critical review on work's own terms when gender unknown, 72; as travel writers, 104–5

artwork by ES: Lake District scenery, 234, 242, 244–45; as relics and remembrances, 234

Atlantic Monthly, Martineau article on ES's legacy, 202, 221, 226–27

Austen, Jane, 14, 263n7

Bainbridge, Simon, 276n63, 277n80

Balfour, Clara Lucas, 219, 296n69; *Women Worth Emulating,* 218

Ballitore, Ireland: *Fragments*'s sales in, 159; Smith family stay in, 107–8, 201, 236

Baltimore Repertory on ES's commendation in *American Lady's Preceptor,* 215–16

bankruptcy. *See* Smith, George (father)

Bannet, Eve Tavor, 73

Barbauld, Anna Laetitia, *The Correspondence of Samuel Richardson,* 129

RECENT BOOKS IN THE SERIES

Jeffersonian America